Peasants and Politics
in the Modern Middle East

Peasants and Politics
in the Modern Middle East

Edited by

Farhad Kazemi
and John Waterbury

Florida International University Press / Miami

The Florida International University Press is a member of the University Presses of
Florida, the scholarly publishing agency of the State University System of Florida.
Books are selected for publication by faculty editorial committees at each of
Florida's nine public universities: Florida A & M University (Tallahassee), Florida
Atlantic University (Boca Raton), Florida International University (Miami), Florida
State University (Tallahassee), University of Central Florida (Orlando), University
of Florida (Gainesville), University of North Florida (Jacksonville), University of
South Florida (Tampa), and University of West Florida (Pensacola).

Orders for books published by all member presses should be addressed to
University Presses of Florida, 15 Northwest 15th Street, Gainesville, FL 32611.

Library of Congress Cataloging-in-Publication Data

Peasants and politics in the modern Middle East / edited by Farhad
Kazemi and John Waterbury.
    p.   cm.
   Includes index.
   ISBN 0–8130–1088–8. — ISBN 0–8130–1102–7 (pbk.)
    1. Peasantry—Middle East—Political activity. 2. Middle East—
Politics and government. 3. Middle East—Rural conditions.
   I. Kazemi, Farhad, 1943–. II. Waterbury, John.
   DS62.4.P4 1991   91–17014
   956—dc20   CIP

Contents

Acknowledgments

The editors acknowledge the generous financial support of the Department of Near Eastern Studies of Princeton University for helping to defray the cost of translating Reinhard C. Schulze's article from German into English and of the Graduate School of Arts and Sciences of New York University for covering the cost of preparing an index for the volume. They are also indebted to Walda Metcalf for pursuing this project and to Judy Goffman for overseeing its completion. Special thanks are due to all the authors for their contributions, perseverance, and good humor, and for putting up with two nagging editors.

Permissions to use previously published material were received and are acknowledged as follows.

Chapter 3, "Rural Unrest in the Ottoman Empire, 1830–1914," by Donald Quataert, is part of a chapter in *The Ottoman Empire: Its Economy and Society, 1300–1914*, Halil Inalcik, editor, and Donald Quataert, associate editor (Cambridge, England: Cambridge University Press, forthcoming). It is used with permission from the publisher.

An earlier version of chapter 7, "War, State Economic Policies, and Resistance by Agricultural Producers in Turkey, 1939–1945," by Sevket Pamuk, appeared in *New Perspectives on Turkey* 2, no. 1 (1988).

An earlier version of chapter 10, "The Ignorance and Inscrutability of the Egyptian Peasantry," by Nathan Brown, appeared in Nathan Brown, *Peasant Politics in Modern Egypt: The Struggle against the State* (New Haven, Conn.: Yale University Press, 1990). It is reprinted by permission of the publisher.

Peasants Defy Categorization (As Well as Landlords and the State)

JOHN WATERBURY

As the societies of the Middle East entered the twentieth century (for our purposes the Middle East is an area stretching from Morocco in the west to Afghanistan in the east, and including the Sudan), their economies and populations were overwhelmingly agrarian. In that sense the Middle East did not differ appreciably from other regions of what has come to be called the Third (or developing) World. On a priori grounds alone, then, one can argue that the involvement of rural producers in local and national politics must have been, and perhaps still is, of commensurate importance. By politics, I mean the active involvement of groups and individuals in those processes by which valued goods are distributed, such distribution taking place at all levels of social and economic hierarchies.

Yet it is extraordinarily difficult for small-scale rural producers—whether owners, tenants, sharecroppers, or laborers—to exert political pressure, violently or otherwise, that accurately reflects their numbers or their economic significance. The fact that peasants, in and of themselves, have not been the force driving economic and political change has evoked a great deal of scholarly attention to what might be called their plight—that is, that their numbers and their aggregate weight in economic life have not been remotely reflected in their political influence. Our effort in this book is at least partially an analytic approach to this imbalance.

It would be easy, but not very illuminating, to elaborate a multibox matrix with types of rural actors running down the left side and types of political actions running across the top. The matrix might account for nearly all possible combinations, but there would surely be many boxes in which only one data point would be located. It is for this reason that I speak of peasants defying categorization. What I will stress in this essay, and what I suspect the reader will find in the other contributions, is in fact the variety of experiences and interactions that characterize peasant politics and violence in the last century and a half of Middle East history. We shall not find any overarching paradigm that explains most of what has transpired, and, in specific cases, we shall seldom find monocausal explanations of events. Indeed, if we could convert our matrix from a two- to a three-dimensional format, we could add an axis called explanatory propositions to those of types of actors and types of actions. At that point we might encounter a few empty boxes.

The words *peasants* and *peasantry* are shorthand for what is usually a highly differentiated population of small producers. The Middle East is second to no other region in the diversity of actors frequently clustered under the label "peasant." Although I suspect this word defies useful definition, I will furnish one advanced by one of the foremost analysts of these actors (Eric Wolf 1966:3–4): "[P]easants . . . are rural cultivators whose surpluses are transferred to a dominant group of rulers that uses the surpluses both to underwrite its own standard of living and to distribute the remainder to groups in society that do not farm but must be fed for their specific goods and services in turn." I would add that the term surely implies some of the following characteristics: (1) that peasants are primarily sedentary village dwellers, (2) that their own operations are small-scale, (3) that frequently they yield up surplus in the form of tribute, (4) that their sales to markets are frequently under duress (to pay off debt or taxes) and not in search of profit, and (5) that they are politically subordinate and vulnerable. It follows that I would not treat as peasants those producers who have variously been qualified as kulaks, bullock capitalists, middle peasants, and so forth, precisely because they generally have recourse to markets on a voluntary basis and in search of profits. Not all the authors in this volume would agree with that judgment, and it is everywhere the case that peasants, as I have defined them, are not easily separable from somewhat wealthier market producers.

Peasants in this sense are never short of adversaries. Traditionally these have been the landlord and the moneylender who occasionally are the same person. The state is also frequently an adversary, conscripting young men into the army or, as in Egypt, into forced labor gangs (*corvée*), extracting taxes and tribute, and, in its modern form, setting the prices for agricultural inputs, credit, and crop purchases. Until fairly recently, peasantries have been victimized by rural bandits and, in the Middle East, by the raids and extractions of the bedouin. Finally, the peasant faces the elements: flood, drought, wind, locusts, and disease. The peasant does not have the resources to combat any of these adversaries effectively and often has to face all of them simultaneously.

Sometimes the word *peasant* elicits images of venerable traditions, rootedness, and "from time immemorial." But the people who stow away in this definitional vessel are constantly changing, as is the vessel itself. In Iraq, in recent centuries, peasants have reverted to nomadism, while in Egypt, since the middle of the nineteenth century, some nomads have become peasants. In Egypt we encounter a truly ancient peasant way of life, while in Syria's northeast, or in the Sudan's Gezira scheme, we encounter state-created peasantries only a few generations old. An increasingly common feature of rural society in the Middle East is the part-time peasant, with a hold on the land and on the city, on village life and migration, on agricultural and nonagricultural sources of livelihood.

It may simply be that one can no longer speak with any analytic utility of peasants. Hobsbawm said as much more than fifteen years ago (1973:20): "[T]he fundamental fact of peasant politics today is the decline of the traditional peasantry, and indeed increasingly the relative numerical decline of any kind of peasantry."

It may be this perception that accounts for a declining level of interest among historians and anthropologists in rural politics in the Middle East. A generation or more ago, such studies were fairly abundant,[1] but only modest follow-up on them has been done. The editors had difficulty finding anthropologists who felt peasant politics to be a subject worthy of study, and I am grateful to Nicholas Hopkins and Fereydoun Safizadeh for seeing matters differently.[2]

In this collection the reader will find something approaching a critical mass of those who have systematically examined the role of rural producers, including peasants, in politics broadly construed, a role shaped by the profound social and economic transformations that the region has undergone in the last century and a half.

The magnitude of that transformation is borne out by the crude statistics in table 1.1, and it is a process that is still under way. These figures reveal a general, albeit uneven, trend toward an increasingly urban way of life, although many urban agglomerations bear markedly rural characteristics in various quarters and in the shantytowns. They are also a kind of residual category for all those who do not live in cities and large towns. In that sense, and as in the chapters to follow, they comprise far more than peasants (Chaulet 1987:69). The landed gentry, moneylenders, state officials, schoolteachers, petty tradespeople, migrant laborers, and so forth are all present in the coun-

Table 1.1.
Rural Population as a Proportion of Total Population in the
Middle East, 1965 and 1987 (in percentages)

Country	1965	1987
Algeria	62	56
Egypt	59	52
Iran	63	47
Iraq	49	28
Israel	19	9
Jordan	54	34
Lebanon	50	?
Libya	74	33
Morocco	68	53
Saudi Arabia	61	25
Sudan	87	79
Syria	60	49
Tunisia	60	46
United Arab Emirates	59	22
Yemen Arab Rep.	95	77
Yemen PDR	70	58

Source: The World Bank, *World Development Report, 1989* (New York: Oxford
University Press, 1989), 224–25.

tryside and may play crucial roles in rural politics. At the height of the
populist socialist experiments in Egypt and Syria, schoolteachers were used to
try to mobilize smallholders and tenants in favor of the regimes (Harik 1974;
Hinnebusch 1979). The rural middle class, by contrast, has used conventional
patron-client relations to prevent any kind of mobilization among the poorest,
and most dependent, rural producers (Binder 1978; Leveau 1985; Hopkins,
this volume). When peasants act alone, it is generally through foot-dragging,
dissimulation, or surreptitious harassment of the powerful. When they act
collectively, an outside agent of some kind is almost always present.

Peasant protest is as old as peasantries themselves, but in this volume we
focus on the period since the great expansion of European industrial societies
into other parts of the world. For this period, in the general field of peasant
studies, two crucial variables are often adduced in explaining peasant protest:
the penetration of markets into partially subsistent agriculture, and the growing extractive reach of the state. The processes go together and correspond
historically to the phenomenal growth in world trade that sprang from a
revolution in transportation technology involving the railroads and the steamship. Despite a severe downturn in world trade in the 1870s (noted by some

authors here, e.g., Schilcher), between 1840 and 1895 world trade sextupled, and between 1895 and 1913 it quintupled. As Arthur Lewis has shown, "tropical" exports grew between 3 and 4 percent per annum over the same period (Reynolds 1985:33–36; Rogowski 1989:23). The argument is that peasantries were dragged into commercial markets, captured by landlords and moneylenders who sought to extract an ever larger marketable surplus from them, and assaulted by an aggressive state in search of new sources of revenue to sustain military modernization. Peasants resisted as best they could (this volume, Burke, Quataert, Schulze, Schilcher, Havemann).[3] This we might see as phase 1. Phase 2 comes in what Lloyd Reynolds has called "the longest depression" (1985:35), the period 1914–45. Peasants who had in some sense grown accustomed to the market were battered by the slump in world trade, especially in the 1930s, and by drastically declining world prices for primary products. In other parts of the developing world, above all in Vietnam and China, this period gave rise to organized rural-based revolutionary movements. In the Middle East the seeds of the Algerian revolution (1954–62) were planted at the same time, and the insurrections in Egypt in 1919 (Schulze, this volume) and in Palestine in 1936 (Stein, this volume) combined factors of economic privation and opposition to colonial rule.

The rural world should be seen in political terms as both an arena and a protagonist. Protest and violence may occur in rural areas because the terrain is favorable for guerrilla warfare, but on this stage peasants may be relatively passive actors. Extrarural or quasi-rural actors combine with specific, disgruntled sectors of the cultivating population to produce insurrections, rebellions, and even state-toppling revolutionary movements. The bulk of the rural population will be more or less sympathetic bystanders, camouflaging the rebels and even brigands through studied silence (see Brown, this volume) and supplying them with food, shelter, and hiding places. The countryside as the arena for protest and revolution is the subject of Eric Wolf's *Peasant Wars of the Twentieth Century,* and in it he devotes a chapter to the Middle East's most famous manifestation of this phenomenon, the Algerian war. But the Gilan province of Iran (Kazemi, this volume and 1988) and the ethnically defined arenas of the southern Sudan and of Kurdistan provide similar examples.

There are more but less spectacular instances when peasants and other rural producers are the primary actors undertaking acts of protest and violence. In sheer numbers these "acts of everyday resistance" (Scott 1985, 1989) consist mainly in stealing, sabotaging crops, destroying tax and debt records, hiding produce and animals, evading the draft or deserting from the army, and occasional acts of individual aggression (Brown, Mitchell, and Safizadeh, this volume). From the "everyday," however, peasant protest can escalate to levels of widespread and semiorganized violence and insurrection, but almost never in the absence of some form of outside leadership. Two famous episodes are the Tunisian insurrection of 1864 that falls squarely in what I have called phase 1, and the 1919 revolt in Egypt that comes at the beginning of phase 2 (as does the 1920 Iraqi revolt discussed by Kazemi in this volume).

In Tunisia, the Bey (the Ottoman governor of Tunis) gradually increased the fiscal reach of his state from 1831 on, provoking in the process a series of uncoordinated and ineffective rural revolts.[4] The introduction in 1856 of a male head tax, the *majba,* and in 1860 of military conscription triggered a broad movement of violent protest. A new group of state intermediaries, set loose in the countryside to collect taxes and conscript youths, were the targets of peasant wrath. The most notorious of these was Zarruq, the *qa'id* of the Souss and Monastir who quintupled the tax burden on those regions (Slama 1967:142). The revolt of 1864 spread through the Sahel, the center, and the west of Tunisia. For Valensi this insurrection was aimed mainly at restoring a preferred status quo ante, or, in her words, "un sursaut de défense des campagnes tunisiennes pour conserver un ordre sociale ébranlé par l'administration beylicale" (1977:360) [a defensive jolt of the Tunisian countryside to preserve a social order buffeted by the Beylical administration]. The insurgents denounced not only the doubling of the majba and conscription but the new constitution, the abolition of slavery, and the reform of the tribunals.

The insurrection brought together tribes and villages, tenants and landowners, notables and commoners in opposition to the new class of state intermediaries. The alliance was not to survive the harvest, during which the Bey was able to cut deals with various tribal alliances (*sof-s*), turning one against another. It was not to be the last rural insurrection, however; in 1881, at the time the French took control of Tunisia, a new uprising joined the state intermediaries with the local population against the state itself (Cherif 1980).

The 1919 revolt in Egypt represents protest within a more mature form of rural market economy and in the face of a non-Muslim colonial power, Great Britain (cf. the phase 1 insurrections in the Ottoman provinces of Syria described by Schilcher and Lebanon by Havemann, this volume). Schulze's analysis in this volume shows that no monocausal explanations are sufficient. Relative to the rest of the Middle East, Egypt's rural population is remarkably homogeneous, with the partial exception of the Coptic Christian minority. Yet the incidence of revolt was region-, crop-, and even village-specific. There were, nonetheless, two overriding themes: decades of gradual incorporation into the cotton economy, and successive waves of state fiscal assertion, culminating in the forced crop procurements, draught animal seizures, and conscription of World War I (cf. Pamuk, this volume, on similar exactions in Turkey during World War II).

What is most striking in Schulze's account is the sequential unfolding of the "alliance" of the urban *effendiya* in the nationalist movement with the rural notability and the peasantry (cf. Stein, this volume, on the alliances of the 1936 Palestinian uprising). In a sense the effendiya were able to capture briefly for their own purpose the cumulative discontent aroused by incorporation into the cotton economy, which had already resulted in land seizures and growing rural banditry. The alliance led to the formation of short-lived "republics" in various rural areas and towns, but in the face of the British effort to suppress the republics, the nonrural leadership lost its sense of purpose and abandoned its rural allies. Pockets of peasants, rural notables, and bedouin struggled on, seeking to reduce the grip of the state authorities on their everyday lives. The British were then able to deal piecemeal with rural jacqueries deprived of any central leadership.

The 1919 revolt reveals a typical feature of such transregional movements: the outside leaders generally have a different set of objectives, and, indeed, a different vocabulary, than their rural allies. They may share a general sense of who the enemy is and of prevailing injustice but not of the goals to be attained. Outside leaders may have a revolutionary blueprint, as in Algeria or Vietnam, or at the very least will want to gain leverage over the state. Rural participants will more likely be concerned with specific local grievances and with a quest for greater local autonomy.[5]

Apart from these two cases, some general questions and propositions pertain to all forms of peasant resistance and protest. Who acts, how do they act, what do they seek, and in what context do they act? Margaret Levi summarizes a generally accepted understanding: "Outright rebellion reflects improvements in the rebels' organizational capacity as often as it reflects changed relationships between rulers and ruled. However, resistance can take forms other than outright rebellion; for example it can take the form of high productivity, individualistic tax avoidance, or even free-riding. What causes resistance, I argue, is not only the recognition of exploitation but also, and more important, the ability to act. Resistance is as likely—indeed more likely—to come from those with resources as from those without" (1988:53).

Who, then, rebels? For some, like Branko Horvat, it is the oppressed peasantry in a situation of objective exploitation and misery: "[I]n the undeveloped countries . . . the peasants are economically exploited, politically oppressed, saddled with debts, losing their land to the moneylender and the landlord. The salesmen and mass media inform them of a different world and the teacher explains to them that their fate can be changed. As a result, peasants, with the possible exception of a tiny fraction of rich peasants, are ready for revolution" (1981:953).

In a less romantic vein, Scott (1976) emphasized rebellion among the poorest in times of "subsistence crises." The proposition is simple: if one's very life is at risk, one will resort to any means, including violence, to protect it. Scott saw subsistence crises emerging through a combination of market failures and increasingly extractive landlords who eliminated traditional mechanisms such as gleaning rights that could tide the poor over periods of penury. And because the poor were (and are) the most vulnerable to such crises, they are likely to furnish the bulk of the insurgents.

Plausible as this proposition may sound, it seems to break down as often as it holds up. Amartya Sen, for example, points out that the Great Bengal Famine of 1943–44 produced no rural revolt, and its primary victims were fisherfolk, laborers, paddy huskers, craftspeople, and transport workers. The least affected were, in fact, sharecroppers and peasants (Sen 1981:71–72). Similarly, Quataert (this volume) states, "The terrible killing famine of 1873–74 provoked only a few bread riots in various regions." By contrast, near famine conditions in Algeria at the end of World War II provoked large-scale riots (and massive repression) at Setif in the eastern wheat-growing region (Halpern 1948). It could be hypothesized that famines are so cataclysmic that revolt and resistance are not feasible options and that it is, rather, subsistence crises on the margins of survival that induce such action. Pamuk's study (this volume) found that increased grain procurement by the Turkish state during World War II did not produce famine, but it did produce resistance.

In his comparative study of twentieth-century peasant wars, Wolf singled out the "middle peasants" as likely to be political activists because, although they are involved in production for market, they have not attained a scale of operations that can protect them against production or market failures. They frequently act, as well, as intermediaries between central authorities and local populations and may develop nonagricultural economic interests (in housing, transport, or trade) and have family members in purely urban occupations. In short they have a stake in the market economy, in the urban environment, and in national politics, but they are marginal actors in all three. If they lose their stake they are likely to revolt. These are people with resources in Levi's sense, and we can see them at work in the 1919 revolt in Egypt, in the late nineteenth-century insurrections of the Levant, and, as Wolf argues, in the 1954–62 war against the French in Algeria.

Other propositions formalize some of the evidence advanced by Schulze (as well as by Nathan Brown 1990) by linking forms of resistance to various modes of rural production or relations among production factors (land, labor, capital). For instance both Paige (1975) and Stinchcombe (1961) suggest that when tenants (owners of labor power) face landowners (owners of capital and land) with few other economic interests, explosive, even revolutionary, confrontations are likely to follow. However, Egypt since the late nineteenth century has presented just such a context, but with the exception of 1919 has had no explosion. In any event the "modes of rural production" approach has difficulty in accommodating the factor mobility that has characterized the countryside in the last several decades. Labor and capital have become highly mobile, while only land is locked in. Moreover, as we shall see, the portfolio of even the poorest peasants has diversified to an unprecedented extent (although Mitchell, this volume, presents a counterinterpretation). It may be that we should think of a phase 3 emerging sometime after World War II, once the colonial authorities have departed. In this phase the everyday forms of resistance, including migration, nonpayment of loans, and evasion of crop procurement quotas (or what Paige calls market protests) become the prevalent modes of action, increasingly directed at the state itself.

In answering the question "who acts?" in the Middle East, we encounter the particularly thorny issue of overlap between class alignments and ethnic or tribal boundaries. In some instances the economically weak and powerful divide along ethnic or religious lines, as did Sunni landowners and Shi'i tenants in lower Iraq after World War I. More often each "primordial" community contains a full range of economic players, from the weakest to the most powerful, and tribal, ethnic, and religious identity have often been viewed as ideologies manipulated by dominant elites to hold in thrall the weaker members of such communities.[6] The game, Batatu argues, cannot go on indefinitely: "The tribal rebellions of the first decades of the [Iraqi] monarchy—and more so the Arab than the Kurdish rebellions—appear in retrospect as the gasps of a tribal world approaching its end. The rural rebellions of the last decade of the monarchy were of an entirely different character. They were rebellions not under shaikhs but against them . . . and were made by tribesmen whose customary ideas and norms of life had been shaken to their foundation" (1978:469).

One must proceed cautiously with this line of analysis because it is well known that even when the grossest signs of inequality are stripped away, primordial sentiments continue to run deep. Cynically administered ethnic or religious opiates cannot explain Ngorno Karabakh, Lebanon since 1976, or the southern Sudan since 1955.

Two Egyptian peasants playing a strategic game similar to chess in the sand.
Photo by John Waterbury, ca. 1973.

The question of ethnic-cum-peasant protest brings us back to the role of intermediaries. Politicians, even in systems where the ballot is of little consequence, are often tempted to mobilize followers on the basis of primordial appeals in order to extract resources from the center. The Rif rebellion of 1959, shortly after Moroccan independence, can be seen in this light (Gellner 1962), and Clifford Geertz depicted it as a near-universal phenomenon in newly independent states (Geertz 1963; see also Kasfir 1979).

Education and migration have, in recent decades, led to substantial physical and occupational mobility among peasants, yielding what we called earlier part-time peasants. Off-farm employment and incomes have come to be an important, if not the most important, source of livelihood for many rural families. This category includes the middle peasants analyzed by Wolf, but it also includes the rural poor who may be, out of necessity, more heavily involved in off-farm pursuits than the better off (see Taylor-Awny 1984). Saunders and Mehanna (1989) found that in an Egyptian village in 1961, less than half of the adult men indicated agriculture as their primary source of livelihood, while in 1978 more than half did. This surprising change, the authors argue, was because of the increasing prosperity in the village that had seen the landless acquire land through agrarian reform (including women titleholders) and lucrative agricultural pursuits, such as poultry raising, that diminished the attraction of worker migration.

In political terms, the part-time peasant may turn out to be a key player. Hoogland found that in Iran, opponents to the shah were concentrated among middle peasants (in the 7–10 hectare range) and among what he called "shuttle peasants." The former felt left out of the shah's agrarian reforms and were unable to qualify for limited rural credit and subsidized fertilizer. They could not make the transition to capitalist agriculture (Hoogland 1982:138–52). The latter were young men who described themselves as workers rather than as peasants and who shuttled back and forth between their villages and their places of work in nearby towns and cities. They tended to have at least a primary school education and were attracted by the radical programs of Ali Shariati and the militant clergy (Hoogland 1980; Ashraf, this volume).

The ranks of the part-time peasant are bound to grow, and their protest is as likely to be urban as rural. Their economic interests are split among mine, factory, the informal sector, and the field. The phenomenon is not new. Some years ago I summarized the history of the Chleuh, a congeries of Berber tribes of Morocco's Anti-Atlas mountains. Since the beginning of this century they had been able to gain control of most grocery trade in Morocco's northern cities while maintaining a fragile agrarian economy based on arboriculture, coarse grains, and animal husbandry. They were instrumental in mounting the last rural resistance to French "pacification" in 1934 and then in mounting the first urban resistance to the French in Casablanca and elsewhere in the early 1950s (Waterbury 1973).

Regarding our second question, how do they act?, we want to know what forms resistance and protest take, and how we can explain them. Two analytic approaches have gained currency in the last decade, one based on moral economy and the other on rational actor models. Although clearly different in their assumptions, their empirical applications are not mutually exclusive. Scott (1976) wrote of a subsistence ethic that bound poor cultivators to more powerful owners of land and capital. He contended that when the ethic was violated by the powerful (e.g., denial of gleaning rights or increase in the landlord's share of the crop), the weak no longer owed them deference and support. Individual or collective resistance then became legitimate. The assumptions can be easily extended to relations between the peasantry and the state (Hyden 1980; Scott 1989). The alternative view has been advanced most notably by Samuel Popkin (1979), who suggests that both the weak and the powerful should be seen as rational actors attempting to maximize whatever they see as their best interests. If there is an ethic, it is a device invoked to justify an unsentimental contest for relative advantage. In Popkin's view the landowner is best seen as a monopolist or oligopolist who will press his advantage until he meets resistance or causes the flight of his own labor force. Peasants will most often act as families, seldom as larger collectivities, to press counterclaims for a larger share of whatever is being produced (cf. Migdal 1974).

As Hayami and Kikuchi have shown (1982), in specific instances one may discern a mix of the moral economy and rational actor approaches; so, too, in many of the contributions to this volume. For example, in Tunisia and elsewhere in the Ottoman empire in the late nineteenth century, the resistance to state efforts to increase rural tax revenue involved large, communally organized coalitions of rural actors (Druze, bedouin, Sunni peasants, urban merchants in the Hawran of Syria; see Schilcher, this volume), followed by a collapse of these "fronts" as the central authorities cut deals with each of the contenders, sometimes, as in Tunisia, setting one erstwhile ally against another.

The issue here is that of collective action, crucial to understanding any economic or political behavior (Burke, 1988). Collective action will succeed, if at all, only so long as all members of the collectivity remain committed to the cause. But rational actor models tell us that any individual will have an incentive to stand idly by or to act passively, for if the movement succeeds, that person will reap all its benefits without having been exposed to any of the risks. These people become "free riders," and if enough people in the movement follow their rational individual maximizing strategies, the movement will obviously fail. Because peasant movements are so rare, and their successful outcomes rarer still, this simple proposition would seem to have great power.

Individual foot-dragging, or small-scale family resistance to and sabotage of oppressive power wielders, yields benefits that are to some extent "excludable," that is, they do not accrue fully to all members of the oppressed group. The risks of everyday forms of resistance are relatively low, and the payoffs also relatively low and individualized (theft of grain or animals, poaching, desertion, credit delinquency, etc.). Between collective action and individual foot-dragging lie acts that may provide payoffs for certain free riders: destruction of tax records or squatting on the landlord's land.

There is a temptation to place foot-dragging and violent collective protest at opposite ends of a spectrum of forms of resistance with the implication that one might expect an escalation from the petty and the individual to the violent and the collective. In fact it may be that foot-dragging is best seen as an alternative to revolt and insurrection, and in that sense it may be in the interests of the power wielders to tolerate a certain level of foot-dragging in order to prevent a generalized conflagration. This seems to me most apparent in contemporary relations between state agents and small-scale rural producers in which a certain level of credit delinquency, crop rotations violations, black market sales of subsidized inputs, and so forth has become a standard feature in Egypt, the Sudan, Algeria, Syria, and elsewhere.

A romantic figure in Middle East history arises out of everyday forms of resistance—the rural bandit. Yaşar Kemal's novel *Mehmet My Hawk* portrays just such a hero, who not only abducts the landlord's daughter but kills the landlord. Eric Hobsbawm characterized such figures as social bandits, precursors to more organized forms of rural resistance. But David Hart (1987) and Nathan Brown (1990), among others, have argued that bandits have rarely exhibited much social conscience and have stolen from the poor perhaps more often than from the rich. When they are pursued by the authorities, they may benefit from a peasant conspiracy of silence, but they do not appear to have been the catalysts to collective resistance.

The foregoing discussion has partially answered the third question, what do they seek? I will deal here with two simple dichotomies. The first is whether the movements are forward- or backward-looking. Recall that Valensi saw the Tunisian insurrection of 1864 as restorationist, seeking the return to a preferred status quo ante. The subsistence ethic approach also suggests that peasants will seek to restore what are portrayed as venerable obligations and understandings. But other movements and actions, outwardly no different from the restorationist, seek to overturn the basic power structures. Tanyus Shahin's movement in Mount Lebanon in 1859 (Owen 1981:161–62; Havemann, this volume), the Jangali movement of 1920 in Gilan (Kazemi, this volume), the 1919 revolt in Egypt (at least for its leaders), the 1936 Palestinian uprising (Tress 1988; Stein, this volume), and the Algerian revolution begun in 1954 (Wolf 1969) were resolutely aimed at creating new orders. The problem is that a backward-looking movement may look exactly like a forward-looking one.

The same confusion arises with rural ethnic or religious protest (Favret 1972). Sometimes, as with the Iraqi Kurds or Nilotic populations of the southern Sudan, the proclaimed objective is to secede from the state or at least to create regional autonomy. However, more frequently such movements are aimed at extracting more resources from the state, that is to opt in rather than to opt out. The 1959 Rif rebellion in Morocco, the Yemeni civil war of 1962–67, the Lebanese civil war since 1976, and the Sudanese civil war since 1983 can best be understood as struggles, in which rural ethnic or confessional actors are heavily involved, to turn the state apparatus to their own advantage.

The problem of split agendas arises once again. The leaders may have a revolutionary set of objectives while the followers are restorationist. Ethnic brokers may employ the idiom of separatism to get a bigger piece of the state's action, while followers may well see the destruction or evasion of the state as the objective. Leaders can be bought off but so can followers. Collective action problems are compounded by split agendas.

Finally, we must ask "in what context do they act?" Even if one were to agree with Horvat about the revolutionary potential of the peasantry, its ability to undertake action, as well as the nature of the action, will depend on a host of contextual and institutional factors. The most obvious is, perhaps, the nature of the terrain: it is easier for a mountain Kurd to revolt than it is for an Egyptian Delta peasant. More important is the nature of the state and of markets. For some these are the villains of the piece, beating down peasants through heavy taxes and adverse terms of trade. For others, like Samuel Popkin, there is nothing given about states and markets, which in many instances provide mechanisms for spreading risks among producers and for promoting a general improvement in rural welfare. The studies in this volume by and large depict the state in unflattering terms, and because Middle Eastern states have interfered so extensively with markets, these, by extension, have brought as much harm as good to the interests of rural producers.

In this sense many Middle Eastern states adhere closely to a pattern analyzed by Michael Lipton under the rubric "urban bias" (Lipton 1977; see also Bates 1981), whereby the state sets the terms of trade between its agrarian and nonagrarian sectors to generate a net flow of resources from the former to the latter. Agriculture is taxed to finance industrialization and a subsidized standard of living for the urban poor and lower-middle classes. Only the wealthiest rural producers can profit from this bias by selling highly valued produce to upper-income urban consumers or for export. The rural poor, as suggested above, resist the state by defaulting on government loans, sabotaging "government" crops, and so forth. When everyday forms of peasant resistance are aggregated, they can oblige states to change the policies of urban bias (Hyden 1980), although in the Middle East such changes are only at their inception.[7]

Many observers have noted that in the twentieth century, cities have replaced the countryside as the most likely source of challenge to incumbent regimes. The old distinction employed in Morocco, between the land of dissidence (*bled as-siba*) and the land of government (*bled al-makhzen*), has been inverted so that the cities are now the center of dissidence. Student demonstrations, labor agitation, and cost-of-living riots have been common features of Middle Eastern cities in recent years. It was primarily the cities that brought down the shah in 1978–79, and it is in the cities that the Lebanese civil war has been fought.

Years ago Samuel Huntington argued that because of the disruptive potential of the cities, political stability could be assured only through an alliance of the central authorities with the countryside (Huntington 1968:435). Paradoxically such alliances have been forged at the same time that the authorities have implemented pricing policies that penalize rural producers. They are able to do so through control of government patronage, meted out through local brokers and notables who can neutralize the alienation that the victims of urban bias may feel—or, at any rate, keep it individualized. Rémy Leveau (1985) has provided a fine case study of this strategy.

Yet this view of the cities and the countryside is flawed to the extent that it suggests two worlds—two modes of existence and two distinct populations. Migration from the countryside, the phenomenon of the part-time or shuttle peasant, the flow of remittances from the cities to the countryside, all indicate that the two economies are highly interdependent. Balancing rural against urban interests is probably snare and delusion, a point apparently substantiated by the role of recent migrants to Iranian cities in toppling the shah. Conversely some of the benefits of urban bias, such as subsidized consumer goods, find their way back to the countryside in the form of an increased remittance flow. Middle-income urbanites, fighting the erosion of their incomes by inflation, increasingly invest in commercial agriculture and animal raising, bringing new resources to the countryside but also creating a new set of absentee owners.

One arena of state-peasant interaction and confrontation in the Middle East has grown in importance, but, unfortunately, none of the contributors to this volume address it. It is the arena created by large surface irrigation schemes, generally state-owned and -operated, on which the cultivators are tenants dealing with a landlord that is the state itself. Even in those instances when the land brought under irrigation has been alienated to private holders (Turkey, Morocco, Egypt, Iran), the state may try to control cropping patterns and the terms of tenancy and sharecropping. The role of the state as landlord needs systematic comparative study, and, at least for the Middle East, we have some good case studies upon which to build.[8]

Political brokers, licensed, as it were, by the state, in all instances turn out to be crucial actors who serve two masters. They must deliver their rural clients to the mercies of the state, by collecting taxes and outstanding loans from them and by assuring their political quiescence, yet they must serve their clients by assuring a supply of state services and patronage. In hard economic times the broker is in an extremely precarious position and may not be able to serve both masters simultaneously. Throughout this volume we see intermediaries (landlords, merchants, tax farmers, bureaucrats) swinging back and forth between support for the central state and involvement in local resistance. A clever broker can convince both parties that he is acting in their interest. The unclever have short careers.[9]

Even when rural power structures and institutions are extensively refashioned in the wake of revolutions from above or below, new, rigid power relations tend to develop, a new stratum of brokers and functionaries often lapses into corruption, bossism, and rent-seeking, and new forms of footdragging are frequently invented. The most extensive agrarian reforms in the Middle East—those in Egypt and Algeria—support this observation.[10]

The efforts of a number of Middle Eastern states to redistribute rural assets have strengthened the state's ability to intervene in and to control rural markets and have led to coopting or replacing local elites (Ashraf, this volume). In the process peasant grievances have come to focus on the state itself, and because of increasingly blurred rural-urban lines of economic demarcation, resistance may take place in either environment. The point is that urban resistance should not be seen as driven by purely urban interests.

At the same time the ability of the state to control these markets has diminished as producers have escaped into parallel and black markets or have migrated to the cities or to other countries. In general the collective good provided through the redistribution of rural assets has been privatized or familized, on the one hand by intermediaries collecting fees at every point that the regulatory state apparatus impinges upon the producer, on the other by the producers themselves who appropriate and dispose of collective goods (irrigation water, subsidized seed, fertilizers, fuels) for their own personal ends. Those who start the game with better factor endowments usually increase their advantage so that new patterns of stratification emerge in what was intended to be an egalitarian environment.

If phase 3, since World War II, has been characterized by everyday forms of peasant resistance, interspersed on a global scale with spectacular bursts of rural-based, and sometimes peasant-based, revolution, then phase 4 may involve states recognizing their limitations in regulating agricultural production, the distortions introduced through policies of urban bias, and the fiscal constraints on delivering adequate services to the countryside. The state might then quietly relinquish its role as creator and defender of rural egalitarianism and recognize and legitimize what already exists, that is, extensive rural differentiation. The market, though by no means unregulated, will be touted as the best guarantor of increased production and incomes, accompanied by a necessary sorting out of the efficient from the inefficient. Any true equity concerns still alive in the bosom of the state might best be promoted by contested elections in which the weight of numbers of the rural poor can be a factor. With or without elections, we might anticipate that in this phase the resistance and protest of the small-scale producer will once again focus on those in the countryside who own land, movable assets, and capital. The contest will be less naked than in the early decades of this century, for the state will set rules (land ceilings, floor prices) and maintain programs (targeted subsidies on credit and inputs) that will inhibit gross distortions in income distribution.

Whatever shape phase 4 may take, it is still part of the longer process of market and state penetration into the countryside. As in other parts of the developing world, the context is set by the long economic swings of trade and business cycles and by the steady increase in rural population, processes punctuated by short, conjunctural economic crises—sudden increases in taxes, crop failures, privatization of commons, power vacuums in which contenders mobilize rural constituents, forced grain procurements, relative price shifts, and so on, down a long list.[11] Small-scale producers have often been victims in both the long and the short term. The objective conditions of their victimization have not been as important as have fissures in the ranks of their exploiters, whether landlords, the state, or some combination of both. Oppression, rage, and threat of extinction in and of themselves have not been sufficient to drive them to collective action in the absence of outside leadership, resources and organization that can command their commitment, and a favorable terrain.

As we near the end of this century, it is probably no longer useful to speak of peasants in Wolf's sense of the term. Rural production and rural producers will remain highly significant in the political and economic development of Middle Eastern societies, and poverty and vulnerability will probably remain concentrated in their ranks. But to answer the questions now of who acts, how and why they act, and the contexts in which they act will be analytically a much greater challenge.

The only rural violence we are likely to witness will be ostensibly ethnic or confessional in nature; indeed, since the end of the Algerian liberation war, the Middle East has witnessed no other form of sustained rural resistance. We must be attentive to the long-term shift in population from agrarian to non-agrarian sectors, the increasing integration of the lower-income groups at both ends of that shift, and the possibility that the distinction between urban and rural political arenas will be increasingly meaningless. The most aggressive rural political actors may turn out to be the growing ranks of the medium-scale market producers who will lobby collectively for favorable policies from the state. They will have the resources and the organization to give voice to their grievances. For the rural poor, exit to the cities will prevail over protest, while accommodation with the middle strata through clientage will prevail over conflict.

Notes

1. The leader among them was Gabriel Baer (1969), but see also Jacques Berque (1955, 1957), Launay (1963), Couleau (1968), Hamed Ammar (1954), and Jacques Weulerrse (1946).

2. Two good, recent anthropological surveys of the Middle East are Bates and Rassam (1983) and Eickelman (1981). Neither deals with peasant protest, although Bates and Rassam devote a chapter to local politics and patronage (pp. 241–68). An excellent collection of historical articles, some of which deal explicitly with the same

subject matter that concerns us here, is Edmund Burke and Ira Lapidus, eds. (1988). Bridging history, anthropology, and rural sociology is the special 1987 issue of the *Revue de l'Occident musulman et de la Méditerranée*, "La Société, la Terre, et le Pouvoir dans le Monde Arabe" (vol. 45, no. 3).

3. The two best general economic histories of this period are Issawi (1982) and Owen (1981).

4. The primary sources are Valensi (1977:350–68), Cherif (1980), Slama (1967), and Anderson (1986:69–70, 84).

5. Scott (1979:108) explores these split agendas in some detail. Commenting on Vietnam in 1930, he states, "What the party belatedly called 'Soviets' were nothing more, nothing less than the enactment of local autonomy and the vision of an equitable distribution of food and land."

6. This theme is explored in Roberts (1982, 1983), Seddon (1981), and Schilcher (this volume). In a recent collection on ethnicity and politics in the Middle East, only Farhad Kazemi tried systematically to explore the links between ethnicity and the peasantry in Iran (Esman and Rabinovich, 1988:201–14). For an earlier collection dealing only with Berberism in North Africa, see Gellner and Micaud (1972).

7. A difficult empirical and analytic question inheres in this observation. Do individual actors, when they drag their feet, understand their action as challenging political authority, or is it more likely that they are "merely" looking out for their own best economic interests? Answering the question may be impossible, but see Scott (1989:8) and Brown (this volume) for views that support conscious political intent.

8. On the Sudanese Gezira scheme, see Barnett (1977); on Syria's Tabaqa scheme, Hannoyer (1985); on Egypt, Mehanna, Huntington, and Antonious (1984); on Morocco, Swearingen (1987); and on Tunisia, Baduel (1985).

9. An excellent analysis of the Janus-faced intermediary can be found in Zweig (1989:74–97), where he deals with leaders of production teams and brigades in Maoist and post-Mao China.

10. Stinchcombe (1961:173) makes the general point, while Pearse (1975:165) provides case material on the rise of *caciquismo* in the Bolivian countryside following the far-reaching agrarian revolution of 1952. In the flavorful observation of a Nicaraguan peasant after the Sandinistas came to power, "Only the flies change; the crap remains the same" (Colburn, 1986:120). See Ashraf (this volume).

11. In this broad frame the Middle East is in no way unusual; see the excellent collection edited by Friedrich Katz (1988), especially Coatsworth, "Patterns of Rural Rebellion in Latin America."

References

Ammar, Hamed. 1954. *Growing Up in an Egyptian Village*. London. Routledge & Kegan Paul.

Anderson, Lisa. 1986. *The State and Social Transformation in Tunisia and Libya, 1830–1980*. Princeton, N.J.: Princeton University Press.

Baduel, P.-R. 1985. "Action sur les facteurs de production et dépendance paysanne:

L'Exemple du développement hydro-agricole tunisien." In *Les Politiques de l'eau en Afrique,* edited by G. Conac. Paris: Economica.

Baer, Gabriel. 1969. *Studies in the Social History of Modern Egypt.* Chicago: University of Chicago Press.

Barnett, Tony. 1977. *The Gezira Scheme—An Illusion of Development.* London: Frank Cass.

Batatu, Hanna. 1978. *The Old Social Classes and the Revolutionary Movements of Iraq.* Princeton, N.J.: Princeton University Press.

Bates, Daniel, and Amal Rassam. 1983. *Peoples and Cultures of the Middle East.* Englewood Cliffs, N.J.: Prentice-Hall.

Bates, Robert. 1981. *Markets and States in Tropical Africa.* Berkeley: University of California Press.

Berque, Jacques. 1955. *Structures sociales du Haut-Atlas.* Paris: Presses Universitaires de France.

————. 1957. *Histoire sociale d'un village égyptien au XXième siècle.* Paris: Mouton.

Binder, Leonard. 1978. *In a Moment of Enthusiasm: Political Power and the Second Stratum in Egypt.* Chicago: University of Chicago Press.

Brown, Nathan. 1989. "The Conspiracy of Silence and the Atomistic Political Activity of the Egyptian Peasantry, 1882–1952." In *Everyday Forms of Peasant Resistance,* edited by Forrest Colburn. Armonk, N.Y.: M. E. Sharpe.

————. 1990. *Peasant Politics in Modern Egypt.* New Haven, Conn.: Yale University Press.

Burke, Edmund. 1988. "Rural Collective Action and the Emergence of Modern Lebanon." In *Lebanon: A History of Conflict and Consensus,* edited by Nadim Shehadi and Dana Mills. Oxford: I. B. Taurus.

Burke, Edmund, and Ira Lapidus, eds. 1988. *Islamic Political and Social Movements.* Berkeley: University of California Press.

Chaulet, Claudine. 1987. "Les ruraux algériens et l'état." *Revue de l'Occident musulman et de la Méditerranée* 45, 3:67–93.

Cherif, Mohammed Hadi. 1980. "Les Mouvements paysans dans la Tunisie du XIXe siècle." *Revue de l'Occident musulman et de la Méditerranée,* no. 30.

Coatsworth, John. 1988. "Patterns of Rural Rebellion in Latin America." In *Riot, Rebellion, and Revolution: Rural Social Conflict in Mexico,* edited by Friedrich Katz. Princeton, N.J.: Princeton University Press.

Colburn, Forrest. 1986. *Post-Revolutionary Nicaragua: State, Class, and the Dilemmas of Agrarian Policy.* Berkeley: University of California Press.

————, ed. 1989. *Everyday Forms of Peasant Resistance.* Armonk, N.Y.: M. E. Sharpe.

Couleau, Julien. 1968. *La Paysannerie marocaine.* Paris: CRESM/CNRS.

Eickelman, Dale. 1981. *The Middle East: An Anthropological Approach.* Englewood Cliffs, N.J.: Prentice-Hall.

Esman, Milton, and Itamar Rabinovich, eds. 1988. *Ethnicity, Pluralism, and the State in the Middle East.* Ithaca, N.Y.: Cornell University Press.

Favret, Jeanne. 1972. "Traditionalism through Ultra-Modernism." In *Arabs and Berbers,* edited by Ernest Gellner and Charles Micaud. London: Duckworth.

Geertz, Clifford. 1963. "The Integrative Revolution: Primordial Sentiments and Civil

Politics in the New States." In *Old Societies and New States,* edited by Clifford Geertz. New York: The Free Press.

Gellner, Ernest. 1962. "Patterns of Rural Rebellion in Morocco: Tribes as Minorities." *European Journal of Sociology* 3, 2:297–311.

Gellner, Ernest, and Charles Micaud, eds. 1972. *Arabs and Berbers.* London: Duckworth.

Halpern, Manfred. 1948. "The Algerian Uprising of 1945." *Middle East Journal* (April): 191–202.

Hannoyer, Jean. 1985. "Grands projets hydrauliques en Syrie." *Maghreb-Machrek,* no. 109 (July–September): 24–42.

Harik, Iliya. 1974. *The Political Mobilization of Peasants: A Study of an Egyptian Community.* Bloomington: Indiana University Press.

Hart, David. 1987. *Banditry in Islam.* Cambridgeshire: Middle East and North African Studies Press.

Hayami, Yujiro, and Masao Kikuchi. 1982. *Asian Village at the Crossroads.* Baltimore, Md.: Johns Hopkins University Press.

Hinnebusch, Raymond. 1979. "Party and Peasant in Syria." *Cairo Papers in Social Science* 3, 1 (entire issue).

Hobsbawm, Eric. 1973. "Peasants and Politics." *Journal of Peasant Studies* 1, 1:3–22.

Hoogland, Eric. 1980. "Rural Participation in the Revolution." *MERIP Reports,* no. 87 (May): 3–6.

———. 1982. *Land and Revolution in Iran, 1960–1980.* Austin: University of Texas Press.

Hopkins, Nicholas. 1987. *Agrarian Transformation in Egypt.* Boulder, Colo.: Westview Press.

Horvat, Branko. 1981. "Establishing Self-Governing Socialism in a Less-Developed Country." *World Development* 9, 9:951–64.

Huntington, Samuel. 1968. *Political Order in Changing Societies.* New Haven, Conn.: Yale University Press.

Hyden, Goren. 1980. *Beyond Ujamaa in Tanzania: Underdevelopment and an Uncaptured Peasantry.* Berkeley: University of California Press.

Issawi, Charles. 1982. *An Economic History of the Middle East and North Africa.* New York: Columbia University Press.

Kasfir, Nelson. 1979. "Explaining Ethnic Political Participation." *World Politics* 31, 3:365–88.

Katz, Friedrich, ed. 1988. *Riot, Rebellion, and Revolution: Rural Social Conflict in Mexico.* Princeton, N.J.: Princeton University Press.

Kazemi, Farhad. 1988. "Ethnicity and the Iranian Peasantry." In *Ethnicity, Pluralism and the State in the Middle East,* edited by Milton Esman and Itamar Rabinovich. Ithaca, N.Y.: Cornell University Press.

Kazemi, Farhad, and Ervand Abrahamian. 1978. "The Non-Revolutionary Peasantry of Modern Iran." *Iranian Studies* 11:259–304.

Launay, Michel. 1963. *Paysans algériens: La Terre, la vigne, et les hommes.* Paris: Édition de Seuil.

Leveau, Rémy. 1985. *Le Fellah marocain: Défenseur du trône.* Paris: Presses de la FNSP.

Levi, Margaret. 1988. *Of Rule and Revenue*. Berkeley: University of California Press.

Lipton, Michael. 1977. *Why Poor People Stay Poor: Urban Bias in World Development*. Cambridge, Mass.: Harvard University Press.

Mehanna, Soheir, Richard Huntington, and Rachad Antonious. 1984. "Irrigation and Society in Rural Egypt." *Cairo Papers in Social Science* 7, monograph 4.

Migdal, Joel. 1974. *Peasants, Politics and Revolution*. Princeton, N.J.: Princeton University Press.

Owen, Roger. 1981. *The Middle East in the World Economy*. London: Methuen.

Paige, Jeffrey. 1975. *Agrarian Revolution*. New York: The Free Press.

Pearse, Andrew. 1975. *The Latin American Peasant*. London: Frank Cass.

Popkin, Samuel. 1979. *The Rational Peasant*. Berkeley: University of California Press.

Reynolds, Lloyd. 1985. *Economic Growth in the Third World, 1850–1980*. New Haven, Conn.: Yale University Press.

Roberts, Hugh. 1982. "The Unforeseen Development of the Kabyle Question in Contemporary Algeria." *Government and Opposition* 17, 3:312–34.

———. 1983. "The Economics of Berberism: The Kabyle Question in Contemporary Algeria." *Government and Opposition* 18, 2:218–35.

Rogowski, Ronald. 1989. *Commerce and Coalitions: How Trade Affects Domestic Political Alignments*. Princeton, N.J.: Princeton University Press.

Saunders, Lucie, and Soheir Mehanna. 1989. "Smallholders in a Changing Economy: An Egyptian Village Case." *Peasant Studies* 16, 1:5–30.

Scott, James. 1976. *The Moral Economy of the Peasant*. New Haven, Conn.: Yale University Press.

———. 1979. "Revolution in the Revolution: Peasants and Commissars." *Theory and Society* 7, 1 and 2:97–131.

———. 1985. *Weapons of the Weak: Everyday Forms of Peasant Resistance*. New Haven, Conn.: Yale University Press.

———. 1989. "Everyday Forms of Resistance." In *Everyday Forms of Peasant Resistance,* edited by Forrest Colburn. Armonk, N.Y.: M. E. Sharpe.

Seddon, David. 1981. *Moroccan Peasants: A Century of Change in the Eastern Rif*. Folkestone: Dawson.

Sen, Amartya. 1981. *Poverty and Famines*. Oxford: Clarendon Press.

Slama, Bice. 1967. *L'Insurrection de 1864 en Tunisie*. Tunis: Maison Tunisienne de l'Édition.

Stinchcombe, Arthur. 1961. "Agricultural Enterprise and Rural Class Relations." *American Journal of Sociology* 67, 2:165–76.

Swearingen, Will. 1987. *Moroccan Mirages: Agrarian Dreams and Deceptions, 1912–1986*. Princeton, N.J.: Princeton University Press.

Taylor-Awny, E. 1984. "Peasants or Proletarians: The Transformation of Agrarian Production Relations in Egypt." In *Proletarianisation in the Third World,* edited by H. Finch and B. Munslow. London: Croom Helm.

Tress, Madeleine. 1988. "The Role of the Peasantry in the Palestine Revolt, 1936–39." *Peasant Studies* 15, 3:161–90.

Valensi, Lucette. 1977. *Fellahs tunisiens: L'Économie rurale et la vie des campagnes aux 18e et 19e siècles*. Paris: Mouton.

Waterbury, John. 1973. *North for the Trade: The Life and Times of a Berber Merchant.* Berkeley: University of California Press.

Weulerrse, Jacques. 1946. *Paysans de Syrie et du Proche Orient.* Paris.

Wolf, Eric. 1966. *Peasants.* Englewood Cliffs, N.J.: Prentice-Hall.

———. 1968. *Peasant Wars of the Twentieth Century.* New York: Harper and Row.

Zweig, David. 1989. *Agrarian Radicalism in China, 1968–1981.* Cambridge, Mass.: Harvard University Press.

Changing Patterns of Peasant Protest in the Middle East, 1750–1950

EDMUND BURKE, III

To an extent not generally recognized, peasant rebellions and protest movements were recurring features of rural politics in the Arab world in the period 1750–1950. Until recently, the historical literature has emphasized the non-revolutionary character of the Middle Eastern peasantry, stressing the fatalism of peasants and the oppression of corrupt governments and landowners. The elite bias of many sources and stereotypes about the nature of Islamic societies account to a considerable extent for this view.[1]

The Problem: From Peasants to Politics?

Recently this orthodoxy has shown signs of crumbling. A survey of rural protest in Egypt and Bilad al-Sham, for example, concludes that "throughout the last 200 years there was no generation that did not witness a fellah rebellion."[2] Peasant protests were also important in the Maghrib, where their occurrence is somewhat better documented.[3] In some cases, as we shall see, peasant revolts could give rise to challenges to the established agrarian order. Protest has had a far greater presence in the Middle Eastern countryside than previously recognized, even though in comparison to western Europe and China, the area still looks relatively peaceable. What is clear is that overt peasant rebellions were less frequent than resort to various forms of avoidance protest. The weak demography of the Middle Eastern countryside and the proximity of vast unpoliced wastelands in which recalcitrant peasants could hide out helped shape protest along lines different from the European and

Chinese models. The alternation between protest and passivity, it now seems clear, as well as the changing patterns of peasant revolt in the Arab world over these two centuries were both connected to the transformation of agrarian structures. When and how these changes came about, which groups benefited from them and which suffered, are topics that must be explored in order to understand fully their genesis.

We are on the threshold of a new understanding of the processes of rural change in the Middle East and North Africa. In part, this is because new research has called into question many of the old assumptions about the ways Middle Eastern rural society was transformed.[4] In part, we owe this new understanding to significant changes in the social science literature on rural society and peasant protest, which has evolved from an infatuation with peasant revolution to a more complex and nuanced grasp of the realities of peasant protest and avoidance.[5]

In the first part of this essay, I will briefly survey the literature on rural protest and seek to show that not only has rural protest been a recurrent feature of Middle Eastern history since 1750, but also that there were patterns to this protest.[6] Next, I will situate rural collective action and avoidance protest against the background of the transformation of the region's agrarian structures. Finally, I will advance some hypothetical connections between the ways in which Middle Eastern societies were transformed over the long nineteenth century and the outcome of these rural struggles.

Rural Collective Action: Some Preliminary Considerations

For purposes of analysis, one can say that since 1750 social movements in the Middle East have emerged as a result of the intersection of three main kinds of change. The first was the indigenous self-strengthening movement, under whose aegis the state bureaucracy sought to increase its control of the society, establishing modern armies, schools, and methods of communication. In the Ottoman provinces this process was known as the *tanzimat* movement. It inevitably led to a collision between reform-minded state bureaucrats and local elites, eager to defend their traditional rights and liberties. The tanzimat also stimulated conflict with peasants and artisans, who experienced the state's encroachment primarily in the forms of military conscription and increased taxation.

The incorporation of the Middle East into the world economy stimulated a second and in some ways more far-reaching type of change. Although even relatively isolated regions with weak states felt its effects, the consequences were differentially greater for societies like Egypt and the Arab East that stood astride major world communications links. Economic incorporation led to the rise of a new urban middle class whose fortunes were linked to Europe, and of an urban-based class of landowners engaged in commercial agriculture for export. It also caused a decline in the fortunes of artisans and peasants unable to adapt to the changing economic tides. Incorporation in the capitalist world market, therefore, added to the fiscal and other pressures of the centralizing state.

Where the experience of the Middle East diverges with that of Europe to join that of the rest of the Third World is in the colonial context of its coming to modern politics, the third major change to affect the region. European hegemony challenged basic cultural values and distorted the impact of change in significant ways, setting in motion deeply rooted responses throughout the region. One place to evaluate the social impact of Western dominance is in the internal processes of political change, where collaboration with imperialism worked to undermine the legitimacy of local elites even as it strengthened their power. In this ambiguous context, the national struggle tended to take precedence over the class struggle. Thus European dominance shored up the precarious power of old elites, who successfully capitalized on their position to maintain control of the nationalist movement and ensured that when new classes at last emerged on the political scene, after World War II, their impact would be muffled. This era is only now showing signs of drawing to a close.

Each of these vectors of change worked in favor of certain groups in the society and against others. Those possessing privileged ties to the state or to European business interests were often in a position to profit disproportionately, while urban artisans and rural agriculturalists found themselves squeezed from all sides. Following the establishment of European political control, groups willing to serve as intermediaries gained substantially, while overt opponents suffered from various forms of political and economic discrimination. The complex sequences of change thus set in motion intersected with one another, generating powerful crosscurrents and eddies that eroded established interests and molded new ones. Social protest and resistance found fertile ground in the circumstances thus created.

ANY SURVEY of the transformation of protest in the Arab countryside must begin with some basic distinctions in the agrarian structures within the region. Agricultural conditions in Egypt, Bilad al-Sham (greater Syria), and the Maghrib varied considerably according to rainfall, soil type, relief, and proximity to irrigation sources. No less important were social and political realities: the system of land tenure, the precise nature of the connections between governments, intermediaries, and agriculturalists, and the social organization and ethnic composition of rural society.[7]

The agrarian structures of the Arab East were infinitely complex and various. Mamluk Egypt with its system of tax farms and urban-based military elite, for example, differed from the quasi-feudal society of Mount Lebanon with its *muqataji* great families and oppressed peasantry, the tribally controlled irrigated lands of Iraq, and the collectively held *mushaa* lands of the Palestinian villages. The countryside was further marked by the presence of significant ethnic and religious minority communities: Kurds, Druze, and Christian and Shi'ite sects, so that in some districts of Bilad al-Sham and al-Iraq, minorities could outnumber Sunni Arab groups.

The Arab Maghrib was no less varied, ranging from the densely settled olive- and grain-producing Sahel region of Tunisia to the sedentary Berber-speaking arboriculturists of Kabiliya, the pastoralist transhumant sheepherders of the Middle Atlas mountains in Morocco, and, in the southern oases, the quasi-serf black *haratin* populations and their Bedouin overlords. In the Maghrib, the Atlas mountain chain presented an even greater barrier to government control, giving greater weight to tribally organized forces. Also, in contrast to the Arab East with its plethora of ethnic minorities, the Arab West enjoyed substantial homogeneity: the Jewish population was mostly urban, and even the Berbers were Sunni Muslims of the Maliki legal rite. Out of the Middle East's many microecologies and political systems, a profusion of distinctive ways of life developed that at the same time had significant points in common. The conventional image for this diversity—a mosaic of intergroup rivalries and tensions arbitrated by state authorities—exaggerates differences while it downplays the significance of conflict.

Against the background of this diversity, we can attempt to sketch in the broad sequences of rural rebellions in the period 1750–1950. Because Egypt was both the center of state centralization and the most strongly engaged in the expanding world market, the new changes (and the related patterns of collective action) tended to emerge there before they affected the rest of the Middle East. The twin forces of statemaking and capitalism impinged next upon Bilad al-Sham, while Iraq and the Maghrib (except colonial Algeria) went through broadly analogous patterns of change about a generation later.

Rural Collective Action, 1750–1850

If we examine the patterns of rural collective action, the first phase that can be distinguished runs from roughly the 1750s to the 1840s. Toward the end of the eighteenth century Egypt began to experience a sharp increase in the pace of change. In response to the state's increasing fiscal demands on the rural populations, a series of revolts broke out beginning in the 1770s and 1780s in Egypt and Lebanon. Another wave of peasant uprisings followed the establishment of the Muhammad Ali regime in 1805 and of comparable regional dynasties in Lebanon and Palestine—the 1820–23 rebellion of peasants in Qina province in Upper Egypt, the 1820 general rebellion of peasants in Mount Lebanon, and further rebellions in Egypt in the late 1820s. Significant uprisings occurred in Palestine in 1834 and in Syria in 1837–38.[8]

In North Africa the timetable of revolt lagged somewhat. The first decades of the nineteenth century were the scene of major rebellions in Algeria, Tunisia, and Morocco. They took the form of regional resistance to would-be centralizing rulers: the 1803–4 Kabyle uprising, the 1803–12 and 1820s Oranais revolts against Turkish rule in Algeria, rebellions in Tunisia in 1795, 1819, 1824–25, 1840, and 1844 against the fiscal impositions of the Beys, and risings of Middle Atlas Berbers in the 1820s. The onset of the French conquest of Algeria in 1830 significantly altered this pattern in ways that will be explained in the next section.

A finer-grained analysis than is possible here would reveal the crucial importance not only of the new, more systematized demands of the Muhammad Ali dynasty but also of responses to the commercialization of agriculture, the transformation of landholding arrangements, the increased role of urban moneylenders, and, as has been suggested for the Egyptian rebellions of the 1820s, the decline of rural artisans and craftspersons threatened by the incorporation of hitherto largely autonomous provinces into a national economy linked to the capitalist world economy.[9] The local elites proved central in all of these uprisings. In most instances they reached compromises with the established governments that safeguarded their interests or even increased their control locally.

Beginning in the 1840s the Arab countryside was further transformed by accelerated economic changes stemming from the commercialization of agriculture on one hand, and the Ottoman self-strengthening movement on the other. Thus began the second phase of protest, which lasted roughly from the 1840s to the early 1880s (with local variations). A key problem was the absence of security of land tenure anywhere in the region. The system of land rights was based on usufructary rights held by farmers who paid land rents to various intermediaries, with the rest forwarded to the central treasury. As a consequence, surplus revenues were invested in commerce, rather than in land. The changes introduced from the 1840s onward exploded the old agrarian structures. Private property on the European model was introduced and loosened the bonds between cultivator and land and between cultivator and village community. In place of the old class of tax-farmers a variety of social groups emerged, including a numerous smallholding peasantry in Tunisia and a class of urban-based absentee landowners in Egypt and greater Syria.[10]

The extension of government power into the countryside, one of the primary features of the self-strengthening movements throughout the area, gathered force in the 1840s and provoked major rebellions in Lebanon, Egypt, and Syria, among others. Increased security led to the further commercialization of agriculture and rural textile production, undermining local social and economic structures and setting the stage for a major confrontation around mid-century. The extension of regular steamship service between the Middle East and Europe by the 1840s accelerated these changes.

Mid-Century Peasant Collective Action and Avoidance Protest

By the 1850s the agrarian structures of the Arab world entered a phase of sustained crisis. Especially in Lebanon (1858–61), Tunisia (1864–65), and Algeria (1871–72), rebellions broke out that challenged the very basis of the system itself, before they were repressed with European assistance. The scale and radical demands of these mid-century rebellions mark a break with earlier movements. More significantly, their repression led to the crystallization of the coalitions of rural, urban, and state forces within which agricultural development proceeded until the twentieth century. Of these movements, the Lebanese rebellion of 1858–61 is the best known.[11] Both in it and in the more radical Tunisian rebellion of 1864, the cruel pressures of the state's fiscal demands and the commercialization of agriculture can be seen clearly.[12]

Other peasant rebellions in the region merit inclusion in this list. Most important was the so-called Muqrani rebellion of 1871–72 in Constantine province in Algeria, which occurred in the context of the Franco-Prussian war and before it was repressed had seriously threatened French control over Algeria.[13] Lagging somewhat in this sequence was Morocco, which experienced a number of important rural insurrections between 1850 and 1906. The 1894–96 insurrection in the Marrakech region of Morocco by the Rehamna and associated groups challenged the authority of the Sultan 'Abd al-'Aziz and required three years to bring under control.[14] Finally, among the most important Moroccan rural insurrections in this context were the 1902–6 *siba* of the tribes in the Shawiya plain of Morocco adjacent to Casablanca, and the rebellion of Abu Himara (1902–9), a pretender to the throne who gathered substantial support among the tribes of northeastern Morocco and managed to survive two sultans.[15]

Very much in this context was the 1889–90 rebellion of Druze peasants against the supremacy of their Atrash lords, the last great mid-century rebellion. The peasants endured undeniably harsh circumstances. They previously had owned neither their fields nor their homes and could be evicted at will with no compensation. In alliance with anti-Atrash clan heads, they managed in 1889 to wrest ownership of the land from their quasi-feudal Atrash overlords. The resolution of the conflict permitted the extension of new relations of production into the heart of the Jabal, and, in an interesting parallel to the Maronite rebellion, recemented the alliance of Druze peasants with their chiefs in opposing Ottoman policy.

Several common features emerge from the obvious differences among the great peasant rebellions of the middle part of the nineteenth century. One is the common opposition to crushing government fiscal impositions and to the intervention of the state and its agents. Expanding government ambitions and the need for more revenues to pay for them resulted in a sharply increased tax burden on the peasantry. Recent administrative changes that threatened further encroachment on local autonomy is a second common feature. Initially the revolts were supported by disaffected local elites. Often, however, peasant groups sought to turn the revolts into broader attacks on the remnants of the old agrarian structures, as well as on government fiscal repression. Yet as the revolts consolidated their gains, this radicalization lost the rebels the support and sympathy of local elites and urban groups. The opposition of urban landowners and big merchants entailed the eventual opposition of the ulama (in the case of the Muslim rebellions), or of the Maronite upper clergy (in the case of the Kisrawan rebellion in Lebanon). With these defections, the balance of social forces shifted and the rebellions were repressed.

In all cases, the regions in which the revolts broke out were substantially involved in producing agricultural exports, and the local agrarian structures had managed to retain much of their previous character, and the old families, their power. The development of new agrarian relations was thus largely channeled within the old social forms, overlapping and interpenetrating them. In areas that did not experience revolt on such a scale, the old agrarian elites were less tenacious, and the changeover left less opportunity for challenge from below.

Through their demands and their action, one glimpses the hidden world of the peasants. Their targets were the houses and goods of government repre-

sentatives and of particularly disliked wealthy indigenous and foreign landowners. In the case of the Tunisian movement, the rebels were able to forge a
coalition that included at its height most of the Beylik outside the capital,
Tunis. In neither the Lebanese nor the Tunisian case was the leadership drawn
from the agricultural day-workers. Rather it came from the lesser clergy,
smallholders, and rural artisans. (The Lebanese leader Tanyus Shahin was a
farrier, while the Tunisian Ali bin Ghadhahim was head of the local Tijaniya
sufi brotherhood.)

In Tunisia, the explicitly political strategy adopted (collective bargaining
by riot) was directed against Ottoman taxation policies (rather than, for example, against landowners, or toward changing the conditions of landholding or
labor). In Lebanon, the revolt was directed against the excesses of the greedy
Khazin muqatajis and resulted in the ending of feudalism in the Maronite
sections of Mount Lebanon. To defend the allegedly self-sufficient peasant
village, the rebels took up arms, selecting their leaders from among the better-
off peasants, and drafted political demands aimed at forcing a roll-back of
intrusive government reform measures. Their rebellion culminated in bloody
intercommunal fighting between the Druze and Maronites and the intervention
of Ottoman and European forces.

The other face of peasant revolt, as Anton Blok observes with reference to
Sicily, is the intimidation by agents of the landlord or the state of peasants
who might be tempted to rebel. Blok was attempting to explain the so-
ciogenesis of that peculiarly Sicilian institution, the mafia.[16] If we look at the
Arab world through Sicilian spectacles, the extent to which the countryside is
controlled by similar social forces is striking: the Lebanese *zu'ama* and
qabadays, the Palestinian great families, Egyptian *umdahs,* Moroccan *grands
qa'ids.* Violent political middlemen in a myriad of social forms flourished in
the niche created between weak governments uncertain of their power and a
restive and rebellious peasantry. Through their control over the means of local
coercion, such middlemen were able to dominate the countryside, in some
cases into the twentieth century. Through their control over kin, clients, and
confederates, they were able to dominate the labor market and make themselves indispensable to urban absentee landlords and the state. It is no accident
that the development of this group of violent political middlemen reached its
height in Lebanon, with its intense confessional rivalries, oppressive agricultural system, and weak state. The perpetuation of archaic social forms in
the Arab world is to be understood in this context.

As in Sicily, the viability of the old structures was maintained not only by
coercion but also by the availability of emigration as a safety valve in the

explosive countryside. Here we come to the understudied subject of peasant avoidance protest. If the agrarian structures of the Arab world have managed to preserve the shreds and tatters of the old forms, it is as much owing to peasant avoidance as to the maintenance of oppressive structures and social forms. If, unlike the densely settled peasant societies of China and India, the Middle East entered the modern world with a thinly settled countryside, then the dilution of this base by migration is surely an important variable in explaining the patterns of collective action in the region. Without a sea in which to swim, the fish are easily caught.

Peasant Collective Action in the Liberal Age, 1880–1925

By the end of the nineteenth century, beginning in Egypt and spreading to the rest of the region, new forms of collective action begin to emerge. In 1882, the first successful agricultural strike occurred in Sharqiya province. Share-croppers in the district of Zankalun struck against a large renter of lands owned by the Khedive and forced him to give up his lease.[17] The old reper-toire of peasant protest based on the traditional Islamic moral economy and defense of local rights gradually disappeared, to be replaced by new forms of social movements keyed to the new market relations: rent strikes, agricultural worker strikes, boycotts, and an epidemic of rural banditry.

These changes signal the transformation of agrarian relations and mark a new phase in the history of the Middle East. The development of a rural constabulary, the settlement of the nomads, the extension of modern means of communication (railroads and telegraph) into the countryside, and the devel-opment of modern property relations transformed the terrain on which the old struggles were enacted. Agrarian collective action increasingly played itself out in terms of the new model, with the militancy of estate laborers and sharecroppers increasingly replacing jacqueries and older forms of rural vio-lence. With the exception of the mass anticolonial risings that followed World War I, the new forms of protest represent a shift from jacqueries to smaller-scale protests in which economic demands play the major role.

The new forms of collective action were pioneered first in Egypt because that is where the new economic forces had their deepest impact. The agri-cultural laborers who struck at Zankalun in 1882 were part of a wave of agrarian unrest that affected Egypt in the late 1870s and early 1880s. After several decades of worsening agricultural conditions, and encouraged by the ulama and the Sufi orders, Egyptian peasants attacked the estates of the Turco-

Circassian elite and khedival family in Buhaira, Gharbiya, Qalyubiya, and the cotton provinces of Minya and Asyut. Changing agricultural conditions, resulting both from market forces and state fiscal demands, led to a rising tide of foreclosures, with the inevitable human casualties: a growing number of increasingly desperate landless peasants and service tenants. In this context, 'Urabi's promise to cancel peasant debt and "banish the usurers" provoked a widespread series of attacks on foreign moneylenders, and al-Azhar students fanned the discontent. A specific object of peasant wrath was mortgage foreclosure, a hitherto unknown and un-Islamic practice. Only British intervention saved the Turco-Egyptian hold on the land.[18] Not for the last time, a Middle Eastern country would be saved from revolution by European intervention.

By the early 1900s similar strikes were taking place from Syria to Algeria, and by the interwar years the peasant repertoire had expanded to include land invasions and other more radical tactics. By 1900 Algerian agricultural laborers were demanding higher wages. By the 1930s, as a result of Communist party activity, efforts to organize agricultural labor were taking shape.[19]

As the focus of peasant protest turned from the state to moneylenders and landowners, the landed elites (whether European or indigenous) turned more repressive, hiring field guards and other armed retainers to keep order. They also turned increasingly to the courts to enforce their new rights upon a balky agricultural labor force. A plague of lawyers, eager to defend the interests of wealthy clients (and often their own), descended upon the countryside. We catch echoes of this world in such works as Tawfiq al-Hakim's *Yawmiyyat na'ib fi al-riyaf.*[20]

The consolidation of private property rights combined with worsening agrarian conditions to provoke a wave of brigandism in Egypt and elsewhere in the region. The peasant bands that had sprung up in 1879–82 remained active despite the repression of the 'Urabi movement, prompting the creation of an official Brigandage Commission in 1884 to put down the "primitive rebels" who threatened landlords and their estates. Despite punishments, the threat of retaliatory acts by angry peasants remained real into the early twentieth century. Thomas Russell, police commandant of Cairo from 1913 to 1946, noted the reaction of a rural notable to his suggestion of the delights of reading a book on the veranda of a country estate of an evening: "My friend said at once: 'You don't really think that a landlord in the districts could sit out on a veranda after dinner, with a bright light over his head, do you, and not get shot.' "[21]

Algeria also experienced a wave of banditry at the end of the nineteenth century. Especially in mountainous districts like the Aures and Kabilya, bandit gangs functioned with impunity into the twentieth century. Supported by the local populations, groups like the "bande de Belezma" lasted from 1915 to 1921, preying chiefly upon Muslims known to be tied to the French authorities.[22] Social bandits like these may be found throughout the region, testing the limits of the repressive power of the colonial state. They also experimented with new political forms that were later to be adopted in the postwar nationalist movements. (Think, for example, of the armed bands who terrorized landlords in the Palestinian countryside in the 1930s or the Algerian FLN.)

The social movements of the liberal age (1880–1925) reflect not only the tightening grip of state authorities and the heightened pace of economic change but also the looming shadow of the West. A key feature of this period was experimentation with new forms and ideologies of collective action. Increasingly the remnants of the old system were bypassed by new social groups with distinctively different economic bases, cultural reference points, and social experiences. In the countryside, peasant jacqueries began to give way to rent strikes and attacks on local estate agents and usurers. Most important, as portions of the Arab world came under European domination, experiments with new forms of identity and social cohesion, notably secular nationalism, began to emerge.

Conclusion

One way to begin to make sense of the complexity and diversity of the Middle Eastern countryside lies in placing it in comparative historical context. As Barrington Moore, Jr., and Theda Skocpol have shown, the entry into the modern age of states like France, Russia, and China was the occasion of intense social conflict.[23] In these agrarian bureaucratic states, they argue, under certain conditions conflicts could give rise to social revolutions. Whether they did or not, they contend, the manner in which the old structures were transformed in agrarian bureaucracies permanently shaped the sort of modern state that would emerge and the coalition of forces that would sustain it.

The Ottoman Empire, Iran, and Morocco were agrarian bureaucracies similar in some ways to the states studied by Moore and Skocpol. During the period 1750–1950 each underwent intense social turmoil. Yet the Middle East did not experience major social revolution. Why not? The study of the local elites in the Middle East, because they were the chief intermediaries between rural agriculturalists, the state, and the market can help us to begin to assess cases of revolt and nonrevolt in the area. As elsewhere, rural society in the Middle East was connected to the outside world by webs of kinship, religious, state, and market relationships. Local elites were well placed within each of these networks to muffle the impact of change upon themselves, the better to be able to preserve their own fortunes. The adroitness of Lebanese muqatajis, Egyptian umdahs, and rural big men all over the region in penetrating the emerging state structures allowed them to maintain a grip on important political and economic resources and ride out currents of change they could not control. Ultimately, it helped them to survive.

Notes

1. For a summary and critique of this literature, see Bryan S. Turner, *Marx and the End of Orientalism* (London: Allen & Unwin, 1978).

2. Gabriel Baer, "Fellah Rebellion in Egypt and the Fertile Crescent," in *Fellah and Townsmen in the Middle East,* ed. Baer (London: Frank Cass, 1982).

3. See, for example, Muhamed Cherif, "Les mouvements paysans dans la Tunisie du XIXe siècle," *Revue de l'Occident musulman et de la Méditerranée,* no. 30 (1980); Peter Von Sivers, "Rural Uprisings as Political Movements in Early Colonial Algeria (1851–1914)," in *Islam, Politics, and Social Movements,* ed. Edmund Burke, III and Ira M. Lapidus (Berkeley: University of California Press, 1988); and Edmund Burke, III, *Prelude to Protectorate in Morocco: Precolonial Protest and Resistance, 1860–1912* (Chicago: University of Chicago Press, 1976).

4. See, among others, Charles Issawi, *An Economic History of the Middle East and North Africa* (New York: Columbia University Press, 1982); Roger Owen, *The Middle East in the World Economy, 1880–1914* (London: Methuen, 1981); Tarif Khalidi, ed., *Land Tenure and Social Transformation in the Middle East* (Beirut: American University of Beirut, 1984); and Lucette Valensi, *Fellahs tunisiens: L'Économie rurale et la vie des campagnes* (Paris: Mouton, 1976).

5. Joel Migdal, *Peasants, Politics, and Revolution* (Princeton, N.J.: Princeton University Press, 1974); Jeffery Paige, *Agrarian Revolution* (New York: The Free Press, 1975); Samuel Popkin, *The Rational Peasant* (Berkeley: University of California Press, 1979); James Scott, *The Moral Economy of the Peasant* (New Haven, Conn.: Yale University Press, 1976); and Theda Skocpol, *States and Social Revolutions* (Cambridge: Cambridge University Press, 1979).

On avoidance protest, see the special issue of *The Journal of Peasant Studies* 13, 2 (1986), "Everyday Forms of Peasant Resistance in South-East Asia." See also Michael Adas, "Market Demand vs. Imperial Control: Colonial and Southeast Asia," in *Global Crises and Social Movements: Artisans, Peasants, Populists, and the World Economy,* ed. E. Burke (Boulder, Colo.: Westview Press, 1988); and James C. Scott, *Weapons of the Weak: Everyday Forms of Peasant Resistance* (New Haven, Conn.: Yale University Press, 1985).

6. The beginning of modern Middle Eastern history is generally dated from 1798 and the Napoleonic invasion of Europe. Recent research into the economic history of the region, however, has tended to push the date back into the mid-eighteenth century. See André Raymond, *Artisans et commerçants du Caire*, 2 vols. (Damascus: Institute français de Damas, 1973, 1974), and Kenneth Cuno, "Landholding Economy and Society in Rural Egypt" (Ph.D. diss., UCLA, 1985).

7. For a useful overview, see Issawi, *An Economic History*, chap. 7.

8. Baer, "Fellah Rebellion."

9. On the Egyptian rebellions, see Fred H. Lawson, "Rural Revolt and Provincial Society in Egypt, 1820–1824," *IJMES* 13, 2 (1981):131–53.

10. For a summary of our present understanding, see Owen, *Middle East in the World Economy*. See also Dominique Chevallier, "Western Development and Eastern Crisis in the Mid-Nineteenth Century: Syria Confronted with the European Economy," in *The Beginnings of Modernization in the Middle East*, ed. W. R. Polk and Richard Chambers, 205–22 (Chicago: University of Chicago Press, 1968).

On Tunisia, see Muhamad Cherif, "Expansion européenne et difficultés tunisiennes de 1815 à 1830," *Annales* 25, 3 (1970):714–45, and Valensi, *Fellahs tunisiens*.

11. See, among others, Y. Porath, "The Peasant Revolt of 1858–61 in Kisrawan," *Asian and African Studies* (Jerusalem), 2 (1966):77–157; Owen, *Middle East in the World Economy;* D. Chevallier, "Aux origines des troubles agraires libanais," *Annales* 14 (1959):35–64; and Abdallah Hanna, *Qadiyat al-zira'iyyah wa harakat al-fallahiyah fi suriya wa lubnan, 1820–1920* (Beirut: Dar al-Farabi, 1975).

12. See the excellent monograph of Bice Slama, *L'Insurrection de 1864 en Tunisie* (Tunis: Maison tunisienne d'édition, 1967).

13. Von Sivers, "Rural Uprisings."

14. See Ellen Titus Hoover, "Among Competing Worlds: The Rehamna of Morocco on the Eve of French Conquest" (Ph.D. diss., Yale University, 1978), and Paul Pascon, *Le Haouz de Marrakech*, 2 vols. (Tangier: Éditions marocaines et internationales, 1977).

15. On the Shawiya, see the impressive case study of John Godfrey, "Overseas Trade and Rural Change in Nineteenth Century Morocco" (Ph.D. diss., Johns Hopkins University, 1985). On Abu Himara, see Ross E. Dunn, "The Bu Himara Rebellion in Northeast Morocco: Phase I," *Middle Eastern Studies* 17, 1 (1981): 31–48.

16. Anton Blok, *The Mafia of a Sicilian Village* (New York: Harper and Row, 1974).

17. Gabriel Baer, "Submissiveness and Revolt of the Fellah," *Studies in the Social History of Modern Egypt* (Chicago: University of Chicago Press, 1969), 101.

18. Alexander Scholch, *Aegypt den Aegyptern!* (Zurich: Atlantis Verlag, 1972); Alan Richards, *Egypt's Agricultural Development, 1800–1980* (Boulder, Colo.: Westview Press, 1982).

19. Charles-Robert Ageron, *Les Algeriens musulmans et la France*, 2 vols. (Paris: Presses Universitaire de France, 1968), 2:837–47.

20. Abba Eban, trans., *The Maze of Justice* (London: Saqi Press, 1989).

21. Russell, quoted in Richards, *Egypt's Agricultural Development*, 57.

22. Capt. Petignot, "Banditisme au Pays Chaouia" (1921), and M. Bouchot, Sous-Préfet of Tizi-Ouzou, "Rapport sur la répression du banditisme" (1894), both in *Service historique de l'armée. Archives militaires.*

23. Barrington Moore, Jr., *Social Origins of Dictatorship and Democracy: Lord and Peasant in the Making of the Modern World* (Boston: Beacon Press, 1966); Skocpol, *States and Social Revolutions.*

Rural Unrest in the Ottoman Empire, 1830–1914

DONALD QUATAERT

A variety of natural, economic, and political factors affected the pattern of rural unrest in the nineteenth-century Ottoman Empire. Droughts, famines, or locust infestations, familiar parts of life for most of the period, often caused bread rioting but usually not sustained violence or rebellion. The commercialization of agriculture certainly was important. During this period, the growing commodification of the agrarian sector meant a mounting importance of the market economy, aimed at both domestic and international consumers. In its train, this development brought increasing sensitivity to market conditions and to changes in the business cycle. Thus, it is no surprise to find the international financial crisis of the mid-1890s mirrored in rural violence within Ottoman borders, this time directed against Armenians. Shifting demand for Ottoman crops, such as the bust in cotton exports after 1865 or the post-1900 boom in tobacco exports, surely affected the level and frequency of unrest in the countryside, although the microstudies needed to determine these relationships have not been done. Shifts in the terms of trade also influenced the patterns of unrest. Between 1820 and 1873, for example, the terms of trade favored cultivators, then worsened for two decades before turning around again after 1896.

State policy worked variously to aggravate conditions in the countryside. When it settled Muslim refugees from Czarist Russia and its own lost Balkan provinces, for example, the state inadvertently challenged the position of established villagers in areas as widely scattered as Ottoman Bulgaria, the Black Sea coast of Anatolia, and southern Syria. Tribal pacification policies that otherwise were quite beneficial to the body politic and the economy could bring the settling tribes into conflict with village communities—a notable example being the Kurdish settlement in eastern Anatolia. Overall, state policy, often in the form of the centralization of power, exercised a decisive impact on the timing, frequency, and intensity of rural unrest in the nineteenth century.

The Land Law of 1858 certainly affected rural stability but in ways we do not yet understand fully because the actual impact of the law on landholding itself is unclear and the subject of much controversy.[1] The prevailing view has been that it primarily benefited the notables who formed large estates, but this consensus probably is incorrect. The law contained a complex bundle of capitalist and precapitalist features that sought to enhance state control, encourage production, and provide for title deeds and land registration. In certain regions, the law worked to dispossess smallholders. Thus, as is frequently cited, the law did help to promote the agglomeration of land by chieftains and notables in the Iraqi provinces. But elsewhere, it legalized and solidified small cultivators' claims to lands that they had been cultivating. In the Lebanon, around Jerusalem, and in the region of modern Jordan—three case studies for which research has been done—smallholders eagerly flocked to the land registry office and obtained official documents recording their claims. Smallholdings did remain characteristic of Ottoman Anatolia and parts of Syria, while large holdings emerged in some regions of Syria and much of Iraq. But the Land Law did not play the key role, confirming and ratifying rather than creating and establishing, these varied landholding patterns around the empire. What, then, are the correlations between the Land Law and unrest? If smallholders generally sought to register their lands, as the three examples cited above suggest—and it seems reasonable to assume so— then we can see that the Land Law probably raised peasant expectations. Uncertainty over the meaning of the law and who might benefit from its implementation as well as the actual process of land registration may have added to rural unrest.

During the nineteenth century, the state began to encroach upon life in the countryside in a manner rarely, if ever, seen during the long centuries of the Ottoman imperium. This encroachment was part of a larger process, the Tanzimat reform program of centralization and Westernization, that sought to rebuild Ottoman military and civil power to ensure the state's continued survival. Following a long period of decentralized rule in which regional magnates exercised considerable control over the land and the cultivators, the central state sought to reassert its authority, break the autonomous power of the local notables, and regain control over the land, the peasants, and their surplus. In addition, the state adopted policies of equality before the law and equality of fiscal responsibility. It sought to eliminate the tax-exempt status of the magnates and, hoping to increase aggregate revenues, ordered that all pay the same agricultural tax rate. Ironically, these reform programs accelerated, in some respects at least, the pace of Ottoman destruction, for they tore at the loyalty of its long-privileged Muslim subjects while straining relations between Ottoman Muslims and Christians. Vast waves of rural (and urban) unrest were unleashed, shaking the state to its foundation and recasting whole provinces as independent states.

These great cycles of rebellion and destruction were hardly unique examples of nineteenth-century rural discontent in the Ottoman Empire. That protest was an unexceptional part of everyday Ottoman life has often escaped the notice of historians because, in part, they have been bent on rediscovering the history of imperial institutions, reform programs, and Westernizers. Another reason that this history of rural protest has been unrecovered lies in its nature. To begin with, it was located in the (generally illiterate) countryside, away from the urban seats of governmental and other record keepers. Examples occasionally do appear in the written record: in 1880, central Anatolian villagers murdered several government officials seeking to collect arrears in taxes while, further west in the same area, other peasants resisted administrators seeking to transfer grain from their famine-stricken village.[2] Only when it became very large, widespread, or violent, or caused substantial declines in state revenues, might rural unrest become a focus of official attention and outside concern. Because most protest was neither violent nor widespread, it has remained largely invisible—a force surely present but an undocumented one.

Peasant avoidance certainly was the most common form of protest, a refusal to perform duties or pay taxes or enter the military, a posture that might end in flight. But this avoidance could remain unrecorded unless very large numbers were involved, such as the mass movement of Christian peasants from the Ottoman Bulgarian provinces to independent Serbia in the mid-nineteenth century. Other forms of protest included social banditry, which flourished with the support of villagers and nomads whose anger these bandits articulated. There also were frequent open insurrections against the state and rural elites by both peasants and tribes. Intersectarian violence, when Ottoman cultivators fought with one another instead of against the rulers, sometimes was a degeneration of social banditry or insurrection that had begun as anti-elite protest.

RURAL UNREST seems to have been particularly widespread and violent during three periods. The first, from 1839 until about the mid-1860s, was characterized by resistance to the implementation of the Tanzimat reforms. These rebellions were, quite probably, the greatest of the nineteenth-century Ottoman Empire. In the Balkan areas, these struggles mutated into nationalist revolutions. In the Arab provinces, important uprisings occurred around Aleppo and Damascus and in the Hawran; of particular importance was the Kisrawan rising of 1858–61, which also derived from the Land Law of 1858. The next cluster of violence was directed against the Armenians in eastern Anatolia. Beginning in the 1890s and reaching its climax two decades later, in 1915–16, it owed much to the settlement of the Kurds and to Tanzimat promises of equality. The third period includes the growing disorders in the Balkan, Arab, and Anatolian rural areas that characterized the last few years, about 1902–8, before the Young Turk Revolution.

Between about 1863 and the early 1890s, rural rebellions probably were less widespread than at any other time, with the notable exception of Bulgaria, where violence reached new heights in 1875–76, just before the final break from Ottoman control. It seems unlikely that the overall decline in rural violence is only apparent as a result of reporting flaws. If anything, sources for the late nineteenth century are incomparably richer than for the earlier part of the period. Instead, the quiescence derived from several factors. The locus of much unrest had been in the Balkan areas; by the mid-1860s, many of these had achieved de facto independence, with the additional exception of Macedonia, where rebellions continued into the twentieth century.[3]

In the Arab and Anatolian areas, the decreased incidence of social unrest can be explained only partially on the basis of the available evidence. Increasing central control and taxation had been in effect for over three decades and had become institutionalized. More concretely, the military power of the central state was vastly greater than it had been around 1800. The regular army consisted of not more than 24,000 soldiers in 1837; by the end of the next decade, their number had risen to perhaps 120,000 regular troops and came to be supported by the telegraph and, in some areas, by railroads as well.[4] The peasants had thus become accustomed to taxes that evolved from being a novel to a normal part of the rural landscape; in any event, they were less able to resist. The case of the notables is slightly different. In the face of Tanzimat policies, they almost everywhere lost direct control over the land, some revenues, and their tax-exempt status, to boot. Their relative disinclination to open resistance probably owes something to their retention of considerable local prominence, power, and wealth. Toward the end of the century, however, Young Turk resistance to Abdulhamid's regime found support among many provincial notables whose positions had been deteriorating in the face of the increasingly effective central rule of the sultan. The formation of the Public Debt Administration, in 1881, probably also weakened notables' fiscal hold as tax farmers when its salaried agents collected agricultural taxes on behalf of the foreign consortium.

Among the insurrections arising from implementation of the Tanzimat, the Bulgarian peasant rebellions are the best known. Their origins are well documented and arise directly out of the 1839 reform decree. The land regime in the Vidin area combined pre-Ottoman practices with a distorted version of the *timar* system. In a turn of events almost unique in Ottoman history, Muslim lords, descendants of *sipahis,* and urban notables became the true owners of state land during the eighteenth century, when they also seized control of the local administration.[5] In return for a cash payment to a strapped central treasury, these groups emerged as a class of great landlords and took over "all" state lands. The lords were Muslim because the lands earlier had been classified as frontier territories. By customary practice predating the Ottoman arrival, the sipahis collected certain extra dues and taxes not demanded in other provinces, such as one or two months' sowing labor, a cart of wood, or a cartload of corn. Indeed, the peasants owed as much or more to the lord as to the state. When the 1839 decree abolished all forms of compulsory services, peasants in the Vidin region quickly made clear their refusal to perform them anymore. When called in to decide, the state straddled the fence. Like the czar's emancipation of the serfs, the sultan's decree attempted to reconcile the irreconcilable, to abolish the services due without harming the landowners. As a result, landholders generally had their way and, the reform regulations notwithstanding, services and feudal-like dues continued.

In 1850, a revolt erupted in Vidin, its underlying cause confusion and disorder in the land system. In the ten years since proclamation of the Tanzimat, the state had stabilized peasants' possession of state lands by increasing the number of family members who could inherit. The lords, for their part, continued to take dues and services by force, dominating the local councils and thwarting the authority of the governor sent to control them. Peasants demanded abolition of the lords' rule and, apparently, deeds granting them direct ownership of the land. The governor of Vidin concurred, seeing the measure to be essential for peace. But the Istanbul authorities required a three-step procedure: continuation of state ownership of the land, abolition of those obligations to the lords that the central government deemed illegal, and payment of the remaining "legal" obligations that cultivators would render partly to the lords for life and partly to the central treasury. This plan flew in the face of peasants' expectations since they intended to keep the lords' former revenues and pay nothing either to the government or the lords. By the time the state finally decided in 1851 to sell the lords' lands to the peasants, peasants were seeking to obtain the land without compensation. These discontents then meshed with mounting Bulgarian nationalism and culminated in the great revolt of 1875–76 and Bulgarian independence.[6]

A parallel set of events occurred farther west in the Balkans, in Bosnia and Herzegovina. There, as in Bulgaria, a three-way struggle pitted Muslim notables interested in retaining tax revenues against the state, while the Christian peasants sought to take over the land that the notables held. Unrest began immediately after proclamation of the Gülhane decree. The notables orchestrated the first rebellions against the centralizing state but, later on, peasants rose against the lords. In 1858–59, perhaps partially inspired by fear of the Land Law and its provisions for cultivators' registration of lands, long-established feudal families incited the peasants to revolt and prevented imposition of Ottoman central control. With the help of the peasants, these families opposed the Tanzimat reforms and retained their timars or, where they had been converted, their tax farms. They kept the majority of the surplus and dominated both Muslim and Christian peasants, despite strong state efforts in the early 1860s to break landlord power. Over time, however, the programs of the central government weakened the notables. In 1874–75, Herzegovinian Christian peasants rose against Muslim landowners in a number of villages where tax farmers had been trying to collect taxes during a time of bad harvest. The rebellion spread all over Bosnia and Herzegovina. The Great Powers became involved and the rebellions ended with the removal of Ottoman authority, similar to the process that brought about the loss of Bulgaria.[7]

Widespread rural unrest in nineteenth-century Anatolia, on the magnitude of the 1850s and 1860s uprisings in the Balkans or the Arab provinces, seems to have been relatively unusual. Although perhaps underreported by historians, more likely this relative peacefulness stemmed partly from the moral economy of the peasantry in Anatolia, a culture disinclined to use violent protest to register its discontents. Anatolian peasant quietude certainly was tied to the continuing prevalence of small family holdings as the dominant form of land tenure, a distribution pattern inherited from the pre-nineteenth-century era and sanctified by the Land Law of 1858. Not that Anatolia was devoid of unrest: The history of rural Anatolia was one of incessant active and passive protest, from one end of the period to the other. What seems different about Anatolia is the small scale of its protest. Implementation of the Tanzimat reforms there brought immediate and varying forms of resistance. Sometimes the sumptuary aspects of the new state policies were opposed passively: in the small town of Bergama, for example, most people continued to wear their turbans and conical hats, ignoring the example of the Westernizing bureaucracy who adopted the fez.

Against the new fiscal measures, the protests took a more active shape: in 1841, for example, a low-ranking member of the ulema in Adapazari called on the populace not to pay the new, higher, imposts since they already were unable to pay their present taxes. At the same time, notables at Yalvaç, themselves subject to heavier taxes under the new policies, sought to gain allies and urged the populace at large to resist the new levies. A notable in the Bala area south of Ankara understood that the Tanzimat's removal of tax exemptions meant taxes on large state properties in his possession, so he incited a tax revolt among some 400 villagers. When arrested, he complained that although his taxes had increased sharply, those of poor villagers had more than doubled.[8] During the early reign of Mahmud II (1808–39), social bandits had been common, often serving as unpaid military forces responsible for maintaining order. By the 1830s, thanks to the reimposition of central authority and the rise of the larger, salaried military force, many bandits had vanished from western and central Anatolia.[9] But social banditry persisted throughout the period, sometimes focusing on foreign travelers with the connivance of local cultivators and authorities.

Tribal unrest, for its part, faded as the century progressed and had ceased to be an important factor in most areas by the 1870s. In the Armenian massacres of the 1890s, however, several factors seem to have been at work. During the worldwide financial crisis of the mid-1890s, Turkish or sedentarized Kurdish peasants may have sought to escape from Armenian moneylenders through a violence that then focused on the Armenian community in general. There also is the issue of the disintegrating tribal structures as state centralization proceeded: The power of the Kurdish beys over their tribes was fading just as Tanzimat pledges of equality and an awakening nationalism caused some Armenian villagers to become increasingly assertive. The famous Sasun massacre, for example, occurred when the local Armenians refused to continue yielding to the extortionary demands of nearby Kurdish chieftains. Their authority over both the villagers and the tribes threatened, the chiefs resorted to massive force to maintain themselves in power. Using a variety of appeals that may have included shared ethnicity as well as economic advantage, the chiefs mobilized the tribes against the peasants and thus retained control.

The Muslim refugees' encroachment on common lands also contributed to disorders all over Anatolia. In the 1870s, for example, considerable friction existed between the newly arrived settlers and villagers in the coastal areas around Black Sea Samsun. The worst, however, probably was over by the beginning of the 1880s.[10] Factory burnings also are an integral part of the social history of nineteenth-century Anatolia, although these protests focused on particular establishments and never developed into a Luddist variety of protest against factory qua factory. Examples include factory sackings at Bursa in the 1860s, Bergama in the 1880s, and Uşak in 1908.[11] In the carpet-making center at Uşak in March 1908, village spinners marched into the town and sacked three mechanized spinning mills that jeopardized their livelihoods. Crop cycles, by themselves, were not catalysts of major protest. The terrible killing famine of 1873–74 provoked only a few bread riots in various regions. Later, however, a broader series of bread riots accompanied crop failures and shortfalls in 1906–08. In June 1908, for example, Sivas-area villagers marched into the town and with the urban discontented sacked local granaries. The response at nearby Kayseri was more pacific as 12,000 gathered and prayed for rain.[12] At Erzurum, however, fears about food shortages combined with a taxpayers' protest dating back to 1906 over an increase in the poll and animal taxes. The revolt combined rural and urban dissidents and persisted until the 1908 Young Turk Revolution. Without exception, these protests occurred in the presence of failing or threatened crops. But poor crop conditions required a cadre of revolutionaries who mobilized, organized, and articulated the discontents. That is, peasant discontent was a constant but usually required some outside variable to erupt in open revolt or insurrection. These demonstrations eloquently expressed the weakened legitimacy of the state and helped pave the way for the Young Turk seizure of power.[13]

In the Arab provinces, rural unrest erupted with considerable frequency until the 1860s. In 1834, for example, the fellah of Palestine rebelled against forced labor, against the conscription of Muslims into Muhammad ʿAli's army, and against the *ferde,* a levy like the poll tax previously reserved for Christians that Ali imposed on Muslims. Lebanon had four or five rural uprisings between 1820 and 1861. Among these were revolts in Mount Lebanon in 1840, Alawi risings during the 1850s, and Druze insurrections in the Hawran in the late 1870s. Many revolts primarily fought remnants of the old agrarian regime and the increasing fiscal pressures of the reform-minded central state, among them insurrections in Palestine during 1852 and 1854 and in Syria during 1852, 1854, 1862–64, and 1865–66. Peasant rebellions in the Fertile Crescent were most common in remote districts where villages usually were more prosperous than on the plain or near important cities. In many mountainous districts, the local lords, who usually were the tax farmers, led peasant revolts against the centralizing efforts of the state. In this case, the protests were like the early ones in Bosnia and Herzegovina from about 1839 to the 1860s. In other instances, peasants rebelled against local lords or intermediate tax farmers weakened by the intrusion of central power.[14]

Perhaps the best documented example is the 1858–61 revolt of the Maronite peasants of Kisrawan against their Maronite overlords. In Kisrawan, after the Emir Bashir II had removed the tax farmers' judicial authority, Muhammad 'Ali and then the Ottomans further weakened the power of the Khazin family of Maronite sheikhs. The revolt seems to have stemmed from the desire of some prosperous cultivators connected to the Beirut silk trading center to obtain more land to grow mulberries and meet the demand for cocoons. The Khazin overlords, however, refused to alienate land and thus blocked this expanding peasantry. Khazin power had weakened substantially, but, increasingly strapped for money, they demanded all kinds of feudal presents. Still worse from their perspective, massive quantities of European-made arms recently had flooded into peasant hands. When the revolt erupted, its leaders appealed to the call of the *Hat-ti Humayun* for universal equality.[15] The rebellion was a great success for the peasants since, by its end, the Khazins had lost much of their land. In addition, the state abolished feudal privileges and proclaimed equality before the law. Unlike the Kurdish chiefs facing opposition from the state and their own followers, the Khazin lords had not maintained military superiority and so lost the day.[16]

The Kisrawan demands for changes in traditional lord-peasant relations closely paralleled those of the Vidin peasants during the 1850s in their efforts to gain full control over the land. They also are echoed by the actions during 1889–90 of the Druze peasants in the Hawran, who rebelled against their Atrash lords as the Ottoman state sought to subdue the district. In common with the Kisrawan rising, the Druze rebellion ended feudalism and began the extension of new relations of production.[17]

IT SEEMS evident that the peak of open unrest occurred between the 1840s and the middle 1860s, in many cases as popular and notable responses to government fiat. The imposition of the Tanzimat reforms meant a changed agrarian order, with greater (but not full) central control of the land, more of the surplus going to the imperial treasury, and higher taxes for the peasantry. But the notables continued to hang on with considerable success, using their memberships in local councils and other bodies to maintain their influence and power over the peasantry. Extreme confusion reigned in the countryside everywhere in the empire, since the state declared removal of the old order but could not fully eliminate it.[18] As in the Vidin case and that of the Kurdish beys, it may have been unwilling to do so. Programs to eliminate the lords generated strong resistance among the notables while the increase in taxes angered them as well as the peasants. Resistance to the new conscription laws prompted abandonment of Muslim villages in the first decades of the reform era just as the 1908 inclusion of Ottoman Christians in the conscription process led to their large-scale emigration from the empire. Sharecropping expanded at the same time that state taxes on peasants were increasing faster than agricultural productivity. Finally, the peasants demanded that landlordism be abolished and rebelled against a state that was not willing to sacrifice the estate owners. In the Vidin region, the fact that peasants were Christians and the owners were Muslims gave the social conflict a religious and finally a national dimension.[19] Social conflict indeed played a vital role in many nineteenth-century nationalist movements. Peasants hoped to gain from the reform legislation and resented state efforts to acquire coveted notables' lands. Thus, *çiftliks* undermined Ottoman control of the Balkans.[20] Although social struggle between the Kurds and Armenians also took on a religious dimension that incompletely evolved into a national struggle, tendencies toward land agglomeration and market agriculture do not seem to have played a catalytic role.

Lebanon and the Bulgarian lands each were important seats of insurrection. Each possessed unusually high population densities and a strong commitment to commercial agriculture. Whether feudal-like relations were stronger in these two regions than elsewhere is uncertain. In Anatolia, for its part, the prevalence of small peasant family farms played a role in the relative lack of uprisings, as did the relatively low level of agricultural commercialization (compared to that of the European provinces) and the relatively lower economic growth rate after 1850 (compared to that of European and Arab provinces).

A relative absence of open insurrection should not be interpreted to suggest the absence of serious discontents or oppression. Peasant avoidance, not insurrection, was the common form of coping with crisis or difficulties. For many, open revolt remained the exceptional method of expressing rural discontent.

Notes

1. This discussion draws from my analysis and the sources cited in *The Ottoman Empire: Its Economy and Society, 1300–1914,* ed. Halil Inalcik and Donald Quataert (Cambridge: Cambridge University Press, forthcoming).

2. My thanks to Fatoş Kaba of the SUNY-Binghamton Anthropology Department for these references, drawn from the Great Britain Foreign Office reports.

3. Fikret Adanir, "The Macedonian Question: The Socio-Economic Reality and Problems of its Historiographic Interpretations," *International Journal of Turkish Studies* (Winter 1984–85): 43–64. Adanir holds the opinion that socioeconomic factors were not a cause of the Macedonian rebellions.

4. Edouard Engelhardt, *La Turquie et le Tanzimat* (Paris: A. Cotillon et Cie, 1882, 1884), 1:89, 2:281–82.

5. Margaret L. Meriwether, "Urban Notables and Rural Resources in Aleppo, 1730–1830," *International Journal of Turkish Studies* (Summer 1987): 55–73.

6. Halil Inalcik, *Tanzimat ve Bulgar Meselesi* (Ankara: Turk Tarih Kurumu Basimevi, 1943) and "Application of the Tanzimat and its Social Effects," *Archivum Ottomanicum* (1973): 97–128.

7. See, for example, A. Cevad Eren, "Tanzîmât," *Islam Ansiklopedesi* 11 (Istanbul: Maarif Matbaasi, 1970): 709–65; see also the sources cited in Stanford J. Shaw, *History of the Ottoman Empire and Modern Turkey* (Cambridge: Cambridge University Press, 1977), 2: 149–60.

8. Inalcik, "Social Effects"; Osman Bayatli, *Bergama'da yakin tarih olaylari XVIII–XIX yüzyil* (Izmir: Teknik Kitap ve Mecmua Basimevi, 1957), 7.

9. Musa Çadirci, "II. Mahmud döneminde (1808–1839) Avrupa ve Hayriye Tüccarlari," in *Social and Economic History of Turkey, 1071–1920*, ed. Osman Okyar and Halil Inalcik (Ankara: Meteksan L. S., 1980), 237–41; M. C. Uluçay, *Saruhan'da eşkiyalik ve halk hareketleri* (Istanbul: N. p., 1955).

10. Great Britain Foreign Office reports.

11. Donald Quataert, "Machine Breaking and the Changing Carpet Industry of Western Anatolia, 1860–1908," *Journal of Social History* (Spring 1986): 473–89; and Bayatli, *Bergama*.

12. Donald Quataert, "The Economic Climate of the 'Young Turk Revolution' in 1908," *Journal of Modern History* (September 1979): D1147–61.

13. Ibid., and Quataert, "Machine Breaking."

14. Gabriel Baer, "Fellah Rebellion in Egypt and the Fertile Crescent," reprinted in *Fellah and Townsmen in the Middle East: Studies in Social History*, ed. Gabriel Baer (London: F. Cass, 1982), 253–323; Marwan Buheiry, "The Peasant Revolt of 1858 in Mount Lebanon," in *Land Tenure and Social Transformation in the Middle East*, ed. Tarif Khalidi (Beirut: American University of Beirut Press, 1984); Edmund Burke III, "Changing Patterns of Peasant Protest in the Middle East, 1750–1950," paper presented to the 1986 annual meeting of the Middle East Studies Association; and Burke, "Understanding Arab Protest Movements," *Maghreb Review* 11, 1 (1986): 27–32.

15. Buheiry, "The Peasant Revolt of 1858," 299.

16. Account based on Baer, "Fellah Rebellion in Egypt." See article 6 of the 1861 "Regulation for the Administration of Lebanon" in *The Middle East and North Africa in World Politics: A Documentary Record*, ed. J. C. Hurewitz (New Haven, Conn.: Yale University Press, 1975), 1: 347–49.

17. Burke, works cited in n. 14 above. In an otherwise useful analysis, Baer overly stresses the uniqueness of the Kisrawan affair: "Only once in Middle Eastern history

did poor and wealthy peasants revolt together against a feudal-like aristocracy" (294). Here Baer excludes the Anatolian and Balkan areas of the Ottoman Empire from his Middle East.

18. Inalcik, *Bulgar Meselesi* and "Social Effects." Also see, for example, the 1850s reports in A. D. Mordtmann, *Anatolien. Skizzen und Reisebriefe aus Kleinasien,* ed. Franz Babinger (Hannover: Heinz Lafaire, 1925), e.g., 116, 139.

19. Inalcik, "Social Effects."

20. Suraiya Faroqhi, "Agriculture and Rural Life in the Ottoman Empire ca. 1500–1878," *New Perspectives on Turkey* (Fall 1987): 32–33, discussing the research of Stoianovich and Inalcik.

4

Violence in Rural Syria in the 1880s and 1890s: State Centralization, Rural Integration, and the World Market

LINDA SCHATKOWSKI SCHILCHER

*I*n recent decades Syria's rural areas have been the locus of a new political activism and the formation of political constituencies for a new kind of political regime. Historians are now unearthing more primary sources for rural history in an attempt to end the silence of a heretofore voiceless peasantry. There seem to be two complementary approaches: on one hand, we can reconstruct the structures, functions, and routine processes of rural society; on the other, we can investigate particular events or series of events, movements, uprisings, and so forth that were centered in a rural area. In the interplay between these two approaches, we may be able to discover the perceptions and interpretations of shared experiences by particular rural people and what it was or is of these perceptions and interpretations that was and could become influential in subsequent developments.

Having written on the structure and processes of rural society elsewhere, in this paper I pursue the course of rural events with interpretive references to this background.[1] We will follow approximately twenty years of events in a significant district, the Hawran, at the end of the nineteenth century. This district is an important hinterland of the Syrian capital, Damascus, but its population has also been influential in the Lebanon and in Palestine/Israel as migrants and emigrés.

The Hawran: Geography and Economy

The Hawran is an open plain of rich, deep soil, sloping upward toward the east and nearly enclosed by protecting ravines, valleys, and highlands.[2] Taking the plain together with the cultivable hill country, badlands, and desert fringe areas that surrounded it, the Hawran encompassed an area of about 25,000 square kilometers. In the nineteenth century it had a distinct identity as a separate Ottoman sanjak under the control of the vilayet capital, Damascus. As was often the case in remote regions of the empire, however, the actual composition of the Sanjak Hawran depended on the extent of the government's effective control, which, even at the end of the nineteenth century, remained an unresolved military and political issue. To a considerable extent, the history of the Hawran in the nineteenth century is the story of a complex struggle for administrative and economic control as settlement and agricultural production increased.

By the middle of the century the traditional exchange pattern of resource autarchy among bedouin, mountaineers, and plainsfolk was increasingly displaced by production for export.[3] An informal cartel of Damascene merchants and rural government-sanctioned political and fiscal brokers emerged in the course of the bloody Hawran conflicts of the 1860s to disrupt the autarchic pattern, extend agriculture, and "free" surpluses for external markets and for revenues for the Ottoman provincial treasury.[4] This informal cartel was able to exploit not the land, which was plentiful and could not in any case be

A shepherdess, southern Syria. Photo by L. S. Schilcher, 1988.

"owned," being state land (*miri*) or the property of religious endowments (*waqf*), but also the peasantry, who were contracted and manipulated into dependent clientele relationships for ploughing and harvesting. The land unit of production was not necessarily enlarged into plantations (or *çiftliks*, as in other parts of the Empire), but the scale of the managerial unit of production was enlarged as protoindustrial modes of exploitation were extended from the urban and oasis areas into the more distant dry-farming countryside.[5] Since the cartel alternated sales between a number of markets—wherever profits were highest or government pressure strongest—its activities caused the Hawran to oscillate on a varying scale of rural political economy rather than to fall into a fixed or linear pattern of development. Adapting the categories suggested by Pamuk for Ottoman agriculture in Turkish regions for this period,[6] the Hawran could be described as follows, depending on the dispositions of the cartel at any given time: (1) a remote region isolated from the impact of world markets and having small peasant units of cultivation and relatively strong, sometimes quasi-feudal, relations of production; (2) a region drawn into commodity production for world markets, eventually highly commercialized and export-oriented, and increasingly so with the introduction of railways.

The status of the peasants of the Hawran also varied according to these categories.[7] Once autarchy was disrupted, the Hawranites could be exploited as (1) day laborers or (2) servile subsistence tenants, but sometimes they succeeded in remaining (3) semidependent as sharecroppers or (4) fully independent as surplus producers dealing directly in the market.

The cartel required two levels of preconditions for existence and survival. On one level it needed political control, which included cooperation with powerful rural factions, the quiescence or subjugation of the cultivators, and sustained state support, protection, and collaboration. A British consular report of 1869 presents a contemporary description of how the cartel operated:

On orders received from Constantinople, the Governor is selling [to urban entrepreneurs possession and cultivation rights to] land belonging to the government [miri] by public auction. The local treasury has already realised a sum amounting to L[stg]150,000. The lands [for which the cultivation rights are being sold] are in the lower parts of the Hawran, inhabited by the [Sunni Muslim] Hawranites and in the Jabal Ajlun [inhabited by sedentary tribes], where the authorities have but little power. It is to be feared that disturbances will follow any attempt to enforce these sales. The peoples of those districts are bent upon resisting the sales. As the success or failure of this measure depends upon what action the Druze [of Jabal Hawran] will take in the matter, the Hawranites applied to them for protection while the Governor, having allotted the pay of 100 horsemen to the four principal [Druze] shaikhs, which amounts to a salary of 50,000 piasters [to each shaikh], has called upon them to use their influence on his behalf. The Druze shaikhs, in consideration of this pay, have made professions of submission and though they are anxious to retain their salaries, they are unwilling to create enemies so near their home. They will deviate but slightly from their policy which has always been to keep up an alliance with the tribes surrounding their stronghold, since united they are able to live in a state of semiindependence of the government, which singly they could not so easily defy. In order therefore to conciliate their interests with both parties [the Druze shaikhs] will refrain from openly taking part in any contest that might ensue but will secretly assist the Hawranites and perhaps actively aid them under cover of night.[8]

Here the state has ordered sales to urban entrepreneurs and financed the quasi-feudal rural chieftains who were to defend these sales; the rural chieftains hoped to play a double game between the state (and its urban allies) and the peasantry; and the peasantry were likely to be outsmarted and outgunned by the forces ranged against them by the combination of state, urban entrepreneurs, and rural chieftains.

On a second level the cartel also needed economic incentives. Profits in good years averaged 15 percent but could go well beyond that if special conditions applied—as, for example, during the Crimean War, when grain prices skyrocketed in the eastern Mediterranean.[9] The heyday of Syrian grain export in the 1850s and 1860s was gradually reversed in the 1870s and 1880s with the opening of the Suez Canal and as the Great Depression took hold.[10] The consequent slump in world grain prices, which lasted far into the 1890s, was a major disincentive for urban and coastal traders and fiscal entrepreneurs. The profit margin between the price at the port of export and the price on the world market increasingly dwindled in the 1880s and disappeared altogether by 1887. By 1892 the world prices fell below those paid to the cultivators in the fields. For those entrepreneurs who did not grasp the implications early on or had no options even if they did, a long period of struggle and indecision extended from the late 1870s to the late 1880s, climaxing in the 1890s. The best evidence we have of the gradualness of the shift up to 1889 is that in 1879 there was still avid interest in tax farming, and not until 1889 did the government fail to find anyone to bid for the normally profitable tax farms of the Hawran. In the years immediately following, however, the crisis was severe. As we shall see in the next section, many peasants harvested clandestinely or gave up cultivation altogether when they could not reach the terms with their contractors that they considered acceptable. The crisis continued until the late 1890s, and even then profit margins were too low to encourage entrepreneurs to arrange more generous terms with cultivators and transporters. Even though an upturn had begun, the conditions of the 1850s and 1860s had not been restored.

When the price squeeze began in the late 1870s, the cartel's participants put more pressure on their respective peasant clienteles to preserve their own profit margins. The clients sometimes submitted but sometimes responded by resisting or attempting to find new intermediaries. On rare occasions the peasants petitioned the state to champion their cause. The cartel had therefore to consolidate its political and economic control if it were to survive.

Not only the price situation marked 1879 as a turning point. In that year the state introduced direct taxation and the first serious outbreak of rural conflict occurred, bringing to a close a ten-year period of relative peace. The entrepreneurs tended to blame the Syrian peasantry rather than the world market for the relatively high prices of local grain. The trading community expressed its exasperation in a series of articles on grain that ran in 1898 in a semiofficial Beirut newspaper: "Despite the fact that the best lands for the cultivation of wheat [in the world] are in the Ottoman Empire . . . , the prices of our [native] wheat flour in Beirut are now [as high as] those in London and Paris. The reason for that is that our peasants are lazy, stupid and irresponsible."[11]

The state would remain a major player in developments in the Hawran because its grain-based revenues declined and production was disrupted in the course of the ensuing conflicts, raising the specter of famine in the cities and in the desert along the pilgrimage route. Its tactic was to play off one layer of intermediaries against another, sometimes supporting the rural political brokers, sometimes the urban-based merchants and tax farmers. The state also encouraged sedentarization and the immigration into the Hawran of the refugee populations from the Lebanon, Algeria, Tunis, and the Caucasus with the hope that they would be productive and compliant peasants. However, these people produced new sources of conflict and were themselves often turned into intermediaries who challenged state and cartel authority.

Chronology of Events, 1879–1900

The following chronology for the period 1879–1900 was reconstructed from a variety of sources.[12] Though incomplete, it presents ample evidence of the

Wheat cultivators in the Hawran of southern Syria. Photo by L. S. Schilcher, 1988.

impact of the Great Depression, the demise of the cartel, and the resultant scramble for control in the Hawran in the last decades of the nineteenth century.

At mid-century the Hawran's population is estimated to have been somewhat less than 50,000.[13] While the vast majority of its inhabitants were Arabic-speaking Syrians employed in agriculture, there were some important internal differences.

The plainsfolk were villagers practicing grain, seed, and legume cultivation in unirrigated fields. Their attachment to the Hawran was so long-standing that it would be impossible to identify their origins. Their agricultural practices were age-old adaptations to climate, flora, and fauna and triumphed in the production of one of the highest quality preindustrial wheats known.[14] Although the plainsfolk were Sunni Muslims, their religious practices would probably not have conformed to the "high" culture of Sunnis in the Syrian cities.

The nomads of the plain and of the bordering steppe were also Sunni Muslims, but their way of life differed markedly from that of the plains cultivators. The nomads were the chief animal husbanders of the Hawran, providing sheep, goats, and camels and their derivative products in exchange for grain. The sheep- and goat-rearing bedouin frequented the Hawran throughout the year. The camel bedouin came only seasonally but in massive numbers when drought elsewhere obliged them to move their herds into the Hawran's greener pastures and cultivated fields. The nomads often functioned as harvest guards and grain transporters for the villagers' production.

Different again were the inhabitants of the hill country, mostly Syrian Christians and Druze. These were communities of peasants whose faith separated them from the Syrian majority. The Druze were a heterodox offshoot of Shiite Islam, whose adherents concentrated in the hills and mountains in various parts of greater Syria. The Druze of the Hawran sustained ties to other Druze communities, particularly to those in the mountainous regions west of the Hawran in what today is Lebanon. Substantial numbers of western Druze peasants migrated into the Hawran at this time as a consequence of population pressure and political developments in the Lebanon.

The Christians of the Hawran were mostly Greek Orthodox, but there were also some Greek Catholics. They were Arabic-speaking communities with ancient ties to the Hawran who inhabited villages bordering the plain and in the Jabal Hawran. The Christian villagers were often interspersed with the Druze. In contrast to the Druze, however, a substantial number of Christians migrated from the Hawran. Intercommunal tensions combined with economic opportunity in urban and coastal centers and abroad drew Christians from all over Syria into new patterns of migration and settlement in the latter half of the nineteenth century.

All the people of the Hawran would probably have identified themselves exactly as that, as "Hawarna" (the people of the Hawran). This identification would have differentiated them from other regionally defined populations, such as, for example, the "Shawām" (the people of Damascus). Nonetheless they would have recognized that they, the Damascenes, and many other peoples of contiguous regions and towns all inhabited a more general entity, the country of Syria, the "Bilad al-Sham," as distinct from the countries of the Hijaz, Nejd, Egypt, Iraq, or the Turkish-speaking regions to the north. To at least a limited extent, some Hawranites would have been aware of political issues beyond the immediate confines of their own district and would have recognized the importance of their district as a distinct entity in the larger political scheme of things.

The Hawran was a frontier Ottoman district, attached administratively and economically to Damascus, the capital of the province of Syria. Damascene merchants who sought their fortunes in the Hawran usually came from the Maidan, a southern quarter of the city known in this period both for its agricultural trades and its political ferment. Otherwise, the city's presence was increasingly personified by Turkish-speaking Ottoman administrative and military officials and Arabic-speaking Damascene notables. These notables were dispatched by the authorities as mediators in disputes or active in routine administrative matters such as tax collection and conscription. They were also agricultural entrepreneurs, creditors, and land controllers.

As the century progressed, the city dispatched whole groups of newcomers into the Hawran, among them pilgrims who took the overland route from Damascus through the Hawran and into the steppe on their way to Mecca. Some newcomers lingered in the Hawran voluntarily, finding work in agriculture and trade. Others were slaves employed on the Hawran plantations of the pilgrimage officials who had access to this kind of labor supply in the course of their undertakings. More sizable groups of newcomers were the refugees who came to the Hawran from the Caucasus, North Africa, and the islands of the eastern Mediterranean with the blessing of the central government and sometimes, as in the case of the Tunisians and Algerians, the financial support of European consulates. Some of these, though of the Muslim faith and like the Hawranites also Ottoman subjects, were not Arabic speakers; none were Syrians.[15] Their association with Syria would begin with their gradual and not always smooth integration into local society.

Finally, Damascus introduced Europeans and Americans into the Hawran. They came as tourists, adventurers, explorers, missionaries, investors, and aspiring colonizers. Their influence remained largely indirect and, by the later decades of the nineteenth century, was represented by consular officials based in Damascus. The Ottoman authorities often turned to the European consuls to mediate in Hawran affairs, though decreasingly so as time went on.

Phase One (1879–87): Intermediaries Resist the Squeeze, Pressure Their Clients

In 1879 when the British consul reported that the most lucrative form of investment in Syria was still in agriculture, a new cycle of violence began in the Hawran.[16] Three to four thousand Ottoman troops intervened in a dispute between eastern Hawran Druze and the Sunni Muslim villagers of the Hawran plains village of Busra. The Druze were led by the Druze shaikh Ibrahim al-Atrash, who had been the cartel's chief rural collaborator, authorized by the state to collect taxes in the Hawran. Yet the troops fought on the side of the Busrites against the Druze. The outcome was indecisive, and the Ottoman authorities requested that the British consul mediate. A western Druze shaikh, Sa'id Bey Talhuq, was awarded the post of district governor (qaimaqam) of the Jabal Hawran despite opposition from the Hawranite Druze shaikhs.[17]

During this period, the Ottoman government made its first serious attempts to install direct taxation in rural areas. Under Midhat Pasha, the famous Ottoman reform administrator who held the governorship of the province of Syria from 1878 to 1880, the central government ordered the collection of a fixed land tax. Midhat realized that direct cash taxation could not succeed in the Hawran and pleaded with Istanbul that the tithes be farmed as in the past, though not to the members of the cartel. In his first year Midhat was able to find new tax farmers, including some village shaikhs. Even though it was a poor harvest year, the reorganization of tax farming brought in increased revenues, embarrassing the cartel and forming the background to the conflicts spreading in the Hawran, including the dispute between the Atrash shaikhs and the Busrites.[18]

In 1881, about a thousand Hawran Druze led by Shibli al-Atrash, the Druze rival of Ibrahim al-Atrash, attacked the Hawranite Sunni Muslim plains villages of Kerak and Um Walad, seizing cattle and flocks. One hundred villagers and two merchants from the Damascus Maidan quarter were killed. To escape the hostilities, many plainsfolk migrated into the more secure areas of the Hawran such as the Laja' and parts of the Jabal Hawran. Despite renewed negotiations with the Hawranite factions, pursued by the Damascene notable Hulu Pasha al-'Abid on behalf of the Ottoman government, Druze attacks on Hawranite Sunni Muslim villages continued and resulted in the abandonment of fifteen more villages.[19]

At the end of 1881, the Ottomans mounted a military campaign of 10,000 troops into the Hawran to protect the villages, but financial constraints on the provincial treasury obliged them to stop short of engaging the Druze.[20] Probably for the same reason, the authorities reappointed Ibrahim al-Atrash and his supporters to administrative functions in the Jabal in 1882.[21] As legitimate Ottoman governor in the Hawran once again, Ibrahim led his forces, in league with the Sardiya bedouin, in an attack on the Wald 'Ali bedouin. With the hope of provoking Ottoman intervention and restoring their losses, the Wald 'Ali then invaded the plain and attacked Sunni Muslim villages there.[22] But it does not appear that the Ottomans responded as expected.

These events indicate that the Hawran continued in an uneasy state of only quasi-control by Damascus and that struggles between rural factions continued as the government's policies vacillated among authorizing Ibrahim's Druze shaikhs, tax farming through a second echelon of intermediaries, and even direct taxation. In 1883, the authorities reaffirmed their intentions to bring the Hawran to heel. They announced plans for a railway through the Hawran, and proceeded with the construction of military bases at strategic points. They also granted cultivation rights to some bedouin so that they

Plains cultivators, central Syria, at home. Photo by L. S. Schilcher, 1972.

would settle in the vicinity of the bases and serve as a buffer between the authorities and the rebellious Hawranite factions. In 1883, the Ottomans sent a new contingent of troops into the Hawran to adjudicate a dispute over cultivation rights between Sunni Muslim plains villagers and Druze followers of Ibrahim.[23]

In 1884 the authorities once again shifted their support from Ibrahim, this time to the Shibli al-Atrash Druze. Shibli was recognized as the leading shaikh of Jabal Hawran and the adjoining Laja'.[24]

In 1885, Druze demonstrated their objections to the continued settlement of bedouin in the gorges that controlled the access and escape routes to the strategically important Laja' region. Besides being useful in guerrilla warfare because of its gullies and hideaways, the Laja' could offer peasants refuge from attack and oppression. Whoever controlled it could continue to patronize the cultivators of the plain. The Druze attacked the newly resettled villages of Mismiyya and Sha'ra on the fringes of the Laja'. The Ottomans sent troops and successfully intimidated them. When the Druze shaikhs came to Damascus to negotiate in good faith, they were imprisoned by the authorities.[25]

In 1886, the Ottomans attempted to carry out a census of the plains villages but were opposed by the Hawranites, who had ample justification to fear that the census was a measure to facilitate the introduction of conscription. Though Muslims, the Hawranites had until that point been exempt from service in the Ottoman army. Though they justified their exemption by reminding the authorities that they were a frontier peasantry, in fact the state had lacked the power and authority to conscript them. To avoid a confrontation with the 3,000 troops sent to carry out the census, many Hawranites abandoned their villages and escaped to the Laja'. Confident that they controlled the access routes to the Laja', the troops took up positions there to entrap the fleeing villagers, but Druze fighters of Ibrahim's faction attacked them. The Ottoman authorities called in the French consul to mediate. The consul concluded an agreement whereby villagers would return to their fields and the Ottomans would retain control of the Laja' gorges.[26] Plans to take a census were probably dropped, but, as we shall see, these issues were far from settled.

Phase Two (1887–89): The Economic Crisis Peaks

By 1887 the steady decline of world grain prices rendered coastal prices so low that there was no profit margin whatsoever for local merchants and other intermediaries in the export of Hawran grain. The government could no longer find any urban notables interested in farming agricultural taxes in the Hawran and was thus at a loss to raise the funds and grain necessary to sustain troops in the Hawran and eventually in the entire province. Though the urban notables of the cartel may have temporarily lost interest in the affairs of the Hawran, the state could not so easily relinquish its interests. At first the commander in chief for the province paid salaries out of his private fortune, at the same time refusing to pursue any military campaigns into the region. The central government, however, would not concede the Hawran's loss. In the coming years the authorities frequently resorted to sending the gendarmerie to raid villages and seize livestock from nomads in order to extract revenue. The Hawranites often complained of these robber-gendarmes, who were a serious impediment to order and normal economic activity.[27]

During 1887, major battles occurred among the Hawran's factions and between Hawranites and the government's forces based there. For example, 3,000 Druze attacked the newly settled bedouin and drove them out of their camps in the Laja'. The settlers sought refuge in the new Ottoman base there, and troop reinforcements had to be dispatched from Damascus to hold the fort. In the ensuing battle 160 were killed, including the Turkish commander. Though the Ottomans appeared to retain control of the Laja', the Druze retaliated by instigating their allies, the Ghiath bedouin, to attack the Baghdad-Damascus caravan in the desert east of Damascus, causing heavy losses to urban merchants and embarrassment to the authorities.[28]

Supplied by the government with new Martini rifles, the newly settled Laja' bedouin then went on the offensive against the Druze, attacking their grain caravans and seizing their camels. The Ottoman authorities sent Mamduh Pasha and the aged Damascene notable, Sa'id Bey al-Kaylani, to mediate the dispute while rumors spread that the government was planning to resupply the bedouin with the ammunition they needed for their new rifles. The terms negotiated held that the Druze shaikhs were to be restored by the Ottomans to positions of authority in the Jabal Hawran and would exercise judicial, fiscal, policing, and administrative autonomy in their own districts. Ibrahim al-Atrash was to be granted the highest rank, but Shibli was also to have a post. In addition Shibli was expected to adopt Turkish dress and to avoid any contacts with the French consulate. The implication was that the Druze would be restricted to their own districts and a few contiguous regions. For the most part, they would be excluded from economic or political affairs in the Hawran plain, with the central authorities acting directly there. Ibrahim accepted these terms, but Shibli and other subordinate shaikhs eventually rejected them.[29]

No one bid in Damascus for the Hawran tax farms in 1887 and 1888.

Desperate for revenues and grain but unable to collect them directly, the authorities imprisoned the shaikhs of Hawranite villages until the villagers farmed their own taxes. That segment of the Hawranite peasantry that was again subjected to Ottoman control through the shaikhs of Ibrahim abandoned their villages in protest, taking refuge in the Laja' and Jabal. The villagers objected to the share of taxes they had to pay relative to the shares paid by the shaikhs and also to the Atrash shaikhs' attempt to meet their commitments to the state by undercutting the villagers and contracting more compliant, newly arrived Druze immigrants from the west. The authorities were at first inclined to support the peasants in order to obtain the harvest. They applied military pressure on the Druze shaikhs through their new bases, and some villagers returned to cultivation.[30]

Phase Three (1890): Radical Populism in Jabal Hawran

New taxation demands of 30,000 Turkish lire were pressed by the authorities on the Hawranite shaikhs in March 1890. The peasants, however, were even less disposed to cooperate. Grain prices were so low that they could not possibly sacrifice enough of their own supply to raise the cash demanded. In April 300 Christian and Druze peasants converged on the seat of the district governor at Suwaida in Jabal Hawran to seek relief. At that time Ibrahim still held the post. His men fired on the crowd, killing many, whereupon the petitioners forced Ibrahim to flee the fortress, and it was reported that his son was killed in the melee. Ibrahim fled to Damascus and was obliged to accept very difficult terms in order to retain his governmental position, including the payment of the 30,000 lire in taxes from his districts.[31]

In the Hawran, the Druze religious leaders ('aqqal) attempted to mediate the dispute within the Druze community. Their terms held that Ibrahim would remain Ottoman governor of the district but would financially compensate the families that had suffered fatalities at Suwaida for a total of 30,000 French francs. The peasants would be permitted to cultivate the lands they occupied, rather than being displaced, presumably, by incoming western Druze.[32]

But the peasants were not satisfied with these terms either. They wanted assurances that they would not be paid as wage earners on the land they cultivated, exposed to direct taxation. They preferred to return to the share-cropping agreements of previous years whereby the shaikhs paid the taxes and protected them from the Ottoman authorities.[33] In meetings all over the Jabal and in the Hawran plain, many shaikhs began to concede to the peasants' demands regarding the relative shares to be taken in the harvest and for tax

Syrian mountaineer hunter. Photo by L. S. Schilcher, 1972.

responsibilities. At first encouraged by these successes and by the support of some subordinate Druze shaikhs (including Shibli) who had agreed to the justice of the peasants' demands, peasants continued to gather in Suwaida. In April 1890 they held a public meeting and set up a commune ('Ammiyya). In this radical development, the peasants, mostly Druze but also some Christians, announced their intentions to alter the traditional system of agriculture and politics. They wished to elect their own shaikhs, to distribute their own cultivation rights, and to retain three-fourths of the harvest in sharecropping contracts with their elected shaikhs. They were even prepared to accept an ethnic Turk as district governor and expressed their continued loyalty to the Ottoman government, including a pledge to pay their taxes.[34]

Though this might have been the opportunity the authorities were awaiting to establish direct rule, they squandered it. Seizing instead the opportunity to exploit internal Druze disunity, they chose to ignore the 'Ammiyya's proposals and to exert more pressure on the plains Hawranites, who now had no protectors if they attempted flight. Livestock taxes were collected by force, and more village shaikhs were arrested to force the peasants to pay the taxes they could ill afford. These measures only aggravated the Hawranites' discontent with the government. For its part, the government clearly did not trust the communards, for in June 1890 heavy troop contingents were dispatched by the Ottomans to Suwaida. There followed an unprecedented military bombardment that resulted in the reported destruction of three-fourths of Suwaida and approximately 500 casualties. The communards who had broken with their shaikhs were left without protectors as the troops moved in. The commune appeared to have been crushed.[35]

In the aftermath the authorities sent the western Druze shaikh, 'Ali Junblat, to negotiate the terms of submission at Suwaida and called upon the British consul for his mediation. The government's terms were harsh and insensitive to peasant vulnerabilities: land registration (as a preliminary to lump-sum taxation and privatization); the construction of an Ottoman military base directly in the Jabal Hawran at which "foreign" (non-Druze, non-Hawranite, even non-Syrian) troops could be garrisoned; the confiscation of Martini rifles; and the payment of many years of tax arrears in cash. The communards refused these terms, preferring to concede the reinstatement of Ibrahim as district governor and to pay only a lump-sum tribute tax, negotiated through their shaikhs.[36]

Though the Ottomans remained in occupation of Suwaida, they could not handle all the guerrilla attacks on their positions in other parts of the Hawran.[37] The Druze shaikhs could neither control their villagers nor appease the authorities. A fascinating aspect of this phase is the possibility that the central government actually inspired rural populism. As reported locally, the governor in Damascus, Mustafa Assim Pasha, began an open and energetic campaign in the last months of 1890 to support peasants in their disputes over cultivation rights against their land controllers, contractors, and shaikhs. He pressed charges through administrative rather than judicial channels against urban notables with extensive holdings whom he considered to be usurpers, even in cases where they had acquired the land-registration documents. The extent to which the governor's campaign influenced events in the Hawran is not clear. Roughly coinciding with the peasant 'Ammiya of Suwaida, however, his policy added weight to the pessimism of the remaining cartel members. Not only had the government no further intention of promoting their interests, but it had either lost control of the peasants (as in the Hawran) or would promote peasant interests (as in the cases pursued by the governor in Damascus). To the cartel, the situation must have seemed totally out of control.[38]

The uproar in Damascus was significant. Several high-ranking officials of local origin resigned, and the Damascene Administrative Council (*Majlis al-Idara*) refused to convene.[39] The Ottoman Wali responded by exiling four Damascene notables who were alleged to be the leaders of the protest. But other Damascene land controllers and politicians continued to resist rural reforms into the next year, despite repeated deportations. These disputes resulted in yet further difficulties for the Ottomans. Not only did the government fail to farm any taxes in the Hawran, but now the urban tax farmers also refused to deliver the taxes from the rich villages in the vicinity of Damascus.[40] Ibrahim and Shibli both decided to petition their cases at a higher level and left for Istanbul with the hope of having an audience with Sultan 'Abd al-Hamid.[41]

Phase Four (1891–95): Hiatus

In the midst of this crisis, a serious cholera epidemic swept the province of Syria and continued into 1892, especially in the Hawran. Probably as a consequence of the epidemic the Ottoman authorities suspended their new policy in 1891 and 1892, but the duplicity of 'Uthman Nuri Pasha, the former commander in chief who was named governor in 1891, must also have played a role. While accepting bribes from powerful urban tax farmers and land controllers, he pretended to support the peasants' cause in line with the new policy, using the government's reform program as leverage on the wealthy in Damascus to line his own pocket. Also, Istanbul might have thought it wiser to bide its time until the new railway was completed. Though planned and announced, the railway was not actually started until December 1892 and not finished until 1894.[42]

The Ottomans did, however, press ahead with their attempts to register lands in the Hawran plain in 1892, the first and most important step toward

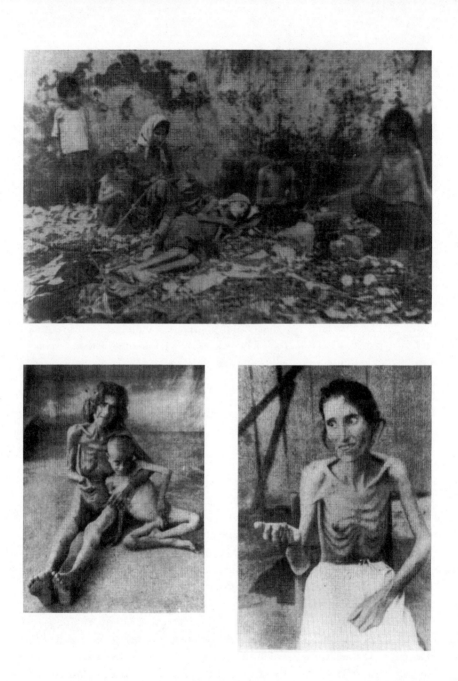

Famine in Syria during World War I. Photos from *L'Asie Française*.

establishing direct control through the further privatization of cultivation rights. They were faced, however, with peasant protest, the abandonment of villages, and covert harvesting. The shaikhs of plains villages received government ultimatums announcing registration, and troops were sent to enforce the measures. Several Druze shaikhs were exiled. By 1893 it was reported that the land registrations had been completed, though they were far from perfect. New revolts in the Hawran involved the bedouin on its southern fringes, who also objected to the land registrations.[43] The Hawranites themselves were confused. Though they objected to the squeeze their shaikhs were applying, they also did not trust the measures the government used to undermine the shaikhs.

Phase Five (1893–95): The Railways

With the railway finally under construction in 1893, the Ottoman authorities revealed yet another plan. They inaugurated the new Sanjak of Maʿan for the administration of the even more remote regions extending south of the Hawran and east of the Jordan River, in what is today the kingdom of Jordan.[44] This move was intended to indicate their commitment to the entire interior region south of Damascus, their determination to bring it under control, and their willingness to offer at least some Damascenes a new field of fiscal and commercial exploitation. A number of Damascene notables were in fact awarded posts and control of lands in the new district. But these measures failed to stem the tide of general rural unrest and the incursions of bedouin into settled areas. Most of the new officials for the Sanjak of Maʿan had to remain in the safety of the fortress at Kerak, a small town east of the Jordan.[45]

Upon the death of Ibrahim al-Atrash, Shibli, who had returned from Istanbul, attempted to form an alliance with some of these rebellious bedouin tribes. In the ensuing raids and counterraids, which included many atrocities, Shibli was captured by the authorities and threatened with imprisonment in Damascus. In a further surprise move, the Ottoman authorities named a Jerusalem Sunni Muslim notable, Yusuf Dia Pasha al-Khalidi, to the governorship of Jabal Hawran. Though he may have been an enlightened and progressive individual, for the Hawranites, he represented the now mistrusted if not despised urban notables. Al-Khalidi was generally rejected by the local population and failed to appease the rebellious factions.[46]

In 1894, the Hawranites and Maʿanites did not pay their taxes, and, with scarcely any revenues coming in, the provincial authorities were hard-pressed to pursue their new policies. They could not even afford to send troops to protect villages close to Damascus from Hawranite raiders.[47] The situation was so critical that it was beginning to evoke panic in Damascus. Though the gendarmerie was dispatched, they punished the wrong Hawranites and only contributed to the general disillusionment with the government and the escalation of violence. Since the gendarmerie chief was a Circassian, outbreaks now occurred between Hawranites and the newly settled Circassians in the western Hawran.[48]

The opening of the railway from Damascus into the Hawran in 1894 did not have the desired effect. For the Damascene grain traders and the authorities, it only exacerbated the situation. Now large quantities of Hawran grain flooded the city's market, depressing prices even further and distressing the producers and merchants from the surrounding villages who normally dominated this market. Coinciding with the depths of the general trade depression in the eastern Mediterranean, the drop in prices severely affected the Damascene commercial community. The situation became even more desperate when news of the 1895 crash on the London and Paris financial markets hit Syria. It was reported that the losses of local investors amounted to at least 20 million francs.[49] Even when, in that year, the branch railway from Damascus to Beirut was opened, grain continued to flood the Damascene market and could not be exported from there with much profit because coastal prices remained depressed. The Beirut market could be supplied more cheaply by sea than from the interior.

'Uthman Nuri Pasha had been assigned to the governorship of Damascus shortly before the completion of the railway into the Hawran. At about the same time, the district governor, Yusuf Dia al-Khalidi, was replaced by Shibli al-Atrash in the Jabal Hawran. These shifts in government assignments indicated a renewal of the policy of supporting peasant cultivation rights. The elite of Damascus was at a loss as to how to respond. Disputes among the notable families broke out as various factions formed and reformed, attempting to place partisans in positions to deal with the government without losing face or vital assets in the Hawran, in the oasis villages, or among urban clienteles.[50]

Given the world trade and financial crises, the Ottomans' ostensibly progressive attempts to undermine the urban land controllers were costly and would have catastrophic political consequences. The provincial authorities could not afford to pay the salaries of troops based even in Damascus and were faced with riots and rebellions in Damascus and its surrounding villages when they attempted to carry out conscription. From their own military officers came open accusations against the sultan, which were read at public gatherings in Damascus. Another serious development was the renewed and brisk trade in arms into the rebel areas of the Hawran.[51]

Not only were taxes not being paid, but the peasants were beginning to abandon cultivation altogether. Either they ignored their contracts with urban land-controlling investors or the investors withdrew from agricultural contracts because of low profit margins. Large numbers of Hawranite villagers left their fields and villages to seek refuge from the general unrest with relatives and allies in more remote parts of the Hawran where the rebels held sway.[52] A general Hawranite uprising was in the air, including not just the Christian and Druze villagers of Jabal Hawran but also the Sunni Muslims of the plain.

Phase Six (1895–96): The State Wages War on Its Peasantry

To regain the confidence of the urban population, the Ottoman authorities had but one alternative: to mount a new campaign into the Hawran. The Damascene ʿulama delivered a *fatwa* expressly naming the Druze as the legitimate target of the state's wrath. Thirty thousand troops were raised, assembled, and dispatched into the Hawran by railway in December 1895. In response, the Hawran unleashed a new kind of weapon. Perhaps the railway's water towers were poisoned, perhaps not, but the Ottoman campaign was crippled at the outset by an outbreak of dysentery among thousands of unfortunate soldiers. Working on a practically nonexistent budget, the authorities now had to interrupt the campaign and were obliged in the end to attempt to negotiate with the rebels.[53]

The government demanded that the rebels surrender their Martini rifles, pay compensation to villagers under government protection, pay twenty years' tax arrears, and submit to conscription. The rebels flatly refused all these demands. The state of health of the troops virtually precluded any further military action. In the early months of 1896, the military authorities struck private deals with the Druze rebels rather than press on with the campaign. As the Ottomans proclaimed themselves the victors, Shibli and the rebel shaikhs agreed to come to Damascus to negotiate in return for a cease-fire.[54]

The Damascenes were disappointed that a clear military victory had not been achieved, and rumors of bribes further undermined the authorities' credibility. The government nevertheless considered the matter closed and disbanded the larger portion of the troops, disregarding the promise of safe-conduct to the rebel leadership, probably under pressure from Damascene notables and public opinion. In the Hawran the remaining Druze and their allies were also exposed to the attacks of progovernment factions with impunity. Their shaikhs telegraphed to Istanbul for protection, but none was forthcoming.[55]

In the following months, more than a thousand Druze prisoners were brought to Damascus and exposed to the abuse of the mob while the authorities stood by. The prisoners had already been mistreated by the soldiers along the trek to the city and many arrived dead. Shibli was publicly displayed, spat on, and heaped with dung. Approximately a thousand Druze, including women and children, were exiled to Rhodes, Bursa, and Castomouni, first transported to Beirut and then overseas.

A few months of bitter discontent in the Hawran followed. Then, though it was harvest time, new hostilities broke out.[56] Reports held that the entire countryside between the Hawran and the Palestinian coast was in turmoil as the Druze carried out retribution on villagers who were considered wards of the state. In one incident the Druze were said to have massacred 600 Ottoman troops.[57] In the middle of the harvest and threshing period, the state mounted a new campaign.

Late in June 1896, Istanbul made a number of major changes in provincial administration. The governor, 'Uthman Nuri Pasha, was removed and replaced by a higher-ranking official from Baghdad, Hasan Rafiq Pasha.[58] Though finances were desperate, civilian salaries were cut in order to mount the new campaign. On July 11, 1896, the troops were given orders to regroup and attack. Some 30,000 soldiers moved on the 9,000–10,000 Druze holding Suwaida. In the battle that ensued, 1,200 casualties among the rebels and 600 among the troops were reported, a result later revised by the governor to 2,000 rebel casualties. The Druze's defense of Suwaida was considered heroic, even in Damascus.[59]

Though the troops swept through all the villages and towns of the Jabal, murdering prisoners, women, and children, raping and pillaging, the Druze still refused to disarm, surrender their leaders, or accept service in the army. At the end of 1896 several thousand Druze rebels still held out in the hideaways of the Laja' and the Jabal while the government had to disband all but six battalions owing to lack of funds.[60]

Fearing retribution, Damascus reached such a peak of panic that the notables pleaded with the authorities to form an urban defense militia. It was known that the Druze had appealed to the western Druze factions to come to their rescue.[61] But the government appeared undeterred. Having defeated the Druze rebels at Suwaida, it pushed ahead with its attempts to tax grain producers directly, without the intermediation of village shaikhs or tax farmers. This system (called *Takhmis*) made production assessments on the basis of a five-year average, taking 10 percent as the government's due. Though the Druze peasants still wished the authorities would reinstitute lump-sum tribute

A street in a southern Syrian town. Photo by L. S. Schilcher, 1988.

taxation through their shaikhs, the plains peasants protested that the tithe assessments were far too high and that they also preferred the previous system of tax farming.[62]

Taxation during 1896 was especially oppressive. As a result of the unrest, the harvest was poor, but the tax assessments did not reflect the shortages. Not only were many fields abandoned but the confiscation by the authorities of 40,000 camels normally used for transport disrupted the delivery of grain to train stations and warehouses. In addition, much money otherwise available for taxation had been spent on bribes to Ottoman officials. Further unrest in the Hawran and resistance to the Takhmis fueled the debate among the local authorities and notables as to the wisdom of the new tax reforms. Damascene opinion blamed Ottoman rule for the difficulties.[63]

As hostilities continued and the general mood of the Hawran remained rebellious, the Druze who held out in the hills spread the message that they were now opposed only to the Ottomans and would undertake to protect any grain merchants traveling in the Hawran and the peasantry in general. The Sunni peasants' loyalties were slowly swinging in favor of the Druze rebels, even though they were now outlaws. The ultimate horror for Damascus and the authorities, a unified Hawranite uprising, was unfolding.[64]

Phase Seven (1897): General Uprising

The peasantry of the Hawran plains abandoned their fields in still greater numbers in 1897 as the harvest was to begin. It was reported that the entire plain was deserted but for the aged and infirm. The Sunni Muslims now migrated en masse to the Laja' and Jabal, seeking alliances with the rebellious Druze and bedouin. Some 8,000 Druze guerrillas had still not submitted to the Ottoman authorities, and when the authorities attempted to cut the water supply to the Laja', the troops were resisted, significantly, by a mixed force of plainsfolk, Druze, and bedouin.[65]

The villagers' threats to abandon their farms at harvesttime were at first not taken seriously in Damascus, where it was assumed that the peasants would not abandon their own food supply. Gradually, however, the scale of the exodus became clear. In addition, a severe grain famine was developing in the desert regions south of the Hawran and along the pilgrimage route—for which the government's policies would be held directly responsible.[66] The possibility of further disturbances involving the bedouin of the Sanjak of Ma'an, the Nejd, and the Hijaz could not be ignored.

The state of the provincial treasury was as desperate as ever, having been exhausted by the previous year's campaign and the increased expenses of escorting and provisioning the pilgrimage through the Hawran. Yet petitions from the Hawranites to the authorities requesting the return to taxation through the intermediacy of rural shaikhs rather than the Takhmis were ignored. The authorities first called on Damascene notables for financial assistance; that proving inadequate, they finally turned to European bankers to float a new loan for the province.[67]

Phase Eight (1898–1900): Détente

These last acts of desperation led the central government to release the provincial administration from the obligation to institute Takhmis taxation and conscription in the Hawran. Though grain prices on the coast recovered enough to make export profitable in 1897 and even more so in 1898, the merchants had little grain to sell in those years. Locust attacks in 1899 extended the production crisis. The government's position was critical, and the civil and military officials quarreled over a course of action. On the eve of yet another military campaign into the Hawran, the sultan himself decided to relent. An order from Istanbul on April 19, 1900, granted a general amnesty, dropped demands for tax arrears, and assigned Druze to the new sub-district posts in Jabal Hawran.[68]

As a result, Jabal Hawran in 1900 had neither a Druze shaikh nor an urban notable as district governor. The Ottomans posted instead an ethnic Turk. As a symbolic gesture of reconciliation, however, this governor held a great banquet in his residence as the exiled Druze shaikhs returned to Suwaida amidst a jubilant peasantry.[69]

The twenty-year period of tension, resistance, and open warfare in the Hawran appeared to have ended with the reconciliation of the Druze shaikhs and at the expense of direct rule. The harvest in 1900 was good, prices had recovered, and relative peace reigned.[70] The Hawranites had won their cause and retained some measure of rural autonomy, a victory won at the expense of considerable hardship and loss for both Hawranites and Ottoman soldiers, many of whom were locally recruited.[71]

Conclusion

The period 1879–99 saw events with causes specific to those years. In this chapter I have attempted to demonstrate that events in the Hawran of the late nineteenth century were strongly influenced by larger economic developments, and especially by those beyond the influence and control of the rural region or even of the larger entities of province and empire. The impact of trends in world markets into which Syria was well integrated by the second half of the century had been crucial to local developments not only in the cities but also in this remote and barely settled rural district.

These events vividly describe patterns of Third World political economy in rural Syria. Coinciding with the accession of the authoritarian and centrist Ottoman sultan ʿAbd al-Hamid, the Great Depression had contributed significantly to tensions in Ottoman provincial politics. In the urban areas, the struggle for survival and control during the depression led to new factionalism within the "politics of notables." The powerful provincial families that survived this period as members of the elite did so by consolidating their positions and increasing their dependence on and identification with the central state. For those who were excluded or who rejected overdependence on principle, the concepts of state decentralization and Arab nationalism presented new political alternatives.[72]

In rural areas, the state was obliged to pursue an expensive policy of military intervention to hold the Hawran in spite of the declining economic value of this chiefly grain-producing region in the new global economic framework of exploitation and investment. Besides losing this struggle economically, the Ottoman state would eventually also lose it politically.[73]

The 1880s and 1890s were a period of serious conflict in rural Syria. Apparent outbreaks of ethnic and religious animosity or of the supposedly endemic struggle between the desert and the sown in fact reflected the scramble for power and profit among several layers of intermediaries and their respective clienteles, a contest played out on a diminishing field of opportunity as both economic depression and state centralism placed rural areas under intense pressure.

I have isolated a number of phases. In the early years of the Great Depression, the provincial cartel of urban-based fiscal entrepreneurs pressured their rural counterparts for more grain as the price squeeze reduced profits. This pressure led to hostilities among rural cultivators who could ill afford to sacrifice more grain. When the state's attempt at direct taxation failed, it turned from the cartel to less demanding fiscal entrepreneurs. Wavering state support undermined the cartel's control at the level of its rural chiefs, and some urban notables of the cartel unsuccessfully conspired with Europeans to sustain their position.

With the drastic decline in world grain prices and with no local profit margins, the cartel disintegrated and the state attempted direct control, taxation, and conscription through its own agents. The state's representatives' harsh measures, corruption, and duplicity reawakened the spirit of rural autonomy, especially among factions with strong communal solidarity. Further state pressure resulted in the declaration of a rural commune in a remote hill region. The communards expressed a form of rural populism that was not only antistatist but antifeudal and antiurban.

Continuing its campaign to reduce the power of urban intermediaries, the state reorganized the provincial infrastructure to permit direct military intervention in remote areas. Following a long hiatus caused by a major epidemic and delays in railway construction, the state mounted a major military campaign into the heart of the rural region. The peasantry reacted with self-sacrificing flight, reaffirming quasi-feudal rural solidarities that bridged the traditional gaps among peasants, nomads, and mountaineers. The state won a military but not a political victory and had to make further political and economic concessions to the rural populations.

Toward the end of these twenty years of struggle and conflict, the depression eased, allowing limited maneuverability and reconciliation. In the meantime, the political community had been transformed, revealing solidarities that reflected and often transcended traditional estate, religious, feudal, and factional allegiances. The cartel's influence was so reduced that neither state nor peasantry would again be as easily fooled by the intrigues of urban notables. The peasantry appears to have developed an even more intense distrust of all urbanites.[74]

The events of 1879–1900 had taught the two groups very different lessons. The local urban notables learned to doubt the imperial state's intentions toward them after a brief era in the 1860s and 1870s when it had actively promoted their interests. Many reacted negatively to the state's policies, withdrew their collaboration, and turned to new political solutions such as decentralization and separatist nationalism. The peasantry was awakened to the possibility that, vis-à-vis the urban elites, the state was a potentially positive force in their struggle for economic survival and political representation, though resistance and survival seemed inevitably linked with hardship, violence, and reversion to quasi-feudal solidarities. The peasants seem to have had only two methods of dealing with their adversaries: armed violence or withdrawal of their labor through flight. Both methods were extreme, but they seem to have been the only ways the peasantry could communicate a desire to renegotiate their relationships with urbanites and authorities.

The rural solidarities forged in the 1890s were further tested in the years leading up to World War I and especially during the famine years of that war, 1916–18. Reorganization of the Syrian rural economy in the interwar period under the French mandate, especially as a consequence of the 1930s depression, and again during World War II under the Allies' Middle East Supply Center would also have a significant impact on rural Syria before independence. If there was a general trend up to the 1950s, it was that the state continued to vacillate in its support of rural political demands depending on the economic indispensibility or expendability of the region concerned. The inability of rural people to express themselves except as factors of production or as disrupters of public "order" forms the sad commentary on urban-rural and state-rural relations of the pre-independence period. It is not difficult to see how the frustrations and bitterness of this little-respected majority of the population might eventually express itself in more organized radical rural populism, even when the peasants were no longer cultivators but had become the newly urbanized petite bourgeoisie of the modern states of contemporary greater Syria.

Notes

1. This paper is one of a series of interrelated papers I have been able to research and write thanks to the financial support of the Volkswagen Foundation during the years 1979–82: "The Hawran Conflicts of the 1860s: A Chapter in the Rural History of Modern Syria," *International Journal of Middle East Studies* 13 (1981): 159–79; "The Grain Economy of Late Ottoman Syria and the Issue of Large-scale Commercialization," in *Large-Scale Commercial Agriculture in the Ottoman Empire*, ed. Faruk Tabak and Çaglar Keyder (New York: SUNY University Press, 1991, forthcoming); "The Impact of the Great Depression on Late Ottoman Syria," in *New Perspectives on Turkey*, ed. Suraiya Faroqhi (special issue forthcoming); "The Famine in Syria, 1916–1918," in *Historical Perspectives on the Middle East*, ed. John Spagnola (forthcoming); "Die Weizenwirtschaft des Nahen Ostens in der Zwischenkriegszeit: Der Einfluss der Ökonomie auf die Politik am Beispiel Syriens," in *Der Nahe Osten in der Zweischenkriegszeit 1919–1939*, ed. L. Schatkowski Schilcher and C. Scharf (Stuttgart: Steiner, 1989), 241–89; "The Wheat Economy of Syria during the Second World War," paper delivered at the International Economic Historians Congress, Budapest, 1982.

I am also grateful to Albert Hourani, Roger Owen, David McDowell, Jean-Paul Pascual, Faris Nasrallah, Chris Eccel, Faruk Tabak, Şevket Pamuk, Eugene Rogan, Henry McAdam, and Charles Issawi for many useful and stimulating comments and discussions. Some of their published works are referred to here in the footnotes, but I am responsible for any misinterpretations or mistakes.

2. To the north lay the valley of Wadi Ajam and the well-settled and ostensibly well-controlled Damascene oasis (al-Ghuta). To the west stood Mount Hermon (Jabal al-Shaikh) and the slopes and valleys of the Anti-Lebanese mountains (Jaulan, 'Ajlun, Aklim al-Ballan) beyond which the Sea of Galilee (Bahr al-Tabariyya) and the Jordan River gorge (Baisan, al-Ghur) presented further barriers. To the northeast and east lay a volcanic badlands region of heavily eroded gullies and redoubts (al-Safa, al-Laja') and the hills, known then as Jabal Hawran, now as Jabal al-Duruz or Jabal al-'Arab, which, together with a lava rock field to their east (al-Harra), built a buffer between the plain and the Syrian steppe. To the south an opening to the Trans-Jordanian plateau and the Syrian steppe existed, though gullies and ravines also provided some protection here.

For a detailed geological, geographic, and land use description of the Hawran see Doris S. Miller, "The Lava Lands of Syria: Regional Urbanism in the Roman Empire" (Ph.D. diss., New York University, 1984), 8–48. See also Eugen Wirth, *Syrien. Ein geographische Landeskunde* (Darmstadt: Wissentschaftliche Buchgesellschaft, 1971), 57–59, 117, 255–60, 409, 417–19, and related figures; Johann Gottfried Wetzstein, *Der Hawran und die Trachonen. Reisebericht über Hawran und die Trachonen* (Berlin: Dietrich Reimer, 1860). Today the Hawran and its previously contiguous or dependent subdistricts are relatively economically depressed areas split among the states of Syria, Jordan, and Israel. Some of its western regions are now disputed among these states. In particular, portions of the Jaulan (Golan Heights) have been annexed by Israel but not relinquished by Syria.

3. If we assume that the average annual per capita consumption of grains among peasants stood then as it does now at approximately 365 kilograms, the Hawran's production to meet the demands of its own population would have stood at about 100,000 tons of grain annually by 1900, when the dependent rural population was probably about 150,000–200,000. In fact, an estimate in 1900 placed the average annual grain production of the Hawran at about 250,000 tons. This would have allowed for a surplus for "export" in an average year of at least 150,000 tons. In years of above-average harvests, that amount would, of course, have been higher. An 1899 estimate of Hawran grain exports to the coastal ports of Haifa and Acre alone stood at an average of 30,000 tons of wheat and 11,000 tons of other grains. See M. R. Hamdan, *Die Versorgung der Bevölkerung in Jordanien mit Grundnahrungsmitteln, Energie und Energie liefernden Nährstoffen* (Bonn, 1979), 110–13, for consumption estimates; Schilcher, "The Grain Economy of Late Ottoman Syria," goes into the problem of production estimates in more detail.

4. Schilcher, "The Hawran Conflicts."

5. Schilcher, "The Grain Economy of Late Ottoman Syria."

6. Şevket Pamuk, *The Ottoman Empire and European Capitalism, 1820–1913: Trade, Investment and Production* (Cambridge: Cambridge University Press, 1987), 96–97, proposes them as mutually exclusive alternatives in nineteenth-century Turkish-Ottoman rural political economy.

7. There are parallels here as well with Pamuk's work; ibid., 106.

8. Paraphrased from consular report of Richard Wood, No. 5, April 10, 1869, FO 195/927. The British consuls often reported on the activities of the cartel in sinister tones, not because they necessarily objected to them in principle but because the cartel successfully blocked the penetration of British protégés. The consul at the time of Midhat Pasha's tax reform attempts reported, "Bids for tax farms are 50 percent above last year due to the energy and personal control of Midhat and to his action in doing away with the time-honored practice of former authorities of selling the tithes of entire districts to favored rings of speculators, the magnitude of which operations prevented the competition of smaller capitalists to the loss of the fisc and proportionate profit of officials and speculators" (consular report from Damascus, June 6, 1879, FO 195/1263; see also consular reports from Beirut, August 16, 1879, FO 195/1264; Damascus, February 6, 1880, FO 195/1306).

9. Schilcher, "The Grain Economy of Late Ottoman Syria," analyzes market factors of supply and demand in further detail.

10. Schilcher, "The Impact of the Great Depression."

11. Taken from an article signed by ʿAbd-al-Wahhab in *Thamarat al-Fanun*, 25, no. 1181 (1898), a government-sponsored, Arabic language weekly published in Beirut.

12. The main sources of information are the reports sent from the French, British, German, and Austrian consulates in Damascus, Beirut, and Jerusalem. (The following abbreviations are used: AE, Archives du Ministère des Affaires Étrangères, Paris [Pol, Correspondence Politique; Comm, Correspondence Commerciale]; FO, Archives of the Foreign Office, London; PPAP, Parliamentary Papers, Accounts and Papers Series, London; AA, Archive des Auswärtigen Amtes, Bonn [O, Oxford Verzeichnis]; OA, Östereichisches Staatsarchiv, Vienna.)

In addition, a valuable source is the Ph.D. dissertation of Najib Elias Saliba, *Wilayat Suriyya 1876–1909*, University of Michigan, 1971 (University Microfilms International, Cat. #7123866), which is based on a survey of contemporary Arabic newspapers.

13. This is a rough estimate. The official statistics quoted in the Ottoman Yearbook (*Salname*) for the year 1316 (A.D. 1898–99) reported the settled male population of the Hawran (including the subdistricts of Hawran, ʿAjlun, Jabal Hawran, Qunaytra, Busra, and Daraʿa) to be 56,429. This number probably indicates a population in excess of 150,000 by that time if we adjust for the underreporting of males and the nonreporting of females, children, and the nonsettled dependent rural populations of the Hawran. A British estimate in 1901 held the population of the limited number of villages in the Hawran likely to be directly affected by the railway to be in excess of 116,630 (Damascus, October 3, 1901, FO 195/2097).

14. The Hawran wheat cultivar is still valued by agronomists today for its resistance to drought and its high protein.

15. See Norman N. Lewis, *Nomads and Settlers in Syria and Jordan, 1800–1980* (London: Cambridge University Press, 1987); Eugen Wirth, "Die Rolle tscherkessischer 'Wehrbauern' bei der Wiederbesiedlung von Steppen und Odland im Osmanischen Reich," in *bustan* 4 (1963): 16–19.

16. Damascus, PPAP/74, 997–1011.

17. Both the British and the French consuls were involved in this dispute and its mediation. Talhuq was considered a French favorite. Damascus, October 22, 26, November 3, 22, 1879, FO 195/1264; August 23, November 1, 5, 11, 25, 1879, July 17, 1880, AE Pol/11. See also Saliba, *Wilayat Suriyya*, 157–65.

18. Damascus, December 31, 1878, FO 195/1202; March 2, 1879, FO 195/1262; April 15, 1879, FO 195/1263. Midhat's tenure in Damascus lasted less than two years. In 1884, the next governor in Syria, Hamdi Pasha, attempted the Takhmis system of taxation in rural areas, but it too was discontinued, not to be tried again until the 1890s. Damascus, April 19, 1884, FO 195/1480; December 16, 1884, FO 195/1480.

19. Damascus, January 31, February 8, March 22, June 20, 1881, AE Pol/12; January 30, February 13, March 21, November 21, 1881, FO 195/1369; from Beirut, February 28, 1881, FO 195/1369.

20. Damascus, June 20, 1881, AE Pol/12.

21. Ibid.

22. Damascus, March 31, 1882, AE Pol/13.

23. Damascus, January 14, 1883, AE Pol/13. The earliest mention of railway projects for the Hawran that I have been able to find is that reported by the British consul in 1869, when a sizable delegation of Damascene notables called on him to launch a company in England for this purpose (Damascus, October 26, 1869, FO 195/927). The inauguration of construction of the Haifa-Acre-Damascus line was not celebrated until December 1892 (Beirut, December 15, 1892, FO 195/1761). On construction of the bases, Damascus, December 8, 1887, FO 195/1583. On bedouin rights, Damascus, November 23, 1881, FO 195/1369; August 18, November 5, 1883, FO 195/1448. On the cultivation rights dispute, Damascus, March 22, 1883, AE Pol/13.

24. Damascus, June 11, 1884, AE Pol/13.

25. Saliba, *Wilayat Suriyya*, 170; Beirut, December 8, 1887, AA(O), Türkei/ 177/1/15977.

26. On the Hawranite escape to Laja', Damascus, April 7, 1886, AE Pol/14. On the agreement mediated by the French consul, Damascus, April 4, May 1, 31, July 25, 1886, FO 195/1548; telegrams of April 7, 10, 11 and report of October 26, 1886, AE Pol/14.

27. On disinterest of intermediaries, Damascus, August 26, 1889, FO 195/1648. On the commander in chief, Damascus, June 25, 1888, FO 195/1613; June 15, 1888, AE Pol/14. On gendarmerie raids, Damascus, December 31, 1888, AE Pol/14; March 17, 1894, FO 195/1839; March 17, 1894, AE Pol/17. On complaints about the gendarmerie, Damascus, June 23, 1896, FO 195/1940.

28. On the Laja' battle, Damascus, November 25, December 12, 27, 1887, FO 195/1583; December 8, 1887, AA(O)/Türkei/177/1/15977. On the caravan attack, Damascus, December 27, 1887, FO 195/1583.

29. On rumors about bedouin ammunition, Damascus, July 6, 1888, AE Pol/14. On the negotiated terms, Damascus, August 23, 1888, AE Pol/14. On the shaikhs' reactions, Damascus, September 18, 1888, AE Pol/14.

30. On the shaikhs' imprisonment, Damascus, August 26, 1889, FO 195/1648; Sidon, July 6, 1891, FO 195/1723. On objections to taxes, Damascus, June 29, 1889, AE Pol/15; July 3, 1889, FO 195/1648; May 13, 1890, FO 195/1683; Pera, June 3, 1890, AA(O) Türkei/177/1/6961. On contracting immigrants, Damascus, July 5, 1889, FO 195/1687; Saliba, *Wilayat Suriyya*, 173. On military pressure on the shaikhs, Damascus, March 14, June 29, 1889, AE Pol/15. See also note 38 below.

31. On March taxation demands and the Suwaida shootings, Pera, June 3, 1890, AA(O) Türkei/177/1/6961; from Damascus, March 31, 1890, AE Pol/15. On Ibrahim's terms, Damascus, June 29, 1889, AE Pol/15; Pera, June 3, 1890, AA(O) Türkei/177/1/6961; Saliba, *Wilayat Suriyya*, 173–74.

32. Damascus, August 8, 1889, AE Pol/15.

33. Saliba, *Wilayat Suriyya*, 175.

34. On shaikh concessions and support, Damascus, November 26, 1889, March 31, 1890, AE Pol/15. On the commune, Damascus, May 3, 1890, FO 195/1687. On Christian peasants, Damascus, July 21, 1890, FO 195/1687. On commune terms, Pera, June 3, 1890, AA(O) Türkei/177/1/6961; Damascus, May 7, 1890, AE Pol/15; Saliba, *Wilayat Suriyya*, 175.

35. On government pressures, Damascus, June 11, 1892, AE Pol/16. On the Suwaida attack, Damascus, June 26, July 3, 7, 1890, AE Pol/15; June 2, 28, July 1, 2, 1890, FO 195/1687; clipping from the Hamburgische Korrespondent of July 28, 1890, included in AA(O) Türkei/177/1/8912. A later report held that the communards had lost only 108 and that the Ottomans had suffered more casualties than originally reported (Damascus, September 27, 1890, AA(O) Türkei/177/1/1035).

36. On the negotiations, Damascus, June 3, July 2, 10, 1890, FO 195/1683; July 7, 1890, FO 195/1687; Saliba, *Wilayat Suriyya*, 177. On the communards' refusal, Damascus, July 1, 1890, FO 195/1687.

37. Beirut, July 23, 1890, AA(O) Türkei/177/1/9141, 11035.

38. At least one previous Ottoman governor had sympathized with the peasants. Rashid Nashid Pasha had unsuccessfully requested that a military campaign be mounted in 1887 to "quell and correct [the Jabal's] leading shaykhs who . . . [kept]

the common folk in serfdom." The governor's report is quoted in Engin Akarli, "Abdülhamid II's Attempt to Integrate Arabs into the Ottoman System," in *Palestine in the Late Ottoman Period,* ed. D. Kushner (Leiden, 1986), 74–89.

39. Damascus, September 15, 1890, AE Pol/15, February 10, 12, 1891, AE Pol/16.

40. Some of these deportees were named. They were members of the well-established notable families: ʿAzm, Bakri, and Dalati (Damascus, September 15, 1890, AE Pol/16).

41. Saliba, *Wilayat Suriyya,* 178. It may be that the impetus for the creation of a new Sanjak south of the Hawran grew out of these representations. See note 45 below.

42. On cholera in Syria, Damascus, November 28, 1891, FO 195/1727; in the Hawran, Damascus, January 23, 1892, FO 195/1765. On ʾUthman Nuri Pasha, Beirut, October 26, 1894, FO 195/1843. On the railway, Beirut, December 15, 1892, FO 195/1761.

43. On peasant protest, Damascus, August 2, 1892, FO 195/1765; July 16, 1892, AE Pol/16. On bedouin involvement, Damascus, October 10, November 7, 1893, AE Pol/17; June 16, 1892, FO 195/1765.

44. Damascus, January 7, 1893, AE Pol/17; October 7, 1893 FO 195/1801; OA 1/35; OA 10/7. For a detailed study of Ottoman planning of the new Sanjak, see Engin Deniz Akarli, "Establishment of the Maʿan-Kerak Mutasarrifiyya, 1891–1894," *Dirasat* (Amman) 13 (1986): 27–42, and Peter Gubser, *Politics and Change in al-Karak, Jordan* (Oxford: Oxford University Press, 1973). For a study of recent farming practices in this region, see *Part-time Farming,* ed., M. Munday and R. S. Smith, Studies in Anthropology, Archaeology, and Epigraphy, vol. 2 (Jordan: Institute of Archaeology and Anthropology, Yarmouk University, 1990).

45. The funds for this new administrative venture were made available to the Ottoman authorities by European creditors through the Ottoman Bank, which would time and again fund the provincial treasury during these decades. Beirut, October 20, 1894 OA/1, and Jerusalem, March 7, 1894, OA 10; Damascus, March 9, 1894, FO 195/1839; Damascus, November 9, 29, 1893, AE Pol/17.

46. On Shibli, Damascus, October 9, 1893, FO 195/1801, OA 11/187, OA 10/7. On al-Khalidi's character, Alexander Schölch, *Palästina im Umbruch* (Stuttgart, 1987), 225–36; on his failure, Damascus, November 7, 1893, AE Pol/17.

47. Damascus, February 3, 1894, FO 195/1839.

48. The Damascene Administrative Council (Majlis al-Idara), on which many Damascene-based Hawran land controllers sat, instigated an investigation of the conflicts in the western Hawran, which led to a cease-fire to permit harvesting (Damascus, June 11, 21, July 31, August 25, 1894, FO 195/1839).

49. On surplus grain, Damascus, July 20, 1894, July 9, 1895, AE Pol/17. On effects on the commercial community, Damascus, June 6, 1895, PPAP/100, 865–71; from Beirut, July 23, 1895, PPAP/100, 945–56; Damascus, August 1896, AE Pol(NS 105/2); December 15, 1896, AE Comm/11. An especially irksome reason for dismay was the conversion of some of the best state land along the railway line in the Hawran into tax- and conscription-exempt private estates, mostly for the benefit of Istanbul personages, including the sultan (Damascus, November 22, 1895, AE Pol/17; March 12, 1896, AE Pol/18). On local losses, Beirut, November 25, 1895, AE Comm/11.

50. Damascus, October 22, 1894, AE Pol/17; November 11, 1894, FO 195/1839;

for land-related disputes between the Mu'ayyad-al-'Azms and the Jaza'iris see the reports from Damascus, July–September 1893, AE Pol/17.

51. On military accusations, Damascus, September 17, 1896, FO 195/1940. On arms trade, Damascus, October 14, 1895, AE Pol/17.

52. Damascus, September 17, October 14, November 6, 8, 15, 1895, AE Pol/17.

53. On the fatwa and the troops, Damascus, November 6, 8, 13, 22, 1895, AE Pol/17. On dysentery, Damascus, December 9, 1895, AE Pol/17; private letter from Consul Hay, Beirut, January 10, 1896, FO 195/1937. On the government budget, Damascus, December 14, 1895, AE Pol/17.

54. Of the 6,000 Albanians among the troops, 4,000 were said to be already dead or dying (Damascus, January 2, 1896, FO 195/1940). The German consul also reported 4,000 troops dead by the end of January 1896 (Damascus, January 28, 1896, AA(O)Türkei 177/2/1471). On negotiations, Damascus, February 12, 1896, AE Pol/18.

55. On bribe rumors, Damascus, January 5, 1896, AE Pol/18. On no safe-conduct, Damascus, December 28, 1895, AE Pol/17; June 2, 24, 1896, AE Pol/18; January 24, February 1, 8, March 12, May 29, June 13, 1896, FO 195/1940. On shaikhs' telegrams, Damascus, February 7, May 7, 1896, FO 195/1937.

56. According to some of the reports, the spark for the new uprising came from the Ottomans. The beautiful niece of Shibli al-Atrash was propositioned by the Ottoman military commander Ramadan Pasha, to whom she had gone to petition the release of her husband. In an attempt to extricate the woman from her predicament, Druze religious leaders approached the Ottoman encampment, but they were fired upon by the Ottoman forces. Now the honor of religion was also involved. The Druze (including this woman and many other women) set up a siege of the Ottoman garrison at Suwaida. This incident escalated the level of hostilities, which were already intense, especially between the Druze and the Circassians. Damascus, January 28, 1896, AA(O) Türkei/177/2; from Jerusalem, July 2, 1896, OA/12.

57. On Druze retribution, Beirut, June 29, July 7, 1896, FO 195/1937. On 600 troops, Damascus, June 19, 1896, AE Pol/18.

58. Some of these new officials had recently been active against the Armenians of Zeitun (Damascus, July 2, 8, 1896, AE Pol/18).

59. On the campaign, Damascus, December 28, 1896, AE Pol/18. Eventually extra taxes would be levied from villages and towns under government control (Damascus, August 20, 28, 1896, AE Pol/18). On the defense of Suwaida, accounts differ on many points of detail: Damascus, July 19, 1896, AA(O) Türkei 177/3/7891; July 15, 1896, AE Pol/18; July 9, 13, 28, 29, 1896, FO 195/1940; Damascus, July 19, 1896, from Beirut, July 20, 1896, OA/2.

60. On the Druze refusal to surrender, Damascus, July 15, 29, August 12, November 13, 17, 1896, AE Pol/18. To fund the campaign, the local authorities had "borrowed" from the budgets of several agencies including the *Awqaf* and the orphans' fund. They had also extracted money from wealthy local inhabitants (Damascus, July 2, November 27, December 28, 1896, AE Pol/18, January 7, 1897, AE Pol/NS104/1; Beirut, July 27, 1896, OA/2). Supplies for the campaign were so short that hundreds of soldiers deserted (Damascus, August 3, 1896, AA(O) Türkei/177/3). Slowly the Syrian soldiers began to sympathize with the Druze, and at

one point they refused to carry out an attack (Damascus, September 13, 1896, AA(O) Türkei/177/3).

61. On panic in Damascus, Damascus, July 20, 1896, AE Pol/18. On western Druze, Damascus, July 13, 1896, AE Pol/18.

62. Damascus, September 19, November 27, 1896, AE Pol/18, January 7, April 26, 1897, AE Pol/NS104/1; June 23, 1896, AA(O) Türkei/177/3/6795; September 10, 1897, FO 195/1984.

63. On the camels, Damascus, November 27, December 28, 1896, AE Pol/18; January 28, 1896, AA(O) Türkei/177/2. On bribes, Damascus, August 6, 1895, AE Pol/17; February 7, 1896, OA/7; from Beirut, February 7, 1896, OA/2. On Damascene opinion, Damascus, September 14, 28, October 29, 1896, AE Pol/18; anonymous report from Damascus, "Situation Politique, 1897," AE Pol/NS 105/2; July 19, September 28, 1896, AA(O) Türkei/177/3.

64. Damascus, April 26, 1897, AE Pol/NS104/1.

65. Ibid., and July 19, 21, 31, 1897, AE Pol/NS 105/2; Damascus, January 1, 1897, FO 195/1980, September 6, 1897, FO 195/1984; June 23, 1897, AA(O) Türkei/177/3/9564.

66. The shortfalls in 1898 were caused by drought, but, under the circumstances, the government would nonetheless be blamed (Damascus, July 23, 1897, FO 195/1984, May 13, June 30, July 5, 1898, FO 195/2024).

67. On the treasury, Damascus, March 1, 1897, April 3, October 11, 1897, FO 195/1984. On petitions, Damascus, August 19, 1897, AA(O) Türkei/177/4/10516. On the loan, Damascus, December 18, 1887, AE Pol/NS 105/2.

68. On the Takhmis, Damascus, October 15, 1897, FO 195/1984; September 17, 18, 1897, AA(O) (Türkei/177/4/11475. On grain supplies, Damascus, December 18, 1897, AE Pol/NS 105/2; May 13, 1898, FO 195/2024. On locust attacks, Damascus, April 4, 1899, FO 195/2056. On the sultan's order, Damascus, April 8, 1898, FO 195/2024, February 23, November 2, December 11, 1899, FO 195/2056, March 9, May 2, 1900, FO 195/2075; April 23, 1900, AA(O) Türkei/177/4; April 9, 1900, AE Pol/NS 106/4.

69. The Ottoman authorities returned exiles to the Hawran with some fanfare and provided new clothes and a cash compensation for each returnee (Damascus, May–June 1900, FO 195/2075; June 11, 1900, AE Pol/NS 106/4).

70. Damascus, October 4, 1900, FO 195/2075.

71. In March 1898 the young Mark Sykes toured the Hawran where he saw mounds of human skeletons (Damascus, May 2, 1898, FO 195/2024).

72. For the late nineteenth- and early twentieth-century activities of members of prominent Damascene families, see my *Families in Politics: Damascene Factions and Estates of the 18th and 19th Centuries* (Stuttgart, 1985), for sketches of the 'Azms (141–43), Barudis (147), Shamdins (147–49), Mahayinis (150), Yusufs (153), 'Abids (155–56), Bakris (160), 'Umaris (181), Hamzas (199), Hisnis (204), Mardams (213), and Jaza'iris (215–18). For an example of retrenchment and consolidation within the elite families in this period, see my "Lore and Reality of Middle Eastern Patriarchy," in *Die Welt des Islams* 28 (1988): 496–512. For the impact of these events on early Arab Nationalists see my "Arab Nationalism in the Frame of Eurasian Nationalisms," in *Arab Nationalisms: Processes of Self-Definition,* ed. Charles Stewart (forthcoming).

73. The connections between the Hawran conflicts of the 1880s and 1890s and the major bedouin revolts in the Hijaz and Nejd have, to my knowledge, never been systematically pursued. The bedouin revolts eventually resulted not only in Arab independence from the Ottoman Empire but also in the emergence of the two leading national Arab dynasties of the twentieth century, the Hashimites and the Ibn Sa'uds. Philby often mentioned the importance of Syrian grain to the political stability of regimes in Arabia, and the British clearly used food as a weapon to win the tribes' support during World War I by blockading the Red Sea ports and by inflating Hawran prices, distributing large amounts of gold there and among the tribes. These measures largely contributed to the catastrophic famine that occurred in Syria in 1916–18 and to the final collapse of Ottoman authority. See my "Famine in Syria."

74. It is interesting to note that the rebels of 1896 specifically requested military (i.e., Turkish Ottoman) rather than civilian (i.e., Damascene notable) negotiators in the aftermath of the revolt (Damascus, September 28, 1896, FO 195/1940).

5

The Impact of Peasant Resistance on Nineteenth-Century Mount Lebanon

AXEL HAVEMANN

Since the early nineteenth century, Lebanon has experienced outbreaks of political violence and civil unrest of varying intensity. All such conflicts, from the rural uprisings and confessional strife in the last century to the civil war of the 1980s, have resulted from internal as well as regional and international causes. They reflect the fragility and precariousness of a pluralistic society, its deficient civility, and its failure to establish a national identity. Although resort to violence has not been unusual in societies of this sort, what is remarkable in the case of Lebanon is the frequency and pattern of such conflicts. Non-confessional, factional rivalries and clashes have almost always been transformed into religious hostilities. Thus, the persisting feature of Lebanon's society is the relative lack of secular and national loyalties and class ties, on the one hand, and the survival of sectarian, communal, and primordial sentiments, on the other.[1]

It is a commonplace that rural unrest has been widespread in Middle Eastern history, but nowhere did it evolve into such sustained movements and so alter society as in the Mount Lebanon region. This study focuses on the origins, developments, and results of Lebanese rural protest movements at three successive times, 1821, 1840, and 1858–61. The conclusions drawn from a systematic comparison and analysis of the movements are based on a broader study of sociopolitical, economic, and ideological continuity and change in Ottoman Lebanon.[2]

The subject will be treated by posing the following questions:

What were the general long-term causes of politico-social unrest and mobilization?

What were the short-term causes that triggered the single movements?
What were the movements' differences and similarities?
To what extent did the movements manifest new phenomena as reflected in
their organization and vocabulary?
To what degree did the movements contribute to positive changes for the
peasants, and what was the impact of rural unrest on society?

THE RURAL movements between 1821 and 1861 must be viewed against the
area's political, economic, social, and ideological structures which underwent
various transformations during the period under study. It has to be stressed
that in the first decades of the nineteenth century both the politico-legal and
socioeconomic organization of Mount Lebanon were singular within the Ottoman Empire. Mount Lebanon was de facto a tributary principality, the
territory of which was in the hands of noble families or clans (patrilinear
kinship groups). They presided over the various tax districts (*muqataʿat*) into
which the entire territory was split; each district or its subdivisions was led by
a *muqataʿaji*. At the top of this hierarchically organized armed nobility stood
the *amir* or *hakim* who represented the principality to the Ottoman sultan.
Internally, however, the amir had no right to interfere in the affairs of the
muqataʿajis' domains.[3]

A formalized hierarchy of nobility existed at the social level, although in
principle the muqataʿajis had equal authority and even the amir was only
primus inter pares. Below him as well as below all the noble families stood
the commoners, mainly peasants and some small artisans affiliated with and
loyal to the houses of muqataʿajis whose duty it was to protect them. The
peasants in turn belonged to a clan and a village and, beyond those, to a
faction or a religious community. However, religion was not a dividing factor;
society was organized in a secular political framework regardless of sectarian
affiliation.[4]

The economy of Mount Lebanon was based on agricultural production and
local handicraft, both oriented toward local consumption and limited regional
exchange. Moreover, a considerable amount of exportable silk was produced.
Small market towns such as Dayr al-Qamar and Zahleh existed in the mountains, but the urban centers on the coast and in the Syrian interior normally lay
outside the sphere of the muqataʿajis. Peasants within a landlord's district
were subject to different forms of socioeconomic and fiscal exactions (irregular, often excessive fees, levies in kind, corvée services, etc.). These exactions differed from place to place according to customary rules. Thus, in
addition to legal ties of personal dependence, peasants were bound by economic constraints.[5]

Regarding the structural levels of Mount Lebanon, one scholar has convincingly demonstrated that it seems possible and necessary to speak of a "Lebanese variant" of feudalism.[6] However, this claim is subject to two qualifications: first, the limited capacity for independent evolution of Mount Lebanon's society because the emirate was located in an empire whose neighboring provinces were structured differently; second, the fiscal connection with the central Ottoman power mediated through the amir and the muqata'ajis who were, however, not mere tax farmers comparable to those in the other provinces of the empire.[7] According to this argument one may say that the muqata'a system was specifically Lebanese, based on a mature social order with roots older than Ottoman sovereignty, and, via the institution of tax farming, artificially adapted to Ottoman law and fiscal practice.

From the first half of the nineteenth century on, Mount Lebanon experienced various internal and external changes that began to dislocate and transform societal structures, with crucial repercussions for the muqata'a system.

On the political level, the centralizing policy of amir Bashir Shihab II weakened the noble families, who were no longer able to contain the power and authority of the emirate. Backed by increasing support from sections of the Maronite church, the amir's position toward the muqata'ajis grew so strong that in the long run it could not be counterbalanced.[8]

With regard to social strata, religious affiliation gained in importance and redefined social boundaries along sectarian lines. Particularly during the 1830s, the time of the Egyptian occupation of Greater Syria, confessional tendencies came to the surface and became even more tense when European intervention sought to curry support among particular local groups. The protective policy of the European powers, especially France and Great Britain,[9] resulted in increasingly differential treatment of the religious communities and aggravated internal conflicts in the Lebanese mountains. In this context, the Maronite church consolidated its position by appealing to Maronite identity. Henceforth, social and religious issues intermingled so strongly that often they could not be separated.

Economically, Mount Lebanon was struck by the disintegration of its traditional mode of production. The dissolution of the economic features of the muqata'a system was linked to both internal economic developments and growing European economic penetration, especially after 1830. New relations of production came into being through the disintegration of the barter economy, the growth of a market-oriented peasant economy, and the appearance in villages of craft workshops employing hired labor. The introduction of cash crops and the monetization of large sectors of the traditional economy caused a gradual change from a "subsistence to a market economy."[10] Such generalizations, however, require comment. First, it is difficult to determine exactly the portion of subsistence existing in Mount Lebanon between 1800 and 1850. Second, with respect to specific products, the transition from old to new modes of economy did not happen at the same time or without interruption. For example, in the production of raw silk and its export to Europe, the transition to a cash economy had already begun in the eighteenth, if not the seventeenth, century. This trade was characterized by sharp fluctuations in silk prices and the emergence of an active class of merchants and money lenders.[11]

The new relations of production evolved and deepened under the growing influx of foreign capital (the circulation of European coins in conjunction with the devaluation of local currency and a general monetary hemorrhage) and the involvement of the country's economy (particularly silk) in the world market. Nothing better reflects these developments than the spectacular rise of Beirut to the leading seaport of the eastern Mediterranean.[12]

In the long run, European penetration proved as detrimental to Mount Lebanon as to all of Syria, exhausting the financial reserves of the country and contributing to the decline of important branches of local handicraft, though this decline should not be exaggerated.[13] One striking example of the European impact was the decline in the production of handmade silk. The establishment by the French of spinning mills in the Lebanese mountains considerably improved the quality of silk. This led, however, to the indebtedness and semi-impoverishment of the muqata'ajis, and, even more, to that of their peasants—bound to their old-fashioned methods of producing silk, they were no longer able to compete with the new technological challenge.[14] The muqata'ajis tried to compensate part of their losses by reinforcing their pressure on the peasants through higher tax demands and forced exactions. Given the general strong population increase, largely a result of improved hygiene and better health conditions,[15] distributional problems were intensified, so that by the middle of the century the struggle for profitable land had become a vital issue.

Altogether, the rupture of the economic basis of the muqata'ajis, the changing patterns of political relationships (between the nobility, the amir, and the Maronite church), and the socioreligious transformations (especially through the Egyptian occupation and the interference of the foreign powers) brought about the breakdown of Mount Lebanon's old order in the first half of the nineteenth century.

ALTHOUGH the short-term causes or precipitants of rural protest differed from one movement to another, the reasons for the outbreak of conflict were related. The *'Ammiyya* riots of 1821 (which consisted of two successive movements, the 'Ammiyya of Antilyas and the 'Ammiyya of Lihfid) were triggered by fiscal policies, amir Bashir's tax demands (both poll taxes and land taxes) that Christian peasants considered excessive and unjust. Bashir's refusal to repeal his demands sparked resistance that evolved into military conflict.[16]

In 1840, the situation was more complicated, and the immediate causes of turmoil were manifold. Starting from a protest against the harsh measures of the Egyptian governors, such as heavy taxation of land and individuals, confiscation of weapons (considered the first step toward conscription into the army), and compulsory labor, the insurgents struggled to throw off foreign rule.[17] A certain degree of patriotic feeling underlay this rebellion.

In the district of Kisrawan in 1858, two factors triggered revolt: first, the sharp and unexpected economic downturn in Kisrawan, beginning two years prior to the rebellion and resulting from climatic difficulties that proved particularly detrimental to cereals cultivation; second, the arming of the peasantry through foreign dealers and smugglers.[18]

According to the Lebanese chroniclers, the oppressive rule of the muqata'ajis over their peasants led to the only rebellion in which the peasants turned immediately against their local landlords.[19] Though this contention may be true, other motives for revolting should be taken into consideration. Participation in or evocations of earlier rural movements may have enhanced the peasants' consciousness and self-esteem. Moreover, the general spirit of reform (for example, that expressed by the Ottoman imperial decree of 1856, which promised equality and freedom for everybody) and the increasing intimacy of the Maronite clergy with the peasants must have impelled the movement further.[20] Together, these factors provided fertile soil for social protest.

WHAT WERE the movements' common features and peculiarities? Regarding social composition, the bulk of the participants in the events of 1821 were peasants and lower clergymen. As for leadership, the villages that were joining the 'ammiyya movements elected deputies (*wukala'*) from the ranks of commoners to advocate their concerns. Above this level, the 'ammiyya movements had leaders from the traditional elite, the muqata'ajis, supplemented by a Maronite bishop who is reported to have initiated the first protest meeting and organized the subsequent campaigns.[21]

In 1840, the peasant mass again constituted and sustained the insurgence. What was new was the appearance of some prominent leaders of low social origin as "popular leaders." But there was still military guidance by some muqata'ajis and by European agents (French noblemen, Catholic missionaries, and British diplomats). Active support in the Maronite church came from the lower clergy, in due time morally backed by the higher clergy, including the patriarch himself. Another innovation consisted of contacts between the insurgents and members of the rising merchant bourgeoisie. For example, merchants and artisans were among the members of the committee that launched the insurgence. Through access to urban centers the bourgeoisie was able to give various kinds of support, such as equipment and provisions.[22]

There seems to be no doubt that the insurrection of 1858 was the most evident manifestation of a popular movement (one is tempted to call it "a revolt by the common man"). Apart from wealthier villagers from the northwestern plains of Kisrawan whose commitment was temporary, the bulk of the rebels who permanently adhered to the movement were poor and perhaps landless peasants from the upper south of the area. Many peasant wukala may have been socially better off but not the majority, and, while indirect support came from higher social strata (above all from wealthier merchants and the upper clergy), the leader of the rebellion was a simple, probably illiterate, man without means—Tanyus Shahin, a former mule driver and blacksmith. His election as general representative (al-wakil al-'amm) and retention of power throughout the period lend credence to the description of the movement in Kisrawan as the culmination of popular uprising in nineteenth-century Mount Lebanon.[23] Not that the role of members from higher social strata was unimportant, but, in comparison to the accounts of 1821 and 1840, the sources' message seems to be that during the Kisrawan events wealthier merchants and upper clergy, including the Maronite patriarch (himself of peasant origins), kept much more in the background. Their suspicion of Tanyus Shahin's character and personal ambitions as well as of the radical groups among his followers was shared by the French consul in Beirut, whose sympathy shifted toward the moderate peasant groups. On the other hand, the moral encouragement or, better, the passive attitude of the Ottoman authorities toward the rebels should be taken into consideration.[24]

As far as religious affiliation is concerned, in both the movements of 1821 and 1840 the Maronites constituted the absolute majority. Temporary participation of some Druze and Shiites was of only minor importance. One of the main reasons for the nearly complete religious homogeneity probably was that no community other than the Maronites was backed by religious institutions comparable to their church. By favoring rebellion and supporting it, the Maronite church intended to strengthen its own influence over the political order.[25] Furthermore, efforts at supraconfessional cooperation had proved unfeasible from the beginning of all such protest movements. In 1858, revolt started in a purely Maronite area and remained limited to it. Direct effects on neighboring districts or followers within them cannot be discerned, although the spirit or mood of revolt spread to other regions.[26]

What of the demands raised by the insurgents? During the first protest meeting in 1821, the peasants demanded the taxes imposed on land and on individuals be levied once a year only, and, above all, not before the crop was mature. Some time later, demands relating to administrative and political problems were added.[27] The matter of personal and land taxes also arose in the 1840 demands along with others: orders to disarm the Christian population should be revoked and inhabitants of Mount Lebanon be exempted from service in the Egyptian army; compulsory labor should be abolished; two members from each religious community should be appointed to an advisory council to help the amir in his affairs.[28] With respect to later developments, this last demand proved the most important, representing the first step toward a confessional order.

Demands advanced in 1858–59 were different. This time, the direct relationship between peasant and master was at stake. Full financial, social, and juridical equality was sought. This meant the repeal of oppressive customary obligations and payments, the abolition of forced labor personal levies (such as gifts), more favorable tenancy terms, and so forth. However, the peasants' claim for social and juridical equality with the muqata'ajis aimed at transforming substantial parts of the traditional social order. In the peasants' view, such equality was established by the Ottoman reform edicts, to which they implicitly alluded in their lists of demands. Radical peasant groups went so far as to demand the settling of the question of who should be *ma'mur* (administrator) by insisting upon his election from the common people. Formerly, the office of ma'mur of Kisrawan had been in the hands of muqata'ajis. The radicals' claim implied much more than political participation; it replaced the muqata'ajis' political authority with self-rule of the common people.[29]

Thus, within a period of forty years, the claim of the "common man" to have his own say in the process of change evolved through an escalation of demands. Starting with a tax issue, it ended with a claim for full equality, which for some implied peasant rule.[30]

The movements possessed certain forms of organization. Unfortunately, beyond the wakil system[31] little is known of their internal functioning, particularly concerning the events of 1821. Sources reporting on 1840 mention a council (*diwan, majlis*) constituted by wakils to take charge of the insurgency and to coordinate its military operations through a fixed headquarters. This organization was shaped through the support of European agents who also helped with better armaments and money.[32] In the Kisrawan rebellion, organization became more refined, with an executive council (diwan) in charge of administrative and judicial tasks. This council, headed by the general representative (*wakil 'amm*) Tanyus Shahin, constituted the basis of the peasant regime.[33] The capacity for warfare was guaranteed by arms deliveries and by purchases and smuggling both from local merchants, and, probably to a minor degree, from foreign dealers. However, it needs to be stressed that the revolt was not mounted or directed by outside forces. There is no support for such a proposition. Apparently, armed men in several villages were ready for quick mobilization.[34] What remains most obscure is the matter of finances. Throughout the peasants' rule there was obviously no tax collection. If, as historical sources suggest, the peasants only subsisted by confiscations, by economizing on their payment of taxes, and by some allowances from merchants, theirs was indeed a rudimentary pattern of financial organization.[35] However, compared to the beginnings of peasant organization in the 1820s, a remarkable development can be discerned.

In conclusion, one may argue that in 1821 there was primarily a fiscal revolt, in 1840 a political insurgence, and in 1858–61 a "social movement," taking this term in its widest sense. Regardless of specific differences, all three were driven by certain present grievances and none was against the whole order. Therefore, the movements were revolts or rebellions but not revolutions. This is also true of the Kisrawan movement, in the course of which even the radical groups demanded neither the expropriation of any of the landlords' estates nor any changes in property rights.[36] On the other hand, in view of some characteristics and given the stages of its development, the Kisrawan movement indeed had quasi-revolutionary traits. In other words, it was the most progressive of all rural movements but still remained "archaic" in the sense defined by Eric Hobsbawm.[37]

Finally, irrespective of progress and continuous evolvement, all the movements were subject to external mechanisms of control: the amir, the muqata'ajis, the Maronite upper clergy, the European powers, the Ottoman authorities. In the frame of the general evolution of society, even rural movements with revolutionary-like claims were tolerated, but only to the extent that they worked in favor of the prevailing tendencies and interests to weaken and overcome those political, social, and economic structures of traditional Mount Lebanon that had become obsolete and dysfunctional.

WHAT WERE the new phenomena revealed by the movements? For the first time in Mount Lebanon's history, members of low social status started to influence the political order by calling into question certain of its basic patterns and by challenging its representatives. The efforts of the common people directed at gaining their own say in political affairs were most evident in the creation of a new form of organization expressed through new terminology and in the adaptation of already existing terms and institutions to their own needs.

The new form of organization was the 'ammiyya, a term that refers both to the movements and to their supporters and is mentioned mostly in the context of the events of 1821, much less in relation to those in 1840, and not at all with regard to those in 1858–61. 'Ammiyya derives from 'amma (common people) and 'amm (general, public). The term suggests the social origin and position of the movements' majority. At the same time, it embodies the political claim to represent the general public and the commitment to its welfare.[38]

It is important to keep in mind that the 'ammiyyas were popular movements directed against the political elite, providing a new source of legitimacy that declared obsolete the old relationship between master and subject (landlord and peasant). Although the 'ammiyya documents familiar to me put forth no clearly formulated program, they contain some rudimentary signs reflected in a specific terminology of a supraconfessional consciousness in the minds of commoners: a completely new phenomenon.[39]

Sources dealing with the events of 1821 and 1840 do use the word *jumhur* in close connection with the word 'ammiyya, perhaps even as a synonym. Jumhur, a word of classical Arabic, means majority (of the people). During the movement of 1858–61, peasants claimed to function "by virtue of the authority of the people's majority" (*bi-quwat al-jumhur*) and "by virtue of the power of the popular government" (*bi-quwat al-hukuma al-jumhuriyya*).[40] It is likely that the term *jumhur* was used by the peasants in its old meaning of "the people's majority" to underline the popular and common character of their movement, irrespective of foreign political influences and ideologies penetrating the country at this time.

The repeated emphasis reported in the sources on acting for the sake of the general interest, common benefit, and public welfare (*al-salih al-'umumi, al-maslaha*)[41] is another hint at the formation of such a political consciousness. The idea of maslaha as a concept of public interest had a long tradition in Islamic law and theology.[42] By the time rural protest was starting, the term *maslaha* was borrowed from Islamic thinking by Lebanese groups, mostly Christians, for their own purposes. Supposedly this was a result of the clergy's influence on the common people.[43] Thinking in terms of public interest indicates an awareness in which the traditional concept of ruler and ruled was no longer acceptable.

There are good reasons to suggest that the ideas behind the terms *'ammiyya, jumhur, maslaha,* and *al-salih al-'umumi* melted into one another, and that with time these terms were interpreted and used in a synonymous or supplementary way. Though this suggestion can hardly be proved, it seems clear that all the terms reflected the social and political background of the rural movements.

'Ammiyya was a new term to signify a new phenomenon; maslaha and jumhur were old words equipped with a new meaning. The same was true of the word *wakil,* that means representative, deputy, or delegate. Like maslaha, the term was borrowed from Islamic law, where the system of representation (*wakala*) was a classical principle. After insertion into the final code of Maronite law around the middle of the eighteenth century, this system of wakil was used by Mount Lebanon's ruling elite.[44] By taking it over from the elite the peasants adopted an instrument for expressing their claim to be represented by their own delegates. This claim embodied a refusal to be "protected" any longer by persons outside their own milieu. The issue reached its climax when peasants of Kisrawan elected Tanyus Shahin as their representative and general commander (wakil 'amm).

A parallel development applies to the word *ma'mur.* Normally referring to a commissioner of the (Ottoman) government, in Kisrawan the term signified muqata'ajis from the Khazin family who were destined to administer the region on behalf of the government. After radical peasants had demanded a ma'mur from among their own ranks, their leader, Tanyus Shahin, had himself appointed ma'mur of Kisrawan.[45] In other words, the representative of the peasants claimed for himself the title and the functions of an official agent.

Finally, the examination of the movements' terminology leads to the question of whether patriotic or even national aspirations were implied. To a certain extent, patriotism underlay the insurrection of 1840. Documents from the period in fact stress the insurgents' resoluteness to regain freedom and independence from foreign Egyptian rule by fighting Egypt's occupation forces "until the end."[46] This aim was the crucial precondition for meeting the insurgents' demands.

However, to attribute to the insurgents nationalism in a civic sense is not at all defensible. What can be recognized from studying the movements is that the idea of "nation on a confessional basis" evolved within the Maronite community, at least in the thoughts of its upper clergy. This concept became clear in 1840 when the Maronite patriarch appealed to his community's feeling of identity. Though he claimed, for tactical reasons, to represent the whole people, including Mount Lebanon's non-Christians, his real intent was the strengthening and superiority of the Maronite church.[47] Thus, what in 1821 had been the first signs of a supraconfessional or nonconfessional concept based on a common benefit was reduced to considerations of political opportunity and advantage. Finally, the movement of 1858–61 in Kisrawan was characterized by confessional (Maronite) uniformity, suggesting even more strongly that efforts to create a common nonconfessional cooperation had disappeared.

FINALLY, let us consider the movements' successes and failures with respect to the conditions of the peasants and of society. With reference to the peasants' demands, no positive results were achieved in 1821. As for society in general, the ʿammiyyas initiated a new and momentous development. For the first time, peasants and low clergy provoked the traditional powers by demanding a system based on public welfare. The first signs of a new, partly supraconfessional awareness became visible.

As there was, apparently, little or no receptivity of these ideas on the part of non-Maronite groups, the efforts at cooperation among commoners from different religious communities failed. Above all from the 1840s, the inclination to think and act along confessional lines was promoted among Lebanon's religious sects, particularly among the Maronites and the Druze—first, by the leaders of the Maronite clergy who aimed at strengthening the Maronite church and weakening the (mainly Druze) muqataʿajis; second, by the European powers who strove for political and economic penetration of the country. To that extent, the insurgence of 1840 initiated long-range effects detrimental to Mount Lebanon's internal balance. In addition, having restored their sovereignty over the area, the Ottomans exacerbated the situation by applying a policy of divide and rule.[48] As in 1821 the movement failed to achieve better conditions for the peasants involved.

Only the Kisrawan revolt succeeded in winning sensible improvements for the peasants concerned, and even these lasted for only a short time in a very limited area of Mount Lebanon. They were not accepted by the other groups of society, or even by all peasants in Kisrawan. It was a de facto, not a de jure, victory. As for the long-range evolution, what general improvements for peasants materialized at all mainly resulted from other factors, namely the developments that had occurred after 1861 when Mount Lebanon started a new phase in its history, the *Mutasarrifiyya*-period. Yet one may argue that the revolt of Kisrawan did share in these new developments by promoting momentous changes on the general level of society and achieving at least some progress for the peasantry.

In the final analysis, the movements' results were ambiguous and double-edged. By exerting a considerable impact on future political and social developments, the rural movements also contributed to the establishment of confessionalism. As genuine social movements, sparked by collective consciousness and concern for public welfare, they failed to bring about the changes intended by the peasants. Their specific interests and aims were deflected into or superseded by confessional rivalry and hostility. Confessionalism today continues to impede Lebanon's national identity and unity on the basis of secular and civic principles.

According to Lebanese historian Kamal Salibi, the fragility of Lebanon's society and the political instability of the country can be overcome only with the creation of a national history based on serious arguments and research and accepted by all groups: "For any people to develop and maintain a sense of political community, it is necessary that they share a common vision of their past."[49] Salibi continues: "History is not merely a search for knowledge. It is also a search for understanding; and the house of understanding has many mansions."[50] Although one can only agree with this position, in view of the continuity and increasing persistence of Lebanon's primordial, communal, and sectarian ties, the application of Salibi's theories in that country seems very remote.

Notes

1. For further details see Samir Khalaf, *Lebanon's Predicament* (New York: Columbia University Press, 1987), esp. chaps. 2, 3, 5.

2. Axel Havemann, *Rurale Bewegungen im Libanongebirge des 19. Jahrhunderts. Ein Beitrag zur Problematik sozialer Veränderungen* (Berlin: Klaus Schwarz Verlag, 1983), esp. 95–103, 124–50, 189–217.

3. See, for example, Iliya F. Harik, *Politics and Change in a Traditional Society: Lebanon, 1711–1845* (Princeton, N.J.: Princeton University Press, 1968), 37–73; Dominique Chevallier, *La société du Mont Liban à l'époque de la révolution industrielle en Europe* (Paris: Paul Geuthner, 1971), 80–89; Toufic Touma, *Paysans et institutions féodales chez les druses et les maronites du Liban du XVIIᵉ siècle à 1914*, 2 vols. (Beirut: Imprimerie Catholique, 1971–72), 2:417–32.

4. Based on Harik, *Politics and Change*, 37–73; Chevallier, *La société*, 80–89, 131–49, and "Les cadres sociaux de l'économie agraire dans le Proche-Orient au début du XIXᵉ siècle. Le cas du Mont Liban," in *Studies in the Economic History of the Middle East: From the Rise of Islam to the Present Day*, ed. Michael A. Cook (London: Oxford University Press, 1970), 333–45; Touma, *Paysans* 2:433–52.

5. Axel Havemann, "Die Entwicklung regionaler Handelszentren und die Entstehung eines Händlertums im Libanongebirge des 19. Jahrhunderts," *Die Welt des Islams* n.s. 22 (1982, publ. 1984): 51–60; Chevallier, *La société*, 131–49.

6. Alexander Schölch, "Was There a Feudal System in Ottoman Lebanon and Palestine?" in *Palestine in the Late Ottoman Period*, ed. David Kushner (Jerusalem: Yad Izhak Ben-Zvi Press; Leiden: E. J. Brill, 1986), 130–45.

7. Ibid., 139; for the whole context see the discussion in Havemann, *Rurale Bewegungen*, 48–65.

8. For Bashir's policy versus the nobility (in particular the Druze families) and his (changing) relations to the Maronite church, see, among others, Harik, *Politics and Change*, 204–7, 222–27, 229–38; also Havemann, *Rurale Bewegungen*, 6–10.

9. Caesar E. Farah, "The Quadruple Alliance and Proposed Ottoman Reforms in Syria, 1839–1841," *International Journal of Turkish Studies* 2 (1981): 101–30; Alfred Schlicht, "The Rôle of Foreign Powers in the History of Lebanon and Syria from 1799 to 1861," *Journal of Asian History* 14 (1980): 97–126.

10. I. M. Smilianskaya, "The Disintegration of Feudal Relations in Syria and Lebanon in the Middle of the Nineteenth Century," in *The Economic History of the Middle East*, ed. Charles Issawi (Chicago: University of Chicago Press, 1966; reprint 1975), 227–47; for the general context see Roger Owen, *The Middle East in the World Economy, 1800–1914* (London: Methuen, 1981), chaps. 1, 2 (76–82).

11. Smilianskaya, "Feudal Relations," 229; Touma, *Paysans* 1: 368; Dominique Chevallier, "Aux origines des troubles agraires libanais en 1858," *Annales E.S.C.* 14 (1959): 35–64, esp. p. 42.

12. Chevallier, *La société*, 184–202, and "Western Development and Eastern Crisis in the Mid-Nineteenth Century: Syria Confronted with the European Economy," in *Beginnings of Modernization in the Middle East. The Nineteenth Century*, ed. William R. Polk and Richard L. Chambers (Chicago: University of Chicago Press, 1968), 205–22; Leila Tarazi Fawaz, *Merchants and Migrants in Nineteenth-Century Beirut* (Cambridge, Mass.: Harvard University Press, 1983).

13. Linda Schatkowski Schilcher, "Ein Modellfall indirekter wirtschaftlicher Durchdringung. Das Beispiel Syrien," in *Geschichte und Gesellschaft* 1/4: *Imperialismus im Nahen und Mittleren Osten*, ed. Wolfgang J. Mommsen (Göttingen: Vandenhoeck & Ruprecht, 1975), 482–505.

14. Chevallier, *La société*, 210–42.

15. Ibid., 44–46.

16. The main Arabic sources are Tannus ash-Shidyaq, *Kitab akhbar al-aʿyan fi Jabal Lubnan*, ed. Fuʾad A. al-Bustani, 2 vols. (Beirut, 1970), 2:400–413; Haidar Ahmad ash-Shihabi, *Lubnan fi ʿahd al-umaraʾ ash-shihabiyyin*, ed. Asad Rustum and Fuʾad A. al-Bustani, 3 vols., 2d ed. (Beirut, 1969), 3:655–94; for the evaluation of these and other reports see Havemann, *Rurale Bewegungen*, 95–103. The Arabic terms for the taxes concerned differ from one source to the other. For the changing meaning of the terms see Chevallier, *La société*, 111–12.

17. Ash-Shidyaq, *Akhbar al-aʿyan*, 2:457–59; Havemann, *Rurale Bewegungen*, 135–40; Caesar E. Farah, "The Lebanese Insurgence of 1840 and the Powers," *Journal of Asian History* 1 (1967): 105–32.

18. Yehoshua Porath, "The Peasant Revolt of 1858–61 in Kisrawan," *Asian and African Studies* 2 (1966): 77–157; Havemann, *Rurale Bewegungen*, pt. B, (esp. 189–

217); and Marwan Buheiry, "The Peasant Revolt of 1858 in Mount Lebanon: Rising Expectations, Economic Malaise and the Incentive to Arm," in *Land Tenure and Social Transformation in the Middle East,* ed. Tarif Khalidi (Beirut: American University of Beirut Press, 1984), 291–301.

19. Antun Dahir al-ʿAqiqi, *Thaura wa-fitna fi Lubnan. Safha majhula min tarikh al-Jabal min 1841 ila 1873,* ed. Yusuf Ibrahim Yazbak (Beirut-Damascus, 1938), 77–78; Malcolm H. Kerr, trans., *Lebanon in the Last Years of Feudalism 1840–1868: A Contemporary Account by Antun Dahir al-ʿAqiqi and Other Documents* (Beirut: Catholic Press, 1959); Mansur Tannus al-Hattuni, *Nubdha tarikhiyya fiʾl-muqataʿa al-kisrawaniyya,* ed. Yusuf Ibrahim Yazbak, 2d ed. (Beirut, 1956), 268–70.

20. Havemann, *Rurale Bewegungen,* 218–21 (see references quoted there).

21. Ibid., 113–16.

22. Ibid., 160–71.

23. Ibid., 223–32 (for Tanyus Shahin see esp. 226–29, 259–61); see also Porath, "The Peasant Revolt," 113–14.

24. Havemann, *Rurale Bewegungen,* 232–43.

25. Ibid., 120–21, 171–74; for the rôle of the Maronite church, see Harik, *Politics and Change,* 74–126, 152–66.

26. Here, the relation of the Kisrawan revolt to the civil war of 1860 has to be considered. However, the question of the extent to which both events interacted needs further research before final conclusions can be drawn.

27. Ash-Shidyaq, *Akhbar al-aʿyan* 2: 401, 408; ash-Shihabi, *Lubnan* 3: 659, 685.

28. Ash-Shidyaq, *Akhbar al-aʿyan* 2: 459; for other references see Havemann, *Rurale Bewegungen,* 347 (n. 167).

29. There are two lists of demands that are more or less identical, except for the question of the *maʾmur:* al-ʿAqiqi, *Thaura,* 161–63 (doc. 3), 178 (doc. 16); another version of the demands is quoted by Touma, *Paysans* 1:269–71.

30. There remains the question of why this assertion of the "common man" did not happen outside of Mount Lebanon. One scholar who has tried to find an answer to this phenomenon stresses that "such a unique revolt could occur only in a country whose social features differed from those of all other areas in the Middle East: an agrarian system with feudal features and private property of land; a relatively high level of education and standard of living of the peasants; and a régime of political autonomy." See Gabriel Baer, "Fellah Rebellion in Egypt and the Fertile Crescent," in *Fellah and Townsman in the Middle East. Studies in Social History* (London and Totowa, N.J.: Frank Cass, 1982), 312. All this is debatable and subject to further research. As long as no new evidence is available, the final answer to this "uniqueness" of the Kisrawan revolt has to be postponed. A critique of Baer's view is offered in Edmund Burke III, "Rural Collective Action and the Emergence of Modern Lebanon. A Comparative Historical Perspective," in *Lebanon: A History of Conflict and Consensus,* ed. Nadim Shehadi and Dana Haffar Mills (London: Centre for Lebanese Studies and I. B. Tauris & Co., 1988), 14–30 (esp. n. 5).

31. The institution of representation exerted by deputies is discussed in Havemann, *Rurale Bewegungen,* 245–47 (see also index, s.v. *wakala, wakil*).

32. Ibid., 137–39, 157, 168–69.

33. Al-ʿAqiqi, *Thaura,* 163–64 (doc. 4), 216–17 (doc. 47); Porath, "The Peasant Revolt," 112.

34. Buheiry, "The Peasant Revolt"; al-'Aqiqi, *Thaura*, 82–83, 184 (doc. 22).

35. Havemann, *Rurale Bewegungen*, 198, 251–52.

36. I dealt with this issue at the 1984 MESA Annual Meeting (San Francisco) in "The Peasant Movement of 1858–61 in Kisrawan (Mount Lebanon): Revolt or Revolution?" forthcoming in a book on nineteenth-century Lebanon edited by Leila S. al-Imad.

37. *Sozialrebellen. Archaische Sozialbewegungen im 19. und 20. Jahrhundert* (German trans., Giessen: Focus, 1979). See also n. 30.

38. Sometimes we find in the sources *'ammiyya* (with a short a-vowel), which is derived from *'amm* (paternal uncle). It seems very likely that the nexus of the conjuration of a relationship, even a fictitious one, and the claim to realize the public interest, which is primarily understood as the interest of the common man, is the reason for the alternate writing of *'ammiyya* and *'āmmiyya*. References for the different writings and implications are in Havemann, *Rurale Bewegungen*, 112–13, 333 (n. 80). This hypothesis is corroborated by a nineteenth-century Palestinian document in which a similar case can be found. Fritz Steppat, "Ein 'Contrat social' in einer palästinischen Stadt 1854," *Die Welt des Islams* n.s. 15 (1974): 233–46.

39. *Lebanese National Archives* (Beirut), doc. no. 5474, reproduced in *Rurale Bewegungen*, 396, 397 (translated and analyzed, 106–8, 110); *al-usul al-tarikhiyya*, ed. Bulus Mas'ad and Nasib W. al-Khazin, 3 vols. ('Ashqut, Lebanon, 1956–58) 1: 145, reproduced in *Rurale Bewegungen*, 400, 401 (translated and analyzed, pp. 153–57).

40. Al-'Aqiqi, *Thaura*, 87; see my discussion of these phrases and what they could have meant in *Rurale Bewegungen*, 247–49.

41. Ibid., index, s.v. *salih*.

42. Rudi Paret, "Istihsan and Istislah," *The Encyclopaedia of Islam*, new ed. (Leiden: E. J. Brill, 1960 ff.) 4: 255–59.

43. One problem is that we do not know much about the authors of peasant tracts; as far as they are reported, they belonged to the Maronite clergy. See Havemann, *Rurale Bewegungen*, 96, 105, 114, 115, 154. No evidence is provided for the hypothesis that members from the notables or merchants might have composed the peasant tracts (as has been recently found for Egypt in Nathan Brown, "Peasants against the State: The Political Activity of the Egyptian Peasantry, 1882–1952" (Ph.D. diss., Princeton University, 1987).

44. 'Abdallah Qar'ali, *Kitab mukhtasar ash-shari'a au al-majalla al-qada'iyya wa-qanun al-ahwal ash-shakhsiyya li'l-masihiyyin fi Lubnan 'ala 'ahd ash-shihabiyyin*, ed. Bulus Mas'ad (Beirut: al-matba'a al-kathulikiyya, 1959), 61–63.

45. Al-'Aqiqi, *Thaura*, 181–82 (doc. 19), 185–86 (doc. 23, 24), 193 (doc. 30).

46. *Majmu'at al-muharrarat al-siyasiyya wa'l-mufawadat al-duwaliyya 'an Suriya wa-Lubnan min sanat 1840 ila sanat 1910*, ed. Filib and Farid al-Khazin, 3 vols. (Juniyah, 1910–11) 1: 3–5 (doc. 3); *Recueil des traités de la porte ottomane avec les puissances étrangères*, ed. Le Baron I. de Testa, 11 vols. (Paris: Amyot, 1864–1911) 3:74–76.

47. *al-mahfuzat al-malakiyya al-misriyya: bayan bi-watha'iq ash-Sham*, ed. Asad Rustum, 4 vols. (Beirut: American Press, 1940–43), 4: 416–17 (doc. 6390); see also Harik, *Politics and Change*, 246–47, 254 ff.

48. On Ottoman reform policy (*Tanzimat*) and its effects on Lebanon after 1840

see, for example, Harik, *Politics and Change*, 266–72; Havemann, *Rurale Bewegungen*, 178–80.

49. Kamal Salibi, *A House of Many Mansions: The History of Lebanon Reconsidered* (London: I. B. Tauris & Co., 1988), 216.

50. Ibid., 234.

6

Peasant Uprisings in Twentieth-Century Iran, Iraq, and Turkey

FARHAD KAZEMI

Three rural uprisings took place in the early twentieth century in certain parts of the Middle East: the Jangali movement in Iran's Gilan province (1915–21), the 1920 Iraqi revolt mainly in the Middle Euphrates area, and the 1925 Shaikh Said rebellion in Turkey's eastern provinces.[1] In this study I analyze factors and conditions responsible for these rural uprisings in the broader context of the countrysides', and particularly peasants', relationship with political authority and the state.

The three uprisings were significant rural revolts with potential impact beyond their immediate localities and as prototype nationalistic movements that combined national sentiments with Islamic religious fervor. They are also important because rural dwellers and, more specifically, peasants have to contend with several major potential deterrents to their radicalism. Eric Wolf (1969) and James Scott (1976), among others, have outlined some of the more general factors that prevent peasant radicalism in most, if not all, rural communities. Economic factors, annual routines, and the peasants' need to devote considerable time to cultivation and harvesting so they cannot leave the land for any length of time serve as important deterrents to revolts. The potential benefits must appear great enough and the chances of success must be reasonably assured before peasants engage in revolts and uprisings. Peasants, like others, are aware of the high cost of violence, whether directed against local landlords or the state. To partake in collective violence is ultimately a choice that peasants make based on some rational calculation of costs and rewards.

Harsh economic conditions in the countryside do not necessarily result in revolts. Peasants frequently find ways to absorb economic hardship, or even a sudden economic crisis, by depending on, to use Scott's words, "an entire range of networks and institutions outside the immediate family" (1976:27). These include generating self-help (in the form of seasonal cityward migration or occasional wage labor), invoking reciprocity among friends, using patron-client ties to secure needed resources, or even depending on various forms of relief that the state (or the landlord) provides (Scott, 1976:26–28). These activities expand the peasants' economic base even though they do not remove the peasants from the inherent limitations of restrictive subsistence economy or economic and social dependency on the landlord or the state. They do, however, give the peasants additional pause before they undertake a decision to revolt. Peasants may decide not to revolt, but they will continue with other forms of resistance when they perceive injustice from those in positions of authority. These struggles, as Scott indicates, are the "ordinary weapons of relatively powerless groups: foot dragging, dissimulation, desertion, false compliance, pilfering, feigned ignorance, slander, arson, sabotage, and so on" (1985:xvi).

In addition to these general deterrents to revolts, several other factors more specifically apply to the Middle Eastern context. Although the inherent relevance and applicability of these factors are somewhat limited, a brief review of their central theses, as possible explanations of deterrents to peasant revolts in the Middle East, is in order.

The first factor concerns the negative impact of the religion of Islam on peasant radicalism. The argument holds that Islam gave the peasants "false consciousness" by channeling their social discontent away from political radicalism and instead inculcated in them a sense of religious subservience to established authority. This explanation ignores the activist and radical dimension of Islam. Although at times Islam has preached passive obedience to authority, at many other occasions it has exhorted active resistance to perceived injustice and economic exploitation. The radical theme in Islam has inspired demonstrations, riots, and rebellions in the cities. There is no reason to expect that the radical dimension would result in submissiveness in the countryside.

The second factor emphasizes the coercive and superior power of the indigenous or colonial state, especially military terror, as a key deterrent to peasant political activity. This is only a partial explanation that becomes relevant mostly after other conditions for peasant radicalism are present. It has more to do with the success and spread of peasant uprisings than with its initiation. Similar to the argument about the coercive capacity of the indigenous state, the colonial power thesis presents only a partial picture. It is correct to maintain that colonial, or dominant external, power used its resources to keep areas vital to its interests from eruption. The colonial state was clearly a mitigating force to any potential unrest that was viewed to be inimical to its economic interests. By the same token, however, many provinces and areas where the colonial state was present became major sources and catalysts for peasant discontent and, in some cases, collective action.

The third factor stresses the negative impact of primordial sentiments and intercommunal cleavages on peasant radicalism. It argues that social fragmentation, tribal lineages, linguistic differences, sectarian ties, and regional sentiments reinforced vertical communal bonds and prevented the development of horizontal cross-regional class consciousness among the peasants. These cleavages have posed major problems for the Middle East, given the diversity of its population and its varied social mosaic. Ethnic diversity and other forms of communal differentiation, however, have not prevented cooperative ventures in urban areas and even occasionally in the countryside. There are many examples of common efforts and joint activities, inspired by major national or regional events in the Middle East, that have transcended communal differences. The relevant concern is to uncover the reasons for greater and more forceful persistence of ethnic sentiments in the countryside among peasants and rural inhabitants.

The fourth factor argues that lack of education and the prevalence of illiteracy in the Middle Eastern countryside created socially unaware and politically passive peasants. This argument can be applied to many different groups in many different situations. Its relevance is limited by the fact that illiteracy, ignorance, and lack of education, even if present, are not insurmountable barriers to collective action. Peasants, like other human beings, are rational actors who are able to calculate costs and benefits. As their behavior in other parts of the world has demonstrated, peasants act when it is in their perceived interest and when potential rewards far outweigh inherent risks of participation in collective violence.

The final factor emphasizes the failure of the urban leftist forces to reach out and help the countryside and peasants organize against the oppressive landlords or the state. It argues that organizations, parties, and groups of the left overlooked the need to mobilize the peasants and ignored the countryside. This explanation is usually advanced for the more recent periods. Its basic thrust, however, is not entirely accurate. Both the "old" and the "new" left in the Middle East have devoted a fair amount of attention to the peasantry and land question. This attention has been expressed both in theoretical discourse and in actual, though sporadic, attempts to organize the peasants in the countryside. The problem has been more the lack of response by peasants than the absence of efforts by the left.

Both the general deterrents to rural uprisings, and what can be called additional deterrents for the Middle East, point to one basic conclusion: rural revolts are not everyday affairs. They take place in the Middle East, as in other parts of the world, when certain factors and conditions are present. I argue that a critical precondition for rural uprisings is significant change in the rural economy—new conditions that emerge from changes in landholding patterns, expansion of the market economy, or increasing commercialization of agriculture. I further argue that peasant collective violence and participation in uprisings and rebellions come about when three other contributing factors are also present: (1) external economic crises that further threaten the newly developed peasant life and its market relations; (2) peasant stratification and the leadership role that is frequently, but not always, assumed by the middle peasantry—defined as independent small landholders who cultivate their land primarily with family labor; (3) weakening of the repressive capacity of the state and its ability and willingness to crush peasant uprisings before they become widespread.

The link between larger economic crisis and specific local conditions that affect cultivation and marketing of produce is a critical factor. There are many intermediaries, in the form of institutions and individuals, that the peasant sees in this relationship. The intermediaries' actions and roles have a lot to do with the way the peasant perceives the impact of macroeconomic crisis. The village social structure and its social organization directly influence collective action by the peasants. The role that the middle peasantry play as articulators of peasant grievance, and as organizers and potential leaders of peasant collective action, is often instrumental in the final decision to revolt. This important role, however, is not necessarily confined to the middle peasants. Other groups, from both inside and outside the countryside, can fill this critical position. Peasants have goals, but these goals have to be articulated and agreed upon before peasants decide to act. They have to be goals that transcend ethnicity and local factionalisms and allow for common action.

The three rural uprisings in the Middle East approximate in varying degrees some of the economic, political, and social preconditions necessary for revolts. They also bring their own particular circumstances to bear on the matter. Their differences and similarities help elucidate some of the problems inherent in applying a common framework to rural uprisings, even to areas that share common cultures and have similar economic conditions.

The Jangali Movement in Iran

The Jangali movement began in the early years of World War I as Russian and British troops occupied the main cities of Iran.[2] The movement was started by a dynamic preacher from Rasht named Mirza Kuchik Khan (see Fakhra'i 1972). An armed volunteer in the constitutional revolution, Mirza Kuchik Khan had joined the proclerical Moderate party in 1909 in opposition to the secular Democratic party. At the outbreak of the war, he established contacts with officials of the Ottoman Empire, formed a Committee of Islamic Unity, and, with weapons obtained from German and Turkish agents, led an armed band into the forests of Gilan to wage guerrilla war against the Russians. He was soon joined by two other bands. The first, headed by a minor Kurdish chief named Khalu Qorban, consisted of Kurds who had been forced out of Kermanshah after an unsuccessful military campaign against the British. The second, formed of Democrats from Tehran, was led by Ehsanollah Khan, a young intellectual who had been influenced by revolutionary political thought, especially anarchism, while studying law in Paris.

These three groups, despite their differences, managed to work together against the occupying armies. They harassed the Russian and British troops, published in Rasht a clandestine paper called *Jangal,* and arrested government officials suspected of collaborating with the foreigners. Moreover, they con-

Mirza Kuchik Khan Jangali, leader of the Jangali Rebellion in Iran. From Ibrahim Fakhra'i, *Sardar-e Jangal: Mirza Kuchik Khan* (Terhan, 1972).

sciously tried to build a popular base among the rural population. They increased the sharecroppers' portion of the harvest, lightened labor services, abolished dues in kind, investigated complaints against landowners, recruited peasants into their bands, paid for the food they obtained in the villages, and even forced wealthy collaborators to distribute some of their estates among the peasantry. They confiscated property of some large landowners, distributed it among peasants in the neighboring area, and levied taxes on landowners' produce (FO 248/1168, 1917). A member of the British expeditionary army sent to northern Iran described Kuchik Khan as the "Robin Hood of the Caspian marshes" who "robbed the rich to feed the poor" (Donohoe 1919:127).

The Jangalis were strengthened further by the collapse of the tsarist regime. As the Russian armies disintegrated, the rebels assumed control over much of Gilan, including Rasht and Enzeli, obtained additional weapons, and recruited more local volunteers. Moreover, as the Red army chased the remnants of the White armies into the Caspian provinces, the rebels found new allies in the recently formed Communist party of Iran. Transferring its headquarters from Baku to Gilan, the Communist party reinforced the Jangalis with its own armed volunteers, most of whom were Azeri-speaking Iranians, intellectuals and oil workers residing in the Caucasus. The party was headed by Haydar Khan Amu Ughlu, a Tiflis-educated electrical engineer who had joined the Russian Social Democratic party, fought in the constitutional revolution in Iran, and helped organize the Democrat party in Tehran. Allying with the Communists, the Jangalis declared the formation of the Soviet Socialist Republic of Gilan in June 1920 (see Yaqikian 1984). The new republic was headed by a coalition cabinet of Democrats, Communists, and local Muslim leaders. Meanwhile, its expanding army of some 1,500 guerrillas was commanded by Mirza Kuchik Khan, Ehsanollah Khan, Khalu Qorban, and Communist representatives.

Internal contradictions soon broke apart the united front. While the Communists called for the immediate distribution of land among the peasantry, Kuchik Khan and his religious supporters talked of the Islamic sanctity of private property. While the Communists initiated an anticlerical campaign and championed the rights of women, Kuchik Khan declared: "Principles, not weapons generate political movements. In the past, the principles that have generated the most meaningful political movements in Iran have been those of Sacred Islam" (Tudeh Party 1969:23).

These differences came to a head after February 1921, when Col. Reza Khan of the Cossack Brigade, the future Reza Shah of Iran, overthrew the government in Tehran, denounced former agreements with Britain, signed a pact with the Russian Bolsheviks, negotiated the evacuation of the Red army, and extended the hand of friendship to all patriotic and progressive groups in Iran. The Communists and many of the Democrats, convinced by the Soviet-Iranian treaty, were willing to accept this hand of friendship. But Kuchik Khan, distrustful of the Cossack officers, foreign intentions, and Tehran politicians, refused to negotiate with the new government. Suspecting double-dealing, he murdered Haydar Khan, tried to murder Khalu Qorban, and forced Ehsanollah Khan to evacuate with the Red army (see Ra'in 1973; FO 371/6406, 1921). Left without allies and confronted with an expeditionary force from Tehran, Kuchik Khan retreated to the snow-covered mountains of Gilan where he froze to death during the bitter winter of 1921. By December 1921, his head was on public display in Rasht to prove to all that the Jangali movement had ended and to preempt future rebels from taking on the dead hero's cause.

Inspired by Kuchik Khan's memory, the Jangali movement revived briefly during World War II. With the weakening of the central government, survivors from the earlier movement regrouped under the name of the Jangali party. They demanded the convening of provincial assemblies, elimination of court influence in politics, and distribution of crown and state lands among the peasantry (*Donya*, January 7, 14, 31, 1945; *Gileh Mard*, May 10, 1946). Moreover, they formed a Farmer's Association and allied with the Tudeh party and its Peasant Union.

By 1945 the local branch of the Tudeh, together with the Jangali party, controlled much of Gilan and the adjacent districts of Mazandaran. While their trade unions dominated the towns, their peasant organizations and armed militias controlled the countryside, setting up roadblocks, imposing fines on landlords, and successfully encouraging sharecroppers not to give up any share of the harvest (*Dad*, December 29, 1946, January 15, 1947). The British ambassador wrote in alarm that the control of affairs in Gilan was rapidly passing out of the hands of the central government into that of local committees, and Soviets dominated the Tudeh party (FO 371/45452-31, 1945). This situation continued until after the end of World War II, when the Soviet troops evacuated the region, allowing the Iranian army to reassert central authority. A foreign visitor to Gilan in 1947 reported that although "few now dared to even whisper the name of the Tudeh party," many peasants were deeply influenced by the demands of the party, especially the demands to increase the sharecropper's portion, open village clinics and schools, and eliminate the "hated" gendarmerie (Hindus 1949:68–69). One peasant implied to a visitor that the local landowner, "who was celebrated as one of the most benevolent in the province," kept a car and frequently repaired the road to his village so that he could make a quick getaway in the event of a new uprising (ibid. 61).

After the victory of the Islamic revolution in Iran in 1979, the Jangalis were once again rehabilitated. The government praised their Islamic orientation and their fight against the oppressors. It republished their newspaper *Jangal,* issued a commemorative stamp honoring Kuchik Khan, and held a memorial marking the sixty-ninth year of his "martyrdom." The minister of culture and Islamic guidance, a cleric, praised Mirza Kuchik Khan for his "Islamic nationalist" uprising and for his attempt to "rescue the people under the shadow of Islam and under the protection of religion" (*Kayhan Havai,* December 6, 1989). A ten-part serial on Iranian television featuring Kuchik Khan's "struggles with Tsarist Cossacks and Victorian lackeys" was also widely shown (*Kayhan Havai,* May 10, 1989). Practically all of these accounts conveniently left out the Jangalis' involvement with the Communists, both domestic and foreign.

The Shaikh Said Rebellion in Turkey

The Shaikh Said rebellion is the largest and one of the most important uprisings that engulfed eastern Anatolia in the twenty years between 1920 and 1940. The rebellion by the Kurdish inhabitants of Turkey was directed against the authorities of the Turkish republic (see Cemal 1955). It affected almost the

Shaikh Said of Piran, leader of the Shaikh Said Rebellion in Turkey. From Great Britain, Public Record Office FO 371/13827.

whole region and included most of the major tribes in the area. There were, however, many who chose to ally themselves with the Turkish republic. For example, the non-Sunni Alevis either remained neutral or actively assisted the government forces. The Alevi nonsupport meant that the Shaikh Said rebellion remained "a Sunni-led rebellion against a Sunni state" (Olson 1989:98). Moreover, some Sunni tribes, such as Reman, Penchinaran, and Reshkotan, that had promised to join the rebellion "remained aloof, gave only token support, or joined the Turks" when the uprising began (Olson 1989:96).

Although the actual uprising lasted only from February to mid-May 1925, its effects were widespread and it was suppressed only by a major government effort. Thereafter, the rebellions that occurred were of relatively limited scope in terms both of their geographic base and their organizational structure. This holds true even for Agre and Dersim rebellions. The forceful government actions during the Shaikh Said rebellion and the ensuing watchful control over local leaders effectively prevented the emergence of any leader aspiring to regional influence.

The rebellion's leadership group was composed of traditional tribal leaders, such as Shaikh Said, and former officers of both Ottoman and republican armies who had defected to the rebels' side. The rank and file of the rebels were composed primarily of peasants and seminomadic rural inhabitants. Most of the rural participants were landless peasants who worked through various arrangements on land owned by local chiefs. The rebellion also attracted certain segments of the urban population of the area who responded to the cry of *jihad* against the Ankara government. At the rebellion's height, the rebels mustered around 20,000 armed men. Some reports claim a larger number of participants, arguing that those villagers who took part in limited operations should also be counted. One Kurdish account put the total number of Kurdish forces at 24,500, divided into units of varying sizes and assigned to nine separate operational districts (FO 371/13827, 1929).

Shaikh Said was a religious, tribal, and Kurdish national leader. He headed the Naqshbandi religious order in the area and founded several religious schools in towns such as Palu and Hinis. He headed four *asirets* (tribes) and had close ties to many of the other clans in the region. He was also viewed by many, including some Turks and Circassians, as a key spokesman for the whole region. Views about his Kurdish nationalist leanings conflict. The Kurds have extolled him as a notable and brave Kurdish nationalist. The Turkish government, and at times others, have maintained that the emphasis on Kurdish nationalist themes is suspect in the absence of convincing evidence and Shaikh Said's support by non-Kurds.

The spark that set off the rebellion was the government request that Shaikh Said turn himself in to the authorities for questioning about his dealings with a band of former Ottoman officers charged with desertion and alleged involvement with a Kurdish nationalist group. Shaikh Said was also suspected of ties with the royalists in Istanbul and of agitation against the government's secularization efforts. When the gendarmes arrived in Piran, a town north of Diarbekir, in search of Shaikh Said and others in his entourage, they were promptly fired upon. The combat soon spread to other areas, where fronts were rapidly organized by the rebels. In the first two weeks of the rebellion, the insurgents captured the towns of Lice, Hinis, Piran, Sivan, Genc, and Harput. Soon the city of Elazig was also taken, and the spread of the rebellion to other areas appeared imminent.

Meanwhile, in Ankara, the government of Fethi Okyar was replaced by that of Ismet Inonu, who became prime minister in early March 1925. Inonu promulgated a new law that gave his government extraordinary powers. The Law for the Maintenance of Order called for establishment of "independence tribunals" composed of government appointees. These tribunals were meant to try those charged with sedition and to reestablish order throughout the country. Soon after, partial mobilization was declared and the government forces moved rapidly to the eastern provinces to quell the rebellion. It is estimated that more than 50,000 troops took part in operations against the rebels (see Olson 1989:103–4). Turkish casualties, in one account, are estimated at 50,000, with the whole operation costing over 60 million Turkish pounds (FO 371/13827, 1929).

According to most accounts, by the end of March 1925 the back of the rebellion was broken. Serious fighting, however, continued for almost another month. Other sporadic uprisings with links to Shaikh Said were reported to have occurred until the late 1920s. Shaikh Said, along with several of his followers, was captured on April 15 in the region of Carpuk spring, north of Varto. He was brought for trial to the hastily convened "independence tribunal" in Diarbekir. Shaikh Said and forty-six of his followers were sentenced to death. The sentence, by hanging, was carried out on June 29, 1925. Shaikh Said's purported last words were, "He who dies for country, lives through eternity" (FO 371/13827, 1929).

In his speech to the Grand National Assembly in November 1925, Ataturk characterized the doomed rebellion as "reactionary propaganda carefully organized" (FO 371/10863, 1925). Similar sentiments were expressed by Ismet Inonu and other Turkish leaders, all stressing their belief in the rebellion's "reactionary" focus and the threat that it posed to the state and its republican form of government. As the British reports from the scene indicate, "The

Turkish Government was at pains during the rest of the year to explain that religious reaction, and not nationalism, has been at the base of the insurrection" (FO 371/11556, 1925). It is clear, as Olson points out, that "the suppression of the Shaikh Said rebellion contributed to the consolidation of the new Turkish republic, the evolution and domination of the Republican People's Party . . . and the one-party state it represented up to 1950, and the greater articulation of the Turkish nationalism on which the party and the state were based" (1989:160).

The Kurdish nationalists and other followers of Shaikh Said, however, did not completely capitulate to the Turkish state. Shaikh Said's son, Ali Reza, visited British officials in October 1925 and informed them that the "Kurds intended to continue the fight for their national independence, led by their sheikhs, and by his family and himself" (FO 371/11556, 1925). He blamed their losses on "lack of ammunition, not of money, of which they then had plenty" (ibid.). Open or clandestine Kurdish struggles against the Turkish state continued in the post-Said era. Many of these battles were fought during Ataturk's reign, but they also extend to the most recent period. Shaikh Said's rebellion, as the most significant Kurdish uprising against the Turks, occupies an exalted position in Kurdish national consciousness and is considered to be "one of the great episodes of Kurdish history" (van Bruinessen 1978:354; see also Mazhar-Ahmad 1983).

The 1920 Revolt in Iraq

The 1920 revolt was the culmination of a general unrest that had engulfed Iraq after World War I. It began in late June 1920 among the tribes of the middle and lower Euphrates against the British presence in the area. It soon spread to other parts of the country including the northern sectors. With important support coming from Shi'i and Sunni religious leaders in urban centers, rural tribal and peasant inhabitants sustained a fierce revolt for about five months. The British mobilized much of their area force of 133,000 troops and even had to call for additional reinforcements to quell the uprising. The revolt was finally crushed by the end of November 1920 but at a heavy cost of lives and great expenditure of funds. British casualties numbered over 2,000, including an estimated 426 who died in combat. It also cost the British treasury about £40 million, twice the amount set aside for the annual budget of Iraq. Iraqi casualties were approximately 8,450. It was a costly insurrection for both sides.

The revolt began on June 30, 1920, in Rumaytha on the lower Euphrates with the Zawalim tribesmen's attack on a government building where their shaikh was detained by the British over disputes on certain agricultural loans and tax payments. The shaikh was set free by his men but the unease did not subside. Within a short time the uprising spread to other areas and gained the support of other tribes. British inability to contain the revolt and relieve Rumaytha encouraged the tribes in their resistance. In Muntafiq, as in many other tribal areas, "men of avowed pro-British sentiments had been openly insulted in the streets; a few had already fled" (FO 371/5230, 1920). A petition drafted by several tribal leaders and presented to the British included a call for the independence of Iraq. As the revolt continued, tenant farmers also became involved and declared their "rebellion against the absentee landlords" (Rassam 1972:137).

A key feature of the revolt was the active participation of Shi'i religious leaders from Najaf, Karbala, and Kazimayn. These Shi'i towns were major centers of agitation before the start of the uprising. Karbala, in particular, had developed a strong climate of hostile anti-British propaganda. When the revolt began, Karbala's "inhabitants expelled British officials and the town became a centre for the distribution of arms and the dissemination of propaganda among the tribes" (FO 371/5069, 1920). The Shi'i leaders issued *fatwas* declaring jihad against the British and were instrumental in getting the Shi'i tribes to participate actively in the organized anti-British insurrection. In one instance a fatwa by Karbala's chief mujtahid declaring that "service under British Administration was unlawful" resulted in many resignations of Muslim employees of the British (FO 371/5071, 1920). British consular accounts often give vivid descriptions of local unrest as Shi'i emissaries, or their forceful messages, reached the faithful. One report concerns the activities of the influential son of a former chief mujtahid, Mirza Muhammad Hasan, as he moved from town to town exhorting the Muslims to rise in a holy war against the infidels. The report notes that when the cleric's son reached Shatrah, where the officer was stationed, "the whole town rose to greet him and a big demonstration with banners took place. . . . Rifle firing from roofs now took place in the daytime" (FO 371/5231, 1920).

The Shi'i leaders' involvement in the revolt was supported to a large extent by Sunni ulema who, setting aside their communal differences with the Shi'is, agreed on a common course of cooperation. At its height, the revolt engulfed much of Iraq including Kirkuk and areas north of Baghdad. The city of Baghdad remained relatively quiet as the British forces were able to establish a reasonable modicum of order.

The revolt was finally brought to an end in late November. Troop reinforcements, heavy expenditures of funds, and the appointment of Sir Percy Cox as the high commissioner in Iraq all played important roles in the revolt's eventual defeat. Cox attempted to reach accommodation with key tribal leaders and responded positively to what he considered to be legitimate concerns about the style and content of British governance. The revolt also paved the way for the establishment of a monarchy in Iraq with Faisal, the son of Sherif Husayn of Mecca, as the ruler.

Several different interpretations of the causes and precipitants of this revolt have been documented in writings of Rassam [Vinogradov], Marr, Wilson, Holt, Ireland, Kedourie, and local sources in Iraq. The most noted of these interpretations propose the following set of explanations. (1) The revolt was another tribal insurrection that "stood in a long line of tribal revolts against government authority" but differed from previous efforts in scale and the presence of religious and nationalistic sentiments (Holt 1960). (2) The tribes rose to protest the twin "evils" of foreign rule and heavy taxation imposed by the British (al-Fir'aun 1952). (3) It was a tribal insurrection fueled and financed by Hashimite agents and agitators from the outside, particularly Syria (Wilson 1931). (4) The revolt can be best characterized as a Shi'i-inspired insurrection against the power and authority of the politically dominant Sunnis (Kedourie 1959). (5) The revolt was the first "primitive, but genuine, national response to fundamental dislocations in the political and socio-economic adaptation of the tribally organized rural Iraqis. These dislocations were brought about through the direct and indirect encroachment of the West" (Rassam 1972; also, with some modifications, the view of Ireland 1937 and Marr 1985).

The interpretation that appears most valid on the basis of the available evidence is that the revolt was a response to major socioeconomic dislocations in the countryside caused by important transformations in the organization of rural economy and the land tenure system. The roots of this development can be traced to changes initiated by the Ottoman ruler Midhat Pasha as far back as the late 1860s and early 1870s. (These developments, along with similar transformations that contributed to the uprisings in Iran and Turkey, will be discussed later.) As far as Iraq is concerned, it is critical to underline the significance of the 1920 revolt as a case of incipient Iraqi national consciousness that combined religious and anticolonial sentiments. The revolt also allowed for cooperation among diverse elements of the population— Shi'is and Sunni, tribes and peasants, townspeople and rural dwellers. For at least a short period, it brought forth the possibility of united action for a common goal.

Observations and Conclusions

The three uprisings present points of comparison and contrast in the context of this study's major thesis. It appears that transformation of land and agricultural holdings and the development of market economy, even though partial, had important effects on the villages' economic and social life. These changes resulted in basic dislocations of the village economy and reoriented the villagers to the world outside. The Ottoman Land Law of 1858 played a significant role in transforming patterns of landholding in many parts of the empire. The law had, of course, no relevance to the Iranian case. However, landholding patterns, village and peasant stratification, and peasant-landlord relationships were also responsible for developments in Gilan.

The Ottoman Land Law of 1858 was enacted as one of the principal laws of the Tanzimat reform. It divided land into five distinct legal categories specifying ownership and use rights. Its first two chief categories made distinctions between *mulk* land (freehold ownership) and *miri* land (state ownership held on lease). The law attempted to regulate and systematize landownership and provided mechanisms for registering titles and deeds that granted legal rights by the state to the owners. It also allowed the state to tax land and increase its revenues. Although there are some disagreements about the exact purpose behind this land law, all observers agree that the law had an important but varying impact on land and taxation in different parts of the Ottoman empire (see Warriner 1966; Baer 1966; Gerber 1987). As Gerber states, the law enabled "for the first time . . . the creation of truly vast estates in the Middle East" through "registration of land formerly held by the accepted legal methods" or "registration of newly acquired land that was formerly unclaimed" (1987:72). Legal right to freehold ownership, now enforceable by the state, allowed for systematic land accumulation and hence, in due time, the creation of large estates in some parts of the empire.

The extent and degree of land accumulation, however, varied from one area of the Ottoman empire to another. A combination of local conditions, practices, and prevailing economic and political factors resulted in different land size developments in Ottoman provinces. In much of Anatolia, for example, many small peasants acquired titles to land. As Issawi points out, "In 1863 small ownership was predominant in the area of the Republic, large ownership being widespread in Macedonia, Kurdistan, and some of the Arab provinces" (1980:202). In Kurdish regions where the Shaikh Said rebellion took place, many local shaikhs became major landowners in the wake of the 1858 land code. The shaikhs were already on their way to political and economic prominence by the slow but systematic destruction of the semi-independent emirates that had taken place in their areas in the previous decades. The departure of the emirates prompted the shaikhs to assume roles beyond their traditional religious and mystical activities. Many of these holy men became significant political and economic figures who also gave vent to incipient Kurdish nationalist sentiments. The shaikhs' hold on their flocks began to assume a multidimensional role that secured and cemented their authority over rural inhabitants.

As van Bruinessen (1978:232) has summarized, the effect of the land code in the Kurdish regions was a reduction in tribal communal economy, an increase in economic stratification within tribes, loss of many cultivators' traditional rights, and emergence of urban-based absentee landlords with their own particular rural patronage network. Rather than becoming the owners of lands that they had traditionally cultivated (as the 1858 land code had intended), many Kurdish peasants became sharecroppers or hired laborers on land owned by others. The local shaikhs were among those who reaped the benefits from these changes. They increased their individual landownership "from gifts, sale or usurpation" (van Bruinessen 1978:318). Many augmented their large tracts of land by treating *waqf* lands "as their own properties" (Olson 1989:4). Rural life in the Kurdish areas was also affected by the decline of nomadic animal husbandry, which contributed to pressures on land settlement and resulted in "a marked deterioration of the living conditions of the common tribesmen" (Lazarev 1980:67). In short, the Ottoman Land Law of 1858 disrupted and dislocated the Kurdish rural economy and helped to usher in a new system of village stratification where effective economic power was wielded by either powerful local shaikhs or by urban-based absentee landlords.

The land law was applied to Iraq somewhat later. It was implemented by the Ottoman governor, Midhat Pasha, whose short reign in Iraq (1868–71) had a profound impact on many areas of Iraqi life, particularly the system of land tenure. He introduced a new land tenure arrangement that differed dramatically from the existing and long-practiced tribal dira system. The traditional dira system allowed the tribes control over an area where they exercised "rights of ownership" that in turn permitted individual tribesmen usufruct rights to a portion of land that was "owned collectively" (Rassam 1972:128).

The new system introduced the concept of miri land, which implied that the land belonged to the state and allowed the state to assign it to others on the basis of freehold rights through title deeds (*tapu sanad*) for cultivation. The buying and selling of title deeds adversely affected tribal practices and in due time resulted in the introduction of "large-scale private property into areas where land was traditionally owned collectively by the whole group. This change set the stage for the emergence of a class of proto-feudal landlords and reduced the free tribesmen to quasi-serfs" (Rassam 1972:128). Expressions of discontent by tribesmen over their newfound lot were common and particularly forceful in the Muntafiq tribal region, a major locus of the 1920 revolt. As Farouk-Sluglett and Sluglett point out, "The Muntafiq tribes were in a state of almost constant rebellion against their nominal overlords, the Sa'dun family, who had obtained tapu sanads in the 1870s, since the Sa'duns lost their authority and cohesion as war leaders in the course of their change of status from warrior-protectors to landowners" (Farouk-Sluglett and Sluglett 1983:495; see also Jwaideh 1984).

In addition to the introduction of this new form of private property, the agricultural areas were also affected by cash crop development and a general improvement in the country's infrastructure and communication system. In short, landownership, forms and patterns of cultivation, and the relationship between landowners and agricultural workers (whether tribal or not) were all seriously affected. The British arrival and their enforcement of a rigid taxation code and revenue collection exacerbated the existing problems. As Ireland points out, the agricultural taxation system "tended to press most heavily on the agricultural worker to whom the burden was eventually passed under the prevailing land tenure" (1937:145). In British eyes, as their reports indicate, taxation was "the root cause" of the unrest (FO 371/5230, 1920).

In Iraq, then, the Ottoman Land Law had a profound impact. It dislocated tribal and nontribal landowning patterns and created a new system of village stratification. The end result was a dramatic increase in large landownership and, at the same time, an important decline in the position of the individual cultivator (see Haider 1966). Conditions were further aggravated by the imposition of a rigid taxation system enforced by an alien power. The final revolt gave focus and direction to the many problems and issues that had been developing for some time.

Landownership and cultivation rights in Iran took a different path during the period under discussion. No land law remotely similar to the Ottoman code was introduced. The Iranian agrarian structure generally operated on the basis of five distinct classes composed of absentee landlords (which included state, waqf, and large and small landowners), rich peasants, middle peasants, sharecroppers with cultivation rights, and poor peasants who neither owned land nor enjoyed rights of cultivation. Although the exact size of these different groups cannot be determined, the general evidence points to development of larger estates in nineteenth-century Iran. The holdings of the peasant cultivators were, as a rule, quite small (Lambton 1969; Keddie 1972). The large estates were owned either by the state and the crown or by religious foundations, court officials, provincial magnates, tribal chiefs, and other notables. Many owned several whole villages and surrounding farmlands or portions of different villages. The tendency was to increase the amount of individual land owned since it was perceived to be the chief source of economic security.

The ever-increasing number of poor peasants carried the major burden of land accumulation by absentee landlords. They became progressively dependent on the absentee landlords for survival. Since for a variety of reasons, as explained by Kazemi and Abrahamian (1978), middle peasantry did not develop fully in most parts of Iran, village stratification tended to contrast the gap between the rich peasants with ties to absentee landlords and the masses of poor peasants. The powerful absentee landlord transcended this division and, in various ways, promoted its perpetuation.

Although this was generally the situation in Iran as a whole, the Caspian littoral province of Gilan—owing to geographic, climatic, and other factors—enjoyed a somewhat different stratification system (Kazemi and Abrahamian 1978). While large landlords existed, their numbers and degree of control over the countryside were considerably less than in other parts of Iran. With abundant rainfall and fairly easy access to foreign ports and markets through the Caspian Sea, peasants with smaller tracts of land had a reasonable chance of survival. Furthermore, the homogeneity of the population coupled with the absence of settled tribes in the villages promoted cooperation and mutual assistance. As a result, middle peasantry developed in Gilan in proportions unlike much of Iran. Even those peasants who worked on the absentee landlords' property were more prone to land leasing with fixed rents than to sharecropping arrangements.

The agrarian situation in Gilan in the nineteenth and early twentieth centuries points to a pattern of development somewhat different from the rest of the country. The strong tendency toward the creation of large estates typical of other parts of Iran was conditioned in Gilan by several important local factors that also allowed for the presence and survival of small holdings and the development (rather than diminution) of middle peasantry. Consequently a modified stratification pattern that permitted some degree of peasant tactical freedom from the landlord began to emerge. It was this tactical freedom and this group of peasants that provided the backbone of Kuchik Khan's Jangali movement.

For the most part, the leadership networks in the Iraqi and Turkish cases were not groups that can be identified readily as middle peasants. In the Iraqi case, the predominant element came from the tribal and religious leaders and tenant farmers. Although some of them qualify as middle peasants, most do not. In the Turkish case, traditional tribal and religious leaders and former officers of the Ottoman and Republican armies led the rebellion. Not many of them qualify as middle peasants. The rank-and-file support for Shaikh Said was provided primarily by poor peasants. It is clear, then, that with the exception of Jangalis, middle peasantry's strong leadership role was not a necessary condition for these rural uprisings.

In the three areas of Iran, Iraq, and Turkey where rural uprisings took place, some common and divergent patterns seem to have occurred. In Iraq and Turkey, the development of large estates was accompanied by important dislocations in the countryside and a significant transformation of traditional land tenure rights. In Turkey the burdens of the new system were borne by poor Kurdish peasants who found themselves increasingly under the control of their shaikhs or absentee landlords. In Iraq, peasants and common tribesmen found themselves squeezed, on one hand by their chiefs who also were becoming major landowners, on the other by the weight of heavy and rigid British taxation. In both Iraqi and Turkish cases, village stratification and communal relationships were seriously affected by these developments. The Iranian case in Gilan, however, presents a different picture. Although large landholding continued to flourish throughout the country, Gilan also witnessed the development of middle peasantry in a way that contrasts with much of the rest of Iran. At least portions of the Gilan peasantry maintained their relative autonomy from the landlords and other powerful claimants. It would be inaccurate, therefore, to attribute whatever dislocation that may have occurred in Gilan to the influence of large estate development.

The more proper answer to Gilan's case may be found in the impact of its developing market economy and agricultural commercialization. An important argument can be made that in the Iranian northern provinces, and particularly in Gilan, commercialization of agriculture had made significant headway. Gilan's market economy had been strongly influenced by raw silk production for some time. Although actual production of silk declined after the silkworm disease of the mid-1860s, "merchant capital, mainly foreign, began to play an important role in the production as well as in the export of silk in the period following the late 1860s" (Seyf 1983:54). Gilan's involvement with market economy, both foreign and domestic, was further extended with the growth of cash crops such as tea and rice and the exploitation of northern forests and Caspian Sea fisheries (Issawi 1971; Nowshirvani 1981; Pakdaman 1983; Rabino 1979). Gilan farmers and peasants had an important relationship with markets and were affected by developments and fluctuations of outside market economies. They were considerably more outward-looking than rural inhabitants in other parts of Iran.

Market economy had also some role to play in the areas of Iraq affected by the 1920 revolt. Although agricultural productivity had not necessarily increased in the 1900s, improvements in Iraq's international trade and transport facilities were readily noticeable. As Issawi indicates, "Steam navigation on the Tigris . . . had made it possible greatly to increase the quantity of the country's exports and imports and to reduce freight rates. The volume of foreign shipping calling at Basra had risen several-fold, in spite of the almost complete lack of facilities in the port" (1966:179). Crops (dates, wheat, barley) and animal husbandry products (hides, wool, skins) accounted for much of the rise in exports. Moreover, introduction of irrigation pumps in the second decade of the century allowed better control over land and eventual increase in agricultural productivity (Farouk-Sluglett and Sluglett 1983:497). Market economy and agricultural commercialization in the areas of Iraq affected by the revolt also influenced rural conditions and had some impact on the rural dislocation process.

In Turkey's eastern provinces market economy and commercialization played much less of a role than in the rest of the country. In addition to wheat and other basic crops, commercially important crops such as tobacco, raisins, and cotton were also raised but on a smaller scale (Shorter 1985:426; Issawi 1980). It would be difficult to argue, however, for significant commercialization of agriculture in the eastern provinces during this period. The effect of market economy, therefore, was far less significant in the rural uprising in eastern Turkey.

It is also important to emphasize that these uprisings took place in areas where the impact of World War I was strongly felt. The economic, social, and political dislocations caused by the war may have been felt most strongly in the Iranian and Iraqi cases, but the Turkish eastern provinces were also affected. All three countries were undergoing important political transformations. In Iraq a new political arrangement was being formulated, in Turkey the republican regime was attempting to consolidate its power throughout the countryside, and in Iran the tired Qajar dynasty was rapidly dying. The weakness of the states, therefore, contributed to rural problems and extended the uprisings beyond their initial confines.

These uprisings also point to several other significant political factors.[3] All three exhibited important nationalistic sentiments. The 1920 revolt was the first coherent expression of a "national" sentiment in Iraq that seemed to transcend ethnic and religious divisions. The cooperation of the Shi'is and Sunnis and the tribes' collective statements for an "independent" Iraq were significant expressions of support for such sentiments. Some of these nationalistic views were nurtured through Iraqi contacts with leaders of Arab nationalist movements. In the Shaikh Said rebellion, the Kurdish factor was an important feature even though support for the rebellion also came from non-Kurdish elements. It is also possible to view the forceful and committed actions of republican Turkey as an attempt to solidify the sense of a national entity within the designated post–World War I boundaries. The Jangali movement in Iran had a clear nationalistic theme, articulated by Kuchik Khan at critical junctures during his rebellion. This theme sometimes took the form of turning against close allies when they were suspected of goals other than an independent national Iran.

Two of the three rebellions had to contend very closely with external major powers. The Jangalis had to confront both the British and the Russian entrenched positions. Depending on the circumstances, they sometimes cooperated and sometimes fought the two major powers. The Iraqi revolt had a clear anti-British orientation. The British were the country's rulers and the focus of much of the rural inhabitants' discontent. In the Turkish case, the role of major foreign powers was, for the most part, inconsequential. The British were not eager to respond to the overtures of Shaikh Said's followers.

Isolating a political nationalist dimension in these three rebellions has certain inherent dangers. Although nationalist strands were present in all three, and at least two of the uprisings had a clear antiforeign focus, these movements cannot be readily identified as secular political nationalisms as we understand them today. It is apparent that these nationalist sentiments were strongly influenced by an overarching religious perspective. For many of the participants, Islam played an important role in defining the problem and giving it a concrete and understandable ideology.

All three rebellions, then, had significant religious dimensions. The Shi'i ulema and tribes were the key players in the Iraqi revolt. Religious passions and symbols were readily exploited throughout the five-month period of combat. As a religious leader, Kuchik Khan also appealed to Islamic sentiments and regularly preached Islamic solutions. Shaikh Said was an important religious leader and expressed dismay with the republican regime's secularization efforts. In all three rebellions the leaders used religion to mobilize followers' support.

All three rebellions had unusual alliances and strange political bedfellows.

Kuchik Khan cooperated closely with Communists, leftists, and groups outside Gilan; Shaikh Said had Kurds and Turks supporting his cause; and the Iraqis managed to get Shi'is and Sunnis (and even some Kurdish elements) to cooperate with them. Furthermore, all three rebellions had some ties, in varying degrees (Shaikh Said's being the least), with the urban centers adjacent to the areas where the uprisings were taking place.

In the rebellions in Iraq and Turkey, the rural participants were primarily tribal or settled peasants with strong tribal ties. The tribes were not an important force in the Iranian case even though some individuals with tribals links supported Kuchik Khan. Tribal affiliation had been eroding for some time in the Gilan province and was not, in contrast to other parts of the country, a significant force of identity for the local inhabitants.

In sum, having studied peasants and politics in their larger economic and social context and having looked at peasant collective action in the Middle East in light of major economic transformations in land and agriculture, I have concluded that these transformations do not by themselves result in peasant uprisings. Major social factors and political events, both domestic and international, play critical roles in peasants' decisions to rebel. Peasants rebel when their expectation of gain outweighs their fear of loss.

Notes

1. I would like to thank Omar Karasapan for his assistance on the Shaikh Said rebellion and Ouafae BenHallam for her assistance on the 1920 Iraqi revolt. I am also grateful to the Social Science Research Council for a grant that helped make research for this project possible.

2. For the section on the historical overview of the Jangali movement and general comments on peasants, I have freely borrowed from Farhad Kazemi and Ervand Abrahamian, "The Nonrevolutionary Peasantry of Modern Iran," *Iranian Studies* 11 (1978):262–63, 285–87.

3. The following comparative points were raised initially in my paper "Commercialization of Agriculture and Peasant Uprisings in Iran, Iraq, and Turkey" presented at the twentieth Annual Meeting of the Middle East Studies Association, Boston, November 1986. Olson (1989) raises some of the same points in his concluding chapter.

References

Agah. 1982. *Majmu'eh-ye Ketab-e Agah: Masa'el-e Arzi va Dehqani.* Tehran: Entesharat-e Agah.

Alavi, Hamza. 1965. "Peasants and Revolution." In *The Socialist Register,* ed. Ralph Miliband and John Saville. New York: Monthly Review Press.

Antoun, Richard, and Iliya Harik, eds. 1972. *Rural Politics and Social Change in the Middle East*. Bloomington: Indiana University Press.

Baer, Gabriel. 1966. "The Evolution of Private Landownership in Egypt and the Fertile Crescent." In *Economic History of the Middle East: 1800–1914*, ed. Charles Issawi. Chicago: University of Chicago Press.

———. 1982. *Fellah and Townsmen in the Middle East: Studies in Social History*. Totowa, N.J.: Frank Cass.

Al-Basir, M. M. 1924. *Tarikh al-Qadiyah al-Arabiya*. Baghdad.

Batatu, Hanna. 1978. *The Old Social Classes and the Revolutionary Movements of Iraq*. Princeton, N.J.: Princeton University Press.

Besikci, Ismail. 1969. *Dogu Anadulu'num Duzeni*. Ankara: E. Ysayinlari.

Cemal, Behcet. 1955. *Seyh Sait Isyani*. Istanbul: Sel Yayinlari.

Chayanov, A. V. 1986. *A. V. Chayanov on the Theory of Peasant Economy*. Edited by Daniel Thorner, Basile Kerblay, and R. E. F. Smith. Madison: University of Wisconsin Press.

Dad. 1946 (December 29).

———. 1947 (January 15).

Donohoe, M. 1919. *With the Persian Expedition*. London.

Donya. 1945 (January 7, 14, 31).

Fakhra'i, Ibrahim. 1972. *Sardar-e Jangal: Mirza Kuchik Khan*. Tehran: Javidan.

———. 1979. *Gilan dar Jonbesh-e Mashrutiyat*. Tehran: Sepher.

Farouk-Sluglett, Marion, and Peter Sluglett. 1983. "The Transformation of Land Tenure and Rural Social Structure in Central and Southern Iraq, c. 1870–1958." *International Journal of Middle East Studies* 15:491–505.

al-Fir'aun, Fariq al-Mizhar. 1952. *al-Haqa'iq al-Nasi'a*. Baghdad.

FO. See Great Britain Public Record Office.

Fumani, Abdul-Fattah. 1974. *Tarikh-e Gilan*. Tehran: Foroughi.

Gerber, Haim. 1987. *Social Origins of the Modern Middle East*. Boulder, Colo.: Lynne Rienner.

Gileh Mard. 1946 (May 10).

Great Britain Public Record Office. FO 248/1168; FO 371/5069, 5071, 5230, 5231, 6406, 10863, 11556, 13827, 45452-31.

Haider, Saleh. 1966. "Land Problems of Iraq." In *Economic History of the Middle East: 1800–1914*, ed. Charles Issawi. Chicago: University of Chicago Press.

Haldane, A. L. 1922. *The Insurrection in Mesopotamia*. Edinburgh: Edinburgh University Press.

al-Hasani, Abdel Razzaq. 1952. *al-Thawrah al-Iraqiya al-Kubra*. Saidon: Matba'at al-Irfan.

Hindus, Maurice. 1949. *In Search of a Future: Persia, Egypt, Iraq, Palestine*. Garden City, N.Y.: Doubleday.

Holt, P. M. 1960. *Egypt and the Fertile Crescent, 1516–1922*. Ithaca, N.Y.: Cornell University Press.

Hooglund, Eric. 1982. *Land and Revolution in Iran, 1960–1980*. Austin: University of Texas Press.

Husrev, Ismail. 1934. *Turkiye Koy Iktisadi*. Ankara: Kadro Yayini.

Ireland, Philip. 1937. *Iraq: A Study in Political Development*. London: Jonathan Cape.

Issawi, Charles, ed. 1966. *Economic History of the Middle East, 1800–1914*. Chicago: University of Chicago Press.

———. 1971. *Economic History of Iran, 1800–1914*. Chicago: University of Chicago Press.

———. 1980. *Economic History of Turkey, 1800–1914*. Chicago: University of Chicago Press.

Jangal. 1916. Reprinted, Tehran: Entesharat-e Moula.

Jwaideh, Albertine. 1984. "Aspects of Land Tenure and Social Change in Lower Iraq during Late Ottoman Times." In *Land Tenure and Social Transformation in the Middle East*, ed. Tarif Khalidi. Beirut: American University of Beirut Press.

Kayhan Hava'i. 1989. (May 10, December 6).

Kazemi, Farhad, and Ervand Abrahamian. 1978. "The Nonrevolutionary Peasantry of Modern Iran." *Iranian Studies* 11:259–304.

Keddie, Nikki. 1968. "The Iranian Village before and after Land Reform." *Journal of Contemporary History* 3:69–91.

———. 1972. "Stratification, Social Control and Capitalism in Iranian Villages: Before and after Land Reform." In *Rural Problem and Social Change in the Middle East*, ed. Richard Antoun and Iliya Harik. Bloomington: Indiana University Press.

Kedourie, Elie. 1959. "Réflexions sur l'histoire du Royaume d'Irak (1921–1958)." *Orient* 3:55–79.

Lambton, Ann K. S. 1969. *Landlord and Peasant in Persia: A Study of Land Tenure and Land Revenue Administration*. London: Oxford University Press.

Lazarev, M. S. 1980. "Kurdistan i Kurdskaya Problema." In *Economic History of Turkey: 1800–1914*, ed. Charles Issawi. Chicago: University of Chicago Press.

Marr, Phebe. 1985. *The Modern History of Iraq*. Boulder, Colo: Westview Press.

Mazhar-Ahmad, Kamal. 1983. *"Mahiyyat-e Qiyam-e Sal-e 1925 Kurdistan-e Turkiye."* Translated by Abdullah Mardukh. *Alefba* 3:65–77.

Migdal, Joel. 1974. *Peasants, Politics, and Revolution*. Princeton, N.J.: Princeton University Press.

Moore, Barrington, Jr. 1967. *Social Origins of Dictatorship and Democracy: Lord and Peasant in the Making of the Modern World*. Boston: Beacon Press.

Nowshirvani, Vahid. 1981. "Aspects of the Commercialized Agriculture in Iran." In *The Islamic Middle East, 700–1900: Studies in Economic and Social History*, ed. A. L. Udovitch. Princeton, N.J.: Darwin Press.

Olson, Robert. 1989. *The Emergence of Kurdish Nationalism and the Sheikh Said Rebellion, 1880–1925*. Austin: University of Texas Press.

Paige, Jeffrey. 1975. *Agrarian Revolution: Social Movements and Export Agriculture in the Underdeveloped World*. New York: The Free Press.

Pakdaman, Nasser. 1983. "Preface. Studies on the Economic and Social History of Iran in the Nineteenth Century." *Iranian Studies* 16:125–35.

Popkin, Samuel. 1979. *The Rational Peasant: The Political Economy of Rural Society in Vietnam*. Berkeley: University of California Press.

Rabino, H. L. 1979. *Gilan: Valayat-e Dar al-Marz-e Iran*. Translated by Ja'far Khamamizadeh. Tehran: Ta'ati.

Ra'in, Ismail. 1973. *Haydar Khan Amu-Uqli*. Tehran: Entesharat-e Ra'in.

Rassam [Vinogradov], Amal. 1972. "The 1920 Revolt in Iraq Reconsidered: The Role of Tribes in National Politics." *International Journal of Middle East Studies* 3:123–39.

Scott, James. 1976. *The Moral Economy of the Peasant: Rebellion and Subsistence in Southeast Asia*. New Haven, Conn.: Yale University Press.

———. 1985. *Weapons of the Weak: Everyday Forms of Peasant Resistance*. New Haven, Conn.: Yale University Press.

Seyf, Ahmad. 1983. "Silk Production and Trade in Iran in the Nineteenth Century." *Iranian Studies* 16:51–71.

Shanin, Teodor, ed. 1971. *Peasants and Peasant Societies*. Harmondsworth: Penguin.

Shorter, Frederic. 1985. "The Population of Turkey after the War of Independence." *International Journal of Middle East Studies,* 17:417–41.

Toker, Metin. 1968. *Seyk Sait ve Isyani*. Ankara: Ruzgarli Matbaasi.

Tudeh Party. 1969. *Jonbesh-e Komonisti-ye Iran*.

van Bruinessen, M. M. 1978. *Agha, Shaikh, and State: On the Social and Political Organization of Kurdistan*. Published Ph.D. diss. Utrecht: Ryksuniversiteit.

Vedat, Sadillili. 1980. *Turkiye'de Kurtculuk Hareketleri ve Isyanlar*. Ankara: Kon Yayinlari.

Warriner, Doreen. 1966. "Land Tenure in the Fertile Crescent." In *Economic History of the Middle East,* ed. Charles Issawi. Chicago: University of Chicago Press.

Weller, Scott, and Scott Guggenheim, eds. 1982. *Power and Protest in the Countryside: Studies of Rural Unrest in Asia, Europe, and Latin America*. Durham, N.C.: Duke University Press.

Wilson, Arnold. 1931. *Mesopotamia, 1917–1920: A Clash of Loyalties*. Oxford: At the University Press.

Wolf, Eric. 1969. *Peasant Wars of the Twentieth Century*. New York: Harper and Row.

Yaqikian, Grigor. 1984. *Shoravi va Jonbesh-e Jangal: Yaddashtha-ye Yek Shahed-e ʿeini*. Tehran: Novin.

7

War, State Economic Policies, and Resistance by Agricultural Producers in Turkey, 1939–1945

ŞEVKET PAMUK

Agriculture has always been considered a sector of the economy with special importance and vulnerability during wartime. For a number of reasons, wartime conditions create special difficulties for agricultural production and more generally for the food supply. For one thing, during peacetime, most countries rely on imports for at least part of their food needs. The disruption of imports of both food and such agricultural needs as fertilizers and agricultural machinery is bound to affect production adversely. Also the wartime conscription of males and requisitioning of draft animals by the military often create difficulties. Even though women assume a greater agricultural burden, acreage under cultivation and levels of output often decline. At the same time demand for food may actually increase to feed a larger army (Milward 1977, chap. 8; Hardach 1987, chap. 5) Clearly, wartime conditions are likely to create imbalances between supply and demand that may lead to shortages and sharp increases in food prices.

In this respect, the wartime experiences of developed economies differs qualitatively from that of underdeveloped economies. Typically, developed economies show greater flexibility and greater ability to maintain levels of food production close to peacetime levels. Since their agriculture uses a variety of inputs, the reduction in the availability of one or more of them need not affect the levels of output severely. Other inputs can be substituted for the scarce input. For example, if labor becomes scarce, a developed economy substitutes machinery or fertilizers to maintain the earlier levels of production.

This flexibility is usually not available to less developed economies, whose structures of production are much more rigid. Where agricultural techniques of production are rather primitive, machinery can not be easily substituted for labor or draft animals.

Similarly, in developed economies, diet is often more diversified, allowing a greater degree of substitution in consumption, from luxuries to necessities. For example, rather than relying on meat and butter—both of which use more resources to provide a given level of nutrition—more cereals and milk can be used for human consumption. Again, the less diversified and simpler diets in underdeveloped countries do not allow for such substitutions. In addition, less developed economies are unlikely to have developed transportation networks that are so essential for linking the areas with food surpluses to the areas with food deficits during wartime. As a result, underdeveloped economies are less flexible and much more vulnerable to wartime disruptions (Antsiferov et al. 1930; Prest 1948; Lloyd 1956).

Shortages of food and hunger during wartime are not always the result of a decline in food availability, however. As Amartya Sen (1981) has argued, even though total availability of food may remain unchanged or decline only slightly, hunger and famine will result if some groups in society lose their ability to command food. For example, wartime conditions may drive food prices beyond the reach of the urban poor or landless agricultural workers. Food shortages and hunger depend, then, not only on total food availability but also on distribution of the food available.

In short, with or without a decline in total food availability, inequities may emerge in the distribution and consumption of food among different groups in society that would seriously affect the war effort. For this reason, securing the food supply of the urban population and the military and distributing the available food equitably are two of the most important problems facing governments during wartime.

Governments' wartime food supply policies often cover an area ranging from direct intervention in production to the transportation and distribution of food in urban areas to measures aimed at limiting demand and ensuring a more equitable pattern of consumption, such as rationing. In this paper I will focus on only one aspect of this broad picture: government measures to obtain cereals from rural producers, that is, procurement policies and their impact on agricultural producers during World War II. Although Turkey did not participate in that war, full mobilization was in effect there for the entire period. Securing the food supply of the urban areas remained an important and at times critical problem.

My theoretical interests are broader, however. The example of Turkey provides a good case study for looking at the interaction between the formulation and implementation of state economic policies and rural class structure. Equally importantly, it provides insights into the behavior of rural producers in response to market opportunities and economic demands by the state.

In the theoretical framework adopted here, peasant producers attempt to maximize their economic interests subject to social and economic constraints. Subject to these constraints, they attempt to take advantage of whatever market opportunities present themselves. I argue further that the interaction between state economic policies and rural producers can be best understood if the latter are treated not as a homogeneous mass but as differentiated producers who may have diverging interests and who may be affected differently by government policies and market opportunities.

On the basis of landownership, I distinguish three strata of rural producers—large landowners, middle peasants, and small peasants. Large landowners are those who own enough land to avoid direct labor. In Turkey during the period under study, few large-scale agricultural enterprises used year-round wage labor. Most large landowners rented their holdings to sharecropping tenants, although some fixed-rent tenancy was also observed. Middle peasants are owner-producers who, while relying primarily on family labor, cultivate enough land to produce a marketable surplus. I define small peasants as tenant farmers and owner-producers with smaller amounts of land. Wage-laborers constituted only a small fraction of the rural population in Turkey during the interwar period.

Agricultural Production during Wartime

Turkey's economy remained mostly agricultural during the 1930s despite the beginnings of state-led industrialization in response to the Great Depression. Agriculture accounted for 40 to 50 percent of the annual GNP and close to 90 percent of the country's exports. Approximately 80 percent of the country's population continued to live in rural areas as total population increased from 14 million to 17 million.[1]

During the early part of the 1930s, Anatolian agriculture was adversely affected by two developments.[2] Unfavorable weather conditions led to declines in output, particularly in cereals, which accounted for more than half of agricultural production. Equally important were the adverse movements in relative prices brought about by the Great Depression. The intersectoral terms of trade turned sharply against agricultural commodities. Not surprisingly under these circumstances, the impact of the depression was felt most severely by the market-oriented producers.

Recognizing the difficulties faced by cereals producers, the government initiated in 1932 a program of wheat purchases through the state-owned agricultural bank designed to support the price of that leading crop. In 1938, the program was taken over by an independent agency established for this purpose, Toprak Mahsulleri Ofisi (Ofis hereafter). Support purchases of wheat remained limited, however. Not only did the intersectoral terms of trade remain against agriculture, but within agriculture, cereal prices continued to fare more poorly than the prices of leading cash crops until the end of the decade.[3] By allowing the relative prices to penalize agriculture, the state helped create more favorable conditions for industrial accumulation in urban areas.

Despite the adverse price trends, however, the second half of the 1930s witnessed a strong expansion in the levels of agricultural production. According to official statistics, output of noncereal crops during 1937–39 was more than 50 percent higher than a decade earlier. Even more remarkable was the increase in the output of wheat and other cereals. According to official figures, cereal production during 1937–39 averaged 100 percent above 1927–29 levels.[4]

It is difficult to find a single explanation for these trends in production. The demographic recovery following a decade of war (1914–22), the steady expansion of acreage under cultivation, more favorable weather conditions, extension of the railroad network by the Republican regime into the central and eastern regions of the country, and the long-term effects on supply of the abolition of the much despised tithe in 1925 appear to have played their part (Shorter 1985). Whatever the explanation, one thing is clear: the increases in agricultural production were not a statistical artifact. On the eve of World War II, Turkey had become not only self-sufficient but a small net exporter in cereals. Exports of wheat averaged 70,000 tons or about 2 percent of total production during 1937–39.[5]

Although Turkey did not participate in World War II, a number of factors combined to bring about substantial decreases in the output of cereals and, apparently to a lesser extent, of other crops during this period. According to official statistics, the decline in the output of noncereal crops was limited. Even in the poorest harvest year of 1945, levels of noncereal output were only 15 percent below averages for 1937–39. On the other hand, official statistics indicate that a dramatic decline in cereals production occurred during the war years. Whether these figures provide a reliable picture regarding the timing and magnitude of the decline is not clear. Because official statistics are at variance with other, indirect evidence on cereals production levels for two of the war years, 1942 and 1945, they need to be used in conjunction with other evidence in assessing production trends in cereals. What follows is a preliminary discussion based on incomplete evidence.

As shown in table 7.1, the first drop in the levels of agricultural production came in 1941 when wheat and total cereals production fell approximately 15 percent below their 1937–39 levels. In official statistics, 1942 appears as a year of recovery when cereal and noncereal production exceeded prewar levels. However, the twelve months following the 1942 harvest turned out to be the most critical period of the war in Turkey as severe shortages of cereals developed in the urban areas. Press coverage in Turkey also indicates that the 1943 and 1944 cereal harvests were larger than that of 1942. In fact, the urban food supply situation considerably improved after the harvest of 1943. This evidence suggests that the official estimates for 1942 presented in table 7.1 need to be revised downward. It is also possible, however, that official estimates of cereals production in 1942 were not so much in error but that withholding by peasant producers (discussed below) was much larger during that year.[6]

According to the same official estimates, the wheat and overall cereal harvests for 1945 were disastrous. These estimates put the wheat crop at 46

Table 7.1.
Official Estimates of Wartime Cereals Production

Year	Wheat (mill. tons)	Wheat (1937–39 = 100)	Total cereals (1937–39 = 100)
1927–29 (avg.)	1.88	46	48
1937–39 (avg.)	4.06	100	100
1940	4.07	100	103
1941	3.48	86	85
1942	4.26	105	106
1943	3.51	86	88
1944	3.15	78	75
1945	2.19	54	50
1946–48 (avg.)	3.92	97	93

Source: Bulutay, Tezel, and Yıldırım, 1974.

Note: In their national income study, Bulutay et al. argue that the official figures overestimate the actual quantities. Consequently, they deflate the official wheat production figures given here by 10 percent. For the purposes of the present discussion, however, the key issue is not the absolute level of production, but the extent and timing of the year-to-year fluctuations during the war.

percent and the overall cereal production at 50 percent below their 1937–39 levels. Although the 1945 harvest was certainly a poor one, the food supply problems of that year were less severe than those of 1942 and early 1943, so it is not clear at this stage whether production levels in fact declined so dramatically in 1945.

The reasons behind the decline in cereal production are easy to identify. First, there was the shortage of labor in rural areas. Even during the interwar period, labor had been a scarce factor of production in agriculture. During the war years, the government maintained an army of more than one million out of a total population of around 18 million. Most of this burden fell on rural areas where close to 80 percent of the population lived. Many young peasant producers and potential producers ended up spending as many as four years in the military during this period.

Second, the availability of draft animals declined. According to official statistics, the number of oxen in the country declined by about 10 percent during the war.[7] If true, this decline reflects the difficulties associated with feeding livestock at a time of cereal shortages. In addition, according to another estimate, 20 percent of all draft oxen and 40 percent of draft horses were taken by the military during the war years (PRO, FO 371/33357; report cited in note 6). Decreases in the availability of other inputs such as fertilizers were not as critical since they were not an important part of Anatolian agriculture at the time.[8]

A third potential reason for the observed decline in cereal production was government policies. The government pursued policies of in-kind taxation and forced purchases from producers at below-market prices during the war years. Some producers who were in a position to produce cereals for the market may have responded by reducing their acreage or shifting to other crops.

It should be reiterated that the poor quality of the available estimates on cereals output present problems. In the absence of reliable production figures, it is difficult to assess the extent to which the urban cereal shortages of 1942–43 resulted from decreases in production or from hoarding by merchants and middlemen and withholding by peasant producers in response to government policies.

As Amartya Sen (1981) has suggested, however, outbreaks of famines are not necessarily related to decreases in the overall availability of food. Rather, starvation and famines occur when the available food is distributed unevenly and some social and economic groups cannot establish command over the available supply. Although the food supply problems experienced during World War II did not lead to famine levels in Turkey, this conceptual framework is still useful for analyzing where and why shortages occurred.

One important feature of rural Anatolia during this period was that the numbers of landless wage workers remained limited. An overwhelming majority of the rural population cultivated their own land or others' plots either as fixed-rent or more often as sharecropping tenants. Moreover, while the degree of specialization in noncereal cash crops such as tobacco, cotton, hazelnuts, opium, raisins, and figs varied from one region to another, virtually all rural areas in every region of the country were self-sufficient in foodstuffs. It is not surprising, therefore, that rural areas were affected much less than cities by the cereal shortage during the war.

Wartime cereal shortages were experienced most severely in the three largest urban centers, Istanbul, Ankara, and Izmir, and in the urban centers of the Black Sea coast such as Zonguldak and Trabzon, as that whole region was not self-sufficient in cereals. In these urban centers the government adopted rationing in the distribution of bread and flour and adjusted the daily allowances sharply downward as the available supply of cereals dwindled during 1942–43.

The emergence of cereal shortages inevitably led to dramatic increases in prices of foodstuffs, especially of cereals. Prices of cereals—wheat, barley, corn, and others—rose much faster than other agricultural and nonagricultural prices during the war years.[9] It did not mean, however, that all producers with a surplus of cereals benefited from wartime conditions. The distributional consequences of cereals shortages and high cereal prices on rural producers depended on the policies followed by the government in securing the food supply for urban areas. Since the government demanded deliveries of a large part of the cereal output at prices substantially below those prevailing in the open market, not all agricultural producers were in a position to take advantage of rising market prices. In other words, the unusually high market prices for cereals were relevant only to those agricultural producers who were allowed to keep part of their surplus or who could successfully evade government actions. To understand the nature of the urban shortages in cereals and the impact of wartime conditions on peasant producers of different strata, it will be necessary, therefore, to examine the procurement policies pursued by the government.

Government Procurement Policies, Their Differential Impact, and Resistance by Producers

Whether a country actively participates in a war or opts for armed neutrality under full-scale mobilization, two basic approaches to the food supply problem are available to the government. In one, the government relies on the market mechanism to secure the basic foodstuffs. By avoiding controls and other forms of intervention in the agricultural commodity markets, it hopes that producers are willing and able to increase production in response to price increases. In the other, the government intervenes actively in the commodity markets and attempts to control both the production and trade of cereals and other foodstuffs. It demands deliveries from the producers at below-market prices. As agricultural producers and merchants try to evade these measures, scarcities, black markets, and profiteering will spread.

In either case, the securing of foodstuffs from agricultural producers constitutes only one stage in dealing with the problem of food supply. The distribution of these commodities to the urban and possibly rural consumer presents the government with another set of policy alternatives ranging from no intervention in the market to price controls and, finally, rationing. (See, for example, Milward [1977, chap. 8]; this latter issue will not be directly examined here.)

As for the problem of securing foodstuffs from agricultural producers, governments in Turkey during World War II, as in most underdeveloped countries facing similar circumstances, adopted the second approach of forced purchases at below-market prices. While these policies remained in effect from 1941 until the end of the war, their specific forms changed depending on the severity of the food supply problems in the urban areas and the nature and extent of peasant resistance. For this reason, it will be useful to examine government policies, peasant response, and the actual outcomes in four distinct stages.

Stage 1 (September 1939–February 1941): Reliance on Existing Stocks

When war broke out state agencies and private merchants held considerable stocks in cereals. During the following year and a half, the government actively pursued interventionist policies in most nonagricultural markets, attempting to prevent price increases and relieve shortages by administrative fiat. In markets for cereals, however, the abundant harvests of 1939 and 1940 kept prices relatively low. Because of the optimism created by existing stocks and large harvests, producers were left free to sell their crops either to the state purchasing agency, Ofis, or to private merchants. Since Ofis offered prices higher than the prevailing market prices in most localities, however, it had no difficulty purchasing wheat during 1939 and most of 1940. These stocks together with cereals purchased by the merchants were then sold to bakeries in the urban areas. Exportation of modest amounts of wheat and other cereals continued during this early period. During 1940, for example, 60,000 tons of wheat or approximately 1.5 percent of the country's total output was exported to Greece, Belgium, and Germany.[10]

Stage 2 (February 1941–July 1942): Forced Purchases by the Government

By fall 1940, it became clear that cereal prices were edging upward as a result of hoarding by merchants and that at the prices it offered, the Ofis would not be able to purchase enough of the 1940 crop. In October the government issued a decree enabling it to purchase at its own prices all cereal stocks in the hands of merchants and middlemen. In February 1941, it initiated the policy of requiring all producers to sell their entire cereal crop, after allowances were made for household subsistence, seed, and animal feed, to the Ofis at pre-determined below-market prices.

The policy was first implemented in the seventeen leading cereal-producing provinces. By the spring of 1942 it was extended to all sixty-three provinces. In each village, every producer was asked to make a written declaration regarding his output of cereals. Allowances were then made for subsistence, seed, and animal feed, and the producer was expected to deliver the rest to the Ofis (*Resmi Gazete,* May 15, 1942).

In 1940, total purchases of wheat by the Ofis amounted to 157,000 tons or about 4 percent of estimated total production, with one-third of these purchases occurring after the October decree. During 1941, with official prices only slightly below market prices, the Ofis increased the volume of its purchases to 491,000 tons of wheat and 137,000 tons of barley, or 14 and 8 percent, respectively, of the total output of these two crops (Araz n.d.).

Just before the start of the harvest in May 1942, in anticipation of under-reporting by producers, the government dissolved the self-declaration system and instituted a new system of assessment. In every village, a committee of two, a government representative (*subaşı* or *kolcu*) and the headman (*muhtar*), supported by the gendarmes, was to inspect the crops of each producer before or during the harvest, determine the allowances for subsistence, seed, and animal feed, and either seize the rest or demand that the producer surrender the rest to the Ofis (*Resmi Gazete,* May 15, 1942).

However, as the difference between the market prices and the official prices paid by the Ofis began to widen during 1942, it became clear that this policy would face considerable resistance from all strata of peasantry. Peasants tried to surrender as little of their crop as possible. They attempted to smuggle the harvest from the field and hide it. They tried to bribe the local official to underestimate their obligations. They tried to deliver less than the assessed amount. They tried to deliver grains of lower quality.

How successful a peasant producer was in these attempts depended on the power balances between the village and the local government or the representative of the local government and on how the individual producer fit into village social and political structures. Powerful peasants, large landowners, and politically prominent members of the village such as the headman or local representatives of the Republican People's party, the single party in power, received preferential treatment. Obviously, if the government representative was hosted by a landlord or the headman during his stay in the village, he would be sensitive to their suggestions on how to assess their harvests and harvests of others.

As is the case with other more common forms of peasant resistance, little documentation about withholding by agricultural producers exists. Despite close wartime censorship, occasional references to hoarding by peasants appeared in the press.[11] By far the most important macrolevel evidence for the extent of peasant avoidance, however, was the volume of cereal purchases by the Ofis, which remained substantially below government targets. The official government target for purchases of wheat from the 1942 harvest was 800,000 tons, approximately 25 percent of the crop. Considering that 20 percent of the country's population lived in urban areas, such a volume of purchase would have been sufficient to meet urban and military demand. It appears that despite all efforts, government purchases of wheat in 1942 remained below 500,000 tons, less than 15 percent of the total production (Araz n.d.).

What is uncertain and may never be established is the extent to which crops that were not surrendered to the representatives of the government were sold to private merchants and found their way to the black market. Since official policy was to purchase the entire surplus, it was illegal for any amount of cereal to appear in the market-place outside government channels. There was, as a result, considerable risk and it may be that only landowners with large marketable surpluses were willing to sell their crops to private merchants. The rest of the crops not surrendered to the Ofis were probably consumed in the countryside after being bartered among the rural population.

Stage 3 (July 1942–June 1943): The 25 Percent Rule; Coercion of the Small and Market for the Large

As purchases by the Ofis remained substantially below target levels, the food supply situation in urban areas continued to deteriorate. In January 1942, bread rationing was initiated in the three largest urban centers, Istanbul, Ankara, Izmir, and in Zonguldak. When Prime Minister Refik Saydam died in the summer of 1942, there emerged a good opportunity to modify the procurement policy. The new government of Sukru Saracoglu announced that producers would be allowed to keep part of their harvest for sale to private merchants. The share of the cereal crop to be delivered to the government was defined as 25 percent for the first 50 tons, 35 percent for the next 50 tons, and 50 percent of the output above 100 tons (*Resmi Gazete,* August 1, 1942).

When first announced, the new policy was hailed in the press as a move toward the relaxation of government controls in cereal markets.[12] In retrospect, however, why this should be the case is not clear. For one thing, the government maintained a wide margin between the official purchase price and the market price. In 1942 the government paid 20 kuruş per kilo for the wheat it purchased while the market price approached 40 kuruş. The price differential increased considerably during the following year as the government insisted on the same price while inflation and, more importantly, cereal shortages had pushed the market price above 100 kuruş in April 1943. Purchases by the government had indeed become seizures. Clearly, the new policy provided little incentive to producers to surrender their crops to the state.

Second, while appearing to shift the burden toward large landowners, the new policy actually increased the burden of poor peasants. Although the earlier policy had provided allowances for subsistence, seed, and animal feed, the 25 percent rule did not include such a clause. As a result, peasant households that produced barely enough for their own needs were being asked to deliver a quarter of their gross output to the state. In fact, the following simple calculation reveals that 25 percent actually represented the entire marketable surplus and often more for the large majority of peasant producers.

(1) In the late 1930s and early 1940s, average wheat and barley yields in the country were around 0.8 tons per hectare. In other words, all producers who cultivated up to sixty hectares—which included more than 95 percent of all peasant households—were being asked to surrender 25 percent of their cereal output.

(2) In the dry-farming lands where most of the cereal production was undertaken, seed-yield ratios were about one to five. In other words, most peasant producers had to set aside 20 percent of their gross output for seed or a total of 45 percent for seed and the state share.

(3) An average peasant household of five or six consumed close to two tons of cereals a year. Assuming average yields in dry-farming areas, then, a peasant household that cultivated about five hectares of land and obtained an average of four tons of cereals would be left with barely enough cereals for

self-consumption after the state share and the seed was set aside. All tenant farmers and those small peasants cultivating up to five hectares of their own land were in this category. These two groups probably made up more than half of all rural households, although detailed data on patterns of landownership and tenancy are not available for this period.

In other words, the new policy left marketable surplus only in the hands of households that owned and cultivated much more than five hectares of dry-farming land. Middle peasants who cultivated up to eight or ten hectares of dry-farming land while relying primarily on family labor, and who produced a marketable surplus under normal circumstances, may not have been forced to reduce their consumption of cereals. However, the 25 percent rule sharply reduced the amounts they could sell at the market. It was primarily the large landowners, therefore, who could take advantage of the extraordinarily high cereal prices in the marketplace. For them, the new policy had the additional advantage of legalizing all cereals sales to private merchants.

It is often said that wartime benefits farmers, but it was certainly not the case in the episode examined here. The policies adopted in the summer of 1942 and continued until the end of the war distributed the burdens and opportunities of wartime conditions unevenly. Small and middle peasants producing cereals witnessed a sharp decrease in their consumption and real income levels during these years, while large landowners took advantage of the rapidly rising cereal prices in the marketplace. At the same time, incentives for avoiding government demands remained high for all producers, large and small.

In retrospect, the period December 1941–June 1943 emerges as the most difficult and critical of the war in terms of the so-called food supply problem. At least four factors contributed to the cereals shortages of the urban areas during this period.

First, the shortcomings of the transportation network and, more importantly, shortages in storage space made it difficult to distribute cereals around the country from regions and pockets with surpluses to those with deficits, especially the leading urban centers. Second, merchants and middlemen practiced a good deal of hoarding. These speculators did not reduce the total availability of cereals to urban consumers, but by keeping prices higher for extended periods of time, they probably intensified the crisis. Third, cereals production declined particularly in 1942, to an extent that remains unclear. Finally, there is macrolevel evidence that withholding by producers was considerable and played some important role in the emergence of urban shortages. We know, for example, that the actual amounts of cereals the Ofis purchased remained well below initial government targets. We also know that, in the case of wheat, even if the actual 1942 crop was well below official estimates, the share of Ofis purchases in total production remained well below 25 percent, the minimum target established by government policy. In any case, additional evidence regarding the actual volume of the 1942 crop would be helpful in assessing the respective contributions of the last two factors to the urban shortages.

Stage 4 (June 1943–End of the War): The Return of the Tithe

In May 1943, just before the start of the harvest, the government decided to modify the 25 percent rule. Government shares were redefined as 20 percent of the first six tons, 30 percent of the next nine tons, and 50 percent of all cereal production above fifteen tons. This change lowered slightly the burden of poor peasants and increased the level of government demands from large landowners who produced more than twelve tons. In another decision, similar measures were extended to pulses with a flat 25 percent government share for all producers (*Resmi Gazete,* May 15, 1943).

Cereal shortages began to ease in June 1943 as it became clear that the 1943 crop would be abundant, but it did not deter the government from introducing a new in-kind tax in June 1943 that varied from 8 to 12 percent depending on the crop. In practice, this tax was not collected separately but was included in the earlier government shares. In other words, the government simply stopped paying for part of the crop the Ofis continued to demand under the 25 percent rule (*Resmi Gazete,* June 7, 1943). In April 1944 the rates on this new tax were changed to a uniform 10 percent for all crops, including cereals. As a result, the new tax began to be interpreted by the peasant producers as the return of the Ottoman tithe that had been abolished by the Republican regime.

Concluding Remarks

These coercive policies were discontinued with the end of the war in 1945. As the country began to move gradually toward a multiparty parliamentary regime, the leadership of the Republican Peoples party attempted to mend fences. In June 1945, a potentially radical land reform bill, including a clause enabling the government to redistribute any holding over five hectares to poor and landless peasants, was passed by the parliament. The bill was supported by the top leadership of the party over the violent protests of deputies who represented large landed interests. Subsequent efforts by these deputies, however, prevented the redistribution of private land under the bill. As a result, this last-ditch attempt by the single-party regime failed to gain the support of poor peasants (Keyder and Pamuk 1984).

With the first free elections of the new political era in 1950, the peasantry acquired immediate importance for the first time in the country's politics. The newly established Democrat party won these elections. The discontent of large landowners with the urban-based, industrialization-oriented policies of the single party regime during the 1930s and the land reform bill after the war is well known. They responded readily to the Democrats' promise of greater emphasis on commercial agriculture. In fact, some of the leading members of this new party were large landowners. What is more striking and more difficult to explain regarding the 1950 elections was the support the Democrats received from small and middle peasants, although this examination suggests that it was, at least in part, a vote of protest against the wartime policies of the single-party regime.

Beyond the history and political economy of Turkey, this wartime episode has implications for the more general study of peasant economic behavior and for the study of the interaction between state economic policies and rural class structure. For example, in response to peasant resistance, why did the state move from policies of coercion aimed at all producers (from February 1941 to July 1942), attempting to purchase the entire surplus at below-market prices, to a combination of coercion aimed at small producers and market incentives for large landowners?

At least two explanations appear possible. First, it can be argued that large landowners were politically more powerful, with a good deal of influence in the parliament and in the higher echelons of the Republican Peoples party. It is not surprising, in this view, that the government developed a policy package that allowed them to take advantage of high cereal prices. This argument is not entirely convincing, however. It cannot explain, for example, why the government did not pursue this course as soon as the Ofis stocks began to decline and cereal shortages began to appear in the urban areas in 1941.

A more satisfactory argument would emphasize that with the outbreak of the war, the provisioning of urban areas became a matter of military and political survival for the state. Particularly during such crisis periods, state interests transcend those of individual groups or classes. In its policies toward rural producers during the war years, the government was concerned more with extracting the maximum amount of cereals for urban areas and less with the distributional consequences of its actions in rural areas.

From this perspective, the small peasants were not expected to bring cereals to the market. Therefore, the government attempted to take away part of their output by force, even though it meant an absolute decline in the levels of consumption for most small producers. Large landowners, on the other hand, did have marketable surpluses. The measures adopted by the government after July 1942 can thus be interpreted as providing the highest market incentives to those producers most likely to bring cereals to the market. In other words, large landowners were the beneficiaries of these policies not so much because of their political power but because they had marketable surpluses and could successfully resist the government's coercive measures.

Finally, a few words about the implications of this episode on the study of peasant behavior. Until recently, a large part of the literature on peasant politics has focused on peasant rebellion.[13] Despite the importance of these rebellions, they tell us little about the struggles and conflicts of peasants and how they defend their interests under more ordinary circumstances. The resistance of Anatolian peasants of different strata to state economic policies, without any organization and without open protest, provides an important example of how peasants defend their interests most of the time. In the case examined here, macrolevel data indicate a considerable amount of withholding on the part of peasant producers.

The existence of widespread noncompliance, however, does not necessarily mean that peasant producers constitute an undifferentiated mass. For a variety of reasons, the burden of government measures may not fall equally or proportionately on peasants from all strata. For example, large landowners who are more influential and politically better connected will often be more successful in evading the tax collector. In comparison to poor peasants, they may end up surrendering a lower percentage of their crop to the government.

Moreover, agricultural producers belonging to different strata may evade government actions for different reasons. In the case studied here, poor peasants attempted to avoid government taxation in kind in order to maintain minimum standards of consumption for themselves. Middle peasants and large landowners, on the other hand, avoided government taxation and forced deliveries in order to take advantage of market opportunities and sell a larger part of their surplus. Widespread resistance to government measures will not necessarily mean, therefore, a unity of interests among producers belonging to different strata. Any assessment of the significance of peasant avoidance needs to emphasize these characteristics and limitations.

Notes

Author's note: An earlier version of this paper appeared in *New Perspectives on Turkey* 2, no. 1 (1988). I would like to thank Charles Issawi, Reşat Kasaba, Insan Tunalı, and John Waterbury for helpful comments and suggestions. I would also like to acknowledge a research grant received from the Joint Committee on the Near and Middle East of the Social Science Research Council and the American Council of Learned Societies with funds provided by the National Endowment for the Humanities and the Ford Foundations.

1. See the national income study by Bulutay, Tezel, and Yıldırım (1974), which relies on the official statistics; these statistics are available from Turkey, İstatistik Genel Müdürlüğü, *Tarım İstatistikleri,* Ankara and Turkey, and İstatistik Genel Müdürlüğü *Dış Ticaret Yıllıkları,* Ankara, both annual publications.

2. Based on the price and production data available in Bulutay, Tezel, and Yıldırım (1974).

3. Boratav (1981) has recently underlined this point. For a conceptual framework emphasizing the alliances between the state and various strata of rural producers during the 1930s, see Birtek and Keyder (1975).

4. The official agricultural statistics of the period are available in summary form in Bulutay, Tezel, and Yıldırım, 1974. For an earlier study underlining the increases in total and per capita agricultural production, see Hirsch and Hirsch (1963).

5. Turkey, Istatistik Genel Müdürlüğü, *Dış Ticaret Yıllıkları,* Ankara.

6. The British government followed the food supply situation in Turkey closely during 1942–43, not only because of its political and military implications but also because the Turkish government had requested to purchase wheat from the Middle East Supply Centre in Egypt in order to alleviate the urban shortages. Estimates of the 1942 cereal crop undertaken by nongovernment observers in Turkey and cited in the secret British reports of the period suggest that the 1942 cereal harvest was approximately 10 to 15 percent below 1941 levels, which themselves were below the prewar levels. These estimates also need to be treated with caution, however. See Great Britain, Public Records Office, FO 371/33357, Report by Bennett Sterndale in Ankara, December 4, 1942. See also Wilmington (1971, passim).

7. Turkey, İstatistik Genel Müdürlüğü, *Hayvanat İstatistikleri,* Ankara.

8. One would expect that these declines in the availability of labor and draft animals resulted in the reduction of acreage under cultivation during the war years. However, the official statistics are not very clear on this issue. They indicate that the area under cereals cultivation increased by about 7 percent between 1939 and 1942 but then declined by 19 percent in 1943. It is possible that official statistics for 1943 were adjusted in response to the urban food shortages of 1942–43. According to the official estimates, acreage under cereals cultivation in 1945 was 10 percent below its 1939 levels. See İstatistik Genel Müdürlüğü, *Tarım İstatistikleri.*

9. Detailed price data for crops and sectors are available in Bulutay, Tezel, and Yıldırım (1974).

10. Turkey, İstatistik Genel Müdürlüğü, *Dış Ticaret Yıllıkları,* Ankara. In the official foreign trade statistics, exports of wheat to Germany during the year 1940 are given under the category "other countries."

11. For example, "Köylüler Pasif Mukavemet Yapıyor" (The Peasants Are Showing Passive Resistance), *Tan Gazetesi*, July 17, 1942, Istanbul, and "Köylü Malını Saklıyor" (The Peasant Is Hiding His Crop), *Tan Gazetesi*, October 1, 1942, Istanbul.
12. See, for example, the oppositional *Tan Gazetesi* during July and August 1942.
13. For example, Moore (1966); Paige (1975), and Wolf (1969). For a perspective emphasizing more common forms of peasant resistance, see Scott (1984).

References

Antsiferov, Alexis, in collaboration with A. D. Bilimovich, M. O. Batshev, and D. N. Ivantsov. 1930. *Russian Agriculture during the War*. New Haven: Yale University Press.

Araz, Kemal. n.d. "Toprak Mahsulleri Ofisi: Iktisadi Faaliyeti ve Mali Bünyesi 1938–1954." Manuscript, library of Toprak Mahsulleri Ofisi, Ankara.

Birtek, Faruk, and Çağlar Keyder. 1975. "Agriculture and the State: An Inquiry into Agricultural Differentiation and Political Alliances." *Journal of Peasant Studies* 2:446–67.

Boratav, Korkut. 1981. "Kemalist Economic Policies and Etatism." In *Atatürk: Founder of a Modern State*, ed. A. Kazancıgil and E. Özbudun. Hamden, Conn.: Archon Books.

Bulutay, Tuncer, Yahya S. Tezel, and Nuri Yıldırım. 1974. *Türkiye Milli Geliri (1923–1948)*. Ankara: Ankara Üniversitesi Yayınları.

Hardach, Gerd. 1987. *The First World War, 1914–1918*. Harmondsworth: Penguin Books.

Hirsch, Eva, and Abraham Hirsch. 1963. "Changes in Agricultural Output per Capita of Rural Population in Turkey, 1927–1960." *Economic Development and Cultural Change* 11:440–57.

İstatistik Genel Müdürlüğü (Turkey). *Dış Ticaret Yıllıkları*. Annual publication, various years.

İstatistik Genel Müdürlüğü. *Hayvanat İstatistikleri*. Annual publication, various years.

İstatistik Genel Müdürlüğü. *Nufus Sayımları*. Various years.

İstatistik Genel Müdürlüğü. *Tarım İstatistikleri*. Annual publication, various years.

Keyder, Çağlar, and Şevket Pamuk. 1984. "1945 Çiftçiyi Topraklandırma Kanunu Üzerine Tezler." *Yapit* 8:52–63.

Lloyd, E. M. H. 1956. *Food and Inflation in the Middle East, 1940–45*. Stanford, Calif: Stanford University Press.

Milward, Alan S. 1977. *War, Economy and Society (1939–1945)*. Berkeley: University of California Press.

Moore, Barrington, Jr. 1966. *The Social Basis of Dictatorship and Democracy*. Boston: Beacon Press.

Paige, Jeffrey M. 1975. *Agrarian Revolution: Social Movements and Export Agriculture in the Underdeveloped World*. New York: Free Press.

Prest, A. R. 1948. *War Economics of Primary Producing Countries*. Cambridge: Cambridge University Press.

Public Records Office, Great Britain, Foreign Office. 371/33357; Report by Bennett
    Sterndale, Ankara, 4 December 1942.
Resmi Gazete. Ankara.
Scott, James C. 1984. *Weapons of the Weak, Everyday Forms of Resistance*. New
    Haven: Yale University Press.
Sen, Amartya. 1981. *Poverty and Famines*. Oxford: Oxford University Press.
Shorter, Frederic C. 1985. "The Population of Turkey after the War of Independence."
    IJMES 17:417–41.
Tan Gazetesi. Istanbul. Daily newspaper.
Wilmington, Martin W. 1971. *The Middle East Supply Center*. Albany: SUNY Press.
Wolf, Eric R. 1969. *Peasant Wars of the Twentieth Century*. New York: Harper and
    Row.

8

Rural Change and Peasant Destitution: Contributing Causes to the Arab Revolt in Palestine, 1936–1939

KENNETH W. STEIN

*I*n April 1936, Palestine's political temperament was precipitously poised for another outbreak of communal violence. Arab antipathy for Zionist presence and growth was ripe for reaction. Palestinian Arabs had interpreted British policy as a continuous, capricious intent to deny self-determination and to support Zionism's growth. After the August 1929 disturbances had agitated the political status quo, His Majesty's Government (HMG) confronted the pragmatic limitations of constraining Arab political aspirations. Based on British investigations of the economic causes of the disturbances, a new policy statement on Palestine was issued by HMG. The October 1930 Passfield white paper promised to decrease the British mandate's pro-Zionist orientation. Whereas it took HMG more than a year to evaluate and prepare to implement a policy shift that would restrain the development of the Jewish National Home, it took less than four months for Great Britain to rebuke its own intent by issuing the February 1931 MacDonald letter in favor of the Zionists. As a definitive demographic majority expecting the establishment of self-government, Palestinian Arabs were frustrated when Jewish immigration and land purchase were neither stopped nor declined. For the next five years, rather than providing political satisfaction to the Palestinian Arab population and especially the political elite, HMG half-heartedly sought to ameliorate the peasantry's barren economic conditions.

From 1931 onward, the daily press in Palestine predicted an ominous Palestinian Arab political future, attacking Arab leaders for inaction or ineptitude and recounting the economic plight of the peasantry almost daily. Anti-Zionist sentiment intensified among Arab Palestinians, whose antagonism against HMG broadened because of its policy reversal. Antipathy for Zionism and HMG was nurtured by fears generated by the dramatic increments of Jewish immigration and land acquisition. Palestinian anxiety about the future was exacerbated by HMG's public but unsuccessful six-year effort to resettle 1,200 Wadi Hawarith bedouin who had been displaced from their lands near Hadera because of Jewish land acquisition before the 1929 disturbances. By regularly reporting the futile efforts to save land for the Wadi Hawarith bedouin, the Palestine Arab press further fueled Arab aversion to British equivocation and Jewish settlement. In addition to the absentee landowner selling relatively large land areas to Zionists, there was also the small peasant proprietor selling small parcels with increasing frequency to Jewish buyers because of unbearable economic pressures. Both transactions added uncertainty to the contentious political environment. A sense of dispossession and displacement was real for Palestinians, who saw Zionism as continuous and relentless and the future as impermanent, even hopeless.

In October 1935 at the Jaffa port, a secret arms shipment for Jewish paramilitary forces was discovered, providing "demonstrable proof" to apprehensive Palestinians of Zionist intentions to dislodge them violently and physically. The next month, Arab leaders representing five political parties formally demanded that the British high commissioner establish a representative government in Palestine, prohibit land sales to Jews, and cease Jewish immigration. HMG responded to this request by offering to create a legislative council, a move Palestinian leaders criticized as a transparent scheme that failed to ensure majority Palestinian Arab rule free of either dominant British influence or Jewish involvement. Rather than deriving its authority from the majority Arab inhabitants, 75 percent of Palestine's population, the legislative council would have been a political instrument of the British high commissioner in Palestine and the Colonial Office in London. In March 1936, HMG recanted approval for this very limited form of self-government when the House of Commons publicly opposed implementing the proposal. No Palestinian self-governing institutions were established.

During the preceding fifty years, Zionists and Palestinian Arabs had struggled physically and emotionally to acquire or retain control of the same coveted land. Within this context, distinctive conditions prefaced the Arab general strike and revolt. The early 1930s witnessed an unprecedented increase in individual Arab fear about the collective future. For the first time, Arabs of all classes were alarmed by the reality of a Jewish National Home established with British assistance.[1] In 1920, 1921, 1929, and 1933, public

Arab protest against Zionism had manifested itself in civil disorder. What distinguished the 1936–39 Arab general strike and revolt from the previous communal violence? It was the resolve and maintenance of the revolt's dependence on the active and intense participation of a segment of Palestine's rural population.[2] The earlier outbreaks had originated in urban areas and had even been partially instigated by urban notables. In contrast, the 1936–39 revolt originated and was sustained in rural Palestine, with urban political leaders seeking ways to influence uncontrollable bands of roaming peasants.

For the peasantry of Palestine the bleak political future generated despair that their leaders sincerely and carefully nurtured. But my thesis in this essay is that economic and social factors also contributed significantly to the peasantry's individual motivation to participate in the Arab revolt and general strike. (1) A prolonged economic plight with multiple dimensions had afflicted Palestine's peasant population especially in the six years prior to the outbreak of the revolt and general strike.[3] (2) A building anger among the peasantry within Arab villages was directed in general against urban landowning interests and in particular against the grain merchants, moneylenders, and landowners who had disadvantaged the peasantry for decades. (3) A penetrating dislike for Zionism had been fueled by increased physical displacement by Jewish immigration and land purchase. (4) A deep disenchantment had set in with HMG for its belated, meager, and unsuccessful efforts to rescue the peasantry from its economic cul de sac and for failure to sustain the peasant owner and tenant cultivator in agricultural occupations.

What provoked the writing of this essay was an unanticipated discovery of fairly uniform but independent assessments made by Palestinian, Zionist, and British sources acknowledging these problems. Although Zionist leadership tended to focus exclusively on preventing any obstruction to the development of the Jewish National Home, British officials and Palestinian Arab leaders recognized that severe rural economic decline, the peasantry's general disillusionment, and the impact of Jewish growth could blend to produce a volatile mixture of disturbance and bloodshed. In a political environment of anxiety and uncertainty, this combination exploded when approximately 5,000 Palestinian peasants participated in the revolt and general strike from 1936 to 1939.

Major Factors Influencing the Peasantry's Economic Condition: Administrative Reform, the Musha' System, and Indebtedness

Beginning in the late nineteenth century, administrative change in the Arab provinces of the Ottoman Empire transformed the peasantry's relationship to land. Ottoman reforms were aimed at increasing the amount of regional taxes generated from land use, revenue to be collected locally and sent to the Ottoman treasury. These changes caused the peasantry to fear the levying of new or increased taxes on previously unregistered lands. Perhaps more important, they feared recruitment into the Ottoman army if their names appeared on tax rolls.

To avoid having their names placed on the tax/conscription rolls, some peasants asked notables to register their lands with the local governmental authorities. Peasants in perennial financial insolvency chose to pay off their creditors with land, trading accrued debts for the right to remain on the land that their families had been working for generations. Fear of governmental intrusion into their lives compelled peasant proprietors to rely increasingly but uncomfortably upon urban notables, who were by profession landowners, lawyers, local religious leaders, government officials, moneylenders, small entrepreneurs, and grain merchants.

More than half a century before the outbreak of World War I, these groups legally and informally amassed land areas that were peasant-owned, vacant, or previously vacated. In many villages of Palestine, former peasant proprietors evolved into a class of agricultural tenants or agricultural laborers. Because of growing indebtedness, peasants who had owned moderate amounts of land (perhaps 500 dunams or more) were regularly alienating lands to willing buyers. (A dunam was a quarter of an acre.) According to the 1931 census for Palestine, two-thirds of the Muslim Arab population of Palestine, or 465,000 earners and their dependents, relied upon ordinary cultivation or pasturing of flocks for their livelihood. Of the 115,913 earners, 50,552 were owner-proprietors; 29,077 were agricultural laborers; 12,638 were agricultural tenants; 15,419 raised flocks or grew fruit, flowers, and vegetables; 2,000 were orange growers; 43 were estate mangers; and the remainder hunted, fished, or raised small animals.[4]

The bureaucratic reform of the Ottoman Empire ultimately concentrated more political and economic power in the hands of urban landowning interests at the expense of the rural peasantry.[5] After World War I, urban landowning interests in Palestine maintained an economic and financial grip on the rural population. Like their counterparts in Iraq, Syria, and Lebanon, the peasantry in Palestine lived at a level of bare subsistence. The reasons for rural economic stagnation or decline were many, and none ultimately related to Ottoman or British governance or Zionist presence: poor soil quality, drought, intense or sporadic rains, a long or severe sirocco, not enough knowledge or use of intensive methods of cultivation, lack of access to means of irrigation

Arab peasants ploughing rocky fields in Judean Hills, ca. 1921.

and mechanized equipment, insufficient secondary roads between villages and towns for crop transport, irregular marketing arrangements, dumping of Syrian and Egyptian wheat on the Palestine market, meager agricultural yields or complete crop failures, short-term rental agreements, insecurity in land tenure, and wide abuse and fraud in tax collection.[6] The incentive to increase production was low, since a major portion of the agricultural yield inevitably ended up in the hands and pockets of others: the tax collector, moneylender, landlord, or other agricultural laborers who worked on either owner-occupied or tenanted land. In rare years of fair agricultural output, barely 20 percent of a cultivator's gross yield remained after others had taken their shares. Until the late 1920s, lease payments were usually in kind, from one-sixth to two-fifths of the gross yield. Rarely were lease agreements made for a period longer than one year, and usually they were made for only the winter or summer cultivating season, or for both seasons. Agricultural tenants were regularly moved from field to field by their landowners or estate managers, usually corresponding directly to the two- or three-year crop rotations of Palestinian agriculture. Short-term lease agreements contributed to a widespread sense of personal insecurity and almost total reliance upon those who controlled land use and its distribution.[7]

Two additional factors significantly contributed to tying the peasantry to perennial financial struggles: ceaseless indebtedness and a debilitating system of land use. Perhaps no single factor limited the economic development of the Palestinian peasant more than the *musha'* system of landownership and land tenure.[8] Its use throughout Palestine impeded agricultural output, retarded agricultural development, enhanced peasant indebtedness, led to rural insolvency, and generated village apathy and desolation.[9] By contributing to the atomization of Palestinian society into village units, the musha' system also hampered the development of Palestinian national integration and identity, an effect especially evident in the lower lying valley and coastal regions that had both the highest potential for agricultural improvement and the greatest appeal for Jewish land purchase (after the acquisition of large landed estates). In 1933 it was estimated that between 46 and 63 percent of the country's 8,252,900 cultivable dunams were under some form of musha' use.[10]

The central concept of the musha' system was collective ownership or cultivation of common land that was periodically redistributed among various clans, families, or individuals. Repartition of the land was designed to ensure a measure of fairness in the quality and quantity of apportionment. In order to maintain the integrity of a land area, redistribution ensured that ownership or use would involve a whole village group rather than individuals or people outside the village.

Periodic reparceling had many eroding effects. (1) It militated against a peasant's willingness to spend time, effort, or money in improving a plot that would only become someone else's within one, two, or five years. (2) Redistribution meant that a peasant rarely left an area fallow, which would have prevented or at least limited depletion of soil nutrients. (3) Parcels or shares allotted to peasants were not always contiguous, causing inefficient use of time. (4) Musha'-held shares were not individually registered in the land records, so that loans that required a title deed as collateral could not be made for more than half of the cultivable land in Palestine. This forced musha' shareholders to rely on the usurious rates charged by money-lenders. (5) The size of the overall musha'-held or musha'-owned areas did not change, but the populations who participated in redistribution did. Therefore, the number of people expected to sustain themselves within a musha' area increased while their land area per capita decreased. Over several generations, populations grew due to increased health care and decreased infant mortality. A specific area of musha' village lands that had once sustained several dozen people had to sustain several hundred people generations later. (6) Since not all of the lands within a musha' area were of uniform quality, the peasants who tended to prevail were those stronger, more powerful, and socially connected to the person who oversaw the distribution process. As a result, village and clan harmony was regularly and repeatedly strained during and after the repartition procedure. Quarreling and fighting frequently developed at the time when the areas, shares, or parcels were allotted.[11] Finally, (7) collective ownership of musha' shares proved illusory. Local indebtedness forced many peasants to "give" personal, family, or clan shares to interests outside the village. Over time, especially in the Ottoman period, landowners and moneylenders acquired participatory rights in the redistribution process. It was estimated that as early as 1923 more than 75 percent of musha'-held lands were owned not by peasants themselves but by individuals who lived in the towns.[12] Eventually, the combination of a deteriorating rural economy with the introduction of Jewish immigrant capital saw both urban landowning interests and Jewish purchasers acquire portions or entire musha' villages.

The Palestinian peasant's perennial indebtedness was a pervasive burden. In 1930 British sources estimated that the volume of the individual peasant's indebtedness represented the full value of his annual income from crops and agricultural stock—in other words, his temporary wealth. It was not uncommon in Palestine for the peasant to pay interest rates of 30–60 percent over periods ranging from three months to a year.[13] In early 1930, an official in the Palestine Commissioner of Lands Department recounted in general terms the depth and constancy of the peasant's debt. "The *fellah* has normally no capital which is an inevitable cause of failure in any farming community, as the farmer is unable to withstand his lean years or profit by his fat ones. The fellah is furthermore bound to dispose of his crop as soon as it is harvested, or sooner at a time when prices are at their lowest in order to pay his debts to government, etc. The fellah buys his seed, on the other hand, when prices are at their highest and he is thus unable to benefit by the normal yield. It seems that the Arab farmer in Palestine pays his bills in arrears and sells his crop in advance and until such time as this can be remedied, success [in provision of credit facilities] cannot be hoped for."[14]

Requisite sums to alleviate peasant indebtedness were not allocated on the administrative level. Ottoman authorities did not offer loans through their agricultural bank, nor did the British provide funds from Palestine revenues, even when HMG enjoyed large surplus revenues in Palestine, as in the early 1930s. The Palestine administration's claim in the mid-1930s that it helped reduce peasant indebtedness by at least 60 percent cannot be substantiated. By 1930 the rural earner population of Palestine exceeded 100,000, and total rural indebtedness was estimated at £2 million for less than a quarter of the total rural population.[15] From 1930 through March 1936, the eve of the 1936 general strike and revolt, the British provided only £169,214 in agricultural loans, less than 5 percent of what had been needed in 1930 alone to offset rural indebtedness.[16]

In Palestine, the peasant's indebted condition was further aggravated by the seepage of a monetary economy into the rural barter sector: payment for rent, taxes, and supplies was traditionally made in terms of the yield produced. From 1931 through 1936, the money supply in Palestine increased sharply because of Jewish immigration, Jewish land purchase, additional tourism, accelerated building activity, and growth of the citrus industry. As cash became the measure of economic value, the peasantry's barter-oriented economy was gradually supplanted by the assignment of monetary values to goods and services. As the peasants' need for cash increased, they relied more on the landlord, grain merchant, and moneylender, a financial dependency that forced them deeper into debt and caused them to relinquish ownership, tenancy, or mushaʿ participation rights in exchange for cash and possibly relief from accumulated indebtedness.

By the early 1930s, the peasantry found itself increasingly unable to convert its crop value into money. The most common medium of exchange in rural areas, wheat yields, was in exceedingly short supply. Wheat production accounted for 40 to 50 percent of the winter income from all Arab farms. Thus, when domestic wheat production and prices fell precipitously (see table 8.1),[17] many peasants could not pay their debts. As Syrian wheat dumped on the Palestinian market in the late 1920s and early 1930s drove down the price of Palestinian-produced wheat, creditors refused to accept wheat as debt repayment and insisted instead upon cash or land as a cash equivalent.

Table 8.1.
Principal Cereal Production in Palestine, 1930–37 (in tons)

Year	Winter crops		Summer crops	
	Wheat	**Barley**	**Dura**	**Sesame**
1928	65,288	46,697	32,732	1,978
1929	87,873	46,420	31,439	4,169
1930	87,339	60,071	37,058	2,365
1931	51,159	26,243	25,389	3,000
1932	56,186	29,496	21,203	894
1933	48,305	32,580	8,635	292
1934	85,171	70,308	46,830	2,658
1935	104,353	68,905	46,135	6,914
1936	76,059	55,169	22,122	1,847
1937	127,420	75,417	61,023	9,317
1938	44,000	86,230	61,000	4,000
1939	136,000	102,000	—	—

Source: Government of Palestine, *Annual Reports of the Palestine Department of Agriculture for Years 1928–1940.*

Peasant Attitudes and Relationships with Landowning Interests

In the nineteenth and early twentieth centuries, social classes in Palestine and throughout Arab regions in the Fertile Crescent were sharply divided.[18] Peasant proprietors, agricultural tenants, and per diem laborers were usually bound legally and economically to the urban elite. The control of urban landowning interests over Palestinian peasants survived the shift from the Ottoman to British administrations. These Arab landowners who did not work the land physically and for whom possession of land had only a distant meaning numbered perhaps only several hundred. For this group, landed property was an investment—a means to ensure access to capital, maintain a certain lifestyle, retain social prestige, and sustain political influence. Those who saw land as a tradable commodity did not possess the sense of deep attachment to it held by peasants dependent for their livelihood on tilling the soil and grazing herds.

When land changed owners between Arabs in the nineteenth and twentieth centuries in Palestine, peasant farmers or tenants who had occupied the land for long periods often left unwillingly and sometimes expressed themselves violently against their new landlords.[19] More often, they stayed on the same land they had always worked, changing only the intermediary to whom they paid rent and taxes. Palestinian notables with landowning interests felt little or no obligation to ameliorate the peasants' economic condition. Landowning classes offered minimal guidance about how to achieve better yields, but landlords or moneylenders expressed little interest in improving the standard of living of their tenants or of other agricultural workers. For some members of the landowning class, to alleviate or amend the peasants' situation would have altered their own social status, especially the convenient and informal political relationships developed with HMG in governing Palestine.

Although peasant classes throughout Palestine suffered similar deprivations imposed by urban landowning and lending interests, they formed no sense of class consciousness against these urban notables. Rather, each village developed a separate but similar antipathy for the locally connected moneylender, grain merchant, or urban notable. There is evidence, however, that some peasants during the Mandate, though not politically empowered, clearly articulated to HMG their desire to reduce their indebtedness, unemployment, and dependence upon moneylenders. At a farmers' economic conference in November 1929, peasants proposed establishing an agricultural bank, increasing road communications between villages and markets, and improving sanitary conditions and local educational facilities.[20] Though HMG claimed otherwise, it did little to enhance the peasantry's economic condition.

Moneylenders and others external to the village community in Palestine practiced an oppressive control on the rural population that created negative feelings, overt animosity, and sustained sporadic local disputes between the peasantry and various landowning interests. Commenting on the social distance between the notable-*effendi* class and the peasantry, Herbert Samuel, Palestine's first high commissioner, noted in 1920 "a real antagonism between them." In 1923 Sydney Moody, who served in Palestine and in the British Colonial Office, wrote that "the mass of people whose interest is to agree with Government are afraid to speak. A village is at best a personal union and at worst a personal disunion." In October 1935 a Palestinian intellectual, Afif I. Tannous, commented that "the fellah until recently has been the subject of oppression, neglect, and ill treatment by his own countrymen, and the old political regime. The feudal system played havoc in his life, the effendi class looked down upon him, and the old Turkish regime was too corrupt to be concerned with such a vital problem."[21] Among the many hundreds of cases adjudicated in the Tulkarm sub-district under the Protection of Cultivators Ordinance of 1933, dozens were brought by Arab landowners convinced that their life-styles could not be maintained if agricultural tenants continued to work their lands in ways that made so little money.[22] Arab landowners rarely offered tenants land for grazing or agricultural use in order not to encumber it as a potential land sale to a Jewish buyer; instead, they sought special permission from British officials to evict their Arab tenants in order to sell their land. Typical of some landowners with tenanted peasants was Abdul Latif Tabawi, who served in the Education Department of the Palestine administration. He claimed that he had to maintain a higher standard of living than did the tenants and that he should not be expected to suffer merely to provide a tenant with a means of living. The Nablus district officer working in the British administration, Hilmi Husseini, granted Tabawi the right to evict his tenants.[23]

Tension between urban landowning interests and the rural peasantry necessitated the development of intermediaries. Nonresident Palestinian Arabs with landowning interests employed land managers or local village officials to collect rent, taxes, and crop yields. Involvement of these intermediaries put them in highly perilous positions when the level of village discontent increased. When quantities of village lands were offered to Jewish buyers or Arab and Jewish land brokers, village *mukhtars* often used their prominent leverage and power within a village community for their own material benefit. They acted as intermediaries in land sales, had land registered in their names, or gave testimony in boundary disputes within a village, between villagers and urban notables, or between Jewish purchasers and villagers. In addition, local confidence in a mukhtar was hurt by the reality that his salary (until 1934) was based on a percentage of the taxes he collected from the villagers. The local mukhtar was thus not uniformly admired, and, by the outbreak of the 1936 general strike, the British government conceded in the *Peel Report* that "the authority of [village] elders suffered increased diminution."[24]

The Impact of the Jewish National Home on the Peasantry: Displacement, Congestion, and Land Disputes

Before the April 1936 general strike, the peasantry's rural environment was undergoing rapid changes: Arab, Jewish, and British intrusions in village life, cash and capital requirements replacing a barter economy, and village harmony deteriorating because of the disintegration of the musha' system and the avarice of some village mukhtars. As the social fabric of Arab villages slowly unraveled, in the 1920s a number of important members of the Palestinian Arab political establishment publicly protested Zionism and privately sold land to immigrating Zionists and Jewish land purchasing institutions.[25] Some peasants displaced by these land sales found temporary work in the urban areas of the Palestine coastal plain, burgeoning with the influx of Jewish capital. Others migrated eastward to the more sparse cultivable land of the hill regions, where physical distance from the developing Jewish National Home made many peasants feel more secure. From 1929 through 1936, sustaining existence in the villages had proved difficult. As early as 1931, one-quarter of the rural population of 108,000 earners indicated that they needed a secondary income to maintain their standard of life. The relevance of this number is that, of these 27,000 earners, almost 25,000 found their subsidiary income in a nonagricultural activity such as grocery vending, semiskilled labor, or work in the urban building industries.[26] A significant portion of the Arab village population in Palestine thus needed to augment its income by working outside the village, sometimes in Jewish citrus groves and settlements and frequently outside the rural economy.

Obviously, the pace and quantity of Jewish immigration and land purchase influenced both Zionism's achievements and the level of the peasantry's feeling against Zionism and Britain, which was seen as the imperial collaborator in establishing a Jewish National Home. Especially after 1930, Zionism was viewed as a danger to their demographic and geographic existence. Without enlarging the overall area of cultivation in Palestine, from 1922 to 1931 the Jewish population increased by 108 percent and the general population by 27 percent; during the same period, Jewish ownership of registered land increased by almost 50 percent. In the 1930s, while the general population increased by 69 percent, the Jewish population increased by more than 250 percent, mostly before the strike broke out in April 1936. The Jewish population of Palestine grew from 11 percent of the population in 1922 to just over 30 percent two decades later.[27] By 1930, British official reports, Zionist experts, and Arab politicians concurred: a limited amount of cultivable land with existing or potential economic value was available to a population increasing rapidly through immigration and propagation. In January 1930, well-known Zionist land expert Arthur Ruppin acknowledged that an investigation into the amount of cultivable area in Palestine would show that little land was either unused or unoccupied.[28]

During the 1930s, the average land area available to the peasant proprietor and his family steadily decreased. In 1930, official British reports considered 130 dunams necessary for the peasant proprietor to support himself and his family on "average" land throughout Palestine. Because of meager cultivable areas and poorer soil qualities, especially in the central range running from the Galilee in the north through Nablus, Ramallah, Jerusalem, Bethlehem, and

Hebron in the south, larger areas of land would have been necessary in some regions to sustain a family, yet in 1931, the *Census for Palestine* estimated that in the central range a necessary subsistence area for a peasant proprietor was 88 dunams. By the middle of 1935, Jewish Agency and Jewish National Fund officials estimated that each Arab family in these hill districts could count on only 45–56 dunams for its use. While the situation varied from village to village, in the central range the cultivable land available per family had thus declined rapidly since 1930. In January 1936 the Palestine administration considered introducing a law to require the peasant proprietor to retain a minimum portion of his lands for the subsistence of himself and his family, expressing grave concern that without such legislation (which ultimately was not introduced), "the result would be further disturbances in Palestine and probably a good deal of bloodshed." Peasants from these areas in the central range, particularly near Jenin, Tulkarm, and Nablus, participated in the various phases of the 1936–39 general strike and revolt.[29]

In the 1920s, most Jewish land purchase involved large estates bought from large landowners. Negotiations for these sales were relatively simple and private, and Jewish buyers could avoid the stigma attached to displacing Arab tenants by leaving that to the discretion of the Arab seller. However, in the 1930s, Jews bought more land from small proprietors, either directly or through intermediaries. Most significantly, more Arab vendors were involved in the land sale process over a longer period of time. Since Jewish buyers still wanted to acquire blocks of land free of Arab occupation at the time of legal transfer, more intermediaries such as mukhtars, moneylenders, and grain merchants plied their trade. Land disputes between Arab peasants and Zionist settlers increased, and the Arab political leadership in general was indicted for its ineptitude and nonaction in the face of prolific Zionist development.[30]

Palestinian Arabs of all classes were despondent about their future as a people. The Palestinian newspaper, *al-Hayat*, noted in September 1930 that "an Arab village shall tomorrow be a Jewish one. Where is the [Supreme] Moslem Council? Where is the Arab Executive?"[31] Regardless of political leaning, virtually every newspaper in Palestine throughout the early 1930s repeatedly acknowledged and fretted about the fate of the Palestinian Arab peasant in light of the Jewish presence and Zionist growth. One article noted in 1931, "We are selling our lands to Jews without any remorse. Land brokers are busy day and night with their odious trade without feeling any shame. In the meantime the nation is busy sending protests. Where are we going? One looks at the quantity of Arab lands transferred daily to Jewish hands, [one] realizes that we are bound to go away from this country. But where? Shall we move to Egypt, Hijaz, or Syria? How could we live there, since we would have sold the lands of our fathers and ancestors to our enemies? Nobody could show us mercy or pity, were we to go away from our country, because we would have lost her with our own hands."[32]

Palestine's rural atmosphere was dominated by frequent local disputes over control and use of sparse land areas available for grazing and cultivation. Not just between grazers or cultivators and landowners, but between villages and between clans within a village, these disputes were prompted by a variety of causes: land encroachment for grazing or cultivation purposes, conflicts over water use, quarrels over crops handled at the threshing floor. They were manifested in uprooted trees, trampled crops, selectively looted personal possessions, wounded and stolen cattle and plow animals and, occasionally, people maimed and stabbed. Village disharmony was particularly recurrent and sufficiently dangerous for nonresident Arab landlords to hire local village mukhtars, land brokers, and intermediaries to collect their rent and taxes.

In the several years before the outbreak of the Arab revolt and general strike, Palestine's rural environment was increasingly susceptible to frequent, numerous, intense, violent land disputes. From early 1930 through 1936 the press regularly reported the plight of the 1,200 bedouin at Wadi Hawarith, whose pending eviction sustained a high level of anxiety among the Palestinians. Unlike the 1920s, the mid-1930s witnessed more land transactions and eviction proceedings, which in turn created greater apprehension about the present and fear about the future.

Beginning in the early 1930s, major protracted land disputes between Palestinian peasants and Zionist settlers either occurred initially or resurfaced as unresolved conflicts at Wadi Hawarith (Tulkarm), Shatta (Beisan), Yajur (Haifa), Hartieh (Haifa), Wadi Ara (Haifa), Um Khalid (Tulkarm), Infiat (Haifa), Damireh (north of Hadera), Damun (Acre), and Ein Harod (Beisan). These conflicts involved issues of eviction, trespass, squatting, boundary disputes, ownership, taxation payments, cultivation and grazing rights, Arab tenancy privileges, Jewish right to plow lands, and the use of "state lands." These conflicts and most other land disputes occurred where the local economies were among the worst during the 1930s and where Jewish land purchases had focused after the August 1929 disturbances; here the Arab peasant bands were recruited during the 1936–39 general strike and revolt.

HMG's Failed Effort to Keep the Peasantry Tied to Land

With their rural economy collapsing around them, the peasantry looked toward the British administration for economic assistance. Already, many in the

Contemporary view of terraced and strip parcellation of land in the Judean Hills, similar to the 1930s landscape.

Palestinian Arab political elite (mukhtars, tribal shaykhs, urban notables and village leaders) had either ignored or failed to answer their needs. Particularly after the 1929 disturbances, the British decided to implement a policy aimed at preventing the peasantry from becoming landless while allowing Jewish immigration and land purchase to continue, for the revenue that Jewish development brought to British tax coffers was necessary to maintain HMG's strategic presence in Palestine. Furthermore, restricting Zionist land sales would have angered the Arab landowning establishment, despite demands by some Palestinian politicians that Jewish land purchases be halted in order to end Zionist development. The British became convinced, however, that peasant displacement from land would create a restless and unemployed population that would ultimately become a source of unrest, violence, and political instability. This situation would, in turn, require HMG's dispatch of additional troops to Palestine, a costly exercise that obviously needed to be avoided.

HMG thus introduced a series of limited bureaucratic and legislative measures aimed at keeping the peasantry tied in one way or another to their lands. It was a trilateral effort: restructuring fragmented holdings into larger parcels, legislating means to leash the peasants to land or at least to delay their eviction from it, and trying to reduce the peasants' indebtedness. Bureaucratically intrusive, HMG efforts exacerbated village disharmony because they were only partial and temporary aids. HMG's promises of economic relief through large financial expenditures remained unfulfilled. Nonetheless, a general unrealistic expectation grew among the peasantry that HMG would protect them against Zionism and those social and economic forces arrayed coincidentally against them. But HMG could not control a plummeting rural economy. In terms of political will or available manpower, HMG did not want or was incapable of ameliorating the peasantry's indebtedness through surplus tax revenue. Concurrently, HMG fully rejected the notion of ending the development of the Jewish National Home. HMG's efforts only added disillusionment to the charged political environment.

In 1927 and 1928, the process of "land settlement" was initiated to survey land and adjudicate land rights, thereby increasing agricultural output and augmenting rural tax revenue. Land settlement was designed to amalgamate small land fragments into larger parcels and to replace the musha' system with individual tenure or ownership of land. Land settlement proceeded almost exclusively in the coastal and valley regions of Palestine, adjacent to areas where Jews had purchased lands. Therefore, the wrong perception was easily sustained that the land settlement process of adjudicating legal land rights was ultimately aimed at preparing the "best land" for acquisition or use by the Jewish National Home.[33]

In addition to initiating the land settlement process, the Palestine administration responded directly to the means already used by Arab sellers and Jewish buyers in transferring land occupied or owned by peasants. The June 1931 Law of Execution (Amendment) Ordinance was designed to prevent the eviction of tenants through satisfaction of a mortgage debt. Arab vendors would take a mortgage on a parcel of land for a short period of time and intentionally fail to pay the mortgagee. The lender would then ask the court for financial relief by ordering the mortgagor to sell his land in satisfaction of the debt created by the short-term mortgage. This method of selling land to Jews through a court-ordered transaction was favored by Arabs: the vendor could blame the British administration for forcing the unwanted sale and would also not be liable to compensate agricultural tenants occupying the mortgaged land. But the ordinance filled this loophole in tenants' legal protection by stipulating that land sold in execution of a judgment debt was to be sold subject to, and with the benefit of, any lease or tenancy agreement.[34]

Another piece of legislation, the Protection of Cultivators Ordinance of 1929, was extended, amended in 1931, thoroughly revised in 1933, and amended again in 1936 in an effort to ensure that a tenant receive land, not money, as compensation for leaving a particular land area. But in spite of the 1933 ordinance, compensation in land was circumvented: Jewish purchasers were paying substantial compensatory amounts to willing tenants and other seasonal agricultural laborers to quit their lands in advance of a sale. Although these ordinances and their amendments did restrain some of the circumventions employed by vendors and purchasers, they were not sufficient to deter Jewish land purchase or Palestinian Arab land sales. By 1941 these ordinances for tenants' protection were considered to be among "the most contentious pieces of legislation on the statue books for Palestine."[35]

The 1932 Land Disputes Possession Ordinance was another legislative attempt to keep Arabs on land. In response to increased civil and criminal trespass, this ordinance empowered a British official to issue a stay of eviction when trespass was likely to cause a breach of the peace. In many cases the holder of title deeds (a potential Arab seller or recent Jewish buyer), reluctant to bring public and obviously embarrassing eviction proceedings, wanted the Palestine administration to put the land in his or her possession by executive action.[36] If those in current possession of the land could demonstrate that they were in past possession of the disputed lands, then the British administrator could confirm the occupants in possession until eviction proceedings were effected through the courts.[37] Jewish purchasers complained that the Palestinian peasant believed that, if he seized land purchased by Jews, he could

somehow manage to keep it; or, failing to keep it, he could at least blackmail
the Jewish purchaser for payment to vacate the land, perhaps even after a
former proprietor or tenant had already received been paid by the Jewish
purchaser to vacate it a first time. Although the Land Disputes Possession
Ordinance was aimed at reducing breaches of the peace, it encouraged conten-
tiousness and trespass.

In a highly publicized and unsuccessful effort to return peasants to rural
occupations, the Palestine administration instituted a landless Arab resettlement process in 1931. For a variety of reasons, the very public landless Arab
inquiry succeeded neither in identifying landless Arabs or in resettling them:
insufficient funds to buy lands for resettlement, a narrow definition of "landless Arab," Arab landowners who not want to encumber their prerogative to
sell leased land, and unwillingness of the "landless" to be resettled far from
their traditional lands. By 1937 only 74 of the 900 Arabs classified as "landless" were resettled on alternative lands in Palestine. HMG gave so much
overt publicity to the resettlement of "landless" Arabs that many Palestinians
believed land would be provided to them by the Palestine administration.
When the Palestine administration ruled that the majority of the 3,000 submitted cases were invalid, there was strong disappointment among peasants.
Many had believed that, even though lands had passed out of their ownership
or use, the British would confiscate them from the Zionists and return them.
These unrealistic expectations were never met.[38]

Noble but unsuccessful efforts were made to liberate the peasant from
payment of usurious interest rates, to reduce his indebtedness in general, and
to have him retain more of his yield. To the administration's credit, it remitted
the tithe to the peasant in the early 1930s and reformed taxation categories for
his benefit; but the administration provided only meager capital amounts for
crop loans, seed loans, and long-term credit assistance. An Agricultural Mortgage Bank and contemplated financial cooperative were either not formed or
were capitalized with too little money to act as an alternative to moneylenders.
Among these efforts was the 1931 Imprisonment for Debt Ordinance, which
allowed a debtor to pay off his indebtedness in installments after he had
proved his inability to satisfy his liability in one amount. This ordinance was
aimed at preventing further satisfaction of indebtedness through the sale of
land. Another such effort, the 1934 Usurious Loans Ordinance, was intended
to reduce interest charges imposed by moneylenders. But by the provisions of
this ordinance, the court ruled that sufficient evidence was needed to label
rates usurious. Inevitably the debtor gave sworn but unsupported testimony,
whereas the moneylender provided documentation. Testimony under oath was

not enough to satisfy the court in rendering a decision against a moneylender who had written evidence.[39]

While trying to improve the land regime, HMG generated profound disillusionment through its well-intentioned efforts. Failure to assist the peasantry's plight fostered the widespread impression that HMG supported only Zionism. A Palestine Arab newspaper editorial noted in early 1932, "If government intended to help the people, it would have not shelved the recommendations of the Commissions of Inquiry [*Shaw Report* and *Hope-Simpson Report*] which gave a deplorable account of the distressing conditions of the *fellaheen*. All this willful negligence drives the people to suspect every act or scheme which the government signifies to carry out . . . and its biased attitude toward the Zionists."[40]

HMG's intervention in the land regime forced British administration officials to arbitrate and intervene between communities. This change to an action-oriented policy generated three significant consequences.

First, it evolved into a committed, paternalistic defense by HMG of the Arab population in general, with the ultimate imposition of Jewish land transfer and immigration prohibitions through the May 1939 white paper. The consensus of British policy was that "the Arab landowner had to be protected against himself and the Arab tenant protected against land sale motivations of the Arab landowner."[41]

A second result of the Palestine administration's steady intervention in the land sphere was the exacerbation of existing disputes in Arab villages. By establishing new laws and bureaucratic procedures, the Palestine administration official became the ultimate arbitrator on matters such as trespass, imprisonment for debt forfeiture, agricultural tenancy claims, and boundary disputes. When these laws and procedures were implemented in the early 1930s, British officials who perhaps personally sided with the plight of the Palestinian peasant generally ruled against peasants' claims for tenancy privileges for lack of written proof of a rental or tax record. HMG's earlier promises of assistance to the peasantry then rang hollow, insincere, and characteristic of a governmental policy interested only in furthering Zionist development. Rural Arab attitudes toward HMG grew increasingly unfriendly.

In a third result of additional British support for the peasantry, the Zionist leadership increased internal coordination among its sometimes disputatious organizations and their directorates. Jewish Agency officials demonstrated that they were not responsible for creating an Arab landless class. On the other hand, whenever possible, Zionists privately tried to dilute the contents or delay the implementation of HMG ordinances intended to tie the peasantry to

the land. The more overt British policy in the land sphere renewed the
Zionists' drive to create a Jewish National Home.

Conclusions

Numerous unrelated factors deferred another outbreak of communal violence
until 1936. HMG created a false sense of hope that it would assist the rural
population by extricating it from financial misery and by halting development
of the Jewish National Home, adopting a series of procedures and laws to keep
the peasant on land and creating administrative processes that resulted in the
postponement of evictions or court judgments against the peasantry. When the
process of Jewish land purchase involved acquiring smaller parcels from more
buyers, land sales negotiations were prolonged and the peasantry's physical
displacement was delayed. The time from initial contractual agreements to
possession by the new Jewish owner could be three to five years. On legally
purchased Jewish land, Arab tenants remained until the land was transferred
in the land registry offices; sometimes they stayed until physically evicted.

In most rural areas of Palestine, sustenance for the peasantry reached
sufficiently low levels in 1931 and 1932 that municipal councils in Beisan,
Nablus, and Hebron distributed free flour for bread. In 1933 and 1934, peas-

Peasant transport to market in Jordan, ca. 1936.

ants and tribesmen south of Jerusalem, in the plateau west of Nablus, in the Jordan Valley, and east of the Jenin-Tiberias road were despondent because of heavy stock losses, unexpected cold weather, lack of pasture, and a succession of bad harvests. In 1935, wheat and barley were again distributed by British officials to meet the peasants' needs.[42] There were four consecutive years of inadequate and flawed seeds for coming agricultural seasons. Despite the full or partial remission in the tithe each year from 1931 through 1935, the peasantry remained generally impoverished. Many could not pay back their outstanding debts. Government public works projects helped to absorb Arabs displaced because of either economic woes or Jewish land purchase.

In 1935, British officials in Palestine concurred with High Commissioner Wauchope that rural destitution was linked to the potential for communal violence. Prior to the outbreak of the general strike the situation was bleak: "An air of poverty and depression pervades most Arab villages. The fellah bears a heavy load of debts which robs him of most of his earnings and deprives him of the capital required for the amelioration of his land or the improvement of his crops. Any additional effort made merely increases the usurer's share in the produce but does not benefit the cultivator himself to any great extent. . . . Extortion and maladministration extending over many generations have had their inevitable effect. The combination of these factors have reduced the fellaheen to a state of overwhelming poverty."[43]

The British high commissioner realized that the land dispossession process would continue to create a "universal depression among Arabs, particularly in the hill districts." HMG had a foreboding that "with a disconcerted population there [was] always liability to disturbance and a sense of injury now directed against the British Government." The most senior Zionist officials associated with land purchases and Jewish settlement in Palestine—Menachem Ussishkin, Moshe Shertok, Arthur Ruppin, and Abraham Granovsky—agreed at a meeting in February 1936 that land disputes had reached unparalleled frequency and proportions in part because there was no "empty" land to purchase. Hajj Amin al-Husayni, the Mufti of Jerusalem and the head of the Supreme Muslim Council in Palestine, injected into the already charged political environment Islamic religious symbols as motivational platforms to fuel political activism against the Jews and against land sales. In Palestine in 1934, a *fetwa* issued against land sales to Jews said that selling land was "a grave sin" and that whoever sold land "necessarily commits infidelity and apostasy" as well as "treason." People engaged in land brokerage and land sales were not to be accorded Muslim burial privileges.[44]

From April 1936 through early 1939, the general strike evolved into a peasant rebellion against British rule, Zionist development, and landowning interests. There was the muffled fervor of unfulfilled political aspirations. Equally important, the general strike and revolt were also a class and inter-communal struggle, for the peasantry rebelled against the urban elites and often against their local village leaders. In commenting on the violence perpetrated in the 1936–39 general strike and revolt, W. F. Abboushi noted that there was "an unleashing of rural anger against urban timidity. The worst casualties were among city dwellers who had government affiliations, such as Arab policemen, civil servants, and mayors. But there were also casualties among members of the wealthy big families."[45]

The armed bands that composed the backbone of the rebellion were re-cruited almost entirely from the peasant classes. Roving and mobile gangs attacked Jewish settlements and British institutions. From the standpoint of the urban hierarchy, the duration and scope of the general strike and revolt were unanticipated and, at least initially, unmanageable. Urban notables, grain merchants, landowners, and moneylenders who had exerted tight rein over village life three or four decades earlier had lost considerable control over portions of the countryside in Palestine by the mid-1930s. Within the rural setting, the revolt revealed vicious struggles between peasant bands just as traditional leaders were assassinated for collaborating with either the Brit-ish or the Zionists. In 1938 campaigns of murder, sabotage, gang warfare, and terrorism seriously impaired economic life in the country.[46] Mukhtars were killed, landowners attacked, British officials assassinated, old village scores settled, Zionist immigrants murdered, and land brokers intimidated. These manifestations of violence were profoundly different in intent and intensity from the periodic minor land disputes that occurred during harvest time or that resulted from trespassing.

Acts of violence and intimidation by the rural bands caused many promi-nent Arabs to leave Palestine. The voluntary departures, the assassinations, and expulsions of the urban political elite left the Palestinian Arab community virtually leaderless. As a result of the general strike and revolt, the Arab Palestinian national movement was shown to be vulnerable to the influence and political control of neighboring Arab states. Some traditional sources of authority, like the local *shaykh* and mukhtar, were by this time politically or socially inconsequential or thoroughly discredited, leaving villagers "un-protected" against British governmental intervention and growing Jewish domination.[47] Divisiveness between village bands added to the fragmentation of Palestinian Arab society.

Embedded in the general strike and revolt were a variety of disparate

components, including racial, religious, anticolonial, anti-Zionist, and famil-
ial factors, as well as peasant destitution and rural change. Village populations
were angry, jealous, and fearful of the Jewish immigrants; they were frustrated with the inability or unwillingness of their urban and local leaders or the
British to assist them in any substantive fashion. High Commissioner
Wauchope believed that the unrest from 1936 to 1939, while certainly contain-
ing a distinctly political component, had economic destitution as its core.[48]

Repeatedly, HMG and the Palestine administration found themselves unable to validate their public promises of assistance to the peasantry. British
officials were naturally but unfairly viewed as totally prejudiced umpires
"controlled" by the Zionists, who themselves had taken control of land that
the peasant and his ancestors had once farmed. The peasant could not compete
against these inhospitable forces. He could not manage the emerging monetary economy.

Palestinian rural communal bonds wilted under the dual stresses of external
intrusion and internal village degeneration. The decline of the mushaʿ system
and the decrease in authority of the mukhtar and even the moneylender left the
peasantry adrift, landless, destitute, and dependent on British paternalism.
From 1936 to 1939, the Palestinian peasantry expressed its anger and frustration in part against all those it considered responsible for creating, maintaining, and reinforcing an oppressive and irreparable rural environment. The
general strike and revolt saw Palestinian Arab society go into a collective
convulsion from which it would emerge with its only unanimity its hostility to
Zionism and an emerging Palestinian Arab national feeling.

At the conclusion of the revolt, Great Britain formalized its position as
paternalistic protector of the Arab population in Palestine with the passage of
the May 1939 white paper. By the end of the 1930s, overwhelming rural
changes and destitution engulfed the Palestinian peasantry and left rural Palestine irresolute, leaderless, and incapable of competing with Zionism's relentless thrust forward into the 1940s.

Notes

1. See Great Britain Command Papers, Palestine, *Palestine Royal Commission
Report* (hereafter *Peel Report*), cmd. 5479 (London: His Majesty's Stationery Office,
1937); W. F. Abboushi, "The Road to Rebellion: Arab Palestine in the 1930s,"
Journal of Palestine Studies (Spring 1977): 23–46; Yehuda Bauer, "The Arab Revolt
of 1936," *New Outlook*, pt. 1 (July/August 1966): 49–57, pt. 2 (September 1966):
21–28; Tom Bowden, "The Politics of the Arab Rebellion in Palestine 1936–1939,"

Middle Eastern Studies (May 1975): 147–74; Zvi el-Peleg, "The 1936–1939 Disturbances: Riot or Rebellion?" *The Wiener Library Bulletin* (1978): 40–51; Yehoshua Porath, *The Palestine Arab National Movement, 1929–1939* (London: Cass, 1977), 109–273; and Theodore R. Swedenburg, "Memories of Revolt: The 1936–39 Rebellion and the Struggle for the Palestinian National Past" (Ph.D. diss., University of Texas at Austin, 1988), 110.

2. See Abboushi, "The Road to Rebellion," 42; Yuval Arnon-Ohanna, *Fellaheem Bamered Ha'aravi Beeretz Yisrael [Fellaheen in the Arab Revolt in Eretz Yisrael (Palestine)]* (Tel Aviv University, Shiloah Institute, 1978); Yuval Arnon-Ohanna, "The Bands in the Palestinian Arab Revolt, 1936–1939: Structure and Organization," *Asian and African Studies* (1981): 229–47; Ghassan Kanafani, "Thawrah 1936–1939 fi Filastin," *Shu'un Filastiniyyah* (1972): 45–77; and Subhi Yasin, *Al-Thawrah al-'Arabiyyah al-Kubra fi Filastin [The Great Arab Revolt in Palestine]* (Cairo: Dar al-Kitab, 1967.)

3. See Sarah Graham Brown, "The Political Economy of Jabal Nablus, 1920–1948," in *Studies in the Economic and Social History of Palestine in the Nineteenth and Twentieth Centuries,* ed. Roger Owen (Oxford: At the University Press, 1982), 88–176; Ylana Miller, *Government and Society in Rural Palestine 1920–1948* (Austin: University of Texas Press, 1985); Roger Owen, "Economic Development in Mandatory Palestine, 1918–1948," in *The Palestinian Economy,* ed. George T. Abed (London: Routledge, 1988), 13–36; and Kenneth W. Stein, "Palestine's Rural Economy, 1917–1939," *Studies in Zionism* (Spring 1987): 25–49.

4. Kenneth W. Stein, *The Land Question in Palestine, 1917–1939* (Chapel Hill: University of North Carolina Press, 1984), 20–21.

5. For an exceedingly informative history describing the development of large private estates and tenant-landlord relationships in nineteenth-century Palestine, see Leon Schulman, *Zür Türkischen Agrarfrage Palästina und die Fellachenwirtschaft* (Weimar, 1916), esp. 44–57. On Syria and Iraq, see Philip S. Khoury, *Syria and the French Mandate: The Politics of Arab Nationalism, 1920–1945* (Princeton, N.J.: Princeton University Press, 1987), 8–10, 60–63; Abdul Latif Tabawi, *A Modern History of Syria* (London: St. Martin's, 1969); and Hanna Batatu, *The Old Social Classes and the Revolutionary Movements of Iraq* (Princeton, N.J.: Princeton University Press, 1978), 83–152.

6. Government of Palestine, *Report by the Registrar of Cooperative Societies in Palestine on Developments During the Years 1921–1937* (Jerusalem: Government Printing Press, 1938), 10–11.

7. Government of Palestine, *Report of a Committee on the Economic Conditions of Agriculturalists in Palestine and Fiscal Measures of Government in Relation Thereto* (hereafter *Johnson-Crosbie Report*) (Jerusalem: Government Printing Press, 1930); and Stein, *The Land Question in Palestine,* 26–28.

8. Schulman, *Zür Türkischen Agrarfrage Palästina,* 65; Ernest Dowson, *Preliminary Study of Land Tenure in Palestine* (1924), Israel State Archives (hereafter ISA), box 3571/file 1; Government of Palestine, *Report by Mr. C. F. Strickland of the Indian Civil Service on the Possibility of Introducing a System of Agricultural Cooperation in Palestine* (Jerusalem: Government Printing Press, 1930), 11; Arthur Ruppin, *Syrien als Wirtschaftsgebiet* (Berlin: Kolonial-Wirtschaftliches Komitee Verlag, 1917), 31.

9. Gad Frumkin, *Derech Shofat Beyerushalaim* [The Path of a Judge in Jerusalem] (Tel Aviv: Dvir Company Ltd., 1954) 305.

10. Letter from High Commissioner Sir Arthur Wauchope to Secretary of State for the Colonies Phillip Cunliffe-Lister, April 15, 1933, Colonial Office (hereafter CO) record group 733/box 230/file 17429, pt. 1.

11. Ernest Dowson, *Progress on Land Reforms, 1923–1930*, 27–28, CO 733/221/97169; *Report on the State of the Ghor Mudawarra Demarcation Commission*, March 19, 1932, ISA, Box 3548/file 1; Albert Abramson, former Commissioner of Lands in Palestine, "An Aspect of Village Life in Palestine," *Palestine Post*, July 6, 1937.

12. Letter from Hilmi Husseini, Inspector of Lands, Northern District to Director of Lands, July 14, 1923, ISA, box 3317/file 6.

13. Great Britain, *Palestine Royal Commission Memoranda Prepared by the Government of Palestine*, memo no. 13, "Rural Indebtedness" (London: His Majesty's Stationery Office, 1937), 41–43.

14. Maurice C. Bennett, Land Officer, Office of the Commissioner of Lands, *Memorandum on the Village Congress of 1929*, February 3, 1930, ISA, M 3380/file 2.

15. Ibid.; Great Britain, *Palestine Royal Commission Memoranda Prepared by the Government of Palestine*, memo no. 14, "Measures Taken to Provide Agricultural Credit" (London: His Majesty's Stationery Office, 1937), 45–48.

16. Ibid.

17. See Sa'id B. Himadeh, ed., *Economic Organization of Palestine* (Beirut: American University of Beirut Press, 1938), 125.

18. See Albert Hourani, *Syria and Lebanon* (Oxford: At the University Press, 1945), 86–87; Philip S. Khoury, *Urban Notables and Arab Nationalism: The Politics of Damascus, 1860–1920* (Cambridge: At the University Press, 1983), 27, 28, 94; Stephen Longrigg, *Iraq, 1900 to 1950* (Oxford: At the University Press, 1968), 30–31; Taysir N. Nashif, *The Palestine Arab and Jewish Political Leaderships* (New York: Asia Publishing House, 1979), 1–58; and Alfred Bonne, *State and Economics in the Middle East* (London: Routledge and Kegan Paul, 1960), 117–38. See also Paul J. Klat, "Musha Holdings and Land Fragmentation in Syria," *Middle East Economic Papers* (1958): 12–23; David Ben-Gurion, Remarks before the Palestine Royal Commission, Notes of Evidence, January 7, 1937, Central Zionist Archives (hereafter CZA), record group S25/file 4642.

19. See Schulman, *Zür Türkischen Agrarfrage Palästina*, 47.

20. Salim al-Tabir, *Village Congress Proposals*, November 14, 1929, ISA, box M3380/file 2.

21. Letter from Herbert Samuel to Lord Curzon, April 2, 1920, Herbert Samuel Archives, ISA; note by Sydney Moody, Political Report for January 1923, minute sheet, February 23, 1923, CO 733/42/8933; Afif I. Tannous, "The Arab Village Community," *Annual Report of the Smithsonian Institute* (1943), 236.

22. For an example of cases brought before administrative review in the Tulkarm subdistrict that shed light on the social gap between landlord and tenants, see ISA, box 3384/files TR/41/33, TR/204/33 and TR/441/33, and dozens of others.

23. See letter from Abdul Latif Tabawi to Assistant District Commissioner Nablus, November 16, 1934, in the case of *Abdul Latif Tabawi* vs. *Tenants Kamil Amrur, Abdul Fattah Amrur, and Abdul Hafiz Amrur*, ISA, box M 3922/file TR/114/33.

24. On danger to mukhtars, see notes by A. T. O. Lees, Palestine Land Settlement Officer, October 10, 1937, CO 733/329/75072/11; letter from High Commissioner Sir Harold MacMichael to Lord Moyne, Secretary of State for the Colonies, November 10, 1941, CO 733/447/76117. For examples of mukhtars seeking personal enrichment in village land matters, see Al-Jami'ah al-'Arabiyyah, April 22, 1931; Gaza Settlement Officer to Commissioner of Lands, June 17, 1938, ISA, box LS 274/file 4/folio 33; "Land Speculation," ISA, box 2637/file G536. See also Miller, Government and Society in Rural Palestine, 56–62; and Gabriel Baer, "The Office and Functions of the Village Mukhtar," in Palestinian Society and Politics, ed. Joel S. Migdal (Princeton, N.J.: Princeton University Press, 1980), 103–23. On mukhtar salaries, see letter from Wauchope to Cunliffe-Lister, December 7, 1933, CO 733/244/17270. Peel Report, 345.

25. 'Adb al-Wahhab al-Kayyali, ed., Wathi'iq al-Muqawama al-Filastiniyyah al-'Arabiyyah didd al-Ihtilal al-Baratani wa al-Sahyuniyyah, 1918–1939 [Documents of Palestinian Arab Resistance against British and Zionist Occupation, 1918–1939] (Beirut: Institute for Palestine Studies, 1968), document #142, January 14, 1934, 357–58. See also Stein, The Land Question in Palestine, 65–79, 228–39.

26. Government of Palestine, Census for Palestine, 1931 (Alexandria: Whitehead Morris Limited, 1933), 1:291.

27. Census for Palestine, 1931 (Alexandria: Whitehead Morris Limited, 1933), 2:10–11; Stein, The Land Question in Palestine, appendix 2, "Absolute Increase of Registered Jewish Land Purchase Excluding Government Concessions, 1882–1945," 226–27; Anglo-American Committee of Inquiry, A Survey of Palestine (Palestine: Government Printer, 1946), 1:141; Esco Foundation for Palestine, Palestine: A Study of Jewish, Arab and British Policies (New Haven, Conn.: Yale University Press, 1947), 1:497.

28. Letter from Arthur Ruppin to Chaim Weizmann, January 30, 1930, CZA, Z4/3450. See also findings from Government of Palestine, Commission on the Disturbances of August 1929 (hereafter Shaw Report), cmd. 3530 (London: His Majesty's Stationery Office, 1930); and Government of Palestine, Report on Immigration, Land Settlement, and Development (hereafter Hope-Simpson Report), cmd. 3686 (London: His Majesty's Stationery Office, 1930).

29. On the decline in land, see Johnson-Crosbie Report, 22; Hope-Simpson Report, 64; Census for Palestine, 1931 1:22; The Jewish Agency, Land Policy in Palestine (1936), CZA S25/6916; Joseph Weitz, Yomani [My Diary] (Ramat Gan, Israel: Masada Publishing House, 1965), 1:119. On the proposed law, see Memorandum on points likely to be raised with the Secretary of State for the Colonies by the Arab Deputation from Palestine (January 1936), CO 733/297/75156, pt. 1. On the peasants in the revolt, see League of Nations, Permanent Mandates Commission Minutes, 25th session, May 31, 1934, 14, 27th session, June 2, 1935, 39. See also Abboushi, "The Road to Rebellion," 40–46; Arnon-Ohanna, "The Bands in the Palestinian Arab Revolt," 229–33.

30. See Kenneth W. Stein, "The Jewish National Fund: Land Purchase Methods and Priorities, 1924–1939," Middle Eastern Studies (April 1984): 190–205. For statistics on the increased number of smaller sales in the early 1930s, see the British administration monthly land sale statistics in Stein, The Land Question in Palestine, 181.

31. *Al-Hayat* (Jerusalem), September 8, 1930.

32. *Al-Ikdam*, January 19, 1931.

33. See Land Settlement Ordinance, 1928, *Official Gazette*, January 26, 1928. On the "best land" concept, see Government of Palestine, *Department of Surveys Report for Years 1940–46*, CO 814/40.

34. *Official Gazette*, June 16, 1931, 471.

35. "Report of the Committee on State Domain on the Proposal to Exempt State Domain from the Provisions of the Cultivators (Protection) Ordinance," enclosure in a letter from Sir Harold MacMichael, High Commissioner for Palestine, to Lord Moyne, Secretary of State for the Colonies, June 28, 1941, CO 733/447/76117.

36. Note on Land Disputes Possession Ordinance, 1931, CO 733/209/87343.

37. Michael F. J. McDonnell, *Law Reports of Palestine, 1920–1933*, High Court no. 92 of 1932, 2:860–64.

38. Extract from Annual Report of the Palestine Government for 1933, CO 733/278/75156, pt. 1, folio 75; letter from Lewis Andrews to Chaim Arlosoroff, head of the Jewish Agency, March 4, 1933, CZA, S25/7622. For a full discussion of the landless Arab inquiry see Stein, *The Land Question in Palestine*, 146–68. On peasants' disappointment, see *Al-Jami'ah al-Islamiyyah*, September 2, 1932.

39. Government of Palestine, *The Banking Situation in Palestine* (London: Westminster Bank Limited, 1936), 80.

40. *Merat al-Shark*, February 3, 1932. For some of the many cases in the Palestine Arab press showing the belief that the British intended to change aspects of the land regime in order to assist Zionist growth, see *Al-Carmel*, January 27, 1932; *Al-Jami'ah al-'Arabiyyah*, October 10, 1934, June 17, 1935; *Filastin*, February 2, 1935; *Al-Liwa*, February 12, 1936.

41. Minutes by J. E. Shuckburgh, Colonial Office official, January 14, 1940, CO 733/425/75872/2.

42. See remarks under "Land Regime" in *Report(s) by His Majesty's Government in the United Kingdom of Great Britain and Northern Ireland to the Council of the League of Nations and the Administration of Palestine and Transjordan for the Year(s) 1930, 1931, 1932, 1933, 1934, 1935, 1936, 1937, and 1938*, colonial nos. 59, 75, 82, 94, 104, 112, 129, 146, and 166 (London: His Majesty's Stationery Office). See also Stein, "Palestine's Rural Economy," 40–43; and *Al-Jami'ah al-'Arabiyyah*, March 4, 1934.

43. Government of Palestine, *Report by the Registrar of Cooperative Societies on Developments During the Years 1921–1937* (Jerusalem, 1938), 10–11.

44. On HMG's forebodings, see letters from Wauchope to Cunliffe-Lister, February 11, December 7, 1935, CO 733/278/75156. On the Zionist meeting, see Protocol of a Joint Meeting between the Jewish Agency Executive, the Jewish National Fund, and the Palestine Land Development Company, February 19, 1936, CZA S25/6538. On Islamic religious activity, see Criminal Investigation Department Reports, August 30, October 7, 1933, Foreign Office (hereafter FO) 371/file 16926, and December 19, 1933, FO 371/17878; *Al-Jami'ah al-'Arabiyyah*, September 16, 1932; and *Al-Difa'*, November 5, 1934. See also Uri M. Kupferschmidt, *The Supreme Muslim Council Islam under the British Mandate for Palestine* (Leyden: Brill, 1987), 242–47.

45. Abboushi, "The Road to Rebellion," 42–44.

46. Anglo-American Committee of Inquiry, *A Survey of Palestine* (Palestine, 1946), 1:44. See Stein, "Palestine's Rural Economy," 44–46.

47. This conclusion is arrived at independently by Miller, *Government and Society in Rural Palestine,* 88.

48. Letter from Wauchope to Secretary of State, December 29, 1936, CO 733/297/75156, pt. 5.

9

Colonization and Resistance: The Egyptian Peasant Rebellion, 1919

REINHARD C. SCHULZE

To date no other anticolonial movement in the Near East has been as clearly defined a national revolution as the so-called Egyptian revolution (*thawra*) of 1919.[1] The consensus is that this revolution was fought for all those goals that are the essence of the struggle for national independence—independence, self-determination, freedom, and national identity. As in all national movements, the Egyptians personified their national identity in the figure of a leader, the former president of Parliament and minister of education, Saʿd Zaghlul.[2] With the creation of a national alliance in autumn 1918 the Delegation (al-Wafd) party had established the organizational prerequisites and platform for the movement. With a structure, platform, and leadership in place, mass support had to be mobilized to transform goals into realities without compromising individual social, ethnic, or economic interests.[3]

The nationalist interpretation of history holds that the latent support of the Egyptian masses became active when the British authorities prohibited the public activities of the Wafd and exiled Zaghlul and three other leading figures of the movement to Malta. As Nadav Safran summarizes the revolution, "The whole nation, fellah and pasha, illiterate and educated, Muslims and Copts, men and women, stood behind Saʿd Zaghlul, fighting with great courage and heavy sacrifice in apparent support of the Liberal Nationalist ideals he represented."[4] This struggle lasted two months, until the masses were defeated by the military power of the colonial regime. The nationalists, however, turned to other means, which finally led to Egypt's independence in 1922–23.[5]

Various theoretical and methodological problems make it difficult to shift our viewpoint away from the elite classes to the rural population, which is generally regarded as producing the foot soldiers of a national revolution. Historical records of direct observation of the rural population are rare. Even oral history does not help much in this respect.[6] The peasant's understanding of the world is connected to a specific structural system consisting of the media, forms of discourse, and procedures tied to a semiotic system, which can only be understood in context.[7] As long as this system is not accessible, the conclusions drawn to reconstruct the historical heterogenity of any process have only limited validity. The following discussion of the events of March and April 1919 should be understood with this in mind.

Colonization of the Egyptian Agrarian Society

If the term *colonization* is used to mean the systematic restructuring of a regional economy, whereby the ultimate goal is to integrate it into a superimposed division of labor, hierarchized and centralized on the basis of capitalist production, then Egypt was being colonized in the second decade of the nineteenth century. The starting point was 1820–21, when long-staple cotton was cultivated as an irrigated summer crop for the first time. Simultaneously, rents drawn from land entered the capital circulation process as the new mode of exploitation obliged the privatization of land, and the villagers' collective responsibility for taxes and conscription strengthened the bonds of the individual to the expanding state.[8]

Colonization created a new social sector within the three traditional social estates, the city dwellers, the country or agrarian class, and the nomads. This new sector was economically dependent on the extensive cultivation of the two most important cash crops, cotton and sugarcane.[9]

The colonization of the Egyptian agrarian estate was actually an uneven process that took place over a period stretching from 1820 to the beginning of World War I. This unevenness was caused by the pace of geographical expansion, but the agricultural potential of the various regions within the colonization project, and by the degree of urbanization within the respective social estates.[10]

Regionalization of the Agrarian Estate

The process discussed here, limited to only the most important events, had far-reaching consequences for Egyptian agrarian society. The most noticeable manifestation on the social level was the urbanization of the former autarchic social relationships of the village community. The village shaikh lost much of his power to the representatives of the colonial bureaucracy, creating a sort of double administration in the village.[11] The village watchmen, for example, previously agents of the village shaikh, became salaried agents of an anonymous state. Property control and cotton cultivation increasingly became the decisive factors in social differentiation,[12] determining an individual's material worth and defining his living standard and social position within the village. In the new cotton latifundias (*'izab*) the level of one's salary replaced the existing measures of socioeconomic differentiation. Simultaneous with the social changes, until the beginning of the twentieth century (that is, up to the conclusion of the first colonization phase) the geographical and economic asymmetry of colonial expansion superimposed various new regions over traditional divisions.

Four criteria allow us to measure the specific historical relationship of a region, even of each locality, to the colonization process: per capita production,[13] extent of cotton cultivation,[14] property structure,[15] and division of labor.[16] Seen from an economic point of view, regionalization did not mean creating autonomous units but rather incorporating labor into the overall colonial system. Regions such as southern Upper Egypt, where subsistance farming predominated, were integrated into the system by providing the needed reserves of migratory labor for cotton cultivation areas of the Delta. Around 1910 the following regions had been formed.[17]

I. The Central Delta
   Per capita production (PCP) LE 11–13
   IA. South: Southwest-Gharbiyya, North-Manufiyya, South-
       Daqahliyya, Southwest-Sharqiyya
       Cotton cultivation: since 1821
       Social structure; well-balanced, tendency toward farm
       labor/property ownership
       Land tenure: almost 50 percent of the cultivated area (CA) under
       large property ownership (LPO)
       (direct cultivation)
   IB. North: East-Buhaira, Central-Gharbiyya, Central-Daqahliyya, Kafr
       Saqr (Sharqiyya), Southeast-Qalyubiyya
       Cotton cultivation: since 1850–60 on poor soil with low yield per
       feddan
       Social structure: as in IA, with more farm labor

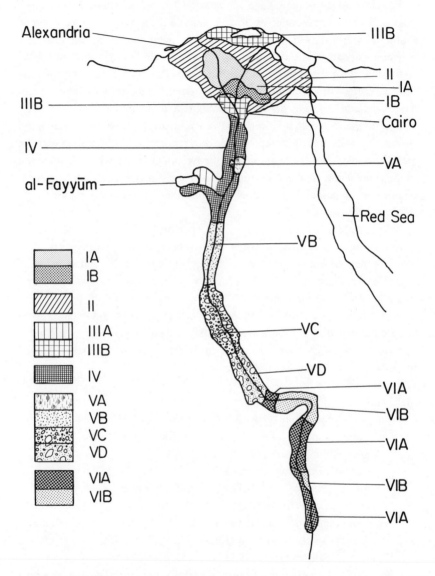

MEDITERRANEAN

Alexandria — IIIB

II
IA
IB
Cairo

IIIB

IV

al-Fayyūm

VA

Red Sea

VB

VC

VD

VIA

VIB

VIA

VIB

VIA

	IA
	IB
	II
	IIIA
	IIIB
	IV
	VA
	VB
	VC
	VD
	VIA
	VIB

Map of the colonial regionalization of Egypt, ca. 1910.

Land tenure: up to 70 percent of the cultivated area under large property ownership (direct cultivation) on large commercial properties ('izab)

II. Inner Delta Periphery
PCP: LE 11–12
West Buhaira, North-Gharbiyya, North Daqahliyya, North, East, and South Sharqiyya
Cotton cultivation: since 1880–90 in the course of land repossession
Social structure: dominated by leasehold on large properties (*isti'jar*)[18]
Land tenure: up to 70% cultivated area under large property ownership, 'izab (indirect culture)

III. Outer Delta Periphery
PCP: LE 8–10
IIIA. Southern Delta
IIIB. Delta coastal areas
Cotton cultivation: less than 10 percent of cultivated area in III(A), none at all in III(B)
Social structure: predominately land owners
Land tenure: predominately medium [III(A)], small [III(B)]

IV. Middle Egypt
PCP: LE 8–10 (exception, Fayyum: PCP: LE 12.8)
Giza (excluding al-'Ayyat), Bani Suwaif (excluding al-Wasita)
Cotton cultivation: less than 7 percent of the cultivated area
Social structure: predominantly leasehold (isti'jar)
Special case: Fayyum
Land tenure: large property ownership up to 23 percent of the cultivated area
Cotton cultivation: 28 percent of the cultivated area
Social structure: most probably as in IB, i.e., large number of farm laborers, statistically, however, not recorded
Property ownership: 40 percent cultivated area under large property ownership

V. Upper Egypt I
PCP: LE 9–13
VA. al-'Ayyat/Giza, al-Wasita/Bani Suwaif
Cotton cultivation: as much as 20 percent of the cultivated area;

sugarcane especially at al-'Ayyat
Social structure: predominantly leaseholders and farm labor
Property ownership: predominantly medium-sized holdings
VB. North-Minya
Cotton cultivation: 30 percent of cultivated area
Social structure: farm labor and *musharaka*-lease, hardly any
property owners
Land tenure: large property ownership up to 50 percent of
cultivated area
VC. South-Minya, North-Asyut
Cotton cultivation: up to 30 percent of cultivated area
Social structure: farm labor far above average, very little
leasehold
Land tenure: large property ownership over 50 percent of
cultivated area
VD. South-Asyut
Cotton cultivation: less than 10 percent of cultivated area
Social structure: well-balanced

VI. Upper Egypt II
PCP: LE 6–7
VIA. Girga; Qena/Qena, Luxor/Qena, Isna/Qena; Idfu, Aswan
Cotton cultivation: none; sugarcane as monoculture
Social structure: leasehold predominant, farm labor slightly
above average
Property ownership: small holdings predominant
VIB. Nag' Hammadi/Qena, Dishna/Qena, Qus/Qena; ad-Dirr/Aswan
Cotton cultivation: none
Social structure: predominantly large property owners
Property ownership: widespread traditional large estate holdings

The statistical units used in this summary are certainly too general to define
the various structural entities clearly. The districts that determined the statistical boundaries had, nevertheless, an average of 123,000 inhabitants in 1910.

A comparison of the statistical data of the nineteenth century provides
evidence concerning the geographical expansion of the colonial economy.
Accordingly, incorporation began in Region IA (southern Delta Center) and
by 1880/90 had been extended as far as Region IB (northern Delta Center) and
farther to include Region II (Inner Periphery). The decisive factor here was

the improvement of the year-round irrigation system,[19] a prerequisite for extensive cultivation of the long-staple cotton needed for the specialized looms of the textile industry in Lancashire.

The areas of the outer Delta Periphery were either incorporated in the metropolitan area (Region IIIA) or marginalized (Region IIIB). Around 1870 the incorporation of the Fayyum Basin began. It was not followed by Upper Egypt until after 1900, with the construction of the first Aswan dam and the Asyut barrage. This incorporation was first confined, however, to Regions VB and VC (Minya and North Asyut) and afterwards expanded northwards.

The general heterogeneity of the Upper Egyptian area (the provinces Girga, Qena, and Aswan) is noteworthy. At the beginning of the twentieth century these districts had a high concentration of small landholders, farm laborers, and sharecroppers crowded into a small area. Girga can be regarded as a center for leaseholders, while the diversity in Qena, especially between Nag' Hammadi and Qus, is notable. Here only the area around the districts of Balyana/Girga and Nag' Hammadi/Qena is treated. Only about 45 kilometers apart, they exhibit two different social structures: in Balyana (or in the villages of Sahil al-Balyana),[20] few property owners cultivated their own land (the statistics register only 320 out of 48,570 recorded households, 0.7 percent). More than half the peasant households leased their land while the rest made their living through farm wage labor (36.1 percent). In the adjacent district of Nag' Hammadi/Qena, on the other hand, an area of approximately the same size (Balyana at 60,000 feddan, Nag' Hammadi at 80,000 feddan), were 28,800 landowners. Only 1.2 percent of the population was recorded as farm labor.

Similar variations existed in the bordering districts of Baba al-Kubra/Bani Suwaif and al-Fashn/Minya. Baba al-Kubra had a relatively high portion of landowners and an above-average share of leaseholders, with only 10 percent of the peasant households engaged in farm labor. In al-Fashn on the other hand, the proportion of landowners was almost as low as in Balyana, while that of farm workers reached almost 50 percent.

Such distinctive divisions could also be found in the Delta provinces, for example in the districts of Abu Hommos and Tah al-Barud, both in the Buhaira province. More than 77 percent of the households in Abu Hommos lived on leased land, and 20 percent were engaged in farm labor. Conversely, in Tah al-Barud the relationship was 20 percent and 62 percent, respectively. The distance from Region IB to II must have been especially short, since both Abu Hommos and Tah al-Barud represented the outer extremes of each region. Similarly, the distance from Region IIIA (Zifta) through IA and IB

(Talkha) (both in the province of Gharbiyya) to II (Mansura) was only 35 kilometers. While in Zifta almost 60 percent of peasant households could be identified as landowners, more than 60 percent of the families in Talkha were farm laborers.

The transformation of the social structure in the rural community depended, of course, on the form of land tenure and the agrarian economy of each region. In certain provinces, such as Gharbiyya, Minya, Fayyum, and Buhaira, the proportion of peasant private ownership to cultivated area lay between 50 and 70 percent. The rest was under state, semistate, or foreign ownership or divided among religious orders, which controlled their lands directly.[21] The provinces of Gharbiyya, Buhaira, and Daqhliyya were especially favored by larger agricultural firms and banks for capital investments. In the Upper Egyptian provinces of Fayyum, Minya, and Qena the social structure of the villages was formed by the semistate ownership (so-called *da'ira saniyya*)[22] of most of the land (a total of 338,536 feddans, 75 percent of which was located in these three provinces). Other large estates (especially in Region II) were leased to individual farmers (50–92 percent).

Likewise, the growing of cotton as a monoculture determined the form of the peasant social structure. In regions with good soil and an optimally functioning summer irrigation system (within a year-round irrigation system) yielding high net profits, the employment of farm laborers was profitable. In areas with poor soil and insufficient summer irrigation, however, the tendency toward leaseholds on large estates predominated. One feddan of cotton produced the following net profits in 1897:[23]

Region VB and VC	LE 11.45
Region IA and IB	LE 7.35
Region VA, Fayyum	LE 5.30
Region II	LE 2.20

Sugarcane, the major economic factor in Regions VIA and VIB, produced similar high net profits (LE 14.00 per feddan) but supported the leasehold system (for example, in Balyana).[24]

Opposition and Resistance

The schematic outline presented here of colonial expansion within Egyptian agrarian society not only led to a new classification of the regions based on the capitalist economy but also shaped the agrarian community's perceptions of the system of rule, of the state, and of the regime. The actions of each community and its reactions to increasing incorporation depended on three conditions: the relationship of the rural area to the economic nature of incorporation; the historical experience of the rural community with resistance; and the relationship of the rural areas to the bridgeheads of colonial society within their own world.

Incorporation created an objective reality for a new system of social interaction. The experimental introduction of cotton cultivation in the fields of Ottoman governor Muhammad 'Ali was at first passively opposed by the *fellahin* affected. Their resistance was directed against the cotton plant itself, since it was seen as a threat to wheat, until that time the predominant crop. Usually it sufficed to pull the cotton seedlings a few centimeters out of the ground to kill them. But financially motivated *dirigisme* on the part of the regime—which secured the monopoly of the cotton crop—and finally the linkage of private title to land to cotton cultivation in order to stimulate investment broke down resistance at an early stage.[25] If incorporation created a new reality based on the introduction of year-round irrigation (by 1897 this covered 100 percent of the cultivated area in the Delta regions and 37 percent in the area between Giza and Asyut),[26] the reaction of peasant communities often corresponded less to this reality and more to their own historical experiences of resistance. The extent of this discrepancy was a function of the type of colonial intervention and of the solidarity and survival power in each rural community. Rural areas that had been recently forced into a new social hierarchy during the process of increasing colonization and whose economies were based almost completely on cotton usually did not attack the new system, even in the worst of times, instead directing their resistance against the distribution of the new wealth and against the draining of this wealth into the cities.[27] At the other end of the spectrum were the regions where cotton cultivation was not very productive, which were primarily affected by the presence of a regime that wanted to incorporate them in the colonization process by military force. Here, the regime's main concern was not to institute a new agrarian system but to mobilize unexploited resources. At first the fellahin themselves were exploited as a new resource, conscripted into the army of the governor and assigned to forced labor. Then uncultivated fields were exploited by privatization and distribution among the officials of the regime. Finally, the region was exploited for its revenues. The result was that in the earlier colonial settlements, especially in the Delta Regions IA and IB, fellahin resistance was directed mainly against injustices, while in the occupied territories (especially Regions VIA and VIB) it was directed against the regime itself. Between these extremes fell numerous regional and local forms of resistance that also had their historal dimensions.

Without disregarding these specific differences it can be generally concluded that between 1820 and 1910 a gradual change from collective to individual resistance took place. Between 1820 and 1865 almost all resistance in the regions took the form of millenarian movements. From 1865 to 1907 British officials spoke of an "endemic trend" toward brigandage.[28] Finally, in the years from 1907 to 1914, one finds only records of so-called individual agrarian criminality.[29] Corresponding to the individualization of each *fellah* within his community, this trend was accelerated in regions with a large majority of migrant workers (*tarahil*). The fragmentation of the resistance, which could mobilize as many as 30,000 fellahin in the second decade of the nineteenth century, resulted from an increasingly present colonial regime, facilitated by a new multifaceted infrastructure that included the railroad.[30]

The investment boom in infrastructure and irrigation lasted approximately 60 years. During that time 30 million LE were invested in irrigation technology, 18 million LE in the Suez Canal, and at least 30 million in the railroads.[31] The fellahin had to carry the burden of increased taxes and to endure forced labor; they were forced to relinquish their subsistence base through the sale of land that had been privatized; they were confronted with a new technology that had little relevance to their rural interests.

The introduction of steam pumps and steam machines to aid the mechanization of farming failed, as did ambitious plans to develop a cotton- and sugarcane-processing industry in Egypt.[32] The boom lasted from 1861 to 1873. That year's worldwide recession presaged the decline of British industrial monopoly and led indirectly to diminished industrial investments in Egypt. At the end of the nineteenth century Egypt had approximately a hundred cotton gins and fifteen sugar refineries. About 60 percent of the cotton gins were located in Regions IA and IB; the refineries were mainly in Minya and Qina provinces.[33]

Colonization was personified by the civil servants and administrative authorities (irrigation inspectors, government inspectors, tax agents) posted to villages following the British occupation.[34] Transport improvements helped them to surface in "problem areas" in a relatively short time and to disappear after their duties were completed. Permanent administrative offices were established only in the larger provincial cities. For rural communities this meant a loss of the security that had been ensured by distance. State officials now appeared in the villages and forced themselves into the structure of district authority, replacing earlier forms of delegated authority. Such intervention in village regimes was not new, however; the eighteenth century had its traveling surveyors and tax collectors and the early nineteenth century its agrarian engineers, who tried to implement the decrees of the the regime. In almost every case such people acted under orders of a regional tax farmer (*multazim*), in most instances a person known in the district. The representatives of the colonial government who now appeared in the villages, however, were subordinate to an anonymous regime and could no longer be personally identified. This impersonality coupled with the efficiency of the infrastructure reduced the possibility of resisting the orders and decrees. Next to the old concept of *dawla* (regime), the new concept of *hukuma* (government) was added to the peasant consciousness to signify everything that constituted a state. The abstract character of the government, however, reduced the peasant perception of the state to those symbols and terms against which the rural population could defend itself.

At first the formation of the state crippled fellahin maneuverability. Only in circumstances where historical conditions forced the presence of the colonial regime to decline was it possible for them to revert to their traditional methods in order to improve their social and economic conditions. Convincing examples can be seen in the revolts of the fellahin during and after the British occupation of 1882. The following actions taken by peasants were recorded for March to September 1882: seizure of arms, partly by force, partly to strengthen the troops of the Egyptian military leader, Ahmad 'Urabi; seizure of harvests, generally organized by the village shaikhs, supposedly to supply food for the army; takeover of large estates with the declared objective of land redistribution; attacks on individual stewards of large estates.[35]

Documented revolts took place in the Delta provinces of Gharbiyya, Buhaira, Daqahliyya, and Qalyubiyya, as well as in the Upper Egyptian provinces of Bani Suwaif, Minya, and Asyut. In the Delta area it appeared that people revolted only between March and October, the interval between cotton planting and harvesting. In the Upper Egyptian provinces, on the other hand, fellahin occupied properties more continuously, even after military intervention by the British. The historical treatments of this period generally attempt to relate peasant resistance to larger political events, but when the so-called political background of such rebellions is unclear, peasants' actions become difficult to trace and are recorded only as "security problems" by police authorities.[36]

Peasants as Part of the Political Scene

With the expansion of colonial society into the Egyptian provinces after 1882, members of the so-called *afandiyya*—professionals such as doctors, lawyers, journalists, students from secular schools, and civil servants[37]—began to have direct contact with peasant society. Around the turn of the century the literary world began to discover and study the Egyptian peasant. The fellahin, however, were seldom understood within their real world but were viewed as symbols of millenial Egyptian history (the "eternal fellah") or as the heroic "son of the land" (*ibn al-balad*). In 1906, when a few fellahin from the village Dinshawai/Manufiyya defended their village poultry against British soldiers on an unofficial hunting excursion, one soldier was beaten and later died of sunstroke.[38] Colonial authorities and Egyptian intellectuals both reacted in a manner corresponding to their perception of peasant society. The authorities (British and Egyptian) condemned four peasants to be hung, imprisoned twelve others, and had another nine publicly flogged. The Egyptian intellectuals regarded the peasants as martyrs for the nation; hymns of praise for patriotism finally included the Egyptian peasant.[39]

From this time forward, the peasant seemed to become an important political factor, regarded as the object of politics by both the colonial regime and Egyptian intellectuals. The regime promoted integration of the peasant communities into the colonial society through a more or less successful agrarian policy. The intellectuals, however, believing themselves to be the representatives of all social groups and classes, felt their patriotism was sufficient to mobilize the peasants against the British colonial regime. Moreover, the structure of agrarian production provided the intellectuals with an opportunity to assail the local notables and to introduce their plans for cooperatives.[40] The political ambitions of the afandiyya, however, were not so quickly fulfilled. During the military revolt of Ahmad 'Urabi in 1881–82 it was already evident that the peasant community was not willing to mobilize simply as a tool of the elite.

As late as 1904 Egypt had still been considered a model of successful British colonial politics, but the economic crisis of 1907 initiated a sudden change. As in 1873 it was a crisis caused by overspeculation that ended in the bankruptcy of several large investment companies. The 294 companies established in Egypt between 1898 and 1907 had little capital at their disposal, with the greatest portion concentrated in the Compagnie Universelle du Canal de Suez, Bank of Egypt, and Société des Raffinéries. In the summer of 1907 overspeculation led to the collapse of more than 300 firms.[41]

This collapse certainly did not mean the end of the colonial system, but it did mark the high point of the first phase. The expansion of cotton production had reached a critical turning point. Profits per feddan stagnated as did yields (maximum 5.2 qantars/feddan).[42] Further expansion of the cultivable area was economically and technologically infeasible. At the same time the political crisis in the country reached a new high point. The events in Dinshawai ushered in a gradual decline in the loyalty of the colonial society to the British regime. The competition for power between the British authorities and the native economic and political elite (notables and afandiyya) threatened to undermine the ruling system in effect since 1882.[43] The British authorities withdrew from the countryside and confined themselves to the control of the

The Dinshawai incident took place in June 1906 when British officers, off on a pigeon-shoot, wounded the wife of the village *imam* (prayer leader). Angry villagers in turn wounded two British officers, and the other officers opened fire on the villagers. In the aftermath 52 villagers were arrested and put on trial. The special court at Shibin al-Kom condemned four to death, and on June 28 the sentences were carried out. Reprinted from *sahifa min tarikh Injiltarra fi Misr* (N.p., May 1, 1915).

most important cities, and the vacated positions gradually filled by local notables and colonial agents such as district officers or village chiefs. Security in the countryside was no longer guaranteed. Agrarian criminality reached a new high.

The Second Colonization

The Egyptian crisis was part of a global crisis that precipitated World War I and the restructuring of the world economy, a process that included Egypt. Not only were the colonial government restored and a consolidated colonial state created within four years, but a second phase of colonial expansion followed. After the Egyptian government declared war on the Austro-Hungarian and German Empires in August 1914 (despite the country's belonging to the Ottoman Empire by international law), four British officials assumed all legislative, executive, and later judicial powers.

The cotton harvest of autumn 1914 set the second phase of colonial restoration in motion. A sudden decline in world market prices caused the export value of cotton to drop 50 percent and the size of the harvest 15 percent. Capital investment in agriculture came to a standstill, and the irrigation system was jeopardized.[44] At this critical impasse, the military authorities fell back on the *étatist* intervention methods of Muhammad ʿAli. Cotton cultivation was put under state control to create an artificial shortage. By autumn 1915 the effects could already be felt. The demand for cotton on the world market in the summer of 1915 caused prices to climb steadily, quadrupling within four years. Alternating restrictive and liberal policies, the authorities were able to guarantee affordable and adequate cotton exports to Great Britain. Finally, in 1918 the state appropriated the entire cotton crop.[45] With the restoration of a state monopoly on cotton, the regime was also able to control the cultivation of foodstuffs in Egypt. Their availability helped guarantee the supply for British troops stationed in the country during the war, whose numbers peaked at about one million at the time of the Gallipoli campaign (figures from German archives). High cotton prices and payment of the British troops led to considerable inflation in Egypt and to a twentyfold increase in the amount of capital in circulation between 1913 and 1919.[46] Among the peasantry, new taxes, artificially deflated produce prices, and increasing rent, interest, and mortgage rates led to an increase in the debt level and to the confiscation of land and property by the leading agrarian and mortgage banks.[47] The Agricultural Bank of Egypt alone confiscated 47,571 feddan valued at £E 1,353,942. Approximately 10–15 percent of peasant property owners lost their land in this manner.[48]

Through the expansion of infrastructure many villages and cities formerly not incorporated into the central bureaucracy were now invested by the state authorities (military as well as civil). Government agencies stationed in the regions included the British army (British forces in Egypt approximately 100,000), a small Egyptian army (approximately 12,000),[49] special police forces (approximately 1,000–2,000), and, indirectly, the "watchmen" (*ghufara'*) (33,000 in 1913, 42,000 in 1919). After 1915 these units were sent into the villages to look for hidden weapons despite a ban on weapons since 1904. Allegedly, more than 100,000 firearms were confiscated.[50]

Colonial Administration Concerns

Having reasserted its control, the colonial administration had at least three areas of concern.

Control of cotton production. The Cotton Commission had several hundred agents at its disposal distributed over the entire cotton belt. Although its agents were actually paid by the military authorities, the commission was subject to the directives of the large trading companies of Alexandria and London.

Provision of food for the British troops. On November 3, 1917, Edmund Allenby, commander of the Egyptian Expeditionary Forces since June 27, 1917, ordered that all supplies for the British troops be provided by Egypt. To this end a Supplies Control Board was established on October 13, 1918, to control the requisition and confiscation of livestock and grains.

Conscription. Initial recruitment began in April 1915. Although the British Foreign Office had declared on August 4, 1914, that no Egyptian citizens could join the forces of the warring parties either as soldiers or sailors, the first 6,000 Egyptian volunteers were stationed in Gallipoli in August. In the summer of 1916 this number had increased to 40,000 and was incorporated into the Egyptian Labour Corps (ELC). The daily pay in 1916 of PT 3 was so inviting that enough Egyptians volunteered for the ELC or the Camel Transport Corps (CTC), also established in 1916. In autumn of 1916, however, the compulsory draft was extended, and 100,000 fellahin, especially from Upper Egypt, were already mobilized in January 1917. The Egyptian civil authorities painstakingly supported the compulsory draft. Between 1916 and 1919 more than 1.5 million fellahin were recruited, approximately one-third of the male population between seventeen and thirty-five.

Changing Nature of Peasant Resistance

This second phase of incorporation, pressed forward by the wartime emergency, was reflected in the gradual change in the character of peasant resistance already evident by 1915. Direct military control of the villages initially prevented any substantial collective revolt. At first resistance came from individual village headmen (*'umdah/'umad*), who passively disregarded the directives of the military authorities. In spring 1918 collective resistance to the presence of grain confiscation agents and draft officers could be seen in the villages of the Faqus and Sharqiyya districts.

More prominent was the rebirth of bandit groups, especially in the provinces of Buhaira and Minya. Several groups succeeded in controlling villages for long periods of time, although the already documented symbiosis between village and bandit group that had led to a sort of offensive/defensive alliance seemed to be declining. Instead, economically self-sufficient bandit groups developed, attacking even their own villages. Attacks on the railway were a speciality of the bandit groups of Upper Egypt.

The crime statistics of 1914–19 give little indication that the number of criminal cases in the countryside had changed. A preliminary analysis of classified criminal cases, however, indicates a shift from 1914 to 1919 in the types of crimes committed, from personal injury to murder (associated with revenge) and from petty theft to robbery (revenge and possession). From November to February of those years the number of murders and attempted murders averaged 100 per month, from March to October, 156 cases per month, reaching a highpoint in July with over 200 cases. As with large-scale revolts, it seems the willingness to settle conflicts by force increased in March and declined toward October, a pattern that coincided with the cotton cultivation cycle.

Despite statistical problems involved in the recording of criminal cases far from the seat of government, a sudden increase in the crime rate can be seen in 1918. Between 1914 and 1920, the following cases of murder, attempted murder, and robbery were recorded:

1914	1,677	(other cases 2,092)
1915	1,904	(" " 2,288)
1916	1,857	(" " 2,123)
1917	1,961	(" " 2,280)
1918	2,523	(" " 2,111)
1919	4,600	(" " 3,020)
1920	5,326	(" " 2,304)

These figures included only so-called crimes. Cases of agrarian crime (especially theft of crops, destruction of crops, poisoning of livestock) also increased significantly after the spring of 1918 (1917, 49,396; 1918, 56,303; 1919, 62,805). They were registered in greater numbers in the Central Delta regions and in the Upper Egyptian provinces of Bani Suwaif, Fayyum, and Minya (especially in Upper Egypt south of Asyut) than in the other regions.[51]

Competition for Control of the Colonial State

The reassertion of colonialism in Egypt during World War I promoted the development of a state consciousness within the native elite, since the state had now established itself as an important economic entity. Capital accumulation in Egypt increased as a consequence of the war economy and the mobilization of raw materials through development of infrastructure. Capital savings doubled and bank deposits quadrupled. The crisis of 1907, which led to the first concentration of capital and the establishment of a small number of large industrial concerns, was now followed by this new phase of accumulation and concentration.[52]

The greatest obstacle to further industrial development appeared to be the colonial state itself, whose policies ran counter to the interests of Egyptian capital.[53] Paralleling the struggle of the economic elite for control of the colonial system's economic structures was the afandiyya bid for political control of the state. The two groups established a political union on November 12–13, 1918. This relatively small group took the name al-Wafd, the Delegation, under the leadership of former Minister of Education and Justice Saʿd Zaghlul.[54]

The colonial authorities and the British Foreign Office rejected categorically all demands for independence. Britain's economy needed political control of the country as a guarantee of access to Egyptian resources.[55] As a result, the war economy was preserved after the end of the war. Conscription and grain confiscation were as commonplace as during the war years. Numerous commissions and authorities impeded the natural development of Egyptian capital and increasingly censored all political demands of the afandiyya and wealthy notables.

In response, the members of the Wafd tried to refute the accusations of the authorities that their group did not represent the people, in whose name they allegedly spoke. They organized a countrywide campaign to establish their legitimacy, whereby the leaders of the various districts, professional groups, and tribes acknowledged in writing the Wafd members as their representatives.[56] With the aid of the transportation infrastructure, the afandiyya were able to gather signatures in numerous villages. In contrast to 1881–82, when Ahmad 'Urabi, with the help of the provincial notables, attempted to persuade the fellahin to support the army, the fellahin in 1918–19 were expected to surrender their interests to the afandiyya and the economic elite. Of the political concepts that filtered into the rural communities through this petition campaign, three found expression: independence, freedom, and justice.

Within the rural community these three concepts (istiqlal, huriyya, 'adl) indicated a reality other than that perceived by the afandiyya. When a nationalist representative from Cairo came to a village and delivered an impassioned speech about Egypt's freedom, the fellahin in the audience applied these concepts to their own environment. They understood such a speech as a challenge to liberate their district from the oppression formed by the restrictions and repression of colonization. If the same speaker demanded justice, the fellahin heard a call for revenge, which in their minds brought about justice. Freedom meant to the fellahin release from the so-called three C's: *corvée* (forced labor),[57] *courbash* (whippings), and corruption. Corvée represented the state, courbash institutional violence, and corruption the members of the afandiyya and the nouveau riche in the villages ('isamiyyin).

To the afandiyya the fellahin appeared to react positively to their political campaign, and as a result a general strike was planned for March 1919. In case the military authorities did not meet nationalists' demands, at that time limited to the dispatch of an Egyptian delegation (al-Wafd) to the peace conference in Versailles, a boycott was to begin on March 15. The British authorities arrested Sa'd Zaghlul and three other members of the Wafd on the evening of March 18 and exiled them to Malta, throwing the political plans of the afandiyya into disarray. The badly planned, hectic student demonstrations of the following days underlined the national movement's own lack of authority to control the growing and diverse social movements and revolts that broke out within the week.[58]

The Rebellion of March 1919

The revolts of spring 1919 that began between the March 9 and 15 and lasted until May 1919 resulted in the deaths of over 3,000 Egyptians.[59] More than 100 villages were destroyed, 63 railroad stations were burnt, and the railway itself was damaged at over 200 points. It is impossible to summarize these revolts under one rubric, although they can be classed as neither a national revolution nor a national social revolution.[60] Their only common characteristic was simultaneity connected to the reassertion of colonialism in Egypt and its deep penetration into all levels of society. The afandiyya increasingly regarded the colonial state as the object of their efforts, while the heterogeneous agrarian societies saw the state as a negative entity. Egyptian peasants did not react as the nationalists had expected. They did not share the perception of colonial society as the object of the revolt. They perceived the danger to be the wholesale colonization of their economic life.

Political Autonomy

The demands for political autonomy—the seizure of control and decision-making positions within the colonial state—provided the basis for the numerous demonstrations that took place March 9–20 in Cairo and Alexandria.[61] Supported, led, and organized by the younger members of the afandiyya and students from the Islamic al-Azhar University, the demonstrators marched in orderly formation through the cities and returned afterward to the al-Azhar University, where representatives of the national movement addressed them. The economic elite limited itself to well-formulated written protests and sent telegrams throughout the world with their demands for the release of the exiles.

The British military authorities regarded the demonstrations as a danger to general security and as proof of the ingratitude and disloyalty of the colonial elite, who owed their existence to the colonial system. The military authorities broke up all demonstrations and almost all ended in a bloodshed. On the other hand the afandiyya failed in their attempt to integrate the "Egyptians" into their operations. Members of the traditional urban sectors of inner Cairo and Alexandria exploited the opportunity to attack the symbols of the colonial presence during demonstrations and later at random. At first only in the inner cities, later in the new urban areas, mobs looted stores, attacked police and members of the military, ransacked hotels, and finally attacked even the afandiyya. Behind these actions were primarily the so-called rabble (*ghawgha'* or *awbash*), the urban poor who made up nearly half the population of Cairo and had suffered the most from inflation in the years 1916–19. Numerous artisans had lost both their jobs and their workshops and were most affected by the general level of impoverishment.

However, a large-scale revolt by the urban poor never materialized, though signs of increasing social and communal autonomy could also be seen. Several quarters of the cities were systematically closed off to the outer world.

Trenches were dug right through the streets to prevent the intrusion of tanks and mounted troops.

Finally, industrial workers from the Cairo suburb of Buluq and from the city of Suez, who had already gone on strike before March 9, extended their strikes into May.[62] The introduction of an eight-hour day was the main demand. They succeeded in bringing to a standstill industrial production and public transportation in Cairo as well as the loading of coal in Suez. The political demands of the afandiyya were only superficially embraced by the workers and relegated to the last place on their long list of demands.

The afandiyya ended demonstrations on March 18, 1919, when they realized that they had failed to forge a mass spontaneous movement. For nine days, individual members of the afandiyya continued to organize their own demonstrations and protest rallies and to issue protest manifestos at key points in the provinces. They succeeded mainly in the cotton centers of Lower Egypt and in the provincial cities of Upper Egypt.

Village Autonomy

In at least fourteen cities throughout Egypt, the afandiyya and the notables used the newly created municipalities to protect their social and economic positions against the attacks of peasants and nomads as well to defend themselves against the British troops.[63] The municipalities were often dubbed "national committees," which were later depicted by British authorities as pockets of bolshevism within the national movement.[64] The afandiyya's attempt to dominate the provincial towns through the national committees soon reached a critical point. Local notables who had profited most from the colonial agrarian society, but who had also suffered a loss of power and authority through the state intervention of 1914–19, regarded the activities of the afandiyya with mixed feelings. Their initial support gave way to the fear that they could lose the patronage of the colonial regime on the one hand and on the other their position of authority in the provinces. In almost every case they rather quickly took over de facto control of the national committees (table 9.1). In Zifta/Gharbiyya the notables collaborated with the British army to drive out the afandiyya. The notables resisted the British troops only in Minya and Qalyub/Qalyubiyya.

Two other places in the province of Girga, Suhag and Girga itself, also had national committees. The most active was in Minya, which on March 16 established branches in the district towns of al-Fashn, Abu Qurqas, and Bani Mazar. The political concept of independence introduced by the afandiyya in

Table 9.1.
National Committees, March 14–April 2, 1919

Place	Province	Date	Leading groups	Other groups
Bani Suwaif	Bani Suwaif	March 21–?	Notables	Azhariyyun
Minya	Minya	March 15–25	Notables	Afandiyya
Asyut	Asyut	March 18–19	Notables	
Aswan	Aswan	March 14–April 5	Afandiyya	Notables
		March 17–April 1		
Qena	Qena	March 15–?	Notables	
Zaqaziq	Sharqiyya	March 15–?	Notables	
Mansura	Daqahliyya	March 18 ?–April 2	Notables	
Qalyub	Qalyubiyya	March 15–22	Notables	
Zifta	Gharbiyya	March 17–April 5	Afandiyya	
Mit Ghamr	Daqahliyya	March 15–?	Afandiyya	
Rashid (Rosette)		March 17–19	Notables	(Merchants)
Matariyya	Daqahliyya	March 15–?	Notables	(Fishermen)

October 1918 thus became a reality. In at least five cities and towns the national committees declared their independence from the British colonial regime (Minya, Zaqaziq, Zifta, Qalub, and Matariyya, and possibly Aswan).

The assertion of city and town autonomy by notables who were dependent on the afandiyya was not limited to the provincial capitals. Village communities operated in this manner primarily in the southern Central Delta and southern Delta periphery. Led by the local Azhariyyun, clan leaders, and village officials (usually low-ranking police officers), the fellahin destroyed the railways and roads that led to or near individual villages. Their goal was to prevent an invasion by British troops. The villagers, under the leadership of the local notables, assembled outside the village, waited for the British troops to arrive, and attacked them. The resistance was usually brought quickly under control, and the village occupied, looted, and burned.

The destruction of infrastructure was designed to cut villages off from the colonial world. It did not mean, however, that the fellahin attacked the inner-village social framework or even opposed the authority of the notables. On the contrary, the notables seized the opportunity to restore and expand their authority within the village that in the previous decades had become increasingly limited to economic control. In some places such as Qalyub they reorganized the tax levies, introduced village councils (diwans), and extended their power to the surrounding villages.[65]

Village autonomy in the southern Delta succeeded because the village structure itself was firmly established. The notables, at least the owners of middle-sized properties, were for the most part not absentees but had direct contact with the peasant population. The minor "troublesome" elements were the so-called *'isamiyyun,* "foreign elements," who had come to the villages and towns in the process of agrarian incorporation and had established themselves as merchants, traders, store owners, coffeehouse proprietors, or agents of absentees. Usually of Greek origin, they personified for the fellahin the foreign, distant colonial society within the agrarian community. Pogrom-like attacks by the fellahin against Greeks and other 'isamiyyun broke out, and the latter were expelled from the villages. Around March 26 the state of affairs stabilized somewhat when the notables, in cooperation with the British troops, were able to reestablish the status quo.

Peasant Autonomy

After several thousand fellahin ransacked a police station in Kafr ash-Shaikh/Gharbiyya, they left the village and attacked several large estates (in this case, 'izab). Using captured weapons they looted granaries and cotton silos, burned down the buildings, and stole the harvest. The migrant laborers who had just come from Upper Egypt to help with the cotton planting fled and returned to their homes. In the province of Daqahliyya almost every 'izab was destroyed. The fellahin sabotaged the irrigation system, drove away the cattle, and robbed local bank branches. Instead of planting cotton the fellahin inundated the cotton fields around Simballawain/Daqahliyya and planted rice.

Unlike the revolts in the southern Delta the fellahin in Regions IB and II did not make the village the center of action, concentrating rather on the economic forms of colonization—the cotton itself, irrigation installations, and the 'izab economy. In only a few cases is it possible to determine whether the rebelling fellahin were tenants or farm laborers. Many indications suggest, however, that the fellahin came not from the ranks of the 'izab workers, but from the surrounding villages. In any case they tried to reestablish their autonomy by destroying the economic forms and symbols of colonization. Autonomy in these regions seemed, however, not to base itself on the traditional structure of the villages, which indicates that here the village community had experienced a deeper transformation through the 'izab economy than had the village communities of the southern Delta. The rebels did not operate within the context of the village but as fellahin, pure and simple, whose goal was to liberate the fellahin from the 'izab organization and restore their economic position as peasant farm workers or share-croppers. Unfortunately the records do not indicate if the flight of the ʿizab migrant workers was caused by the actions of the local fellahin or if the ʿizab migrant workers used the situation to effect a change in their social situation. That the workers who fled returned in the autumn for the harvest suggests that the rebelling fellahin also turned against the Saʾidi workers from Upper Egypt.

Bedouin Autonomy

One of the most remarkable manifestations of the spring rebellion was the revolt of the Egyptian bedouin tribes between March 17 and 27, 1919. The last phase of the Delta rebellion began with this "threat of the bedouins," as the British authorities called it. The reason for the insurrection is unclear. Between March 17 and 19, the tribes advanced on the provinces of Buhaira and Fayyum and occupied them the following day. On March 17 they engaged in battle with the British forces in Damanhur/Buhaira and Madinat al-Fayyum; in Madinat al-Fayyum over 400 bedouin died. They halted their advance in Buhaira on the west bank of the Nile on March 23. Although the British military feared that they would actually attack Cairo from the southwest or northwest, the tribes remained in position for four more days, then withdrew on March 27. Only the Harabi tribe, which settled in the northern Fayyum basin, continued to fight on into April.

The unexpected and coordinated attack by the four larger tribes, Aulad ʿAli (Buhaira), Harabi, Baraʾisa, and Rammah (Fayyum), gave the impression that these attacks were a continuation of the unsuccessful insurrection of the Sanusiyya tribe in 1915–17.[66] At that time Cyrenaican tribes associated with the Sanusiyya tried, with the help of Ottoman troops and several German officers, to establish a second front in western Egypt. Fifteen thousand bedouin invaded Egypt on December 1, 1915, but were defeated between January 24 and 26, 1916, near Marsa Matruh, approximately 200 kilometers west of Alexandria. A second attack was supposed to be carried out into northern Egypt from Sanusiyya strongholds in the western oases, but disease and lack of replacements decimated the groups to the point that the offensive from the Dakhla oasis was aborted. British troops recaptured Siwa oasis on February 5, 1917. Nevertheless, the British military had to employ more than 50,000 soldiers for this desert war.

Presuming that the Sanusiyya perpetrated the Buhaira and Fayyum offensives, between 1917 and 1919 the British military authorities had all Sanusiyya settlements closed down or destroyed, but the affiliation of other tribes with the Sanusiyya naturally could not be similarly dismantled within a few years. Apparently the Rammah tribal faction from Fayyum was responsible for the offensive. Among the exiles in Malta was the former shaikh of the Rammahs, Hamad al-Basil, who had been replaced in 1906 by his younger brother, 'Abd al-Sattar al-Basil.[67] He is supposed to have contacted Sanusiyya agents in Cairo concerning plans for a revolt.[68] He also plotted in Bani Suwaif and took part there in meetings of the national committees. It is unlikely, however, that the Aulad 'Ali actually had any close contact with the Rammah in Fayyum or that they even recognized the authority of the al-Basil family. Even the Sanusiyya themselves in March 1919 had little room for maneuver, especially since their leader, Ahmad ash-Sharif, had just been replaced by his pro-British nephew, Muhammad Idris.[69] In the course of the tribal attacks in March 1919 many individual factions seized the opportunity to attack villages and steal cattle to augment their modest subsistence level. It seems that the tribes used the offensive to stake out territory and to demonstrate their independence and autonomy.

Antistatism

In the Upper Egyptian regions IV and V and especially VB and VC the rebellion was based on issues much more complex than in the Delta regions. From March 15, 1919, fellahin and bedouin groups left their villages and camps and marched on provincial cities. Here they first lay siege to the cities and then invaded them. The institutions of the British and Egyptian authorities were attacked, and the strongholds of national politics in the provinces were taken. Village groups collaborated with bedouin tribal factions to liberate the provinces from colonial rule or, in some cases, from all foreign presence.

The following methods characterized the rebellions in the provinces of Bani Suwaif, Minya, and Asyut: fighting against the colonial powers (British and Nationalists); revenge for conscription and confiscation; revenge for murdered rebels; destruction of the economic power of the 'isamiyyin (usually Copts), most often by looting; de facto occupation of towns by mere "presence"; attacks on infrastructure (railways, steamships, vehicles, telegraph and telephone lines); "liberation" of arsenals and grain silos; and attacks on irrigation infrastructure. Not all these methods were employed by the fellahin everywhere, but they provide an aggregate picture. These actions were usually accompanied by the call "There is no government!" (*ma fish hukuma!*).[70] Anyone in any way connected to the government was a potential enemy.

After a week of de facto occupation (March 15–22) the fellahin changed tactics and attacked openly, often aided in procuring weapons by local police officers. The various stages of the revolt are evident in a survey of events in Minya:

March 10–15   Demonstrations by the afandiyya.

March 15–25   Minya ruled by a national committee made up of members of the local notables and several prominent afandis. On March 22 the first fellahin groups appear, having previously gathered outside the city.

March 25–30   Tribal groups and fellahin occupy the city and drive out the national committee and British troops.

March 30–April 15   British reinforcements force the fellahin into retreat. Radical fellahin take refuge in their villages, which are reconquered one by one by the British troops.

Whereas in Minya the fight was aimed mainly at the colonial state, the revolt in Asyut (March 23–25) was oriented mainly against the Coptic 'isamiyyin and the large estate owners who resided as absentees in the city. In Bani Suwaif, the destruction of infrastructure was the goal of fellahin action.

Particularism

Little is known about the revolts in the Upper Egyptian provinces VIA and VIB, Girga, Qina, and Aswan. Only developments in the city of Aswan are documented. Most remarkable is the local national committee's absence of difficulties with the peasant community. As a precaution the notables and the few members of the afandiyya protected the substantial British colony, but there was no uprising as in Minya. The peasant and bedouin communities did not take part in any demonstrations and apparently did not occupy the towns. Only Luxor was said to have been besieged by "bedouins." Instead of large-scale revolts, groups of bandits appeared in various districts and looted villages and large estates. In Qina several clans exploited the situation to settle old, internal conflicts.[71] The clan feuds and the bandit attacks undermined the authority of the national committee in Qina, which could no longer provide protection for the railway to Luxor. When this was destroyed near Luxor, loyal bedouin tribes from the eastern shore of the Nile took over the security of the railway.

The Political Victory

Simultaneous with the end of the major demonstrations in Cairo was the repossession of the provinces by the military. As early as March 18, a frigate under the command of General Huddleston left al-Wasita/Bani Suwaif and sailed up the Nile to Qina, where on March 28 the troops joined units under the command of General Grigg returning from the Sudan. At the same time several units traveled overland through the Delta provinces, where they occupied villages and forced the fellahin to repair the damage to the railway. The reoccupation of the villages in the Delta was completed by April 12; in Upper Egypt individual villages put up resistance long into May.[72]

Edmund Allenby, the so-called Victor of Palestine, was installed as the new special high commissioner on March 21. He immediately contacted representatives of the afandiyya and notables. The common interest of the colonial system and economic order was expressed in a declaration of capitulation published on March 24 by forty-eight notables and the five most important religious leaders of the Muslims and Copts.[73] The afandiyya had this declaration distributed throughout the land. The local notables, who in many places had been able to reestablish their positions of authority as a result of the rebellion, accepted this declaration, since their local power had been restored and the necessity to compete with the afandiyya, as well as the danger of a more far-reaching social revolution within the peasant community, seemed to have been averted.

Even for the afandiyya and the Egyptian economic elite the suppression of the peasant rebellions brought about a needed respite in the conflict for control of the colonial state. The British regime also seemed appreciative. General Allenby's March 25 declaration allowed the afandiyya and the notables a certain influence (and share of responsibility). On April 7 it was announced that the exiles had been released and allowed to travel to Paris.[74]

Further concessions by the British military authorities were a partial result of the new strike activities of the afandiyya, beginning in early April. The struggle for control of the colonial state, which ended in 1922 and with the declaration of independence, was at this point limited, however, to the colonial sector of Egyptian society. The peasant community was divided. Many landowners felt that the national movement represented their interests,[75] while sharecroppers, agricultural laborers, and small-scale farmers experienced the political colonization of their world through the afandiyya and the local notables. In the course of the military reconquest of the provinces, branches of the Wafd party were established, donations for the nationalist campaign were collected, and, later, elections for the constitutional assembly were even held. In the conflict between the politicians of the colonial elite and the revolt of the fellahin, the politicians were clearly the victors.

With this victory the last phase of colonization of the Egyptian agrarian society began. It led to the elimination of autonomous forms of social organization in the countryside and the assertion of central control in the hands of the British, mediated by the monarchy, the notables, and the afandiyya.[76]

Notes

1. In Egyptian nationalist historiography, see ʿAbdal ʿAzim Ramadan, *Tatawwur al-haraka al-wataniyya fi Misr, 1918–1936* [The Evolution of the Nationalist Movement in Egypt, 1918–1936] (Cairo: an-nahda al-misriyya, 1968); ʿAbdarrahman ar-Rafiʿ, *Thawrat sanat 1919, Taʾrikh Misr al-qawmi min 1914 ila 1921* [The National History of Egypt from 1914 to 1921] (Cairo: an-nahda al-misriyya, 1374/1955); ʿAbdal ʿAziz Rifaʿi, *Thawrat Misr 1919* [The 1919 Egyptian Revolution] (Cairo: dar al-katib al-ʿarabi, 1966); Muhammed Sabry, *La révolution égyptienne d'après des documents authentiques et des photographies prises au cours de la révolution,* 2 vols. (Paris: J. Vrin, 1919–21); Husain Muʾnis, *Dirasat fi thawrat 1919* [Studies in the Revolution of 1919] (Cairo: dar al-maʿarif, 1974); Mahmud Sulaiman Ghanam al-Muhami, *Adwaʾ ʿala ahdath thawrat sanat 1919* [Light on the Events of the 1919 Revolution] (Cairo: dar al-fikr a-hadith, 1969); Fathi ar-Ramli, *Thawrat 1919 fi dawʾat-tafsir al-madi lit-taʾrikh* [The 1919 Revolution in the Light of the Materialist Explanation of History] (Cairo, ca. 1978); ʿAsim ad-Disuqi, *Thawrat 1919 fil-aqalim, ʿan al-wathaʾiq al-britaniyya* [The 1919 Revolution in the Provinces, from the British Documents] (Cairo, 1401/1981); and ad-Disuqi, *Kibar mullak al-aradi az-ziraʿiyya wa-dawruhum fi l-mujtamaʿ al-misri (1914–1952)* [Large Agricultural Landowners and their Role in Egyptian Society (1914–1952)] (Cairo: dar ath-thaqafa al-haditha, 1975). The last two titles address the rebellions of spring 1919 in a more sophisticated manner than the others listed. It should be noted that the concept Thawrat Misr 1919 usually refers to the time period between 1918 and 1922/23.

2. The best biography is ʿAbdal Khaliq Lashin, *Saʿd Zaghlul wa-dawruhu fis-siyasa al-misriyya* [Saʿd Zaghlul and his Role in Egyptian Politics], 2 vols. (Cairo and Beirut: dar al-maʿarif, 1970–75).

3. Nadav Safran, *Egypt in Search of Political Community: An Analysis of the Intellectual and Political Evolution of Egypt, 1804–1952* (Cambridge, Mass.: Harvard University Press, 1961), 105–7.

4. Ibid., 101.

5. Fawzi Tadros Awad, *La Souveraineté égyptienne et la Déclaration du 28 février 1922* (Paris, 1935).

6. Ronald J. Grele, "Ziellose Bewegung. Methodologische und theoretische Probleme der oral history," in *Lebenserfahrung und kollektives Gedächtnis,* ed. Lutz Niethammer (Frankfurt a.M.: Syndicat, 1980), 143–61.

7. Compare Michael Gilsenan, *Recognizing Islam* (London: Croom Helm, 1982), and Ernest Gellner, *Muslim Society* (Cambridge: Cambridge University Press, 1984).

8. Concerning the origins of the colonial society, see my essay "Mass Culture and Islamic Cultural Production in 19th Century Middle East," in *Mass Culture, Popular*

Culture, and Social Life in the Middle East, ed. Georg Stauth and Sami Zubaida (Frankfurt a.M.: Campus, 1987), 189–222.

9. See my thesis, *Die Rebellion der ägytischen Fallahin 1919. Zum Konflikt zwischen dem kolonialen Staat und der agrarisch-orientalischen Gesellschaft in Ägypten 1820–1919* (Berlin: Baalbek, 1981). This chapter augments two basic themes in that thesis—a clearer definition of Egypt's colonial regionalization and a more precise description of the rebellions in the northern Central Delta and in the Inner Delta Periphery.

10. Ibid., 19ff.

11. See Gabriel Baer, *Fellah and Townsman in the Middle East* (London: F. Cass, 1982), 49, and Baer, *Studies in the Social History of Modern Egypt* (Chicago: University of Chicago Press, 1969), 30–61.

12. In regard to the development of land ownership see, among others, Gabriel Baer, *A History of Landownership in Modern Egypt* (London: Oxford University Press, 1962); ʿAli Barakat, *Tatawwur al-milkiyya az-ziraʿiyya wa-atharuha ʿalal-haraka as-siyasiyya fil-fatra min 1813–1914* [The Evolution of Agricultural Ownership and Its Effect upon the Political Movement in the Period 1813–1914] (Cairo: dar al-muʿallim, 1977); Yacoub Artin-Bey, *La propriété foncière en Égypte* (Cairo: Impr. nationale de Boulac, 1883); and Ahmad al-Hitta, *Taʾrikh az-ziraʿa al-misriyya fi ʿahd Muhammad ʿAli al-kabir* [Egyptian Agricultural History in the Era of Mohammad ʿAli, the Great] (Cairo: dar al-maʿarid, 1951). Concerning the history of cotton, see François Charles-Roux, *Le coton en Égypte* (Paris: Armand Colin, 1908), and E. R. J. Owen, *Cotton and the Egyptian Economy, 1820–1914* (Oxford: Oxford University Press, 1969).

13. Muhammed Fahmi Lehita, *Taʾrikh Misr al-iqtisadi fil-ʿusur al-haditha* [The Economic History of Egypt in the Modern Age] (Cairo: lajnat at-taʾlif, 1944), 566, based on the evaluation of the eight most important cultivable plants.

14. Schulze, *Rebellion,* 35ff.

15. *Annuaire Statistique,* edited by the Ministry of Finances 1920 (Cairo: 1921), 60–64. The average ratio of the three social segments "property owners" (1–3 feddan) to leaseholders and to agrarian laborers (in Egypt as a whole) was 1 to 1.8 to 1.6.

16. Ministry of Finances, *The Census of Egypt,* taken in 1907 (Cairo, 1909), 278ff. The concept *fellah* should include the following social groups: property owners holding property of 0–3 feddan, leaseholders, and agrarian laborers. Three feddans represented approximately the minimum subsistence level for an average agrarian household.

17. The basic unit is the district (*maʾmuriyya*). The 77 districts considered here had an average size of 69,000 feddan (289.8 km²). In 1907 Egypt was administratively divided into the following provinces:

Lower Egypt		Upper Egypt	
Buhaira	Sharqiyya	Giza	Girga (Suhag)
Gharbiyya	Qalyubiyya	Bani Suwaif	Qena
Daqahliyya	Manufiyya	Minya	Aswan
		Asyut	

With special emphasis on irrigation, William Willcocks, *Egyptian Irrigation* (London and New York: F. N. Spon, 1899), 208–28, provides a valuable survey of the agrarian structure of the individual provinces.

18. Henry Labib Ayrout, *Moeurs et coutumes des fellahs: Études sur le milieu et la vie des paysans d'Égypte* (Paris: Payot, 1938), 55.

19. Willcocks, *Egyptian Irrigation*, passim; Ju.D. Dimitrevskij. *Nil. chozjajstvennogo ispol 'zovanija* (Vologda: 1958).

20. Large landownership in Balyana dates from the *'uhda* (a kind of tax form) imposed in 1840. See 'Ali Mubarak, *al-Khitat at-tawfiqiyya al-jadida li-Misr al-qahira wa-muduniha wa-biladiha al-qadima wa-l-haditha* [The New Tawfiqiyya Plan for Egypt the Victorious and its Cities and Country, Ancient and Modern], 20 vols. (Cairo: al-'amiriyya, 1886–88), 9:82f. For *'uhda*, see Artin-Bey, *La propriété foncière*, 128ff.

21. Willcocks, *Egyptian Irrigation*, 20, 21.

22. Originally this concerned the private property of the Khedival family which was mortgaged in 1877 and sold off to private agrarian companies in 1898. See Earl of Cromer, *Modern Egypt*, 2 vols. (London: Macmillan, 1908), 2:313–15, and Alan Richards, *Egypt's Agricultural Development, 1800–1980: Technical and Social Change* (Boulder, Colo.: Westview Press, 1982), 58ff.

23. Willcocks, *Egyptian Irrigation*, 379ff.

24. After the military conquest of Upper Egypt in 1824, Muhammad 'Ali ordered the extensive cultivation of sugarcane on an experimental basis. Allegedly 95,000 Feddans had already been planted with sugarcane by 1833. See al-Hitta, n. 12, 205.

25. See Max Eyth, *Lebendige Kräfte*, (Berlin: 1918), 8:59ff.

26. Willcocks, *Egyptian Irrigation*, 23. The proportion of perennially irrigated fields to cultivated area was Fayyum, 100 percent; Bani Suwaif, 22 percent; Minya, 40 percent; and Asyut, 7 percent.

27. See Baer, "Studies," 92–108.

28. Ibid., 89ff. The district of Balyana in particular produced several influential bandit groups.

29. See Mohammed El Kolaly, *Essai sur les causes de la criminalité en Égypte* (Paris: Jur. Diss., 1928).

30. Concerning the history of the railway, see Lionel Wiener, *L'Égypte et ses chemins de fer* (Bruxelles: M. Weissenbruch, 1932). On the text of the treaty see ibid., 641–44. The railway network was extended in 1858 to 353 kilometers, in 1869 to 1,338, in 1890 to 1,797, and in 1914 to 4,314. By 1914 Egypt had a rail density equivalent to that of France (9.6 km:km^2). The telegraph network was set up at the same time as the railway was under construction. Further expansion of the railway system through central Egypt to the south was not taken up until after the British military conquest in 1882. In 1888 the railroad reached Asyut, in 1891 Girga, and in 1897 Qina. See "The Construction, Development, and Organization of the Egyptian State Railway, Telegraphs, and Telephone System," in *L'Égypte Contemporaine (EC)* 24 (1933): 87–138.

31. Schulze, *Rebellion*, 41.

32. Rosa Luxemburg, *Die Akkumulation des Kapitals, Ein Beitrag zur ökonomischen Erklärung des Imperialismus* (Berlin: Paul Singer, 1913), 376–78, based on footnote 377/1.

33. Leheita (n. 13), 446; Charles-Roux, *Le coton en Égypte*, 395ff; and Willcocks, *Egyptian Irrigation*, 208. Nine of the fifteen sugar refineries were administered by the da'ira saniyya.

34. See Jeffrey G. Collins, *The Egyptian Elite under Cromer, 1882–1907* (Berlin: Schwarz, 1984), 242.

35. According to Barakat (n. 12), 423–28.

36. See for example Thomas Russell, *Egyptian Service, 1902–1946* (London: Murray, 1949).

39. See Collins, *The Egyptian Elite*, 221ff.

38. Schulze, *Rebellion*, 94f.

39. See Rotraud Wielandt, *Das Bild der Europäer in der modernen arabischen Erzähl- und Theaterliteratur* (Beirut: Steiner, 1980), 194–200. For photographic documentation, see *Sahifat min ta'rikh Inkiltarra fir Misr* [Pages from the History of England in Egypt], ([Istanbul]: n.p., 1915). Similar events the year before were hardly even noticed by the *afandiyya*. In 1887 an Italian doctor on a hunting expedition was shot by fellahin in Shubra, near Cairo. Two days later, two British officers out hunting in a village in Giza (Kufra) wounded a child. In the ensuing attempt by the fellahin to disarm the culprits, the father was shot. The fellahin then beat up the two officers. A commission of inquiry was immediately established, and twelve farmers were sentenced to forced labor and public whipping. See Edouard Plauchut, *L'Égypte et l'occupation anglaise* (Paris: Plon, 1889), 218.

40. See ʿAbdarrahman ar-Rafiʿi, *Niqabat at-taʿawun az-ziraʿiyya* [Agricultural Cooperative Unions] (Cairo: an-nahda al-adabiyya, 1914).

41. Hossam Issa, *Capitalisme et sociétés anonymes en Égypte* (Paris: Pichon/D. Auzias, 1970), 88.

42. One qantar unginned cotton = 157.5 kilograms; 1 q (qantar) = 44,928 kilograms.

43. A survey of the Egyptian national movement can be found in Arthur Goldschmidt, "The Egyptian Nationalist Party, 1892–1919," in *Political and Social Change in Modern Egypt*, ed. P. M. Holt (London: Oxford University Press, 1967), 308–33.

44. A. E. Crouchley, *The Economic Development of Modern Egypt* (London: Longmans, Green & Co., 1938), 182.

45. See Muhammed Fahmi Leheita, *Ta'rikh Fu'ad al-awwal al-iqtisadi* [The Economic History of Fu'ad the First], 2 vols. (Cairo: lajnat at-ta'lif, 1945), 1:117–269.

46. For British troop strength, Auswärtiges Amt, Bonn, Politisches Archiv, IA-die ägyptische Frage-7, Neapel to Auswärtiges Amt, December 27, 1914, and IA 11496, March 15, 1918. For inflation, Parliamentary Papers, Annual Reports of Commissioners (PP/ARC), Report for 1914–1919 (Egypt no. 1, Cmd. 957li75) (London, 1920), 5.

47. Property taxes increased in some instances by 20 to 100 percent.

48. Schulze, *Rebellion*, 119.

49. The Egyptian army consisted of 85 English officers, 415 Turkish/Arab officers, and 8,612 troops, as well as 1,931 women and 518 male "camp followers." See Lothar Rathmann, "Aspects of British Military Policy in Egypt (1919–1939)," in *The Arab World and Asia between Development and Change*, ed. Günter Barthel and Lothar Rathmann (Berlin: Akademie-Verlag, 1983), 53.

50. In order to clear out their arsenals, the British army sold off various weapons to Egyptian arms dealers in November 1886 and July 1887 (including 10,000 Remington rifles). See Plauchut, *L'Égypte et l'occupation*, 211.

51. See El Kolaly, *La Criminalité en Égypt*, 205–56, and 305–39; PP/ARC, Report for 1914–1919, 58ff; Report for 1920 (Egypt no. 2, Cmd. 1487) (London, 1921), 8off, 100ff. For a summary of court cases that would still have to be individually evaluated see *Bulletin de Législation et de Jurisprudence égyptienne*, red. p. Th. Lebsohn et D. Palage, Table alphabetique des Sommaires des arrêts et jugements, 1–4 (every ten years) (Alexandria, 1899, 1909, 1919, 1929).

52. Robert L. Tignor, *State, Private Enterprise, and Economic Change in Egypt, 1918–1952* (Princeton, N.J.: Princeton University Press, 1984), 15–48.

53. This objective was especially advocated by the Commission for Commerce and Industry (founded in 1916). Its president was Isma'il Sidqi. In addition to several British colonial civil servants, other members included Amin Yahya (businessman), Yusuf Aslan Qattawi (financier), and Muhammad Tal'at Harb (entrepreneur).

54. See 'Abbas Mahmud al-'Aqqad, *Sa'd Zaghlul, sira wa-tahiyya* [Sa'd Zaghlul, Path and Remembrance] (Beirut: dar ash-shuruq, n.d.). The coalition was represented by the combination of people on the executive panel: Isma'il Sidqi and Sa'd Zaghlul, both former ministers, the former an industrialist, the latter a judge with vast property holdings; Muhammad Mahmud and Hamid al-Basil, both absentee landlords; 'Ali Sha'rawi and 'Abdallatif al-Mikabbati, both large landlords; finally representatives of the afandiyya, Ahmad Lutfi al-Sayyid and 'Abdal'aziz Fahmi; and two members of the Khedivial family, Muhammad 'Ali and 'Umar Tusun.

55. This position was especially defended by the British foreign secretary, Arthur James Balfour.

56. Text can be found in Schulze, *Rebellion*, 133.

57. Often-used synonyms are *sukhra* (corvée) and *sulta* (force, power, state).

58. A general picture can be found in Ahmad Baha al-Din, *Ayyam laha ta'rikh* [Days of History] (Cairo: Dar al-katib al-'arabi, 1386/1967), 119ff.

59. This is a moderate estimate. The British figures are somewhat lower, the Egyptian higher.

60. See Jacques Berque, *L'Égypte: Impérialisme et Révolution* (Paris: Gallimard, 1967), 318.

61. The subsequent description of the events is based on Schulze, *Rebellion*, 139–209. Sources are listed there.

62. The best sources regarding the workers strikes are: Amin 'Izz ad-Din, *Ta'rikh at-tabaqa al-'amila al-misriyya* [History of the Egyptian Working Class], 3 vols. (Cairo: vol. 1, dar al-katib al-'arabi, 1970; vols. 2–3, ash-sha'b); Ra'uf 'Abbas, *al-Haraka al-'ummaliyya fi Misr, 1899–1952* [The Labor Movement in Egypt, 1899–1952] (Cairo: dar al-katib al-'arabi, 1965). [Editors' note: Beinen and Lockman come to somewhat different conclusions than Professor Schulze. They see significant links between labor agitation and strike activity with nationalist political objectives, especially during the month of March. See Joel Beinen and Zachary Lockman, *Workers on the Nile: Nationalism, Communism, Islam, and the Egyptian Working Class, 1882–1954* (Princeton, N.J.: Princeton University Press, 1987), 84–100.]

63. See M. M. Delcroix, "L'Institution municipale en Égypte," in *Égypte Contemporaine* 13 (1922):278–323.

64. Public Record Office, London, Foreign Office (PRO/FO), 407–184–92, Cheetham to Curzon, March 19, 1919.

65. The term *Diwan* refers here to a sort of advisory board.

66. In regard to *'izab* see G. Hug and J. Lozach, *L'Habitat rural en Égypte* (Cairo: IFAO, 1930). Using 4,000 questionnaires, they describe the settlement structure of the Delta (which was divided into three regions, more or less corresponding to the above-mentioned Regions I–III) and Upper Egypt (from Minya to the northern district of Qinas). The survey was done in 1926.

67. Ilyas Zakhura, *Kitab mir'at al-'asr fi ta'rikh wa-rusum akabir ar-rijal li-Misr* [The Book of the Reflection of the Age in History and the Traces of Egypt's Great Men], 3 vols. (Cairo: 'umumiyya, 1898–1916) 2:204–6, 333–34. Regarding the history of the Sanusiyya in Egypt, see my essay "Sanusiyya in Egypt, 1840–1920." A description of the campaign from a British point of view can be found in W. T. Massey, *Desert Campaigns* (London: Constable, 1918), 132–71. The second phase of the war is treated more objectively by Archibald Murray, *Sir Archibald Murray's Despatches (June 1916–June 1917)* (London: Dent, 1920), 204–6.

68. PRO/FO, 141–581–9137, Dossier Qalini Fahmi. In this case it was most certainly a denunciation.

69. Compare the treaty between Great Britain and Muhammad Idris from April 14, 1917, in FO 141–652–340/637.

70. Cf. Tawwaf, *Egypt 1919, Being a Narrative of Certain Incidents of the Rising in Upper Egypt* (Alexandria: Whitehead Morris, 1925), 36.

71. Ibid., 77.

72. Compare "Egyptian Delegation to the Peace Conference," *White Book*, 12 Appendices (Paris, 1919).

73. Text in *al-Ahram* [The Pyramids], 27 December 1919.

74. Allenby stated, "My intentions are: First, to bring the present disturbances to an end. Secondly, to make careful inquiry into all matters, which have caused discontent in the country. Thirdly, to redress such grievances as appear justifiable. It is you who can lead the people of Egypt. It is your duty to work with me in the interest of your country." Archibald Percival Wavell, *Allenby in Egypt* (London, 1944), p. 43. For release of exiles, ar-Rafi'i, *Thawrat sanat 1919*, 2:5.

75. The Wafd was supposed to have promised the abolition of the property tax; see PRO/FO, 407–184–363, Encl., Summary of events, May 16, 1919.

76. For further developments see, for example, Reinhard Schulze, "Ägypten 1936–1956: Die Nationalisierung eines kolonialen Staates," in *Das Ende der Kolonialreiche. Dekolonisierung und die Politik der Großmächte*, ed. Wolfgang J. Mommsen (Frankfurt a.M.: Fischer, 1990), 134–67,225–31.

The Ignorance and Inscrutability
of the Egyptian Peasantry

NATHAN BROWN

*P*easants in many areas of the world have long frustrated those who study them. To many, the peasantry appears as a passive and unthinking yet almost insurmountable obstacle to reform and development. Social scientists have noted peasant obstructionism, and many have written of the difficulties caused by the attachment of peasants to traditional methods and leaders. For societies attempting to develop, peasants seem to fail in their duties, blindly unaware or even suspicious of the benefits brought by new techniques and leaders.

Social scientists have frequently sympathized with reformers confronting the obstacle of peasant ignorance. In 1971, Joseph LaPalombara wrote of peasants and the "crisis of penetration" of state authority: "There is both great irony and great challenge here, for peasants are likely to manifest their fiercest opposition to center-determined programs designed to improve their lot. Generations of agricultural field administrators or community development agents have marveled at the obstinate refusal of the peasant to have his material condition improved. The language of animal husbandry, or of agronomy, or of public health is alien to him—an outside, hostile force, considered hostile simply by reason of communicated symbols that are completely outside [his] ken. Lacking both knowledge and empathy, he can only react to outsiders with suspicion and fierce hostility. He represents in this sense the most ubiquitous aspect of the crisis of penetration."[1]

Even scholars whose sympathies seem to lie more with peasants than their rulers often bemoan peasant ignorance as an obstacle to revolutionary change. Eric Hobsbawm has mentioned the "sheer ignorance and helplessness of peasants outside the confines of their region"; Eric Wolf wrote that "past exclusion of the peasant from participation in decision-making beyond the bamboo hedge of his village deprives him all too often of the knowledge needed to articulate his interests with appropriate forms of action."[2] Social scientists writing from a variety of perspectives share a frustration with the failure of peasants to recognize their true interests.

In particular, those who study Egypt have often exhibited this frustration. For instance, a study by an Egyptian social scientist portrays the political culture of the peasantry as lacking a secular, activist, egalitarian, national spirit; Egyptian peasants lack a political perspective conducive to democracy and freedom. Raymond Hinnebusch has described Egyptian peasants as "the most politically crippled by the traditional political culture of passivity, deference and particularism."[3]

Few of those who write in this vein seem aware of the history of such complaints. These authors, however, are heirs to a tradition of decrying peasant ignorance. The complaints that social scientists have recently echoed originated from those seeking not simply to understand peasants but to dominate them. Peasant ignorance was created—and continues to be sustained—by the desires and frustrations of ambitious rulers. Peasants are ignorant not because of what they do not know but because of what they refuse to believe.

Because peasants would not cooperate with officials, felt no loyalty to the state, and seemed impervious to reform, they were routinely branded as ignorant and inscrutable. Yet they were denounced as ignorant largely because their political outlook differed from that of their rulers and as inscrutable largely because few observers sought to discover the nature of their outlook.

The relationship between ambitious rulers and ignorant peasants can best be illustrated by an examination of writings on Egyptian peasants over the last century (and is especially clear in writings of the period before 1952). Indeed, ignorance forms the theme of most of these writings; the ignorance of the peasantry was obvious to all of those who cared to look. Since the British occupation of Egypt, occupiers and Egyptian rulers have participated in an attempt to remold Egypt into a modern nation. While perceptions of what this effort required have varied considerably, both the British and the Egyptians have seen the need to reeducate peasants in modern values.

The Meaning of Ignorance

Lord Cromer, the British consul-general in Egypt between 1883 and 1907, and his fellow colonialists often doubted the peasants' awareness of benefits brought by the British occupation. They generally believed that some of their works inspired gratitude but almost always added a qualification: "Ignorant though he may be, [the *fellah*] is wise enough to know that he is now far better off than he was prior to the British occupation." Yet Cromer was not entirely sanguine. Because the peasant lacked logical skills, the consul-general observed, "he is incapable of establishing clearly in his mind that, for the time being at all events, good administration and the exercise of a paramount influence by England are inseparably linked together."[4]

Not just the British traced much peasant behavior to ignorance. An article written in 1908 in the Cairo daily *Al-Mu'ayyad* (purporting to be written from the peasant's perspective) listed ignorance as one of the principal burdens of the peasant. In 1940, Dr. Muhammad Mustafa al-Qulali wrote that the most important causes of rural crime were social in nature and that ignorance lay at the root of these. One year later Ahmad Hamdi Mahbub Bey also concluded that a lack of instruction and education was partly behind the high crime rate.[5] The high crime rate and peasant ingratitude were not the only problems brought on by peasant ignorance. Contemporaries saw poverty, apathy, and susceptibility to usury as all stemming from ignorance. In the minds of their fellow Egyptians and of foreigners, ignorance was the defining condition of peasants.

This stress on ignorance seems curious at first. Peasants may have been ignorant of many world events that occupied the attention of their countrymen, but why was it ignorance that explained peasant reluctance to pay taxes or be impressed by the corvée? On points such as crime and exploitation by usurers, the role of ignorance is still less obvious. Certainly peasants knew that murder and theft were crimes. Similarly, it is hard to believe that peasants were too ignorant to realize that loans contracted with moneylenders would have to be repaid with interest.

The ignorance of which the British and Egyptians wrote was something more than a narrow lack of knowledge. It was a moral failing, a spiritual torpor. Cromer saw it as a failure to appreciate progress and Western civilization and as a general phenomenon throughout the Islamic East: "Progress, such as Western people more or less eagerly seek for, the Muhammedan of Egypt or of India does not put in the front of his desires; nor does order offer to his mind the advantages which Europeans ascribe to it. System and method, which to us seem indispensable, are apt to be tiresome to people long debauched by the excitement and surprises of chance and circumstance." Cromer's opinions were understandably offensive to a large number of Egyptians. His insulting, sometimes even racist, language provoked controversy and reaction in Egypt. Yet many Egyptians did see moral decay, apathy about progress, and lack of order in their country. They saw these vices as widespread among their own lower classes, especially the peasantry.[6]

Thus the ignorance of the peasantry meant more than an inability to read and write or a lack of awareness of world events. It was a failure (again really a refusal) to meet the demands of a modern society and state. In Cromer's eyes the task of the British was to bring justice and other benefits of civilization to a society ignorant of its needs for them: "Egypt is now passing through a period of transition. On one hand, the country is far too advanced to admit of anything but a civilized system of justice being applied. There can, of course, be no question of returning to the practices of the past, under which order of a kind was maintained by the simple process of making but little attempt to discriminate between guilt and innocence. On the other hand, any system of civilized justice which can be devised is, to a certain extent, beyond the comprehension and in advance of the moral and intellectual status of the mass of the inhabitants."[7]

The British believed the peasants had to be taught how to behave; they needed to be educated on the nature and proper use of freedom and other benefits of civilization. Shortly after the Dinshawai affair of 1906 (in which some villagers had been hanged and others flogged after they had clashed with a group of pigeon-hunting British troops), the acting consul-general wrote, "The Fellah has awoke to the fact that he is free. He has not yet learned that liberty has its limits, and he must be brought to respect them."[8]

The contemptuous terms used by the British were rarely repeated by the Egyptian elite, but all shared the belief that rural dwellers were morally backward. The peasantry was both deplored and feared. Even a writer sympathetic to the peasantry, Yusif Nahhas, declared that "the social morals of the peasant are what oppression and ignorance have brought to be."[9] In contemporary writings this concept of ignorance appears most prominently in discussions of rural crime. The British and the Egyptian elite shared a desire to impose a new definition of crime on the country, and the peasants' continuing refusal to accept this definition appeared ignorant to their rulers.

Ignorance and Crime

Prior to the late nineteenth century, crime was generally defined as an affair that concerned only the local community. Local authorities and practices prevailed in matters of crime and punishment. Although higher officials may have concerned themselves with specific cases, local leaders had no obligation to refer routine crimes to their superiors.

The construction of the modern Egyptian state (which had certainly begun by the 1870s, prior to the British occupation of 1882) required a redefinition of crime. Part of the problem was the increased mobility of the population. Large numbers of Upper Egyptians migrated to the north on a seasonal basis. A purely local authority could not apprehend and punish such migrants when they committed a crime. Yet a larger part of the problem was that the mores of the elite increasingly clashed with those of the peasantry. Most often discussed was *tha'r*. Largely a rural practice, this concept involved a family avenging an offense or murder by attacking or killing the original offender or a member of his family. The deed and the response it provoked were personal or family matters; they were not crimes requiring the attention of the authorities. Such, at least, was the view from the village. The practice of tha'r drew increasing denunciation in the contemporary political debate; it also drew the increased attention of the authorities who were generally frustrated in their attempts to suppress it.[10]

Tha'r was not only seen as barbaric; a deeper opposition to the practice stemmed from the very idea of such weighty matters being dealt with outside the national system of justice. Tha'r symbolized the villagers' definition of justice. As murder and theft were offenses against the village and its residents, villagers seemed to believe that the proper response to these offenses had to come from village leaders and residents. Village leaders considered it within their authority to apprehend criminals and administer justice, and up to the end of the nineteenth century the Egyptian state conceded to them authority in these matters. Many offenses did not even get to the level of the village leaders but were settled instead by compensatory payments or retaliatory attacks. Tha'r was therefore part of a system of local justice.[11]

Thus the most important reason that crime was redefined, that the definition, investigation, and punishment of crime were no longer local matters, was that both British and Egyptian rulers believed crime and order to have become national concerns. The extent of rural crime was a national problem and a national disgrace. Statistics on crime were collected and classified. Rural crime became a leading political issue. Courts were established.[12] The state asserted its authority over law enforcement down to the village level and established a police force in the provinces. It also assumed responsibility for the supervision, training, and finance of guards and watchmen. Most important, it demanded that crimes be reported. The 'umda (village mayor) retained the authority to deal with minor violations, but his failure to report crimes became a serious matter. 'Umdas were slow to learn—or accept—the diminution in their authority and routinely faced suspension or fines for failing to report crimes. What the new national legal code defined as criminal took precedence—in the eyes of the state—over local customs. Violations of the code were to be reported by ʿumdas, investigated by the Parquet, and tried by the courts.[13]

The new definition of criminality also required cooperation from the population. The peasant response to the redefinition, however, was silence. Lord Lloyd wrote that "co-operation in the suppression of crime can only come where there is a widespread sense of civic responsibility, and in the provinces no such sense had as yet been engendered. The villagers were still children, and the only way to preserve order among them was by discipline imposed from above." Peasants would usually neither report a crime nor cooperate with those investigating it. Generally, peasants denied knowledge of crimes and the identity of criminals to officials. The British believed that the peasantry would have to be reformed. In his 1916 report, the British judicial adviser stated that "if the problem of crime is ever to be solved, I imagine that the solution must be found in some new basis for the orderliness of village life."[14]

Like the British, Egyptians writing in the press attributed this refusal to act as citizens of a modern state to a mixture of cowardice, ignorance, and resistance to modernity. In 1914, *Al-Ahram* called for education as a long term solution to the problem of crime. Twenty-seven years later, Muhammad al-Babli, the director of the police academy, wrote that the poor in both the cities and the countryside were victims of ignorance who were consequently short-sighted and did not realize their public duty. Their ignorance led to a lack of feeling of involvement—al-Babli believed that this was why they neither helped the police nor obstructed them.[15]

Even when the police could bring a crime to court despite peasant silence, peasants remained completely ignorant of legal procedures. They hardly regarded courts as instruments of justice. Tawfiq al-Hakim, who wrote sympathetically if ironically on rural problems, registered his frustration with a system of justice in which "the guilty did not realize at all that he was guilty; I did not see one of the violators [of the law] show that he believed that he had truly committed [a crime]; indeed, the fines fell upon them from heaven just as do natural disasters."[16]

Ignorance and Civilized Politics

Crime was not the only effect of ignorance. A host of social ills appeared to stem from the moral backwardness of the peasantry, who seemed incapable of civilized political attitudes. The British often looked upon peasants as ill-mannered children. One British official wrote in such terms when attempting to explain the quiescence of the peasantry during the economic crisis of the late 1920s. "When the Fellah is well and prosperous he is truculent towards the landowner but when he is poor and things go awry he whines without taking action."[17]

Such personalities were not the sort on which democratic institutions could be built. The British repeated this with satisfaction; Egypt was not a country whose inhabitants could dispense with tutelage in civilized politics. A British official reported that the general reaction among the peasantry to the 1913 elections for the Legislative Assembly was that "the Government has said: Let there be elections, and there is an election. We are poor people. What have we to do with such things?" If this was the real reaction of the peasants then they were far from ignorant: the British had devised an indirect election system to ensure that poor people would have little to do with such things. The British, however, saw lack of interest in elections as symptomatic of the failure of peasants to widen their political horizons. One observer claimed that even after the benefits brought by British rule, the Egyptian peasant "has remained in many ways and with rare exceptions that same totally illiterate peasant that he was, working during the critical seasons of the agricultural year as hard and with as thorough an understanding of his business as any other peasant in the world—the Chinaman himself perhaps not excepted—but otherwise abysmally ignorant and with no interests outside the village and the price of land and its produce."[18]

Some blamed the misgovernance of Egypt on the ignorance of its victims. Lord Milner, a high British official whose various tasks in Egypt spanned thirty years, wrote in 1892:

> I have often been asked whether British influence is popular with the mass of the Egyptian people. It would be absurd to reply to that question in the affirmative; but to answer it with a simple negative would be no less misleading. . . . On the broad political issue they are much too backward to have any opinion one way or the other. The ordinary peasant has probably only the vaguest notions as to how the government is really carried on. That he is satisfied with the results, that he is well aware of being treated much better than formerly, cannot be doubted. But he is not in a position to reason about the causes of the change.
>
> The docile and pacific disposition of the race, their ignorance, and their lack of independence, increase enormously the responsibility resting on their governors. There is nothing in the character of the people to check the abuse of power, nothing to guide its exercise.[19]

Yet while the British cited the absence of what would later be called a participant political culture as a justification for their presence, members of the Egyptian elite displayed embarrassment. They saw a need for education to combat ignorance and raise the moral level of the people. Peasants were supposed to want to vote even if their votes did not matter.[20]

Ignorance and Responsibility

Like apathy in elections, peasants' borrowing was also a sign of moral weakness. An economic structure that denied most peasants sufficient capital to operate farms seldom drew attention. Rather, peasants were portrayed as too improvident and even too debauched to save or work for self-improvement. In spite of the efforts of some in power, peasants seemed incapable of banding together to form cooperatives. Even after the 1920s when the government undertook the promotion of cooperatives on a large scale, peasants seemed uninterested in the idea. Again their ignorance was to blame.[21]

The refusal of the peasantry to be educated in the new morality of the state led the British to abandon the attempt during the 1919 revolution. When the peasantry seemingly rose as a body to expel the colonialists, the British felt compelled to repudiate—or at least suspend—the ideals of justice and responsibility that they had used to justify their presence. Having failed to teach the peasants these ideals—indeed, having done little more than bemoan peasant ignorance of such civilized concepts—the British abandoned their ideals themselves. They tried and sentenced Egyptians who had worked to maintain order during the rebellion. British troops burned and pillaged entire villages in accordance with the official policy of holding villages collectively responsible when nearby railroad tracks or telegraph lines were disturbed. It should be noted that it was not only the British who felt frustrated in the face of the resistance of ignorant peasants. As late as 1944, a prominent Egyptian lawyer called for a return to the policy of collective responsibility of families and villages for crime.[22]

In short, the British and the Egyptian elite wanted the peasantry to become a citizenry able and willing to meet the requirements of a modern state. The peasantry lacked the civic consciousness and sense of loyalty to the state necessary to meet these requirements: they did not report crimes, exhibited little interest in national politics, and failed to respond to reform and development efforts. Cromer perceived that "Egypt had to be Europeanized"; European civilization was a bed, and as "the bed could not be made to fit the Egyptian the Egyptian had to adapt himself to lying on the bed." He called

upon his countrymen "in Christian charity [to] make every possible allowance
for the moral and intellectual shortcomings of the Egyptians, and do whatever
can be done to rectify them."[23]

Few Egyptians wanted their country to become English, but some did want
to change their countrymen to fit what they perceived to be the modern bed.

Egyptian peasant women in Al-Minya province balancing water from the Nile
in jugs on their heads. Photo by Muhammad Hanafi, 1985.

Peasants were to be educated to abandon superstition, cooperate with the state, and be loyal to their nation and their religion rather than their families and fellow villagers.

Ignorance and Reform

This examination of the writings of British and Egyptian observers has revealed a peasantry whose ignorance consisted of a rejection of the new public morality that the state required. Cromer's observation of the "Easterner" is more applicable than most of his comments about the peasantry: "He does not want to be reformed, and he is convinced that, if the European wishes to reform him, the desire springs from sentiments which bode him no good."[24] The peasant refused to be reformed not out of lack of knowledge but out of suspicion of the real intent of the reformers.

The suspicion had a firm basis. Poverty and social reform did receive much attention toward the end of the period, but the reformers did not differ fundamentally from those who had earlier expressed distress over the ignorance of the peasantry. While reformers displayed great interest in the peasantry's material condition, they still desired to remold it. Reform always had a didactic and moral content. Berque observes of the reformers: "They believed above all in education and a moral code inculcated from above, without taking too much account of the basic desires of the people. They thus retained a pedagogic, indeed an authoritarian attitude, 'taking an interest in' the people rather than arising out of them."[25]

Egyptian intellectuals began to take a strong interest in social reform in the 1930s, and began to portray crime as a result not only of ignorance but also of poverty. In 1936, for instance, an *Al-Ahram* reporter, after spending a week in the countryside, wrote that he realized that "poverty is among the most powerful causes in pushing the people to steal—they who, if not for their needs and poverty, would lead honorable lives."[26]

In the 1940s several influential books were published promoting the new theme of the poverty of the peasantry. Calls were issued for minimum wages for agricultural workers, limits on landholdings, promotion of agricultural cooperatives, and, as always, rural education. Indeed, the stress on raising the economic level of peasants reinforced rather than supplanted the older theme of raising their moral and intellectual level, of raising them out of their ignorance.[27]

In concluding his demographic study of Sharqiyya, ʿAbbas ʿAmmar wove together the two themes of rural poverty and peasant ignorance. "To people of this class life presents such a hard front that the struggle for existence cripples intellectual and spiritual growth. . . . Efficiency and mental alertness are at a minimum and nervous reactions are slow. . . . There is no surplus of energy because it is all used up in meeting the hard conditions which make mere survival a difficult matter. . . . Ignorance, overreproduction, congestion, low position of women, lack of sanitation, and a tremendous loss of potential ability—this is the price they pay."[28]

The new reformist ideas began to have an impact on those in power. In 1946 the king and cabinet ostentatiously established the Higher Council of Ministers to Deal with Poverty, Ignorance, and Disease. The king instituted reforms on his own estates and encouraged large landowners to do likewise. He visited the estates of the Badrawi family, the largest private holdings in the country after those of the royal family. The king's approval of the conditions on the Badrawi did not convince the residents. In January 1951 a full-scale battle broke out between the estate management and the tenants; afterwards, the Badrawis were forced to rely on the protection of a large and heavily armed police guard.

Cromer found Egyptian peasants illogical and unpredictable, and they were just as unfathomable to the Egyptian elite. In retrospect, it seems that it was not the peasants alone who were ignorant. The rulers lacked knowledge of the values of those they ruled. Ayrout noted that, "faced with the simplest queries about [the *fellahin*], the rich often display an ignorance which shows quite clearly that such questions have never occurred to them and arouse no curiosity at all."[29]

This ignorance on the part of the rulers was recast as inscrutability on the part of the peasants. Even as perceptive a writer as Berque characterized the Egyptian peasant as "a withdrawn inscrutable character," and he noted of the period that "if many people spoke of progress, if a few acquired education, if the word Freedom resounded in countless speeches, the great mass of the population remained something unknown, shunned and menacing."[30]

Peasants against the State

Egyptian peasants, then, operated according to their own moral outlook. Their outlook was not simply different from the outlook of those who ruled them; it was an outlook to which they clung tenaciously, earning them the contempt and abuse of those on whose writings we must rely to understand them.

Taxes

Taxes are a natural point of conflict between a state and its subjects. Historically, however, the Egyptian peasantry had particularly strong cause for complaint. Taxes were heavy, and collection methods made them even more burdensome. They might be collected in advance; irregular surtaxes might be added, or the same tax payment collected twice; corporal punishment was often used on suspected tax evaders. There was also substantial room for abuse by local officials.

Everything from the amount of tax to the schedule of collection was dictated by the financial needs and appetites of the state and its tax collectors—concerns the peasants would have found irrelevant to their own lives. Under the British occupation the tax burden on the peasantry grew lighter in terms of both absolute amount and collection. Taxation thus became a less sensitive issue in peasant-state relations. Yet the residue of this history of capricious extractions from the peasantry contributed to the mistrust and fear with which most Egyptians viewed the state.

Conscription

Conscription left a similar bitter residue although the conflict was of more recent origin. Before the nineteenth century peasants were expected to pay for the military ambitions of their rulers, but they were rarely expected to participate in any fighting. In the early nineteenth century, however, the Egyptian state began taking not only the peasants' crops but the peasants themselves. Rivlin reports, "An average of 100,000 men or 4 percent of a population estimated at 2,500,000 had been withdrawn from agriculture to serve in Muhammad Ali's armed forces. In all of Europe only in the Austrian border provinces did there exist an army of comparable size in relation to the total population. In terms of modern warfare and a highly industrialized society an army of 4 percent would be considered large; in the first half of the nineteenth century, particularly in a country with an agrarian economy, the percentage appeared enormous."[31]

Rivlin also notes that peasant feelings against conscription were strong enough to provoke a grotesque form of resistance: "So unwilling were fellahin to enter military service that mothers mutilated their children, blinding or crippling them, so that they would not have to serve. Adult men often cut off the index finger of their right hand or destroyed their right eye, or pulled out their front teeth to avoid conscription."[32]

In 1841 the European powers, fearful of the threat to the Ottoman Empire posed by growing Egyptian power, stepped in to limit the size of the Egyptian army. Although forced to scale down its military ambitions, the ruling house did not abandon them altogether. Even after the occupation of 1882, when the British disbanded the army they had defeated, a small army was reconstituted and conscription continued. As with taxation, the occupation lightened the burden. In 1901, for instance, 47,944 individuals were registered for military service (after exemptions for family reasons, payment of the exemption fee, and so on). Of these, only 2,334 were actually enlisted.[33]

The British had no qualms about enlisting the peasantry in their own plans, however. In World War I hundreds of thousands of peasants were "volunteered" to support the British army in various areas where the war was being fought. Again, the needs of the state (and the colonial power)—with which the peasantry had little cause to sympathize—dominated the peasant-state relationship.

Corvée Labor

The corvée, or forced labor by villagers, had maintained the Egyptian irrigation system since ancient times. During slack agricultural seasons, peasants were required to furnish labor to clean canals and repair levees and basins. As long as the peasants were required to work only on local projects the relationship between peasant welfare and corvée labor remained clear. Yet the corvée was also used to construct new irrigation projects from which the peasants who had worked on them would not benefit. This practice was greatly expanded in the nineteenth century beginning with the reign of Muhammad 'Ali. Irrigation was extended to uncultivated areas, major new canals were dug, and irrigation projects were undertaken (such as the Barrage at the head of the Delta). Already existing canals in the Delta were deepened to permit summer irrigation. These projects represented a change in the nature of the corvée. No longer could the peasants look upon such labor as necessary if onerous. It became a system in which peasants were required to expand cultivation for the benefit of the state and of those awarded ownership of the reclaimed land.

The corvée was gradually abolished in the period immediately before and after British occupation. Abolition represented recognition of the changes in Egyptian agricultural production that the corvée itself had brought about. Perennial irrigation and thus year-round cultivation became possible; for large parts of the year no idle labor was available. In deepening the canals the corvée had, in this sense, dug its own grave. The British were responding to pressure from the Egyptian elite as much as to their own liberal conscience when they abolished forced labor, for peasant labor was needed on the large estates during the summer. Also, the abolition of the corvée saw large irrigation projects taken over by private contractors who employed seasonal labor from Upper Egypt. Local maintenance of canals and levees continued to be the work of locally organized groups of peasants.[34]

Thus even the abolition of the corvée did not decrease the amount of labor expected from peasants, who spent their summers cultivating cotton rather than maintaining the irrigation system. Nor did the gradual abolition of the corvée bring peasants to trust their rulers. In 1891, when the gradual abolition of the corvée was already well under way, *Al-Muqattam* noted that the government's attempt to carry out a census frightened peasants into fleeing.[35] For peasants, the only reason the government might want to count them was that it needed their labor.

The abolition of the corvée did not even give peasants greater independence. Since its abolition was linked with the replacement of basin and flood irrigation by perennial irrigation, the end of the corvée was also linked with increased government control over water. After a 1928 visit to Upper Egypt, a

Egyptian peasant men with cattle on the banks of the Nile in Al-Minya province. Photo by Muhammad Hanafi, 1985.

British official noted that there might exist a feeling that perennial irrigation puts the cultivator "at the mercy of an official. With basin irrigation, the opportunities for prejudiced intervention by an inspector, and for discrimination in distribution, are comparatively low."[36]

Justice

A fourth point of contact—and source of resentment—between peasants and the state was the administration of justice. It has already been shown that the state and the peasantry clashed over the definition of crime. Particularly in the period after the British occupation, Egyptian laws and policies were to determine not only what was criminal but also who would investigate and punish crime. The peasantry defined crime as an offense against an individual, a family or the community norms that demanded a response on that level. The state sought to recast crime in national terms; it also punished those who did not share its perspective and refused to cooperate. Not surprisingly the police quickly came to be feared as much as the criminals. Ammar reports that in Silwa most disputes were settled by local institutions and councils rather than courts. Some did bring conflicts to court, but most villagers viewed this with disdain.[37]

Reform and Development

A final element affecting relations between the state and the peasantry was the series of reform and development projects undertaken by the British and the Egyptian government. Tignor's observation on the peasant view of the new system of justice could be generalized to all government measures of the period. "The peasantry built up a great fear and resentment against centralized authority over the years and did their utmost to isolate themselves from the government. When the new system was introduced, they were not well enough prepared to see its advantages."[38] Peasants were not prepared to see the advantages because most were illusory or, at best, double edged. The irrigation reforms may have increased agricultural production, but the peasantry shared in this prosperity only to a limited extent.[39] Any material benefits for peasants were partly offset by the burdens of the reforms—first the corvée, and then perennial irrigation under which "what had been a seasonal rhythm became a daily task."[40]

Peasants viewed the projects of which Cromer and the British were so proud with suspicion, then, for good reason. The loudly proclaimed prosperity was a product of a policy aimed at raising production. The condition of the peasantry was incidental. It was the land, not necessarily the population, that was to be enriched.

The same can be said of most of the reform programs proposed in the mid-1930s and later. If some Egyptians began to notice and write about rural poverty, few inquired into the fundamental economic and social relations producing it. Most concern was with the problems that poverty was said to produce, such as crime and lower agricultural production. Sometimes the concern with the superficial reached comic proportions. In the 1940s, Prime Minister Husayn Sirri proposed to meet the problems of the peasantry by launching a campaign to distribute shoes among them to combat barefootedness.[41] For the peasantry reform meant either a substitution of new burdens for old or frequently ineffectual attempts to improve standards of living. It is little wonder that government was still feared and resented even after all that it claimed to have done. Fear and distrust of government were thus central to the political outlook of the peasantry, products of their historical experience both recent and distant.

Conclusion

Egypt's experience with ignorant peasants hardly stands alone. In other areas of the world, ambitious elites pursuing centralization or development programs have encountered rural obstacles. Çağlar Keyder has written of Kemalist Turkey, "When the center became more oppressive in its ideological obtrusion, the peasantry and the petty bourgeoisie of small towns took refuge more resolutely in tradition, thereby inviting the bureaucracy conveniently to label their behavior as obscurantist reaction."[42]

Peasants throughout the world display their ignorance in the eyes of their rulers when they reject the statist or developmentalist ideology required of them. Knowledge is equated not with a given body of factual material but with a particular ideology that legitimizes political domination. Those who accept the authority and program of the central authorities know their place; those who resist are ignorant. Ignorance therefore constitutes more than a passive lack of knowledge; it is a defiant act of resistance that has threatened the ambitions of ruling elites throughout the world.

Social scientists who have reproduced peasant ignorance in their own writings therefore participate unwittingly in a process of domination that they purport only to describe (or even denounce). Goran Hyden has observed that both Western development experts and Western socialists hoping for revolution "create images of the African peasantry that suit our models. . . . Most of this is wishful thinking, if not outright ignorance."[43] Peasant ignorance is a creation of rulers; those who perpetuate ignorance choose sides in the struggle between ruler and ruled.

Notes

1. Joseph LaPalombara, "Penetration: A Crisis in Governmental Capacity," in *Crisis and Sequences in Political Development,* ed. Leonard Binder et al. (Princeton, N.J.: Princeton University Press, 1971), 226–67. In a similar vein, Samuel Huntington and Joan Nelson write of the attachment of the "poor and ignorant" to traditional leaders more concerned with self-promotion than with the betterment of their followers. They claim the influence of such leaders is still strong in Africa and the Middle East. See *No Easy Choice: Political Participation in Developing Countries* (Cambridge, Mass.: Harvard University Press, 1976), 126.

2. Eric Hobsbawm, "Peasants and Politics," *Journal of Peasant Studies* 1 (1973): 9; Eric Wolf, *Peasant Wars of the Twentieth Century* (New York: Harper and Row, 1969).

3. Kamal al-Minufi, *Al-Thaqafa al-Siyasiyya li-l-Fallahin al-Misriyyin* [The Political Culture of the Egyptian Peasantry] (Beirut: Dar ibn Khaldun, 1980). Raymond A. Hinnebusch, Jr., *Egyptian Politics under Sadat: The Post-Populist Development of an Authoritarian-Modernizing State* (Cambridge: Cambridge University Press, 1985), 249.

4. Earl of Cromer, *Modern Egypt* (London: Macmillan, 1909) 2:194.

5. Nasim Fahmi, "Al-Fallah al-Misri, Ra'y fi al-Hukuma al-Hadira" [The Egyptian Peasant, An Opinion of the Present Government], *Al-Mu'ayyad,* August 12, 1908. "Al-Ajram fi al-Rif" [Crimes in the Countryside], *Majallat al-Shu'un al-Ijtima'iyya* (1940): 20. "Al-Amn al-'Amm fi al-Sana al-Madiya" [Public Security during the Past Year], *Majallat al-Shu'un al-Ijtima'iyya* 2 (1941): 106.

6. Cromer, *Modern Egypt,* 2:211; also quoted in Jacques Berque, *Egypt: Imperialism and Revolution,* trans. Jean Stewart (London: Faber and Faber, 1972), 236. For the urban side, see Timothy Mitchell, *Colonising Egypt* (Cambridge: Cambridge University Press, 1988).

7. Lord Cromer, *Report by His Majesty's Agent and Consul General on the Finances, Administration and Conditions of Egypt and the Soudan,* report for 1902, 41. British officials often saw the problem as "Oriental" rather than simply Egyptian in nature. Indeed, Percy F. Martin, a contemporary British official in the Sudan wrote, "To offer these unfortunate people a new and merciful mode of exaction meant at once the gaining of their confidence, for the Orientals infinitely prefer a form of light taxation to the bestowal of European gifts of 'progress' which they neither understand nor appreciate" (*The Sudan in Evolution: A Study of the Economic, Financial, and Administrative Conditions of the Anglo-Egyptian Sudan* [New York: Negro Universities Press, 1970], 93).

8. Findley to Grey, July 7, 1906, FO 141/397/113.

9. As an example of peasants' bad social morals, Yusif Nahhas cited their proclivity to lie. See *Al-Fallah: Halatuhu al-Iqtisadiyya wa-l-Ijtima'iyya* [The Peasant: His Economic and Social Condition] (Cairo: Khalil Matran, 1926; originally published 1902), 59.

10. For example, a British Inspector for the Egyptian parquet linked the lack of morality and fear of vengeance with the widespread refusal by peasants to give evidence. See Kershaw, "Difficulties of Criminal Investigation in Egypt," FO 371/43863/16, file 68.

11. See Muhammad al-Babli, *Al-Ajram fi al-Rif Asbabuha wa-Turuq 'Ilajiha* [Crimes in the Countryside, Their Causes and Methods of Treating Them] (Cairo: Matba'at Dar al-Kutub al-Misriyya, 1941), 241–43.

12. Indeed, rural crime was often described as the most important national issue. See *Al-Muqattam*, June 9, 1891, February 18, 1897, November 18, 1908. Civil courts (*al-mahakim al-ahliyya*), established in 1883, assumed most of the judicial functions formerly assigned to the 'umdas and other local officials.

13. Newspapers in the late nineteenth and early twentieth century regularly reported the suspension and fining of 'umdas for failure to report crimes.

14. Lord Lloyd, *Egypt since Cromer* (London: Macmillan, 1933) 1:153; "Report of the Judicial Adviser for the Year 1916," FO 371/151213/16, file 2927.

15. *Al-Ahram*, July 23, 1914; al-Babli, *Al-Ajram*, 241.

16. Tawfiq al-Hakim, *Yawmiyyat Na'ib fi al-Aryaf* [Diary of a Prosecutor in the Countryside] (Cairo: Maktabat al-Adab, n.d., originally published 1937), 33.

17. Section of report from Kafr al-Zayyat contained in R. M. Graves, "Precis of Reports from the Provinces on the Current Situation," November 3, 1926, FO 141/620/9353.

18. Ronald Graham, "Note on the First Elections for the Egyptian Legislative Assembly," December 29, 1913, FO 141/683/9353; Sir Valentine Chirol, *The Egyptian Problem* (London: Macmillan, 1921), 161.

19. Alfred Milner, *England in Egypt* (London: Edward Arnold, 1904; originally published 1892), 317–18.

20. While both the Egyptian elite and the British felt that the peasants needed to be taught better morals, the British did not share the Egyptian view that formal education was the best means. When the British controlled Egyptian policy, they generally obstructed the spread of formal education. They saw the police, the courts, and bureaucratic firmness and fairness as the tools best suited to inculcate civic virtues in the peasantry. Formal education, in the eyes of the British, only taught the peasants insolence. As late as 1940, a British official favorably reported to the Foreign Office in London the view of a British businessman that "with the spread of education and the increased mobility of the people, the day was not far off when the fellahin might give serious trouble" (Report by Hamilton, assistant Oriental secretary, on his tour in Lower Egypt, contained in Lampson to Halifax, March 8, 1940, FO 371/J818/92/16, file 24623). Most Egyptian writers felt that the spread of literacy and formal education would instead support order in the countryside.

21. See 'Abd al-Ghani Ghannam *Al-Iqtisad al-Zira'i wa-Idarat al-Mazari'*

[Agricultural Economics and Farm Administration] (Cairo: Matba'at al-'Ulum, 1944), 85.

22. 'Aziz Khanki, "Hawadith al-Ightiyal fi al-Aryaf" [Incidents of Assassination in the Countryside], *Al-Ahram*, October 23, 1944.

23. Cromer, *Modern Egypt*, 2:226, 227.

24. Ibid., 161.

25. Berque, *Egypt*, 643.

26. *Al-Ahram*, November 3, 1936.

27. See, for example, the speech of Muhammad al-Basyuni before the Parliament, "Shu'un al-Fallah wa-Islah al-Qarya" [Peasant Affairs and Village Reform], printed in *Al-Ahram*, January 9, 1935. The most prominent works were Ibnat al-Shati' (pseudonym for 'Aysha 'Abd al-Rahman), *Qadiyyat al-Fallah* [The Peasant Issue] (Cairo: Maktabat al-Nahda, n.d.); and Mirit Ghali, *Al-Islah al-Zira'i* [Agrarian Reform] (Cairo: Jama'at al-Nahda al-Qawmiyya, 1945).

28. 'Abbas M. 'Ammar, *The People of Sharqiyya: Their Racial History, Serology, Physical Characteristics, Demography, and Conditions of Life* (Cairo: La Société Royale de Géographie d'Égypte), 323.

29. Henry Habib Ayrout, *The Egyptian Peasant* (Boston: Beacon Press, 1963), 19.

30. Berque, *Egypt*, 129, 484.

31. Helen A. B. Rivlin, *The Agricultural Policy of Muhammad 'Ali in Egypt* (Cambridge, Mass.: Harvard University Press, 1961), 211. Rivlin did overstate the burden slightly as she probably underestimated the Egyptian population.

32. Ibid, 205.

33. Cromer, *Report* for 1906, 68–69.

34. See Nathan Brown, "Who Abolished Corvée Labor in Egypt and Why?" in *The Impact of the 1838 Anglo-Turkish Convention*, ed. Donald Quataert and Çağlar Keyder (forthcoming).

35. *Al-Muqattam*, August 5, 1891.

36. Grafftey-Smith, "General Situation in Egyptian Provinces," FO 371/ J1125/4116, file 13118.

37. Hamed Ammar, *Growing up in an Egyptian Village: Silwa, Province of Aswan* (London: Routledge and Kegan Paul, 1954), 60.

38. Robert Tignor, *Modernization and British Colonial Rule in Egypt, 1812–1914* (Princeton, N.J.: Princeton University Press, 1966), 141–42.

39. See Alan Richards, *Egypt's Agricultural Development 1800–1980* (Boulder, Colo.: Westview Press), esp. 92–98.

40. Berque, *Egypt*, 45.

41. See Muhammad Ibrahim Al-Shawarbi, *Dawr al-Fallahin*, chap. 6.

42. Caglar Keyder, *State and Class in Turkey: A Study in Capitalist Development* (London: Verso, 1987), 121.

43. Goran Hyden, *Beyond Ujamaa in Tanzania: Underdevelopment and an Uncaptured Peasantry* (Berkeley: University of California Press, 1980), 211.

11

The Representation of Rural Violence in Writings on Political Development in Nasserist Egypt

TIMOTHY MITCHELL

The discussion of peasant politics and violence has always been strangely one-sided. Studies of rural resistance and rebellion continue to thrive.[1] But it seems to be a convention of the literature that rural violence refers to the violence of the poor and the powerless. The phrase is not usually taken to mean violence used against these groups. Although the latter may be discussed in explaining the context of rebellions or the reactions they provoke, it is seldom itself the focus of analysis.

Part of the reason for this one-sidedness is that any attempt to write about the everyday use of violence against the powerless faces the problem of evidence. Violence directed against people within a small community often relies on the power to impose silence. Victims can disappear, relatives may fear to speak, investigations, if they occur, produce only accusations and hearsay or are organized to serve larger political purposes. The original act of violence is therefore easily lost, and writing about it becomes an almost impossible effort to reconstruct events out of fragments and recover the voices of the missing.

Yet the silence imposed by local forms of violence is seldom total. A violence that erased every sign of itself would be remarkably inefficient. The death, the disappearance, the physical abuse, or the act of torture must remain present in people's memory. To acquire its usefulness in the play of domination, violence must be whispered about, recalled by its victims, and hinted at in later threats.

Within a culture of fear, the evidence lies in what is missing. To elaborate a cultural economy that can manufacture fear and submission depends on ever-present references to what has disappeared, upon deaths remembered and violations recalled. Paradoxically, the void that seems to undermine the foundations of a scholarly account of political violence turns out to be a crucial empty space— "the space of death" as Michael Taussig (1984) calls it, invoking a phrase of Walter Benjamin. By reference to this space the construction of an economy of fear can proceed. It also follows that the recollections, reports, and rumors that refer us to what is missing are not just secondary evidence offering partial and unreliable access to the original event. Without these patterns of recollection the original event would lose effect. It is the combination of violence and its recollection, of the absent and its representation, that constitutes the event.

Realizing the hybrid nature of its occurrence, we can perhaps become more attentive to the problem of political violence against the poor and begin to question the ways we write about rural politics. In this chapter I reread some accounts of village politics in the Middle East, taking the well-studied case of Egypt in the 1960s. I consider the kinds of writing through which this period has been represented, particularly in the United States, looking for the signs of violence that have been missed and asking how far the narratives we have been given are capable of addressing the question of violence. I begin by presenting some fragmentary evidence of political violence against the poor, gathered in rural Egypt in the 1960s.

The evidence consists of accusations made by the inhabitants of Ghazalat 'Abdun, a village in Sharqiya governorate in the Nile Delta, as recorded in a secret report drawn up in October 1966 by the Criminal Investigation Department of the Egyptian army and reproduced, twenty years later, in an appendix to Hamied Ansari's *Egypt: The Stalled Society* (1986). The report is one of about three hundred such reports submitted to the so-called Higher Committee for the Liquidation of Feudalism set up in 1966 by President Gamal 'Abd al-Nasser in response to demands that the government investigate and curb the provincial power of large landowners.[2] The report accuses Ahmad Hasan 'Abdun, a former member of Parliament and the largest landowner in the village, of eleven "criminal and terrorist" offenses.

"Approximately ten years ago," according to the report, Ahmad Hasan "was accused of killing Muhammad al-Qalshani Ibrahim from the village." The victim "vanished from sight and no traces of him were ever found. No one came forward to testify against him out of fear. The investigations were suspended for lack of evidence." Ahmad Hasan then "took possession of the land belonging to the slain peasant, which amounts to more than four feddans

of the village *zimam* [cultivated area]." (One feddan equals 1.04 acres, or
0.42 hectares.) Five years later, the report claims, Ahmad Hasan "beat and
tortured the farmer Hasan Ahmad 'Ali, known at Hasan Naqah, who was his
private guard." The torture "led to bleeding and death," but "no one in the
village dared to lodge a complaint against him." He dealt with another farmer
"by tying him to his car and dragging him along the village roads until he
reached the front of his store. The victim was naked and he was beaten and
maimed in front of his mother. This took place because the victim demanded
the conversion into *hiyaza* [registered tenancy] of a plot of land he was
cultivating," of which Ahmad Hasan was the owner (Ansari 1986: appendix
D, 257–58).

Three years ago, the report further claims, Ahmad Hasan "beat and tortured the lawyer 'Abdel 'Azim 'Idrawis by burying him up to the shoulders in
a cemetery at night. He was rescued by his relatives. But as a result of this
incident the aforementioned lawyer lost his mind. He now lives as an insane
person in the village." On another occasion Ahmad Hasan "beat the citizen
Ahmad Yusif in the mosque while he was praying. He also assaulted his
wife." When the local schoolteacher, a nephew of the wife, intervened,
Ahmad Hasan assaulted him as well, "hitting him with a liquor bottle which
he held in his hand." In some cases the accusations refer to sexual harassment,
including a murder alleged to have taken place "because the victim refused to
comply with the wishes of the feudalist's wife, who was known for her bad
behavior," and the claim that Ahmad Hasan himself enticed "the wife of the
fruit seller 'Abdel Latif 'Ali to run away from her marital abode and coaxed
her to stay with him for a long time until her husband was forced to divorce
her." Ahmad Hasan then married the woman, "and she continues to be his
wife until now" (Ansari 1986:258–59).[3]

What can we learn from this kind of fragmentary evidence? In the first
place, the report seems to indicate that the typical cause of violence in the
village was a conflict over the control of its land. More than half the crimes it
mentions occurred in response to the victims' demands for cultivation rights.
Such struggles over access to the land appear again and again in the reports on
other powerful families that were submitted to President Nasser's committee,
not included in Ansari's appendix. The Salih family, for example, who owned
extensive property in the village of Beni Salih and nineteen neighboring
villages and hamlets in the district of Fayyum, south of Cairo, were accused
by the local villagers of dozens of acts of violence and exploitation—including at least six killings and the shooting of the village carpenter (Rashad
1977:311–13). A summary of some of the other complaints against members

of the family seems to reveal behind their use of violence the same conflict over cultivation rights. Complaints were made against Salih 'Ali Salih by Mursi 'Abd al-Qandil ("appropriated the produce of the land"), by Mujawir 'Abd al-Ghani Mujawir and his mother ("illegal seizure of half a feddan"), and by the heirs of Muhammad Radwan ("arrested and evicted from the land"); against Anwar 'Ali Salih ("eviction of 'Abd al-Qawi Sanhabi after he demanded a rental contract in writing"); against Anwar Mahmud 'Ali Salih by 'Abd al Tawwab 'Ali Muhammad 'Abd al-'Aziz ("illegal seizure of land he owned, which the former then sold"); and against 'Abd al-Zahir 'Ali Salih by Muhammad Muhammad 'Abd al-Rahman Hasanain ("land illegally seized"), by Mizar Makkawi ("appropriated the produce of the land"), by Naish Tusun 'Awad ("land illegally seized"), by Sufi Muhammad Muhammad Mus'ad and his father Muhammad Muhammad Mus'ad ("blocking a canal from which they used to obtain free irrigation, after which they had to pay for water") and many others (Rashad 1977:314–15).

The logic of these disputes seems clear. The demands for secure access to the land come from those who, like most villagers in Egypt, own virtually no land or none at all. Government figures suggest that in 1965, after the agrarian reform laws of 1952 and 1961, 45 percent of agricultural families were still landless (Radwan 1977:23).[4] Among those owning or renting land, 95 percent held less than five feddans, at an average of just over one feddan per holding, while the top 5 percent of owners continued to control 43 percent of the cultivated area (Radwan 1977:19). (After 1965 the degree of inequality among landholders appeared to decrease, not through land reform but through subdivision [Zaytoun 1982:277].[5] Yet by 1982 a census showed that the area of land in holdings of five feddans or larger had increased to 47.5 percent of the cultivated area, controlled by just 10 percent of landholders [Springborg 1990:29].)

These official figures, moreover, are an unreliable measure of the inequality of ownership. As we have seen, the villagers' complaint is that large landowners have the power to misrepresent the extent of their control.[6] Studies of individual villages almost invariably indicate a far greater inequality and a widespread evasion of the legal limit on landownership (which by 1969 was set at 50 feddans per individual, or 100 feddans per family). A study in 1980–81 of an upper Egyptian village showed that the village's 4,500 officially registered landholdings were consolidated into about 1,250 farms, including two of more then 300 feddans each (Hopkins 1983).[7] A study of three Delta villages in 1984 found that the official landholding records in one village "only began to hint at the degree of concentration of economic and

political power." Although the largest dozen owners officially farmed an
average of less than 15 feddans each and none controlled over 50 feddans, in
fact one individual farmed an estate of 150 feddans and his extended family
controlled three times that amount, or about one-quarter of the village's cultivated area (Commander 1987:53–55). Another village study, conducted in
1979, found that the largest landowner in the village owned about 200 feddans
but was registered as owning only 30 feddans. The study concludes that
widespread fear of a future lowering of the land ceiling "leads most rich
farmers to register their land under more than one name" (Adams 1986:89).[8]
The family of Ahmad Hasan 'Abdun owned 290 feddans, according to the
report from which I have been quoting, although the village registers showed
him owning only 100 feddans. He too had violated the agrarian reform laws
by registering the land under different names.

    This kind of control of the land can be seen as the means, in turn, for
constructing a broader economic and political power. In the case of Ahmad
Hasan it enabled him to monopolize both the village's labor and its agricultural produce. "Tenancy contracts do not exist between him and the peasants," the report notes, "and he exploits them in the worst manner because he
appropriates all the crops, while leaving to them only meager amounts of rice
and wheat." Also, "he imposes forced labor on peasants to work in his
orchards without payment of wages or against very low wages. Whoever
opposes him is punished by beating and torture to be followed by expulsion
from the land and the village" (Ansari 1986:257). Ahmad Hasan's power was
further extended through his control of an irrigation pump and the supply of
water to the fields, and through an attempt to monopolize the supply of
fertilizer from the government cooperative in the village. When the clerk of
the cooperative, a relative of his, tried to resist his demands for more fertilizer
than his quota, Ahmad Hasan "put the warehouse of the cooperative on fire
causing damage amounting to £180 which was paid by the aforementioned
clerk. This incident took place in 1963. He also instigated some of his assis-
tants to let the water flow into the warehouse which damaged the fertilizers
stored there, in order to mete out vengeance on the cooperative's clerk"
(Ansari 1986:259, translation modified).

    The significance of these forms of violence, however, is not simply a
question of their economic utility. In fact, as Taussig remarks (1984:469), it
would be a mistake to make do with a neatly utilitarian explanation of such
events. Although most of the violent incidents in the report on Ahmad Hasan
can be related to a particular dispute over land, labor, or crops, the violence
seems to exceed this kind of utility: a man is buried alive, another is tied to a

car and dragged naked along the village streets, other forms of torture are even worse. The excess appears inexplicable, and leads one to question the reliability of the reports. The Egyptian army's Criminal Investigation Department, after all, was notorious for its own use of terror in collecting information. Yet despite the problems of reliability in such circumstances, the accusations against Ahmad Hasan include a kind of detail that suggests the reports come from the villagers themselves. A certain beating takes place in front of the victim's mother, another occurs during the month of Ramadan, the weapon used in a third case is a liquor bottle. The dates, the locations, the financial sums, and the relationships between the parties involved are all precisely recalled. The details suggest, if not the absolute reliability of the events, their status as stories that have been placed carefully in memory and told and retold among the victims. The accounts, by what seems to us their excess (something we have no way of measuring), reveal a culture of fear.

It is in this context that we should consider the question of reliability. Our impulse is to get to the bottom of such stories, to establish their truth. But as I suggested at the start and as the accusations against Ahmad Hasan seem to confirm, the truth of a culture of fear is built upon absences, upon tortures "no one dared to report," victims who "vanished from sight" and investigations "suspended for lack of evidence." "Despite all these criminal incidents," the report on Ahmad Hasan concludes, ". . . no one dared to accuse him, out of fear" (Ansari 1986:259). To take these accusations seriously as the signs of a culture of fear is not to imply that such fear and violence is typical of all Egyptian villages. But it does raise the question of what exactly, in that case, such reports can be taken to represent.

Some writers on rural Egypt have taken these reports, in a sense, as highly representative. They are taken to represent not the typical landowner, but the very limited extent of this kind of exploitation and its essentially feudal nature. In a country of about 5,000 villages, it is pointed out, the Higher Committee for the Liquidation of Feudalism produced reports on only some 330 families. From this the conclusion is drawn that there were only "pockets" of illegality and resistance to land reform and that exploitation in the countryside was "successfully ended by the reforms of the Nasserist period." Any further reference to "exploitation," therefore, "cannot be other than political propaganda" (Harik 1974:9–10; 1984:46–47). The problem with this use of the higher committee's reports is that conflicts over control of the land were not confined to those villages the committee investigated. On the contrary, its investigations were deliberately limited to families subject to the first agrarian reform law of 1952 (those owning over 200 feddans, or 300 if they had dependent children) in order to divert a far broader popular discontent with the exploitative conditions of rural capitalism, whose power the land reforms had strengthened, by misrepresenting the problem as the survival of the remnants of a pre-1952 "feudalism."[9]

We should not be misled into making the reports represent, in this way, the near absence of violence in rural Egypt after 1952. Although the degree of coercion was no doubt less severe in many other cases, conflicts over the land may have been endemic. In a study of local conflict in three villages in Middle Egypt between 1967 and 1970, 'Abd al-Mu'ti found constant disputes in each village focused on the same three issues: tenant farmers falling behind in the payment of rent, the consequent attempts by the owners of the land to evict them, and the demand of the tenants to have their rental agreements put in writing ('Abd al-Mu'ti 1977). It is true that these disputes were handled by village committees, whose records were the only available evidence for such a study, rather than by the more invisible methods of violence favored by Ahmad Hasan. Like other local institutions, however, the committees were dominated by the landowners and generally ruled in their favor. They thus served the useful function of diverting and dissipating the grievances of tenant farmers (they did nothing for the landless), while legitimizing the underlying relations that are the source of coercive power.

Given the nature of the subject, we cannot resolve the question of how far the reports of violence like that of Ahmad Hasan 'Abdun are representative. To ask how many other large landowners were like Ahmad Hasan or how many other Egyptian villages endured a similar culture of fear would be fruitless. What we can do is to employ what this case tells us about the elusive nature of rural violence against the poor to interrogate and perhaps unsettle other accounts. Rather than passing over the details found in the reports of the Higher Committee for the Liquidation of Feudalism, I want to use them to examine the representation of violence against the poor in Western academic accounts of rural Egypt. I will argue that we have developed ways of writing that, given the nature of rural violence, tend systematically to exclude it from the picture.

A symptom of this exclusion is that in Ansari (1986) the report on Ahmad Hasan is consigned to an appendix. Nowhere in the text itself are its details laid out and examined. The book opens with another case of rural violence, a detailed recounting of the story of a murder in the village of Kamshish, to which I will come back; but even this account is strangely disconnected from the rest of the text. Despite an avowed concern with "local community relations" (xiii), Ansari follows Binder (1978) in examining the national influence of the rural bourgeoisie rather than the local construction of its power. Other studies of rural politics in Nasserist Egypt show a similar neglect.[10]

The only passage of which I am aware describing the role of violence in creating a culture of fear is the following paragraph from Iliya Harik's study of a village in the Nile Delta summarizing the conduct of Mustafa Samad and his brother, who until the end of the 1950s were the village's dominant family.

> The conduct of the two brothers in governing the village was harsh but not ruthless; only two cases of major violence perpetrated by the Samads were reported to me. The first involved a peasant cultivator who had urgent business with Mustafa Samad and pursued him persistently, causing Mustafa to lose his temper and beat him. This incident accidentally led to the man's death, but the issue was settled privately by Mustafa and was never discussed by the villagers with outsiders, a practice quite common in Egyptian villages. A second case involved the accidental shooting of a woman by a member of the Samad family. Again, no official investigation followed the incident, and Mustafa settled the matter with the woman's family. The only other use of violence attributed to the Samad's government involved the beating, intimidation, and blackmail of villagers who caused problems or dared challenge the Samads' authority. (1974:52)

Harik's account of the village he calls "Shubra al-Jadida" is by far the most thorough study we have of Egyptian rural political life in the 1950s and 1960s. But remembering the report against Ahmad Hasan, one begins to wonder how many more cases of "harsh but not ruthless" behavior, privately settled "accidents," and routine violence against those who "caused problems" would need to be reported for all this to merit proper consideration as belonging to the book's central concern, described as "the structures of power in the community" (Harik 1974:27). By the time the author arrived in Shubra in the late 1960s the Samad family had been displaced by another powerful land-owning family, the Kuras. The book mentions in passing that one of the Kura men was "given to violent expressions of his feelings" (73) and that the two lieutenants on whom the Kuras relied "for contact with villagers" were "known for their short tempers" (75). But the question of a culture of fear or the use of violence is simply not raised.

The failure to examine the question of political violence against the poor in Western academic writing on rural Egypt is not merely a matter of oversight or neglect. Rather, as the rest of this essay argues, the literature has generally constructed its object of study in such a way that any evidence of such violence, given its elusive nature, has inevitably been discounted or transformed into something else. This has occurred in several ways, which I will illustrate through a close reading of the two major American works analyzing the period of Nasserist intervention in the countryside, James Mayfield's *Rural Politics in Nasser's Egypt* (1971) and Harik's *Political Mobilization of Peasants* (1974). I have chosen these two works because they deal with the period in which the reports of the Higher Committee for the Liquidation of Feudalism were compiled and will enable us to consider in more detail our understanding of rural violence in that critical period.[11]

Mayfield's *Rural Politics in Nasser's Egypt* is a study of the Arab Socialist Union, the single political party set up in 1962 as part of the process of state-capitalist intervention in the countryside, and of the "psychological barriers" that this process encountered in the form of the Egyptian peasant's "personality and culture." The structure of the argument, as I will show, converts fragmentary evidence of rural political violence into the symptoms of a cultural psychopathology.

The book explains the peasant personality as an unstable mixture of violence and submissiveness. The submissiveness is said to be created by the peasant's general inability to comprehend the forces shaping his life and by the way he raises his children. "The main objective of child training," we are told, "is to cultivate a docile and yielding disposition" (61). The child learns to cherish authority, being discouraged from "independent thinking" by the "feelings of uneasiness or anxiety that may develop in a person making a decision outside the accepted framework" (62). Trained from childhood "to obey without questioning," the peasant's inevitable resentment toward superiors "can be relieved only on inferiors—even if it is only the village animals" (63). Thus an inbred submissiveness in turn breeds violence. "When a complaint does occur, it is likely to be in the form of an emotional protest, or even in the form of violent behavior. With rare exception there is little training in the kind of pragmatic give-and-take that a democratic polity requires" (62).

The violence lying beneath the villager's submissive surface explains other psychological traits, such as what the American visitor experiences as the peasant's "excessive" politeness and generosity. The hospitality and generosity of the Arab, explains Mayfield, quoting the sociologist Morroe Berger (1964:142), "ward off expected aggression. One has the feeling, indeed, that the hostility that becomes overt aggression is so uncontrollable that such measures as excessive politeness (a form of avoidance) or hospitality (a form of ingratiation in a situation where intimacy cannot be avoided) are at times absolutely necessary if social life is to be maintained at all" (cited Mayfield 1971:70). Given this risk of an uncontrollable aggression threatening the very possibility of social life, the peasant "expects the superior to be strict and firm," Mayfield says. "This attitude is often forgotten by bureaucrats and government workers who try to be friendly and kindhearted. Such behavior immediately creates distrust, since they are not playing the role the peasant expects of them" (71). If villagers seem distrustful of authority, in other words, it is because they are not getting enough of it.

The peasant's inbred desire for authority produces not only a spasmodic violence but also a permanent dishonesty of character, termed the "*fahlawi* personality." The fahlawi is a peasant skilled in "deception and trickery," who adapts himself according to the situation. He is sycophantic toward his employer, "kissing his hand and caressing him with flattering words," but as soon as the employer's back is turned the fahlawi "satisfies his ego and frustration" by making him the butt of his jokes (68–69). Given this dishonesty and the fact that "superficiality is the accepted behavior" (68), the fahlawi peasant cannot be trusted as an employee. He has a "wondrous" ability to evade work and responsibility, to find "the 'shortcut' way of doing things," and to "finish his job quickly" without seeing to "the 'finishing touches' " (72). The fahlawi's dishonesty even explains evidence that seems to contradict these racial stereotypes. When the author makes the unexpected discovery that many villagers with whom he talked desired a modern education for their children, he interprets this as a sign of the fahlawi's ability "to perceive what he must do, say and believe in order to be accepted and therefore not bothered" rather than a serious desire for the advantages of schooling (67).

The author cautions us that not every rural Egyptian is necessarily a fahlawi. The more general characteristics of the peasant's psyche include "the obstinate conservatism and parochialism, the suspicion and mistrust, the general apathy and unconcern" together with his "hopelessly avaricious" preoccupation with just two objects of desire, "the acquisition of land and money," a preoccupation "by which his whole personality is twisted." The greed and suspicion combine in the peasant personality to produce "that frantic jealousy which, from passionate and personal causes in the villages, saps the vitality of private enterprises and government institutions, and makes mutual confidence and cooperation almost impossible" (72–73).

The reasons for the failure of policies of rural modernization already seem clear. But the flaws in the peasant personality will cause him not just to weaken the vitality of state-capitalist development, but to reject the very authority of landowners, agricultural experts, and the state. In compensation for his "feelings of inadequacy" the peasant develops an immense egoism, visible in "the tendency to exaggerate one's self-importance, abilities, and control of the situation." The peasant ego is enhanced by making "private attacks on the governor, the landlord, or the village doctor" and expressing "indignation toward anyone or anything that emphasizes difference in status" (69–71). While outwardly respectful toward his superiors, "inwardly he rejects their authority. This feeling can be noted in conversations among the fellahin and the young agricultural engineers who wear 'the western suits' and about whom the *fahlawi* will say *fulan 'amil rayyis* ('such a person acts like a boss')" (71). The end result of this pathology of submissiveness, violence, distrust, greed, and exaggerated egoism is that the rural Egyptian "does not look upon government authority as necessary to society" (71). The state therefore faces in an acute fashion the problem confronting all "newly emerging nations": how to develop among these abnormal personalities "a deep and unambiguous sense of identity with the national government." The name for this problem is invoked in the book's subtitle, "A Quest for Legitimacy," which is defined as "the process of inculcating and deepening the belief among members of a society that the present political institutions, procedures and ideals 'are right, are good, and are appropriate' " (5).

The traits of character described in *Rural Politics in Nasser's Egypt* are in many cases simply an accumulation of earlier Orientalist stereotypes, which are a major source for the book's observations.[12] These stereotypes probably tell us more about the political frustrations of those involved in organizing the capitalist transformation of Egyptian agriculture over the preceding two centuries than about the particular experiences of Egyptian villagers. Nevertheless, texts of this sort can be made, despite themselves, to reveal something of that experience. What appear to the outsider as patterns of docility and dissimulation, of distrust and disrespect for authority, of conservatism and suspicion, can be read as the characteristic symptoms of a culture of fear. Forms of coercion that leave no explicit trace may nevertheless reveal themselves to strangers through negative signs: silence, avoidance, extreme formality, and outward submissiveness.[13] As I suggested at the start, there is no way to establish the truth of these signs, for they are marks left by what is missing. But a writing addressed to the question of "personality and culture" commits itself in advance to interpreting them at face value, as inbred features of the peasant "character." This inevitably transforms what may be the fragmentary evidence of everyday coercion into the symptoms of a cultural pathology. In fact, an "avaricious" preoccupation with acquiring land and money might actually be a sign of abject poverty; "indignation" at differences in social status might indicate the harshness of the inequality; an unwillingness to "finish the job" might express the alienation of those coerced into producing for others' consumption at the expense of their own basic needs; the view that government is "unnecessary to society" might accurately reflect the way its police and army help suppress all fundamental attempts to improve things. But instead of pursuing such questions, all these marks of violence are turned into the psychological defects of its victims, and the violence disappears from view.

Iliya Harik's *Political Mobilization of Peasants* criticizes the psychological focus of works such as Mayfield's. It covers the same period in Egyptian politics but studies an individual village and concentrates "on behavior rather than personal characteristics" in order to uncover the local power network that implements development plans and shapes their success. Before addressing the somewhat different problems presented by this approach, I will situate the book's discussion more closely within the politics of the period. "Shubra" is located in Buhaira province, whose governor, Wagih Abaza, was a close ally of the Egyptian prime minister of 1964–65, 'Ali Sabri. In March 1965 'Ali Sabri took over as secretary-general of the Arab Socialist Union (ASU), and with the help of men like Abaza began reorganizing it as an instrument of mobilization and political surveillance that would simultaneously coopt or neutralize the left and undermine the power of large landowners and provincial bureaucrats. When Harik arrived in Buhaira early in 1967 he was accompanied by the district secretary of the ASU and a public relations official from the Ministry of Agrarian Reform. With their help he chose as his research site a village where the new organizations for rural mobilization had successfully been set up. He also selected a village that was not "strife-ridden," arguing that endemic strife is usually caused by conflict between family groups and can therefore interfere with "normal change processes" (8). For both these reasons, the chosen village turned out to be model of the success of 'Ali Sabri and Wagih Abaza's policies—at least at first.

During the 1950s, Harik found, the control of the village by the Samad family, some of whose methods of violence were described above, had been weakened. Although their own estates had not been subject to the 1952 reforms, land they had leased from an absentee owner, a prince of the royal family, had been confiscated and distributed among small tenants. The Samads found their political position challenged by the only other large resident landowners, the Kuras. The two Kura brothers and their nephew were from a merchant family originally involved in the cotton business. They lived outside the village itself in a large compound on the family estate, land their father had purchased in the village around 1913. As businessmen and politicians they were well connected with the new regime in Cairo, one of the brothers serving as an executive in a nationalized textile company in Tanta and later as a representative in the National Assembly. Thanks to the regime's 1952 reforms the Kuras had become the village's largest landowners, and by 1960 they had used their political connections and their increased influence within the village to replace the Samads as its dominant family. These changes were typical of the way larger rural landowners and the new state bourgeoisie (managers of the expanding state control of politics and the economy) transformed themselves during the dozen years after 1952 into an emergent Egyptian ruling class. It was the consolidation of the political and economic power of this class that the ASU mobilization program attempted to undermine in the years 1965–67. In Shubra, Sayid Kura was replaced as head of the village council by a twenty-eight-year-old party activist from Alexandria, who used evidence of the Kuras' mishandling of council funds and property, together with numerous village improvement projects, an active youth organization, and close surveillance of more militant villagers, to win the political support of Shubra's small landowners and isolate the Kuras.

This was the situation witnessed by Harik in the spring of 1967. By then, however, the mobilization policies were already being slowed down by conservative forces within the regime. They were brought to a halt by the Israeli invasion in the war of that summer, which also cut short Harik's fieldwork in the village after just three and a half months. When he returned for another stay the following summer, he found the party youth organizations had been banned after workers and students had led large antigovernment riots, the young head of the Shubra village council was being transferred elsewhere, and new council elections were under way. With organized campaigning prohibited and only 700 villagers voting (out of a population of over 6,000), the Kuras regained their political control. These developments paralleled those in the country as a whole: the defeat of 1967, the economic crisis it accelerated, and the resulting pressure upon the regime to accept the regional hegemony of the United States enabled the state bourgeoisie and their rural allies to reassert their influence over government policy. The Higher Committee for the Liquidation of Feudalism was disbanded, the lands confiscated from large owners like Ahmad Hasan 'Abdun were restored, and following Nasser's death in 1970 the more populist and pro-Soviet political faction led by 'Ali Sabri was defeated by a faction led by the champion of the state bourgeois and large landowning interests and the future symbol of the country's reintegration into the Western economy, Anwar Sadat.

Part of the value of Harik's account is that he is one of the few scholars to have captured some of these struggles as they occurred and to have illuminated their local complexion. Despite its obvious improvement over Mayfield's psychological and cultural approach, however, the book exemplifies a number of problems with the literature of the late 1960s and 1970s on political development. I will analyze three conventions of that literature. Rather than transforming the symptoms of violence against the poor into a cultural pathology in the manner of Mayfield, these conventions tend to exclude them altogether.

The first convention concerns the question of theme. In any work of political analysis, the account must invoke a larger political phenomenon that particular events are then arranged to illustrate. The phenomenon invoked and illustrated in *The Political Mobilization of Peasants* is a familiar one for American political analyses of this period, "the phenomenon of change." Change is conceived in common Weberian vocabulary as a process of rationalization, initiated by the national government. The regime in Cairo imposed "new normative rules" on the village, it is said, which brought about "the rationalization of its economic and political management" and a corresponding development in the villagers themselves of "new capacities and attributes." The end result is described as "village pluralism" (260–70).

This kind of narrative of the coming of modernity has been frequently criticized, and perhaps Harik himself would say certain things differently today.[14] I do not intend to repeat the criticisms here, but rather to focus on those aspects that seem to me to elide the question of violence. The first problem with the narrative of change is its high level of abstraction. To make events from an individual village portray a phenomenon as general as "change," a lot of detail must be eliminated from the picture—detail that may provide the very clues through which an elusive political violence is revealed. Exactly what gets eliminated depends upon how the movement of change is conceived. Like most such literature, *The Political Mobilization of Peasants* thinks of change as a centralized force intervening in the village from outside. "In Shubra," the book explains, "the major forces that had set in motion the processes of change came from outside the community, namely, the national government" (263). The forces of change are more or less synonymous with a central power, the state, that imposes itself on a resistant periphery.

What this conception excludes is the possibility of thinking of power as essentially local in construction; that is, drawing upon and shaped by the larger logic of Egypt's capitalist development, but built out of the practical relations between farmers and laborers, landowners and middlemen, bureaucrats and merchants, men and women. The fields that villagers own or rent, labor in or supervise, sell or seize control of are the crucial site for constructing and contesting rural power relations—which is why almost every account of violence in the report on Ahmad Hasan 'Abdun mentions fields in one way or another. "Shubra," however, appears to be a village without fields. For all the book's richness of information about village life, from the details of people's travel habits to the closely observed conduct of a local election, one closes *The Political Mobilization of Peasants* without ever having seen a field or learned about the day-to-day relations between the various groups for whom in different ways the fields are the center of their lives.[15]

Seen from the perspective of the fields, on the other hand, the state becomes a more complex set of relations. These no longer appear primarily in the form of a central power intervening to initiate change, but as local practices of regulation, policing, and coercion that sustain a certain level of inequality (not just in the control of the land but in a policy of rural pricing and taxation, for example, that takes from the poor and gives to the rich).[16] The programs of change, from this point of view, appear as temporary interventions that occur in reaction to crises in the local construction of power and are themselves a site of struggle and reversal. The temporary, reactive, and uncertain nature of these interventions cannot emerge from a narrative that seems to generalize such moments, under the name of change, into the unfolding of a unilinear history.

The mid-1960s, as I have suggested, were years of uncertainty and crisis, particularly in the countryside. A postcolonial bourgeoisie had emerged as the dominant force in both the countryside and the nationalized urban economy but had not been able to consolidate its control over the apparatus of government or force upon it the shift, necessary for that consolidation, from dependence on the Soviet Union to dependence on the United States. Even before the disaster of June 1967 an economic crisis had set in, as hard currency reserves dried up, growth rates came to a halt, U.S. food aid was cut off, and the cost of living jumped more than 50 percent in four years. The rural poor were badly hit by the crisis and paid for it in part with their own wages, which were already well below the poverty level and dropped a further 10 percent in real terms between 1965 and 1967 (Adams 1986, 138). Public protests, marches, and hunger strikes were organized in the provinces, particularly in the Delta around large towns like Dessouk, Damietta, Kafr al-Shaykh, and Damanhur, the latter being the market town just a few miles from Shubra. In Damietta in 1965 an incident between local fishermen and the police sparked a large protest in which people marched on the police station and were met with gunfire. Farmers, students, and the unemployed joined in, overturning cars and trucks as barricades, throwing missiles, and ransacking government offices and food cooperatives, until the central authorities intervened and placed the area under martial law (Hussein 1973:231–32). Incidents of this sort persuaded the regime to launch its program of party mobilization, which was intended to divert discontent away from the government and at the same time turn the party into an apparatus of local surveillance.

The narrative of change, focusing on initiatives from the center and abstracting them into a story of development, inevitably tends to overlook the concrete political struggles in which political and economic control is contested or reaffirmed, as well as the forms of coercion and violence such struggles involve. Power is not simply a centralized force seeking local allies as it extends out from the political center but is constructed locally, whatever the wider connections involved. The so-called mobilizing initiatives from the center occurred in response to struggles for specific changes at the local level. The center did not initiate change, but tried to channel local forces into activities that would extend rather than further threaten the weakening influence of the regime.

The adverse consequences of such central intervention can further illustrate this point. The local forces the government attempted to coopt would inevitably overflow the new channels and require further diversion or supervision. This was quickly demonstrated by the famous incident in the Delta village of Kamshish, which is retold in the first chapter of Ansari (1986) and can be briefly summarized. Salah al-Din Husain, a villager from Kamshish who had been seized and then released again in the military-ordered arrest of thousands of political activists in the summer of 1965, was one of those coopted by the mobilization program onto the new ASU committee in the village.[17] He used this position to renew an old campaign from the 1950s against the political power of the landowning family that dominated Kamshish. The government's response was to have Salah Husain immediately placed under surveillance. Investigators discovered that he was the leader of a group of "communists" in his village, who were holding meetings among the peasants at which they "exploited the hatred of the village inhabitants" toward the large landowners and called for "the collectivization of agriculture and the abolition of private property." Two party officials were sent to Kamshish, a surveillance report mentions, to hold a public meeting at which they explained the government's idea of socialism. But Salah Husain "insisted after the conclusion of the discussion in telling the peasants that our socialism is influenced by Marxist thought." He was creating "dangerous divisions" among party members in the village, the report concludes, and was causing a threat to the country's "internal security" (Ansari 1986; appendix C, 251–54). It was such local threats rather than any process of development, as Harik and others would have it, that explains the central government's initiatives.

The following month, April 1966, Salah Husain was shot dead in the village, and his murder was attributed to the large landowners he had denounced. Unlike the killings attributed to Ahmad Hasan 'Abdun, with whose story we began, Salah Husain's death quickly gained attention beyond the village.[18] Party officials and journals took up his case, and the government was forced to respond. President Nasser visited Kamshish and promised an investigation, but once again the government tried to divert popular pressure away from fundamental change and into support for the regime. Instead of allowing 'Ali Sabri and ASU activists to continue investigating the rural bourgeoisie, Nasser set up the Higher Committee for the Liquidation of Feudalism and placed it in the trustworthy hands of his military chief, Field Marshal 'Abd al-Hakim 'Amir. As I mentioned earlier, 'Amir limited committee investigations to the few hundred families that had been liable to the original 1952 land reform. The problem was thus defined narrowly as the survival of individual "feudalists," meaning remnants of the old regime, rather than as the emergence of a rural bourgeoisie nurtured by the new regime. Feudalism could be portrayed as an isolated obstacle to the larger process of development, obscuring once again the more systematic and local forms of coercion out of which everyday domination is built.

The case of Kamshish illustrates how complex, uncertain, and violent can be the struggles in which political control is locally constructed. It also illustrates how the literature on political development, by abstracting such events into the story of how a process of change encounters local obstacles, imitates the language of the regime—a language incorporated into such institutions as the Higher Committee for the Liquidation of Feudalism. The imitation is unsurprising. For the writers on development, "change" is almost synonymous with the exercise of central power. We cannot expect, therefore, that literature of this sort might take as its focus the forms of everyday violence against which the villagers of Kamshish campaigned.

The second narrative technique that tends to elide the question of violence is to construct the story at the local level as an account of interacting individuals. The analysis of village politics, argues Harik, "has to focus on individuals rather than on social classes" (217), a focus that is again a convention of such accounts. One examines the alliances individuals form, the strategies they pursue, and the dominations they attempt. The picture that emerges in the case of Shubra is of a "pluralistic" balance of competing village alliances in which individual allegiances continually shift, rather than any domination of the village by a "power elite" (111, 126). We should note, however, that the individuality taken as the starting point of such analyses is always itself politically constructed. It is a position created out of a certain arrangement of social relations, including relations of subordination and domination. To take the individual as one's starting point renders these unequal relations invisible, and obscures the forms of coercion on which they may depend. (I am not, I should add, going to argue for what is sometimes called "class analysis," which takes the same individualism and looks for its attributes in aggregations of individuals, discovering, needless to say, that such aggregations do not consistently think or behave like individuals and thus appearing to prove that a concept of class has no significance.) In a village such as Shubra, the most significant such relations will be the differing relationship to the land. Although *The Political Mobilization of Peasants* argues that "there is very little social differentiation among the villagers of Shubra" (138) and gives no precise figures, the book provides sufficient information to enable us to outline the different kinds of individuality that social relations in Shubra construct.

Broadly speaking, social relations in Shubra place its inhabitants—or at least its adult males, for women and children are subject to additional forms of subordination about which the book tells us nothing—in one of four different positions. About 40 percent of them, having no land of their own, are employed by others and live in severe poverty. Most sell their labor to middlemen who supply agricultural laborers to village landowners or provide work gangs for governmental irrigation projects out in the desert; others are employed as guards, servants, office boys, vendors and itinerant artisans.[19] Their average income is £3 a month, or £36 a year if they are fortunate enough to find work all year round (47). In 1967, to sustain an average family of two adults and 3.25 children at the poverty line cost £148 per year, or more than four times the annual income of the fully employed landless villager.[20]

A second class of villagers, slightly larger than the first, consists of those with access to small plots of land, either owned or rented.[21] All of them are beneficiaries, directly or indirectly, of the 1952 land reform and farm an average of 2.5 feddans each (43). This provides each farmer with a net income of about £200 a year (47), over five and a half times the income of the landless villager and enough to keep an average family adequately above the poverty line. With a cultivated area of 3,559 feddans, the village has enough land to give every adult male 2.5 feddans of his own and thus end the desperate poverty of the landless (indeed, there would still be a few hundred feddans surplus after such a distribution). A limit of 2.5 feddans would be comparable to the limit imposed in the early 1950s by two of the more successful land reform programs in the Third World, those of Taiwan and South Korea (Powelson and Stock 1987:84, 189). But with the Egyptian government allowing private estates of up to 100 feddans per family, the remaining land in Shubra was concentrated in the hands of a few dozen large owners.

Possessing an average of about 20 feddans, these landowners together constitute the third and fourth social classes. We can follow Samir Amin's (1964) analysis of agrarian class relations in Egypt and divide these landowners into "rich peasants" (owners of 5 to 20 feddans) and "rural capitalists" (over 20 feddans). (We should link with the latter the large shopkeepers and the middlemen, who, as we will see, play a vital role in the exploitation of the poor but whose numbers or place in the village are not described.) No clear boundary separates the "rich peasants" from the wealthier of the small peasant farmers, and in fact in the period of party mobilization it was this uncertain boundary that became the site of the shifting political allegiances that are labeled pluralism. However, the difference between the handful of capitalist landowners—the Kuras, the Samads, and about four absentee owners—and those with little or no access to land is quite clear. The three Kura men, for example, had a registered holding of 136 feddans (115). Leaving aside the question of unregistered holdings and their significant income from other sources, each of them received an annual income from farming alone of at least £3,600, or one hundred times the earnings of a landless villager.[22]

To be an individual in such a village economy means to be already situated in a set of coercive relations. For the landless 40 percent it means being positioned as a victim of poverty, malnourishment, and a desperate need for work—all forms of coercion invisible to a narrative that focuses on interacting individuals. To illustrate the coercive power of these social relations, we can examine the story of an effort to unionize Shubra's agricultural laborers. As part of its attempt to reduce profiteering in the countryside, in 1966 the ASU helped landless laborers in Shubra establish a labor union to replace the system of labor contractors. Instead of selling their labor at a rate below market price to a middleman, who then sold it to government land reclamation projects or agricultural cooperatives at a profit, the laborers' own representative was to deal directly with the employer. Three laborers from the village were trained by the party as union leaders and were shown how "official and semi-official government agencies exploited them no less than did landlords" (253). Despite this outside assistance the effort seems to have failed, at least as regards the village's largest employer, the agricultural reform cooperative.

The workers needed to be paid every day in order to feed themselves and survive, but the cooperative paid wages through a central bureaucracy only once every two weeks. Under the old system, labor contractors possessed sufficient capital to advance the workers their pay daily (and also no doubt to provide small loans to cover medical, marital, or other exceptional expenses that wages well below the poverty level can never cover, thereby creating a typical relationship of debt bondage).[23] The new union had no resources from which to make such advances. The local leadership of the cooperative, which represented the small landowners of the village and was opposed to unionization, refused to advance the union the necessary credit from cooperative funds, and so the attempt to eliminate the middlemen failed (252–54).

The book suggests that we interpret this dispute "without preconceived ideas of social class." The two parties involved have "similar humble backgrounds," it is said, and we should explain their conflict simply as "a contest situation in the context of incompatible interests" (2552–56). It should be read, that is, as one more example of interacting individuals forming competing alliances in a system of village pluralism. In fact the parties' backgrounds appear similar only when compared to outsiders' or to large capitalist landowners'. As we just saw, the small farmers who constitute the membership of the cooperative in fact enjoy an average income over five and a half times that of landless laborers (and the leaders of the cooperative are wealthier than the average member). Moreover, their own relative prosperity depends on maintaining the low wages of the laborers they employ on their farms, which is why they support their forcible exploitation by middlemen (who form a third, but unanalyzed, party to the conflict). It is precisely these kinds of coercive relationships that an analysis of social relations can illuminate, and whose form of everyday violence the "focus on individuals" eliminates from view.

The third and final narrative technique I will examine is the positioning of the author. Like most social science literature, *The Political Mobilization of Peasants* situates its author in the position of an objective outsider, disconnected from the object he describes.[24] My concern with this convention is not to question the writer's integrity, but to examine the means by which the village of Shubra is set up as an object apart from the narrative and its author, and the effect of this on the representation of violence.

An American scholar visiting an Egyptian village is clearly an outsider, but the outsider can also constitute a position within the village. The Kuras are outsiders, set apart by the distance of their family compound from the rest of the village, their political connections, and their large estate, yet these same factors also situate them within the village. The young party activist brought in from Alexandria as the new mayor of Shubra is another sort of outsider situated in a particular way within, as are the district officials of the ASU to whom he submits his regular surveillance reports (92). It was these officials, in turn, who introduced the author to the village, and their close intervention in the villagers' affairs was the context in which he began his observation of their political behavior and administered to them his questionnaire. Such circumstances inevitably situated the author within the complex political struggles of the village.

One can get a sense of the author's situation from the book's account of accusations of corruption among the board members of the village cooperatives. The book describes the accusations as the product of "a community suspicious of holders of public office" and argues that the board members lacked "the tenacity to withstand the pressures and slights to which public servants are usually subjected" in such a community (243). This explanation actually reflects exactly the view of the board members themselves. "People are not appreciative," one of them complained to the author. "They are quite suspicious of a person in office. If a board member repairs the ceiling of his house, buys a water buffalo, or improves his land, they think he is using public funds of the cooperative for personal advantage." Such individuals were "oversensitive," the book concludes (245). "Criticism and suspicion of their record came only from a militant few" (243).

Given the author's situation, we learn little about this "militant few." The accusations against the cooperative came from a group led by "a tractor driver in need of a job, having been laid off from the Kura farm" (247). But we discover nothing about, say, his treatment as an employee, the reasons he was fired, the poverty he may suffer, or the prospects for such a "militant" of ever finding other employment. Still more reflective of the author's situation in the village is the exclusion from the study of women. "Because I observed no involvement on the part of women in the public affairs of the community," the author explains, "and because of practical research limitations, women were not included in the survey" (30). What is termed a question of "practical" research limitations is actually the theoretical issue of the author's status as an outsider and a male. One consequence of this status is the male researcher's conception of politics as "public affairs," meaning activities that are open to the observation of a visiting stranger. The problem in both these cases lies not in the author's failure to report the view of the unemployed or to gain access to the women's realm. Given his situation in the village, this was probably inevitable. It lies in our willingness to accept as a picture of "the structures of power in the community" (27) an account that says almost nothing about the poor and excludes all reference to the experience of women. Once again one must wonder, given the exclusions, how any evidence of the experience of violence among these groups could find its way into the picture.

There is a further aspect to the method of positioning the author in relation to his object. To establish the objectness of the village, and thereby the author's separation from it, the village has to be constructed as something object-like, available to external observation. This means construing it as a system of behavior, something visible objectively to an observer. Its visibility is contrasted to the invisibility of ideas or meanings, which are categorized as "subjective" and converted into visible, objective form by assuming them to consist merely of individual attitudes and recording these in a questionnaire. Behavioralism in political analysis has long been criticized (see, for example, Taylor [1971]—although such criticisms often end up presenting the same material/mental dualism in more sophisticated form), and so has the use of questionnaires in the study of rural development (e.g., Chambers 1983:49–58). My purpose here is to relate all this to the representation of violence. For reasons I will try to explain, behavioralism can never capture a culture of fear.

First, coercion may be articulated in the form of practices that can be reduced neither to observable behavior nor to individual opinions accessible by questionnaire. For example, people in Shubra share a "cultural norm of dignity and self-respect" (227), we are told, expressed not simply in personal attitudes but in a system of deferential practices, appropriate behaviors, and patterns of modesty. Such practices can operate as a subtle coercive force by which dominant families exercise what Bourdieu (1977:191) calls "symbolic violence"—those forms of obligation and compulsion that are never recognized as coercive but are experienced as generosity, piety, personal loyalty, or self-respect.[25] The local elections of 1968 in Shubra were governed by such expectations, which impeded active campaigning and helped ensure victory to the Kuras, thanks to their large accumulation of credit (what Bourdieu calls "symbolic capital") in the system of cultural coercion. This invisible kind of coercion cannot be understood from an observation of the behavior involved, which will appear simply as politeness or decorum. Nor can it be revealed by a survey of attitudes, since the essence of symbolic violence is that it is never recognized as such but is experienced as a system of morality.

Second, attitudes themselves can express far more than they actually say, particularly in the case of those living within the coercive constraints of poverty or political oppression. Although *The Political Mobilization of Peasants* reports little of the views of poorer villagers, much is to be read from what they tell us. The book reproduces part of the transcript of an interview with a fifty-five-year-old farmer, 'Abd al-Mawla. It begins as the author poses question number eight from his survey, concerning the activities in the village of the ASU leadership group:

"I don't know anything about them."

"You mean you have never heard of them?"

"I have, but I do not know anything about them. I just mind my own business."

"How did you hear about them?"

"From my children." He paused for a moment and then said, "I am told they go to meetings and talk politics. They want to appear like big people."

"You don't think this is right for them to do?"

"A peasant should not mix with such things. This is the big people's job. These men have left their fields unattended and are going around doing things that are none of their business." We changed the subject and talked about village problems.

"There are no problems," he said. "We just need a bakery," he added. "Not much grain these days in the village, and people baking at home are causing fires."

"You think you can do something about it?"

"No, I am a poor man and nobody listens to a poor man." (192–93)

Answers of this sort reveal little about "attitudes," and therefore seem to support conclusions about the absence of class consciousness among the poor and hence the pluralist character of village politics. But if one abandons the attempt to render village attitudes as things to be grasped "objectively," that is as solid, measurable objects, then these statements begin to reveal things that they do not consciously say. First, there is the evident apprehension. 'Abd al-Mawla "was courteous though ill at ease" during the interview, we are told, and each of his answers begins in the negative and expresses an unwillingness to speak: "I don't know anything about them"; "There are no problems." When he does consent to speak, his answers express more than anything else a sense of powerlessness: "I just mind my own business"; "A peasant should not mix with such things"; "Nobody listens to a poor man." We cannot gauge from this brief transcript the degree of apprehension or fear, the extent of powerlessness or its causes, or the local forms of violence of which these words might be an indirect expression. What we can judge, however, is that a culture of fear will never emerge from the measurement of attitudes.

A connection emerges, therefore, between the methods of analysis re-quired by the stance of objectivity and the disappearance of any sign of violence. On the one hand, the writer's position as an outsider within the village makes his writing tend to portray the experience of the wealthier male landowners at the expense of the experience of women or the poor. On the other hand, the convention of reducing meanings to those ideas available to individual villagers and expressible in the form of attitudes, so that they may be collected from questionnaires or interviews, tends to exclude the possibility of representing the experience of violence. Those who live intolerable lives, suffering from poverty, unemployment, malnutrition, and other, more direct forms of coercion, must somehow express their condition and yet may be unable to find the opportunity, the courage, or the language to do so. These conditions may express themselves not in attitudes or accounts of observable events, but in silences, an unwillingness to respond, or the sheer inability to narrate. None of this can be explored by the conventional methods of political analysis found in the works on Nasserist Egypt.

FROM A close reading of some of the American literature on rural politics in Nasserist Egypt, I have tried to show how the kind of narrative a particular work adopts can determine whether, and in what way, the question of rural violence is represented. An account of cultural or psychological obstacles to development, a narrative of change, an analysis of interacting individuals, and the construction of an objective view of political behavior and attitudes can in each case transform what evidence there may be of violence into some other pathology or render its effects invisible. This kind of writing contrasts starkly with the report on the violence of Ahmad Hasan 'Abdun. The report is an isolated document, the by-product of an attempt to dissipate broader forms of popular discontent, accidentally preserved in the archives. One need not suppose that its story is representative of capitalist agrarian relations in Egypt, or even absolutely reliable evidence for the particular case it records. But the report does have an important use. Its unsettling details can challenge us to reexamine the way Western scholars have represented rural political life in Egypt during the crucial conflicts of the 1960s, and to question the almost total absence of any sign of, and certainly any investigation of, local violence against the poor.

Notes

1. Besides the contributions in this volume, see the recent work in Middle East Studies by Brown (1990) and Schulze (1981) or the studies of everyday forms of

resistance in Southeast Asia by Adas (1981), Scott (1985), Stoler (1985), and others (cf. Scott and Kerkvliet 1986).

2. The deliberations of the committee and further examples of the reports can be found in Rashad (1977), 209–352.

3. For a discussion of what these reports tell us about the language of powerlessness among the poor, see Mitchell (1987), the source of the preceding two paragraphs.

4. This estimate is corroborated by Radwan and Lee's detailed survey in 1977 of 1,000 households in 18 Egyptian villages. They found that only 36 percent of households owned land, and that even including those households with tenancy agreements, the proportion with access to land was less than 50 percent. What proportion of the remaining households were landless by choice, having access to other sources of income, is unclear. But even if one counts as "landless" only the landless households living below the poverty line, as measured in the same survey, the total is still somewhere between 40 and 50 percent of rural households (Radwan and Lee 1986:48–49, 60–66).

5. The process of subdivision is usually attributed, without much evidence, solely to population pressure and the working of inheritance laws. But of equal importance may be the pressure of poverty, which, coupled with the soaring value of agricultural land, forces the smallest farmers to sell or rent out tiny strips of land to raise the funds needed to survive financial emergencies, to secure marriages for their children (and thus their own survival when too old to work), or to send a son to work abroad.

6. The official figures exclude land an owner legally rents out, which is recorded under the name of the tenant (Hopkins 1987:61). This may tend to reduce the size of large landownerships in the statistics.

7. Besides these two farms, Hopkins estimates that another five or six farmers in the village of Musha, near Asyut, were operating more than 100 feddans, and perhaps another dozen were operating over 50 feddans. Thus about twenty operators, in a village of 2,500 households, controlled somewhere between a third and a half of the village's 5,000 feddans (Hopkins 1983:181–97).

8. An extreme case of land reform evasion was the village of al-Barnugi, in Buhaira in the Egyptian Delta, where the Nawwar family was discovered in 1963 to still control 20,000 feddans (Harik 1974:6).

9. This interpretation of the higher committee was made at the time by Lutfi al-Kholi and other intellectual critics of the regime (see Binder [1978:343], and Baker [1978:108–13]). It is corroborated by the minutes of the committee's meetings, reproduced in Rashad (1977).

10. Studies of rural society in the Nasserist period by Egyptian scholars like Abdel-Fadil (1975) and Radwan (1977) offer a detailed analysis of agrarian reform and its effects on landownership, income, consumption, and prices. But they suffer from having to rely on aggregate quantitative data taken from official sources, whose problems were mentioned earlier. Nor do they examine the actual workings of political power in the countryside.

11. Some important case studies of village Egypt in the late 1970s and early 1980s have recently been published, such as Adams (1986), a study of agrarian poverty and political life in two Egyptian villages, Commander (1987), an analysis of agricultural

18. An alternative version of the Kamshish story later circulated, according to which Salah Husain was murdered at the behest of his wife, a woman of loose morals who hoped to marry into the large landowning family (see Waterbury [1983:340]). This is an example of how political grievances can be delegitimized by transforming them into personal slurs against the victim, the slur depending, needless to say, on impugning the morals of a woman. Anyhow, there is sufficient evidence in the documents collected in Rashad (1977) and in the appendix to Ansari (1986) to corroborate most details of Ansari's version of the story.

19. According to Harik's figures (1974:290, table 2), only 44 percent of the village's adult males cultivate their own land, leaving 56 percent who make their living by other means. It is not clear what proportion of the latter have adequate incomes from other sources and what proportion form the "landless" poor to whom I am referring. My figure of 40 percent is obtained from the table by adding 100% of "agricultural laborers" to 70 percent of "craftsmen and tradesmen" and 70% of "native employees" (70 percent being my estimate of the proportion of these two groups earning less than the poverty level of £12 per month [see note 20], based on the income figures given on p. 47), totaling 539 or 40 percent of the adult male population of 1,350. This figure may underestimate the proportion of families living in poverty because the survey excludes women, even those heading a household (Radwan and Lee's survey of 18 villages found that 8.5 percent of rural households were headed by females and that such households ranked among the poorest [1986:64, table 4.10]), and because it also excludes those who own or rent land in amounts too small to keep them out of poverty.

20. Calculated from the poverty table in Adams (1986:14), adjusted for 1967 using the cost of living index (138, table 6.2). The average family size, taken from population censuses, is calculated by Adams at 4.37 "adult equivalent units" (AEUs), where it is estimated that, on average, 1.0 person equals 0.830 AEUs.

21. Small shopkeepers and the more senior government employees appear to have a similar level of income (Harik 1974:47), but the resources they control may give them a distinct social position.

22. The actual income of the Kuras would have been much higher. Apart from the possibility that they controlled a larger area of land than recorded in the official registers or in answers to questionnaires, they appear to have been involved in several other ventures including livestock trading, and Muhammad Kura earned an income from his position in a government cotton firm in Tanta.

23. The system of debt bondage among migrant agricultural laborers is illustrated in Messiri (1983:88–92) with the case of a laborer who keeps his family alive with loans from a labor contractor and is obliged in return to spend most of the year in labor camps elsewhere in Egypt. Adams (1986:136) offers another illustration, the case of an agricultural laborer who frequently has to borrow money to meet basic needs like food or clothing and must then work for his creditor "a week or more without pay in order to discharge his loans."

24. Only in anthropology has the critique of objectivity been taken seriously by the discipline. For a discussion, see Clifford (1983).

25. Hopkins (1987:175–76, 187–88) includes a brief discussion of how a culture of deference helps maintain social inequality in an upper Egyptian village.

References

Abaza, Mona. 1987. "The Changing Image of Women in Rural Egypt." *Cairo Papers in Social Science* 10, monograph 4.

'Abd al-Mu'ti, 'Abd al Basit. 1977. *Al-Sira' al-tabaqi fi al-qarya al-misriyya* [Class Struggle in the Egyptian Village]. Cairo: Dar al-Thaqafa al-Jadida.

Abdel-Fadil, Mahmoud. 1975. *Development, Income Distribution, and Social Change in Rural Egypt, 1952–70: A Study in the Political Economy of Agrarian Transition.* Cambridge: Cambridge University Press.

Abu-Lughod, Lila. 1990. "The Romance of Resistance." *American Ethnologist* 17, 1:41–55.

Adams, Richard H. 1986. *Development and Social Change in Rural Egypt.* Syracuse, N.Y.: Syracuse University Press.

————. 1987. "The Effect of Remittances on Household Behavior and Rural Development in Upper Egypt." *Newsletter of the American Research Center in Egypt* 139 (Fall).

Adas, Michael. 1981. "From Avoidance to Confrontation: Peasant Protest in Precolonial and Colonial Southeast Asia." *Comparative Studies in Society and History* 23, 2:217–47.

Alatas, Hussein, Syed. 1977. *The Myth of the Lazy Native: A Study of the Image of the Malays, Filipinos, and Javanese from the 16th to the 20th Century and its Function in the Ideology of Colonial Capitalism.* London: Frank Cass.

Amin, Samir [Hasan Riad]. 1964. *L'Égypte nassérienne.* Paris: Éditions de Minuit.

Ansari, Hamied. 1986. *Egypt: The Stalled Society.* Albany: SUNY Press.

Baer, Gabriel. 1969. "Submissiveness and Revolt of the Fellah." *Studies in the Social History of Modern Egypt.* Chicago: University of Chicago Press.

Baker, Raymond. 1978. *Egypt's Uncertain Revolution under Nasser and Sadat.* Cambridge: Harvard University Press.

Beinin, Joel, and Zachary Lockman. 1987. *Workers on the Nile: Nationalism, Communism, Islam, and the Egyptian Working Class, 1882–1954.* Princeton, N.J.: Princeton University Press.

Berger, Morroe. 1964. *The Arab World Today.* Garden City, N.Y.: Doubleday.

Binder, Leonard. 1978. *In a Moment of Enthusiasm: Political Power and the Second Stratum in Egypt.* Chicago: University of Chicago Press.

Bourdieu, Pierre. 1977. *Outline of a Theory of Practice.* Cambridge: Cambridge University Press.

Brown, Nathan. 1990. *Peasant Politics in Modern Egypt.* New Haven, Conn.: Yale University Press.

Chambers, Robert. 1983. *Rural Development: Putting the Last First.* London and New York: Longman.

Clifford, James. 1983. "On Ethnographic Authority." *Representations* 1:118–46.

Commander, Simon. 1987. *The State and Agricultural Development in Egypt since 1973.* London: Ithaca Press, for the Overseas Development Institute.

Cuddihy, William. 1980. *Agricultural Price Management in Egypt.* World Bank Staff Working Paper no. 388. Washington, D.C.: World Bank.

Gendzier, Irene. 1985. *Managing Political Change: Social Scientists and the Third World*. Boulder, Colo.: Westview Press.

Glavanis, Kathy, and Pandeli Glavanis. 1983. "The Sociology of Agrarian Relations in the Middle East: The Persistence of Household Production." *Current Sociology* 31, 2:1–106.

Hamrush, Ahmad. 1975. *Qissat thawrat 23 yulyu* [The Story of the July 23 Revolution]. 5 vols. Cairo: Maktabat Madbuli.

Harik, Iliya. 1974. *The Political Mobilization of Peasants: A Study of an Egyptian Community*. Bloomington: Indiana University Press.

———. 1984. "Continuity and Change in Local Development Policies in Egypt: From Nasser to Sadat." *International Journal of Middle East Studies* 16, 1:43–66.

———, with Susan Randolph. 1979. *Distribution of Land, Employment, and Income in Rural Egypt*. Ithaca, N.Y.: Rural Development Committee, Center for International Studies, Cornell University.

Hopkins, Nicholas. 1983. "The Social Impact of Mechanization." In *Migration, Mechanization, and Agricultural Labor Markets in Egypt*, ed. Alan Richards and Philip L. Martin. Boulder, Colo.: Westview Press.

———. 1987. *Agrarian Transformation in Egypt*. Boulder, Colo.: Westview Press.

Hussein, Mahmoud. 1973. *Class Conflict in Egypt: 1945–1970*. New York: Monthly Review Press.

Mayfield, James B. 1971. *Rural Politics in Nasser's Egypt: A Quest for Legitimacy*. Austin: University of Texas Press.

El-Messiri, Sawsan. 1983. "*Tarahil* Laborers in Egypt." In *Migration, Mechanization, and Agricultural Labor Markets in Egypt*, ed. Alan Richards and Philip L. Martin. Boulder, Colo.: Westview Press.

Mitchell, Timothy. 1987. "The Ear of Authority." *MERIP Middle East Report* 147:32–35.

———. 1990a. "Everyday Metaphors of Power." *Theory and Society* 19:545–77.

———. 1990b. "The Invention and Reinvention of the Egyptian Peasant." *International Journal of Middle East Studies* 22, 2:129–50.

Powelson, John P., and Richard Stock. 1987. *The Peasant Betrayed: Agriculture and Land Reform in the Third World*. Boston: Oelgeschlager, Gunn, & Hain, in association with the Lincoln Institute of Land Policy.

Radwan, Samir. 1977. *Agrarian Reform and Rural Poverty: Egypt, 1952–1975*. Geneva: International Labour Organization.

———, and Eddy Lee. 1986. *Agrarian Change in Egypt: An Anatomy of Rural Poverty*. London: Croom Helm.

Rashad, Muhammad. 1977. *Sirri jiddan: min milaffat al-lajna al-'ulya li-tasfiyat al-iqta'* [Top Secret: From the Dossiers of the Higher Committee for the Liquidation of Feudalism]. Cairo: Dar al-Ta'awun.

Richards, Alan, and Philip L. Martin, eds. 1983. *Migration, Mechanization, and Agricultural Labor Markets in Egypt*. Boulder, Colo.: Westview Press.

Schulze, Reinhard. 1981. *Die Rebellion der ägyptischen Fallahin 1919*. Berlin: Baalbek.

Scott, James C. 1985. *Weapons of the Weak: Everyday Forms of Peasant Resistance*. New Haven, Conn.: Yale University Press.

————, and Benedict J. Tria Kerkvliet, eds. 1986. "Everyday Forms of Peasant Resistance in Southeast Asia." *Journal of Peasant Studies* (special issue) 13:1–150.

Seddon, David. 1986. "Commentary on Agrarian Relations in the Middle East: A New Paradigm for Analysis?" *Current Sociology* 34, 2:151–72.

Springborg, Robert. 1990. "Rolling Back Egypt's Agrarian Reform." *Middle East Report* 166:28–30.

Stoler, Ann. 1985. *Capitalism and Confrontation in Sumatra's Plantation Belt, 1870–1979*. New Haven, Conn.: Yale University Press.

Taussig, Michael T. 1984. "Culture of Terror—Space of Death. Roger Casement's Putumayo Report and the Explanation of Torture." *Comparative Studies in Society and History* 26, 3:467–97.

Taylor, Charles. 1971. "Interpretation and the Sciences of Man." *Review of Metaphysics* 25, 1:3–51.

Taylor, Elizabeth. 1984. "Egyptian Migration and Peasant Wives." *MERIP Reports* 124:3–10.

Tignor, Robert. 1982. "Equity in Egypt's Recent Past." In *The Political Economy of Income Distribution in Egypt,* ed. Gouda Abdel-Khalek and Robert Tignor. New York: Holmes and Meier.

————. 1984. *The State, Private Enterprise, and Economic Change in Egypt, 1918–1952*. Princeton, N.J.: Princeton University Press.

Waterbury, John. 1983. *The Egypt of Nasser and Sadat: The Political Economy of Two Regimes*. Princeton, N.J.: Princeton University Press.

Zaytoun, Mohaya A. 1982. "Income Distribution in Egyptian Agriculture and its Main Determinants." In *The Political Economy of Income Distribution in Egypt,* ed. Gouda Abdel-Khalek and Robert Tignor. New York: Holmes and Meier.

12

Clan and Class in Two Arab Villages

NICHOLAS S. HOPKINS

The comparison of the political evolution of two rural communities in the Arab world—the small town of Testour in northern Tunisia and the large village of Musha in Upper Egypt—illustrates broader trends in the Arab world and in developing cultures generally. By raising questions about the social bases of politics at the village level and about the relations among religion, economics, and politics, I intend to provide an analysis of village level politics that accommodates change. A further question is the place of local politics within the broader question of the relationship between local community politics and the state. The data discussed in this paper are essentially drawn from my work in 1972–73 in Testour and in 1980–81 in Musha, although I have made regular return visits to both communities since the original fieldwork periods.[1]

Although the two cases differ in degree, the general trend of politics in both communities can be summed up as a shift from a *clan* type based on hierarchical or vertical relationships (patron-client) to a *class* type based on horizontal linkages and class opposition. However, there are differences in the way this process has occurred. Part of my task in this paper is thus to explain the difference within the broader general trend.

At the most general level, we are dealing with rupture and change on the political level in Testour and with political continuity in Musha—though their mode of production has changed in similar ways. If the economic trends are similar in the two communities—toward mechanization, wage labor, agricultural credit, secure land tenure, and crops produced for the market—how can one account for the differences in political evolution? Are our analytical tools (e.g., mode of production) simply too blunt? Must factors such as cultural factors or the role of the state be included in the equation?

Testour

Testour is a small town of around 7,500 people in northern Tunisia, about 80 kilometers southwest of Tunis (Hopkins 1983). The town is the central point of a small marketing region, tied into a network of similar regional markets. The historic economic base of the town is agriculture—a mixture of animal husbandry and rainfall and irrigated agriculture. The economy of the local region has been articulated with wider systems through the market, which has developed its own identity. The population includes farmers, farm workers, shopkeepers and merchants, and government workers. There has long been a culture of differentiation, of distinctions between individuals and families. At the time of my fieldwork in 1973 this took the form of a ranking system according to which any individual or family could theoretically be ranked as higher or lower in respectability than any other. Social behavior was oriented to this conception of inequality.

Since the 1920s the agriculture has become mechanized, with animal power giving way to machines, sharing (sharecropping, carrying out particular tasks in return for a share of the product), to wage labor, and ranking to class, or at least the initial stirrings of class. Since 1980 several factories have sprung up, producing bathtubs, socks, and other items, and the Sidi Salem dam (the largest in Tunisia) has been completed less than 10 kilometers away on the Mejerda River (cf. Zamiti 1985).

The community is an Andalusian foundation, a new community in the seventeenth century, and retains a specific identity from that past that distinguishes it from the surrounding countryside. Testour shared in the Tunisian colonial experience (1881–1956) and in the Bourguibist epoch (1934–87). Administratively, it is a municipality and the seat of a "cell" or branch of the Parti Socialiste Destourien (at the time of fieldwork, Tunisia's single party).

While part of mainstream Islam, Testouris have also engaged in the practices of popular Islam. Brotherhoods (*tariqas*) were important in Testour until the 1930s, when they collapsed. At the time of fieldwork, the most evident popular Islamic practices were female-oriented saint cults stressing the solidarity of small groups of kin and friends but reflecting the ranking system that was part of village organization.

Clan to Class in Testour: Rupture and Change

Before the growth of the nationalist movement in Testour, local hierarchies were based on the solidarity of the big Andalusian families. In the 1860s, the town's population was subjected to a census organized along the lines of ethnic categories—Andalusian, Weslati, Zwawi, Hanafi, Jew, etc. (Hopkins 1980a); the dominance of the Andalusian families was based on the control of landed wealth, either directly through ownership or indirectly through the *waqf* (*hbus*) institution. Key members of Andalusian families occupied the principal political and religious posts—*khalifa,* shaikh, *imam, qadhi,* shaikh at-tariqa. Thus around 1900, Taher Handili was khalifa, *naib al-jema'ia,* and shaikh of the 'Issawiyya brotherhood, while members of the Ben Moussa family were notaries, imams, qadhis, and *wkils* of the habous. This is the pattern I refer to as clan politics: big men, combining wealth and office, with a following of clients.

In the early period of colonial rule, the French simply moved in to take charge of this hierarchical system, oriented toward the Bey of Tunis. However, as more land passed into French hands, and especially as the new French colonial owners began to take advantage of farm machinery to farm their land directly rather than through sharecroppers, the economic base of the old elite was destroyed. This process culminated after World War I, when gasoline-powered tractors became available. In 1949–50, 44 percent of the land farmed in the cheikhat of Testour-Ouled Slama was farmed by a handful of Europeans (Poncet 1963:83).

At the same time, colonial political rule led to a dismantling of the traditional political structure. Some posts (e.g., qadhi) were abolished; others were removed from Testouri control, as when the locally chosen khalifa became the centrally appointed *kahia* around 1925. New forms of political conflict appeared. From 1911 to 1913 there was a struggle over naming a new imam for the main Testour mosque in which a protonationalist faction competed with the traditional elite. The protonationalist faction was led by el-Hadi Ben Attia, a landowner with a hereditary claim to the headship of the local Rahmaniyya brotherhood. The faction reappeared in 1925, when Ben Attia pressed his formal claim to head the Rahmaniyya, and again in 1934, when he attended the founding congress of the Néo-Destour party in Ksar-Hellal (Hopkins 1980b:152–56).

Thus the old economic and political (and probably religious) orders had been replaced by an economic system based on large-scale capitalist production, largely in the hands of Europeans, and based on market production, wage labor, credit, secure land tenure, and mechanization. The political system was one of administrative centralization in the hands of the colonial government. Therefore, the independence movement was, at least locally, the expression of new classes—the wage earners and the shopkeepers—whose interests were in some analytical sense opposed to the capitalist farmers, but who established themselves politically by their opposition to colonialism within the framework of the Néo-Destour.

The Testour shopkeepers were involved in the only collective anticolonial episode in Testour's history, a demonstration in 1953 against the French resident general, Jean de Hauteclocque, at a time of high tension between Tunisians and French (see Julien 1985). The event can be interpreted as symptomatic of the shift from clan to class politics, in that those who participated were from the same class situation in Testour, and that collective action was taken by a group organized along lines of similarity.

After consultation with national party officials, the demonstration was planned by the local representatives of the Néo-Destour party. Virtually all the participants I have been able to identify were market people (builders, barbers, shopkeepers of various kinds). Some members of the town's elite were apparently aware of the demonstration but avoided direct involvement. Others welcomed the resident general. Given that the demonstration took place when assassinations were common, such as those of the nationalist labor leader Farhat Hached in December 1952 or of pro-French Tunisians later in the spring of 1953, it was in fact fairly mild—but nonetheless significant for Testour. A number of men, led by the party head, shouted "Long live Bourguiba!" and, according to different versions, slogans in favor of the Bey or of independence. Some say stones were thrown. De Hauteclocque continued on his way. The police arrested all the participants they could find, and they were eventually fined or jailed. The shaikh of Testour was fired for neglecting his job.

After independence in 1956, local power fell to the class that organized the demonstration, organized as a branch of the Néo-Destour. However, within about a decade, a new axis of struggle for local power emerged between the early "militants" and the shopkeepers, on the one hand, and a group of "new intellectuals" (mostly schoolteachers), on the other. During Tunisia's socialist experiment in the late 1960s during the liberal phase that followed, political conditions favored those who were literate, bilingual, and wise in the ways of the state, who could therefore act as local representatives of the state authorities. The new intellectuals and the remaining shopkeepers also became allied with Testour's large capitalist farmers in the liberal period following 1970; the alliance opposed a local protoproletariat.

This marginal class of workers and petty traders in town was concentrated in a peripheral area known as Melassin, where some of them had been forcibly settled during the socialist sixties. These people, mostly of Jbali or "hillbilly" origin rather than Testouri, were stigmatized as different and inferior, yet they provided much of the agricultural labor force.[2] In 1973 one of the political issues in the town was whether to include this class in the town's political system. The issue was symbolic: whether the town authorities should help the Melassin people build a mosque. Behind the actual conflict was the recognition on both sides that building a mosque would symbolize the permanent status of Melassin and its people in Testour. The main confrontation opposed the Testour party leader, who had organized the demonstration against de Hauteclocque twenty years before, to a young shopkeeper and political leader of Jbali origin. The establishment came out ahead, at least in 1973.

In analyzing the political process in 1973, the pertinence of the class concept was apparent in the reaction to a flood, in a local election, in the organization of the annual festival of the patron saint of Testour, and in the organization of an annual festival of popular music (Hopkins 1986, 1987b). In each case, the competing forces could be seen as in some way the expression of class (rather than clan) interests. Some of those class interests were inside the community, others set off the community against the dominant national bourgeoisie. Yet at the same time, individual social action remained primarily oriented toward differentiation by respectability along individual or family lines (ranking) rather than by class (Hopkins 1977a).

The hierarchy of ranking was activated in a number of contexts: who gives charity (zeka) to whom, choices of marriage partners, visiting patterns among women, and men's public behavior in the market. In Testour, men do not visit each other in their homes but can meet only on such neutral terrains as the café, the shop, or the fields. Together with the habit of prefixing all male names with the honorary "si," this helps maintain an illusion of equality that is contradicted in other domains of life.

The symbolizing and conceptualizing role of religion helps explain this contrast between objective class and subjective ranking. While the conventional Islam of the five pillars remained constant, the forms of local popular religious expression changed from male-oriented brotherhoods reflecting the clan-oriented politics of the traditional system (which seem to have disappeared with the underlying economic system) to female-oriented saint cults stressing the solidarity of small groups of kin and friends that reflected the ranking system. One can note, for instance, the importance of visits to saints' shrines triggered by dreams or the desire to escape afflictions. The visitors might be a group of female friends or relatives or an extended family and friends, but usually one woman or more is at the center of the visit. The status claims of the visitors are reflected in the identity of the saint visited, the size of the offering, the size of the visiting group, and so on.

employment and wages based on a survey of three Delta villages, and Hopkins (1987), a detailed analysis of the transformation of labor relations in the Upper Egyptian village of Musha. In the late 1970s the demand for migrant labor in the Gulf and the construction boom in Cairo made it possible for the rural poor to escape the countryside in unprecedented numbers, creating a seasonal shortage of male agricultural labor, a rise in wages (although the figures here are ambiguous), and a burst of rural construction and other economic activity as the migrants returned to the villages with their savings (see Abaza 1987; Adams 1987; Commander 1987; E. Taylor 1984). These sharp though short-lived changes have not ended underlying patterns of inequality and exploitation or the forms of violence they may involve (although the question of violence is still not explicitly addressed in recent studies). Nevertheless, the situation described by Adams, Hopkins, Commander, and others is clearly different from that of the 1960s and will not be dealt with in this essay. For some of the broader theoretical issues in the study of contemporary agrarian relations in Egypt and the Middle East, see the exchange between Glavanis and Glavanis (1983) and Seddon (1986).

12. Baer (1969) offered a critique of one of these traits, the submissiveness of the peasant, but attributed its popularity simply to the superficiality of travelers' observations. On the colonial origins and uses of these kinds of racial stereotypes in another part of the world, see Alatas (1977). For an analysis of their more recent uses in the Egyptian case, see Mitchell (1990b).

13. These remarks may suggest an approach similar to that of Scott (1985). Scott, however, examines the behavior of the poor to find signs of an otherwise unnoticed spirit of peasant resistance, an approach I find troubling (see Mitchell 1990a). I am suggesting that one can examine the same practices for signs of otherwise unnoticed forms of domination. For the latter argument, see Abu-Lughod (1990).

14. For a useful but neglected critique of some of the problems of the political development literature, see Gendzier (1985). Harik remains, however, one of the most optimistic writers on Egyptian rural development. He has recently reiterated the conclusions established by his influential book, describing rural Egypt as a place without exploitation, middlemen, large landowners, or class conflict (1984).

15. A parallel problem exists in studies of urban Egypt, where the workplace has been neglected as a site for the construction of political relations, on the grounds that workers are not an active political force (e.g., Tignor 1982, 1984). The neglect is now being repaired by a number of studies, especially Beinin and Lockman (1987).

16. The state does this by lowering the price it pays for staple and export crops that predominantly small farmers are forced to grow, while subsidizing the cost of seeds, pesticides, fertilizer, and credit, the bulk of which goes to large farmers. On agricultural pricing in Egypt, see Cuddihy (1980).

17. The alleged discovery of evidence that a secret organization of the Muslim Brotherhood was plotting to overthrow the regime, which the Ministry of the Interior refused to believe, had enabled the military to intervene instead, ordering the massive arrests and thus extending its own domestic influence as well as its control over the apparatus of government. It was this same internal struggle for control of the regime that resurfaced the following year in the formation of the Higher Committee for the Liquidation of Feudalism (see Hamrush [1975, 2:240–61]).

This decline of the male-oriented brotherhoods reflects the destruction of the economic system that supported clan politics.[3] The rise of the female-oriented saint cult does not, however, seem to relate closely to the new class-based politics but rather to a system of individual ranks, each relative to all others. In this system, the women generate symbolic capital useful in such arenas as the marriage market. Thus the effort to maintain a set of distinctions inspires political action that regenerates the system by making it seem real, while its relationship to a class structure implied by the economic dimension is obscure or, perhaps better, obscuring. The saint cult seems to provide a basis for social and political action that disguises the underlying class structure and thus promotes the interests of the dominant class in that structure. That class structure has not yet found its symbolic expression in Testour.

Musha

Musha is a village of 18,000 people in Upper Egypt—a village because it is the bottom rung in the ladder of central places, structurally equivalent to all Egyptian villages. It is 400 kilometers upstream from Cairo and 15 south of Asyut. The community is basically agricultural, all irrigated, and animal husbandry has considerable importance. The agriculture is increasingly mechanized, meaning that some operations such as plowing and threshing are always done mechanically, while others are still done by hand (Hopkins 1987a). In addition to farmers and farm workers, there are substantial numbers of government clerks and other workers (though none in the village ranks high in the hierarchy) and a lively network of merchants and traders; many government workers and merchants are also, of course, farmers.

Administratively, Musha is the seat of a village council that includes one other village. There was no overt party organization in 1981 ("We are all one party," I was told, so no organization was needed). One may have appeared in time for the 1984 and 1987 elections, which were contested locally by several parties—the Wafd, the Socialist Labor party, and the National Democratic party—though if so it remained marginal.

The culture of differentiation here stresses the patron-client relationship rather than generalized status ranking as in Testour. Next to mainstream Islam, male-oriented religious brotherhoods built on hierarchy and discipline have predominated and affected the political structure, supporting the clientelism produced by the political and economic systems.

Clan to Class in Musha: Continuity

I have little information on the history of Musha before the present generation. The village appears to have a Pharaonic name and was mentioned in the
Middle Ages. Market involvement and responsiveness to price do not appear
as new features (Girard 1824:142). A pattern of labor migration to Cairo, at
least, is attested from the nineteenth century (Baer 1882:76; cf. also Willcocks
1889:247), and the village participated in the gradual improvement and transformation of the irrigation system that began in the Muhammad Ali period.
These changes involved the shift from basin to canal irrigation beginning at
the end of the nineteenth century, here completed only in 1964–65.

Other comments about Musha are a series of negatives. Apart from the
Christian minority of around 10 percent, no groups in the village are distinguished on the basis of origin. There is no evidence that Musha participated
in the uprisings in and north of Asyut in 1919 (Schulze 1981:165, 188). No
large estates were created in Musha during the period when this practice was
common in the rest of the country.

The main technological change in Musha was the transformation of the
irrigation system in the 1930s, which involved the introduction of diesel
pumps to irrigate during the dry part of the year, although the annual flood
continued. Under the new system, double cropping became possible, and the
value of land as well as the demand for labor increased. Men who had
acquired capital from their control of the labor migration process invested in
agricultural land and joined the agrarian elite. From the 1930s on, farm
mechanization (tractors and pumps) became possible and increasingly common. Land reform had a minimal effect in Musha, affecting only about 5
percent of the land, and that in the second wave in 1961. The mechanization
of some parts of agriculture has destroyed the old household-based domestic
mode of production: the household head has become a farm manager. The
hierarchical control of labor is highly decentralized and so has not yet led to
the formation of a self-conscious proletariat.

Politically, the village has been dominated by large families—political
families or clans, that is to say, including clients as well as relatives.[4] Vertical
relations of a patron-client type are strong, both within and outside the lin-
eage, both internal to the village and as links between the village and the city
and nation. Though rooted in the agrarian social organization, these vertical
relations are not limited to the agrarian sector. The clan elites have long
monopolized relations with the state, articulating the social and political structure of the village with that of Egypt as a whole. The political role of big men,

taken as a group, is reinforced in everyday life, in the brotherhoods, and in dispute settlement, as well as in the organization of work. There is, however, little overt political competition (or cooperation) between the economically dominant farmers in the village. Thus, for most, clientage is restricted to work or personal favors; no confrontation forces the choosing up of sides.

The pattern of political clans goes back at least to the nineteenth century, when historians have chronicled the rise of village notables (Baer 1969:50). One can easily imagine that it goes back much farther, but for the moment there is no positive evidence for Musha. The main recent changes have been the rise of the labor contractors to landed status combined with double cropping and the necessary accommodation of the state, especially after 1952. Political clans persisted through the revolutionary period of the 1950s and 1960s into the 1980s (the Wafdist *umdah* was a member of parliament under Abdel Nasser).

The state's increasing involvement with the village is often channeled through the big families, many of whose members are now respected in urban areas as businessmen and professionals. This is true in such areas as education (where big families donate land for schools), agriculture (where the landed wealth of big families gives them unquestioned clout), or public works (where the siting of paved roads and irrigation canals takes account of the big families' property). Elections for the cooperative and the local council as well as for national office are managed by the village elite, albeit a factionally divided elite. When the state collaborates with the leading men of the village, i.e., with the leaders of the political clans, it consolidates their role.

One of the few examples of strictly political competition between clans concerns the rivalry between east and west in the village. Musha had two umdahs for a while, for the east (in the Bait Shafa' family) and for the west (in Bait 'Abdin). Around 1930 they were combined, with the west dominant. The western headship was held by Bait 'Abdin from 1917 or so until the 1950s, when the post was abolished, but essentially until today, even though the last head died in the mid-1980s. Nonetheless, in a sense, the eastern and western heads led the two opposing factions. This factional politics guided their involvement in party politics, so that the east was Liberal Constitutionalist (with the Asyuti notable, Mohammed Mahmoud), then Saadist, while the west was straight Wafd, linked through the family of the western umdah as well as through the one large outside Christian landowning family, the Khayyats.[5] This pattern of linkage endured until the 1980s, when the village was split in the 1984 election between New Wafd and NDP.

Other evidence exists of a latent polarization between east and west. According to some stories in 1981, Bait 'Abdin won the unified headship in the 1930s not through an election but through a fight, with sticks as arguments. The end of the headship itself, according to one story, came about because Bait Shafa' made an alliance with a junior branch of Bait 'Abdin to formulate an appeal to the national government. When the government-appointed village administrator (*rais majlis al-qarya*) was from the eastern half in the 1970s, men from the western half conspired until he was assigned to a different village; the new head was from the west. Some interpersonal disputes took on added sharpness because they involved families from the east and the west. Whether these stories are literally true is not the issue; they indicate a cultural model for political action on which individuals can pattern their own behavior or interpret the behavior of others.

The social organization of work, based on the concentration of economic authority, is probably more important in shaping contemporary village politics than Musha's peripheral involvement in the nationalist movement, the conflict between east and west, or the growth of a village bureaucracy. Economic power generates political power; the control of a work force leads to political control. However, the big farmers do not attempt to control the work processes of their smaller neighbors directly but work through their control of tractors, pumps, and credit. Since control of labor is decentralized, challenges to that concentration are avoided. The monopolization of economic resources by the large farmers gives them political clout, but this influence is expressed in culturally meaningful terms.

Political power is reproduced, for instance, in visiting patterns (lesser men visit more powerful, never the opposite), so in the evenings big men tend to gather clusters of clients in their reception rooms.[6] This "sitting" is partly an expression of political precedence, establishing shared values and political positions, and partly a matter of organizing the next day's work. There is a vigorous practice of dispute settlement through a form of mediation in which the larger and more senior farmers intervene to settle disputes over land, property, and even marriage. This cultural construction of inequality is reflected also in deferential behavior, especially in speech patterns, and in the titles by which people address one another.

Political power is also reinforced by the religious brotherhoods. Although some elements of a saint cult are present in Musha (the village has a few shrines, their replicas in the village cemetery at the edge of the desert, largely visited by women), the main expression of popular Islam is through the brotherhoods, and the main participants in the brotherhoods are men. Women participate by preparing food, following the ceremony from adjacent rooms, and probably most of all by reminding the men of the family that it is time to invite a brotherhood for a session to commemorate events in the family history and life cycle. Brotherhoods thus express the family and clan structure, whose important events (marriage, circumcision, cures) they validate. Men are the active participants in the ceremonies and hold the leadership roles. Hierarchy prevails. The leaders tend to be middle-range farmers and shopkeepers, while the ordinary members are day laborers and adolescents. The ceremonies are replete with expressions of deference and difference—in the spatial arrangement of the participants or in the kinds of food served, as well as through verbal cues. Thus the brotherhoods can be viewed as an echo of, and a support for, the social hierarchy derived from the mode of production in agriculture. In this context, it is not surprising that the various patterns of Islamic fundamentalism common in Egypt have hardly penetrated villages such as Musha.

The large farmers have an arsenal of techniques at hand for controlling their work force. These range from employing men, women, or children from outside the village, to the use of economic and social constraints on regular workers (speeches to them at work or in the evenings), to the lack of occasions in the village for large gatherings of men in similar social situations—frequenting the few cafés is not valued, and men are anyway preoccupied with their hierarchical relations. No marketplace or single shape-up area exists; few large gatherings of any kind occur, and these are managed and directed by the elite. The dominant man in any gathering tends to control, even monopolize its conversation in what often amounts to a monologue, with others present cast in the role of approving listeners. In the evening gatherings or in the work gangs in the fields, this often means that men agree publicly with opinions they may well privately disagree with, a powerful mechanism for social control and opinion manipulation by the powerful.

Yet, at the same time, "little people" in the system retain or try to retain their sense of personal integrity. One way to do this is to insist that choice exists. People see themselves as constantly making choices—from whom to rent a tractor, for whom to work today, to whom to sell straw—and they resist being classified as permanent workers or regular customers, even when a little analysis shows that they are permanent workers or regular customers, tied by debt, habit, or neighbor or kin relations to one of the powerful farmers. The cultural emphasis on choice works both ways, for it means that the employer can choose not to reemploy his worker, thus providing additional pressure on that worker to adhere to community norms for work and obedience.

Wage labor is extensive in Musha, but the decentralized organization of work precludes the appearance of a class consciousness. The rural proletariat exists analytically but does not act politically. There are capitalist relations of production, without class consciousness or class conflict. How can one account for this relative absence of class as a feature of local politics and social organization? The cultural emphasis on vertical relationships, patron-client ties, and so on, is part of the answer. Here the continuity of brotherhoods as an evident and manifest form of popular Islam contributes to the ideological underpinning for this emphasis. Perhaps the relative facility of movement outside the community is another part of the answer.[7] But all of these explanations revolve around the continuity of village leadership, the big families. Is this continuity part of the explanation or something that itself needs to be explained?

Discussion

Musha and Testour resemble each other in some ways and in others represent alternative reactions to spreading capitalism: in Testour the emergence of class, alliances of the similar; in Musha, the reinforcement of patronage, coalitions of the dissimilar, the retention of clan politics. But capitalism is not a discrete cause with a limited effect—it is a spreading, bifurcating process that produces a range of effects. As the social organization of production changes, so does the precise alignment of relevant classes. Particular forms of consciousness, some direct, others indirect, correspond to this shifting class alignment.

Of course, there is no moment when capitalist relations of production, markets, and so on penetrated these communities; the process was lengthy. Recent historical research has tended to push back the earliest involvement of Tunisia and Egypt in the world market economy to the eighteenth century (Cuno 1984; Richards 1977; Valensi 1985), a limit probably set only by the lack of reliable historical sources and the suspicion that the world market may itself not be that old (Polanyi 1957). For our purposes, this means that no explanation can be based on the presence or absence of capitalist relations of production but only on much more sharply defined factors.

At present the agrarian structure in both communities involves, in Wolf's terminology (1969), market-oriented farmers rather than subsistence-oriented but market-linked peasants and, furthermore, differentiated farmers (Hill 1986:8–15).[8] Perhaps it is this domination of both communities by large farmers that gives meaning to their way of life and ensures the adherence of small farmers, the landless, the shopkeepers, and others to community standards and procedures. Wolf (1969:279) notes, for instance, that "what is significant is that capitalism cut through the integument of custom, severing people from their accustomed social matrix in order to transform them into economic actors, independent of prior social commitments to kin and neighbors." The evidence provided here only partly confirms that statement: people are economic actors, calculating gain and loss, but they are also bound into cultural systems of interpretation of political and economic action. Or, as Polanyi says, "man's economy, as a rule, is submerged in his social relationships" (1957:46).

The precipitate of broad social change ("the spread of capitalism") at the local level can be seen in the pattern of local politics and in the cultural interpretation of interpersonal relations that orients that politics. In this sense we can say that development produces a process (exploitation or differentiation, for instance) that must be understood culturally to provide the framework for meaningful action—action that provides the momentum for the system. This observation indicates how we can combine a transactional approach (e.g., Bailey 1969) that focuses on the structure of interpersonal politics with a political economy approach that stresses the integration of an entire local political system into a wider framework or, again, the congruity of the two. This is both a matter of understanding the processes (mechanization, nationalism, bureaucracy) through which the wider system affects the more local one (and perhaps conversely), and a matter of understanding how local political action is made meaningful—what Geertz (1965:205) calls "the progressive articulation of cultural form—meaning—through the medium of social action."

An example is the analysis by Scott (1985) of a Malaysian village. Scott shows how broader economic forces encourage differentiation of the rural population, while the invocation of charity and cooperation by both the "rich" and the "poor" to manipulate each other reinforces a set of meanings that does not recognize, and may obscure, that process of differentiation. Political action reflects cultural meaning rather than economic interests. Looking at the political economy of development, Scott refers to "state-fostered capitalist development in the countryside" (241) and notes that the ideological conflict is a reaction to the massive transformation of production relations made possible by double cropping and mechanization backed by the state. But people react rather to their own interpretations (305). Still, Scott concludes, "To the extent dominant classes can persuade subordinate classes to adopt their self-serving view of existing social relations, the result will be ideological consensus and harmony that will in turn block the perception of conflicting interests, let alone class conflict" (335).[9]

The Two Communities: A Contrastive Analysis

Here we deal with (1) what these two communities have in common that illuminates either the Arab situation or the situation of rural communities in developing countries generally, and (2) what differentiates or opposes these two communities, so that each case may clarify the other and thus also help in the general formulation. In particular, the contrast of these cases may indicate something of the conditions under which class emerges as a form of social organization in agrarian society.

One of the key underlying social differences between Testour and Musha is the greater sense of identity and unity in the Egyptian village. Premodern Testour, as we have seen, was characterized by the presence of a number of named groups with separate political identities; in Musha the only distinction lay between Muslim and Christian, which, in 1980 anyway, was self-consciously downplayed. One can surmise Testour has a longer history of thinking of politics in terms of group relations, although such thought of itself does not produce classes.[10] Moreover, one can characterize traditional Testour as different from its surroundings (urban and Andalusian as opposed to tribal and country) but integrated with them through market links, while traditional Musha was apparently similar to neighboring villages but poorly integrated with them, with little basis for exchange—an example, in Durkheim's terms, of organic versus mechanical integration.

Testour and Musha nonetheless represent broadly parallel developments. In both, agrarian change involves increased mechanization, wage labor, farm credit, secure land tenure, and market involvement. Both, that is, show a trend toward a more market-oriented form of agrarian economy and a more differentiated role for the state. In both, the key transformation seems to date to the 1920–40 period, with the spread of colonial mechanized farming around Testour and the transformation of the irrigation system and a more capitalist attitude toward farming in Musha. The people of both communities participate in a generalized form of the Arab variant of Islamic culture; though the processes described here are certainly not limited to the Arab world, the common background means that such cultural patterns as hospitality, charity, or the perception of women's role are more or less equivalent.

In fact, the evolution of Testour and Musha parallels that of the great agrarian civilizations, from Japan (Dore 1978) to Mexico (Friedrich 1986), where communities have been drawn into the world economy suffering change, even dislocation, and achieving continuity, even prosperity. However, in both Testour and Musha, population is growing, incomes are up (partly from migration and other extracommunity sources), the standard of living has improved, substantial new construction exists, more children are staying in school longer—and the market economy seems more firmly implanted than ever, with the rich benefiting more than the poor so that income differentials may well be increasing. As communities, both Musha and Testour are among the fortunate of the Third World; yet each has its own poor who are excluded from prosperity. One can gain from these cases some idea of the shape of change in relatively prosperous rural areas in the Arab world and beyond.

In two communities with roughly parallel trajectories, we find class (horizontal relationships) more salient in Testour than in Musha. A century ago this was not the case; the two were in some ways more similar then—or perhaps they were similar in different ways. The explanation for the differential evolution may lie partly in the social organization of production, partly in the local political system, and partly in the changing nature of the encapsulating state. The explanations may be either historical, explaining the present in terms of the past, or functional, explaining the salience of class by differences in the social organization or cultural patterns.

Production

Both Testour and Musha are marked by the role of capital in agriculture and a social organization of work articulated around the relationship between capital and labor. Both are dominated by an agriculture that is mechanized, oriented toward change, and focused on the market. However, Testour is a mixture of agrarian and urban, Musha more purely agrarian. Testour has a more distinct market, and with it a clear shopkeeper class (linked into the market through commerce rather than wages), and a greater symbolic distinction to the working class. Musha is much more a single productive machine. Its shopkeeper class is less distinctive and less segregated, although mercantile activity is perhaps even more important, given the marketing of farm products. Musha produces grains and open field crops, while in Testour vegetables and fruits predominate. Testour is organized around a spatial center, the marketplace street with its characteristic institutions of mosque, café, and shop, where goods and information are exchanged. Musha has no such focus. The nearest parallels do not quite match Testour's market—the *swiqa* in the center of the village and the *mawqef* at the edge, where public transportation into and out of the village operates. Instead, the political centers in Musha are the houses and workplaces associated with the dozen or two largest farmers. This is where people hear certain kinds of news and enter most systematically into contact (and face-to-face communication). The office of the village administrator (rais majlis al-qarya) plays something of the same role but only during daytime office hours.

Testour's agriculture was largely taken over during the colonial period by European farmers, as well as by some Algerians and Tunisians who adopted the same style. After independence, many colonial farms were absorbed into the cooperative system, which itself went through several brief phases (Zussman 1986). In the meantime, the model of the colonial farm survived in the hands of the large Tunisian farmers (Kassab 1979:537–74). But the core of Testour agriculture was in the irrigated gardens, which did not suffer colonial takeover but remained always in the hands of a variety of Tunisian (Testouri) landholders, the larger of whom invested in capital improvements such as motor pumps. Musha's agriculture always remained in Musha hands; even absentee Egyptian holdings were limited. Mechanization was introduced by the existing large farmers, reinforcing their position. The land reform had marginal impact, and Musha never felt the series of shocks to its agrarian structure that Testour suffered. On the other hand, migrant labor was part of the picture early; we can imagine that wage labor in general appeared early.

Political Process

We have seen the rupture of local leadership in Testour and its relative continuity in Musha. This rupture, however, is not the outcome of internal forces but reflects the interference of the state—here the French colonial state. Furthermore, alternative forms of local power were able to emerge in Testour because of the simultaneous emergence of a Tunisian nationalist (anticolonial) party that lent its legitimacy to the local movement while drawing strength from its support. It is interesting to contrast the case of Testour, where nationalist politics (the Néo-Destour) attracted the "marginals" in the community, with that of Musha, where nationalist politics (the Wafd), indeed party politics in general, worked through the existing elite. Nationalist politics in Testour was part of a national movement that eventually produced independence in 1956 and the independent government under Bourguiba thereafter. Nationalist politics in rural Egypt was truncated by the 1952 revolution, in which the military took over the role of the nationalist parties, which had lost their dynamism. This accentuates the difference in the continuing relationship between community and national politics—in Tunisia the rupture operated at both national and local levels, and the two changed in tandem; in Musha the rupture at the national level was not matched by one at the local level, which simply adapted to national level changes.

At present, Musha appears depoliticized compared to Testour, where people are more involved in the official politics of the state and thus engage in more openly political encounters. This is another way of saying that the state penetrated Testour more thoroughly. Yet despite the increasing role of the state, in both communities a strong sense remained that the community was an appropriate arena for politics and that it was in various ways opposed to the state or the wider society.

Testour politics was marked by intraclass elite competition within the party structure—within, that is, the formal institutions provided by the state. Interclass competition occurred between the working class (more or less excluded from the formal political process) and the elite. Politics appeared as competition between groups, which begin to show signs of classes. The transition from clan politics to class politics is well under way.

Testour politics in 1953 thus involved a fight over the nature of the political system—colonial or independent—and a competition between two groups of villagers associated with these two views but also broadly representing social categories such as village elite, large farmers, shopkeepers, and youth. One could aspire to few local offices (that of administrator was filled from outside, for example). In 1973, the nature of the political system was not in question, but the identity of legitimate contestants was. Some of the competition was about position, offices to be occupied in the contemporary party structure (not the administrative ones); some was also a conflict between groups (Testouris vs. outsiders) if not actually between classes. The challenges and confrontations were in the context of the party system and phrased in terms of such normative values as building a mosque. Fair and unfair tactics were discussed: sending a letter over the heads of local officials was resented by the other side, and condemned as an unfair tactic. The question of inclusion in the political community was raised: should the people of Melassin be allowed to join the local political system at all, or were they impossible outsiders?

In Musha, by contrast, patron-client or clan-like politics are dominant both inside the elite and outside it. The key political situation was the hierarchical dyad. Big men kept their positions not by competing with one another, but by maintaining both teams of followers and independent channels to higher authority outside the village. There was some competition for office in the elected local popular council and in the cooperative council, but this seems relatively marginal, especially because the most important men were not involved. An east-west conflict lingered. The politics of dispute settlement operated, a system which in good cases redounds to the credit of those who patronize or endorse the solutions. This came into play particularly when Muslim-Christian relations were at stake. The control of the political process by the village elite has led to the reinforcement of that elite—yet it too has changed by becoming more urbanized, more educated.

The contrast between the collective interests of the top farmers in Musha and the apparent absence of political activity in the community to sustain it presented a paradox. Political competition was certainly less intense then, say, in the Swat valley of Pakistan.[11] Perhaps the capping role of the state was a factor in pushing interpersonal rivalry toward economics rather than politics.[12] Of course, the relative absence of politics (feud, and so on) is itself a form of political action if this restraint tends to support the status quo.[13] Strong personal factionalism would validate the patron-client relations and would tend to undercut the growth of a consciousness of "like" (a class-type consciousness). In fact, actual factionalism is absent, but an ideology of factionalism is maintained through stories about past rivalries coupled with action devoted to maintaining such institutions as the religious brotherhoods that provide ideological support for a hierarchically ordered system. For the large farmers, class-type political action consists in action designed to support the whole system through the nurturing of patron-client relations at home and lobbying for economic interests outside the village.

Symbols and Social Control

Another instructive contrast comes from the role of popular religion. In Testour, the brotherhoods gave way to a more family-oriented saint cult, while in Musha they have remained important. In Musha, their retention is linked to the continuity of political leadership and perhaps to the links between local brotherhood chapters and the national organizations (Gilsenan 1973). The shift in Testour represents an accommodation to the new economic order under colonialism and independence, which gave more weight to individual work and market position.[14] Thus the brotherhoods provide a clear parallel to the social and political hierarchy of Musha, while the saint cult in Testour is more ambiguous. If Gellner (1983) is right, it may correspond to the greater anonymity of the mass society, relatively important in Tunisia, by leaving popular expression of religion in the hands of the believers themselves, without an elaborate social organization. This would be consonant with the increasing salience of a category like class as a feature of social organization: to be treated as a member of a class is to be treated anonymously.

The cultural interpretation of inequality and differentiation distinguishes Testour from Musha. Objective inequalities of wealth and power can only be understood within the context of their meaning to those involved. In Testour a superficial recognition of equality overlies a culturally recognized ranking system based on an implicit respectability index; something of a class system is emerging but is not yet part of the cultural construction of reality. In Musha, the casual form of interpersonal relations openly recognizes inequality, and a good deal of deference behavior goes on. The existence of a male visiting pattern in Musha and its absence in Testour illustrate this difference. The cultural focus on respectability ranking in Testour and clientelism in Musha, as reflected in the predominant form of popular religion, disguises in fact the emergence of a different stratification pattern.

In Musha the poor are enmeshed in a system of social controls that ties them to the rich, and class struggle thus remains a matter of "the weapons of the weak" (Scott 1985). In Testour this has broken down in favor of a more universalistic situation—the class experience of being a worker in Testour is distinguished by the stigma of differences in social origin, by well-defined residential zones, and perhaps by longer periods of working together. Thus one can contrast the techniques for keeping the lower classes in order: by treating them as clients, as in Musha, so that individuals are linked to big farmers and other prominent people, or by marginalizing them as a group, as in Testour, where they are excluded by more or less formal means from the political process.

In the case of Musha, one can wonder why or how the local leadership, the big families, were able to retain their collective power, despite such circumstances as the turmoil in the countryside caused by the socialist experiment of around 1955–65 (Harik 1974, Saad 1988). One can suggest among the explanations the relative isolation of the village, its size (making it relatively impenetrable), and its similarity to other villages (making it harder to know where to begin to undermine local leadership). But it is also significant that the village elite kept in the game, being involved, even if indirectly, in the cooperative movement and in the growing village council process. More important, the village elite managed to maintain its control of the links between the village and the wider society, through its dominance of economic resources, literacy, and government posts at the middle level and above. The village elite also helped sustain the ideological and cultural background of village economics and politics through its (indirect) support for the religious brotherhoods (and perhaps its opposition to the more egalitarian fundamentalists). In other words, it is not enough to say that Musha's elite escaped the destruction of Testour's; its position was enhanced by particular political actions by its members.

The State and Local Politics

The role of the state reflects similarities, or at any rate parallels, between the two countries, despite geographic and other differences. In both cases, the state can be seen as an enterprise in which the bureaucracy is the actual ruler (Weber 1978:1393–94). States are, however, unequally successful at bureaucratizing society. The Tunisian state more than the Egyptian appears to penetrate its society, to be more present on the ground, to enjoy officials who are more inclined to internalize the interests of the state.[15] Impressionistically, I felt in Musha that the state was far away, perhaps even 400 kilometers away, while in Testour one was constantly aware of the projects and the representatives of the state, even without going the 80 kilometers to the capital. During the year I lived in Testour, the ministers of public works, agriculture, culture, and youth and sports all paid brief visits. The governor of Beja also paid several visits. During the year I lived in Musha, no national dignitaries visited. Distance or the scale of the system may certainly play a role here, but I would bet as well on a difference in the ways in which the national system works and in the expectations of its officials.

One issue raised by Bailey (1969:149) is that of the relative congruity of the local and the national systems. Both cases were relatively congruent but in dissimilar ways. Testour politics seemed congruent to the extent that village politics was expressed through the party branch, and the party branch included the same kinds of people as the national party organization. Musha politics was more congruent through the existence of patron-client ties that linked individuals in Musha with individuals in wider structures at a higher level. At any rate, in neither case did the national government feel that it had to intervene to create a local politics more in conformity with its own image of what should be. In both cases, but more obviously in Testour, the political process depended on events at the national level.

The gradual shift toward a class system based on the new capitalist mode of production also presages a different kind of integration of the local community into the state. The integration is through the horizontal structures of class (which are nationwide or statewide) rather than the vertical and personal (and hence particularistic) links of patron to client. The growing class basis for politics implies a greater integration into the state, insofar as that represents the social organization of the nation. If the bureaucratization of the society through the state is to succeed, then patron-client relations (antibureaucratic by nature) must give way to a national division of labor and political system. A national political system requires a different kind of ideological support—one that is more universalistic and stresses the wider society.[16]

Conclusion

To return to the original question: How has it happened that in two communities, with all their differences and parallels, the transition from clan-based politics to class-based politics has been much more complete in the Tunisian case (Testour) than in the Egyptian case (Musha)? The two communities have different historical trajectories. Their starting points were similar but not identical. The one I have singled out here is the greater relevance of ascribed groups (Andalusians, Weslatis) for politics in premodern Testour than apparently in bygone days in Musha. The histories of the two communities have also differed over the last century. Although both were affected by colonialism and spreading capitalism, the colonial state penetrated Testour much more and interrupted the continuity of its economic and political systems. The nationalist movement also affected Testour more than Musha. If one follows this logic, the greater salience of class in Testour thus reflects the greater disruption of the colonial and nationalist periods, perhaps building on a social situation where people were already inclined to think in categorical terms.[17]

Differences in the social organization of production also have implications for the salience of class. The hiring and supervision of workers, in that preeminent class situation of agricultural work, is similar in the two communities. In Testour the workers are seen as outsiders to the community, but they live there. In Musha, they may be outsiders, but they live somewhere else. The Testour workers have a structure that allows them to meet—cafés, a common residence, and so on. The national society has an effect, even if indirect, since national organizations such as the party, the National Farmers' Union, and the labor union are all part of the political environment. The Musha farmers use a series of techniques to divide the workers and maintain their own hegemony; in this they are supported by the willingness of the national structures to work through them in the village. Musha big men work hard to maintain that construction of reality.

The present situation is but a way station in the unfolding of process and development in the two Arab societies. In Eric Wolf's writings on peasants, he stresses that the peasants prone to revolution are the middle peasants, those who have been cut loose from one system without joining another. But by and large, Musha and Testour peasants have made the transition to market-oriented farmers and are now more fully integrated into Egyptian, Tunisian, and world society than Wolf's "middle peasant." The two communities contain definite patterns of differentiation, both at the real level of income and life chances and at the symbolic level of ranking and clientage. Class is simply another way to conceptualize this differentiation and to seek a vocabulary that allows fruitful comparisons that aim at clarifying the long- and short-term processes involved.

It would be wrong to draw from this two-part comparison—and all dual comparisons tend to accentuate differences rather than similarities—the conclusion that Musha and Testour are somehow at different points on the same path, so that the present of one shows the future of the other. Instead, both represent variants of a more general process of transformation of rural societies in the Arab world and in the great former peasant zones of the world. Many other variants may exist. If we are concerned about development with equity, the fate of the poor, or simply adequate nutrition in a healthy environment, we need to understand the variation within the general process of change.

Notes

1. Fieldwork in Testour between 1971 and 1973 was carried out in conjunction with the Centre d'Études et de Recherches Économiques et Sociales of the University of Tunis and with the financial support of the Smithsonian Foreign Currency Program. Fieldwork in Musha in 1982–83 was carried out in conjunction with the University of Asyut, with the financial support of the American Research Center in Egypt and the Population Council. I herewith thank all these institutions and their representatives. I have benefited from comments on this paper by Ferial Ghazoul, Hanan Sabea, and Tim Sullivan. Earlier versions were presented at UCLA, Columbia University, and UCSC.

2. Or *jbali*, meaning from Amdoun and Nefza, north of Béja: on this area, see Hamrouni (1981). Others were affiliated with the great tribes of the center, such as the Ouled Ayar and the Hammama.

3. For comparable observations from Morocco and Algeria, see Geertz 1979:162 and Gellner 1981:159–67. Geertz links the decline of the brotherhoods in Sefrou, Morocco, to the rise of the nationalist party; Gellner sees a swing away from an "associationist" Islam toward a reformist and purist version.

4. One word for these political clans is *'assabiyya*, as in *'assabiyyat al 'omda*.

5. Berque (1957:65–67) tells essentially the same story for the Minufiyya village of Sirs al-Layyan: two shaikhs, then a single 'umdah, clan politics in the village providing the basis for affiliation with the new national parties.

6. Cf. Barth (1959:54) on men's houses among the Swat Pathans.

7. This is the exit option, implying choice in some kind of a market. Hirschman (1986:90) notes, "Exit weakens voice and thus reduces the prospects for advance, reform, or revolution in the unit that is being left." But exit in itself is not a difference between Testour and Musha, since both have experienced substantial out-migration. Perhaps more detailed information on the migrants would uncover a significant difference.

8. Wolf (1969:xiv–xv) notes that "the peasant most often keeps the market at arm's length. . . . In contrast, the farmer enters the market fully, subjects his land and

labor to open competition, explores alternative uses for the factors of production in the search for maximal returns, and favors the more profitable project over the one entailing the smaller risk."

9. However, it is important to keep in mind Weber's comment that "people may react against the class structure not only through acts of intermittent and irrational protest, but in the form of rational association" (1978:929).

10. See Barth (1983) on Sohar in Oman, or Rosen (1984) on Sefrou, Morocco.

11. Barth writes of the Swat Pathans, "Leaders are thus forced to engage in a competitive struggle. A position of authority can be maintained only through a constant successful struggle for the control of sources of authority" (1959:73).

12. This may have happened later in the Swat valley, after political centralization. On the basis of a return visit, Barth writes, "The resulting picture of clientship and patronage in Swat by the mid-1960s was one where landowners as political leaders were drastically weakened, but came out strengthened in their superiority and security vis-à-vis tenants" (1981:143).

13. The classic study of the feud in Upper Egypt was carried out in the village of Beni Smei, only 10 kilometers south of Musha, in the early 1960s (Abou-Zeid 1965). Musha and Beni Smei are thus contrasts, but whether because of difference in time, particular features of village social organization, or research strategy and interests is hard to say. Harik's study of a village in Beheira (1974) also gives a different picture of political activity, perhaps reflecting the active socialist policy of that time, in a village where land reform was an important factor. Party activity and party leaders were prominent there in the 1960s.

14. One can ask, in this respect, what the social implications of modernist fundamentalism in both countries might be. So far neither community has been much affected by it, but future social conditions may lead in this direction (see Gellner [1981, 1983]). For more details on forms of religious experience in Testour and Musha, see Hopkins (1989).

15. Ben Salem (1991) stressed the tendency for local people in Tunisia who become civil servants to drop their local identification and become internalized by the state's project.

16. It could be that fundamentalism is a more appropriate religious style for the new kind of local politics that is being absorbed into the state in a different way. Gellner (1981:165–67), for instance, stresses the shift from a locally oriented saint cult to a universalistic reform movement. In Testour, however, I found that one form of saint cult (the brotherhoods) simply gave way to another (local saints and shrines), and by 1973 I saw no strong sign of a reform movement. In rural Egypt the slow decline of the brotherhoods may yet give way to the reformist fundamentalists, but probably not until village hierarchies also change.

17. This phrasing differs from that of Carl Brown (1975:90–92), who saw Tunisian national development as a continuous organic growth compared to the sudden shifts of direction and intensity in Egypt.

References

Abou-Zeid, Ahmed. 1965. *Al-thar—darasa anthropolojiya bi ahda qura al-sa'id* [The Feud: Anthropological Study in an Upper Egyptian Village]. Cairo: Dar el-Ma'aref.

Baer, Gabriel. 1969. *Studies in the Social History of Modern Egypt.* Chicago: University of Chicago Press.

———. 1982. *Fellah and Townsman in the Middle East.* London: Frank Cass.

Bailey, F. G. 1969. *Strategems and Spoils: A Social Anthropology of Politics.* Oxford: Basil Blackwell.

Barth, Fredrik. 1959. *Political Leadership among Swat Pathans.* London School of Economics Monographs on Social Anthropology #19. London: The Athlone Press.

———. 1981. "Swat Pathans Reconsidered." In *Features of Person and Society in Swat: Collected Essays on Pathans,* vol. 2 of *Selected Essays of Fredrik Barth,* 121–81. London: Routledge and Kegan Paul.

———. 1983. *Sohar: Culture and Society in an Omani Town.* Baltimore: Johns Hopkins University Press.

Ben Salem, Lilia. 1991. "Questions méthodologiques posées par l'étude des formes du pouvoir: Articulation du politique et du culturel." In *Le Maghreb: approches des mécanismes d'articulation,* ed. Rahma Bourqia and Nicholas Hopkins, 187–99. Rabat: Al-Kalam Editions.

Berque, Jacques. 1957. *Histoire sociale d'un village égyptien au XXième siècle.* Paris: Mouton.

Brown, L. Carl. 1975. "Toward a Comparative History of Modernization in the Arab World: Tunisia and Egypt." In *Identité Culturelle et Conscience Nationale en Tunisie,* 73–93. Tunis: Cahiers du C.E.R.E.S., série sociologie #2.

Cuno, Kenneth M. 1984. "Egypt's Wealthy Peasantry, 1740–1820: A Study of the Region of al-Mansura." In *Land Tenure and Social Transformation in the Middle East,* ed. Tarif Khalidi, 303–32. Beirut: American University of Beirut.

Dore, Ronald P. 1978. *Shinohata: A Portrait of a Japanese Village.* New York: Pantheon.

Friedrich, Paul. 1986. *The Princes of Naranja.* Austin: University of Texas Press.

Geertz, Clifford. 1965. *The Social History of an Indonesian Town.* Cambridge: MIT Press.

———. 1979. "Suq: The Bazaar Economy in Sefrou." In *Meaning and Order in Moroccan Society,* ed. C. Geertz et al., 123–314. Cambridge: Cambridge University Press.

Gellner, Ernest. 1981. *Muslim Society.* Cambridge: Cambridge University Press.

———. 1983. *Nations and Nationalism.* Ithaca: Cornell University Press.

Gilsenan, Michael. 1973. *Saint and Sufi in Modern Egypt.* Oxford: Clarendon Press.

Girard, P. S. 1824. "Mémoire sur l'agriculture, l'industrie et le commerce de l'Egypte." In *Déscription de l'Egypte, Etat moderne,* 2e édition, t. 17. Paris: Panckoucke.

Hamrouni, Tahar. 1981. "La paupérisation d'une collectivité montagnarde du Tell: les Amdoun." *Revue Tunisienne de Géographie* 8:99–116.

Harik, Iliya. 1974. *The Political Mobilization of Peasants: A Study of an Egyptian Community.* Bloomington: Indiana University Press.

Hill, Polly. 1986. *Development Economics on Trial: The Anthropological Case for a Prosecution.* Cambridge: Cambridge University Press.

Hirschman, Albert O. 1986. *Rival Views of Market Society.* New York: Viking Penguin.

Hopkins, Nicholas S. 1977a. "The Emergence of Class in a Tunisian Town." *International Journal of Middle East Studies* 8:453–91.

———. 1977b. "Notes sur l'histoire de Testour." *Revue d'Histoire Maghrébine* 9:294–313.

———. 1978. "The Articulation of the Modes of Production: Tailoring in Testour." *American Ethnologist* 5:468–83.

———. 1980a. "Les classes moyennes dans une ville moyenne: le cas de Testour." In *Les classes moyennes au Maghreb*, ed. A. Zghal, 144–65. Paris: Publications CRESM/CNRS.

———. 1980b. "Testour au XIXe siècle." *Revue d'Histoire Maghrébine* 17–18:19–31.

———. 1983. *Testour ou la transformation des campagnes maghrébines*. Tunis: CERES Productions.

———. 1986. "Class Consciousness and Political Action in Testour." *Dialectical Anthropology* 11(1):73–91.

———. 1987a. *Agrarian Transformation in Egypt*. Boulder, Colo.: Westview Press.

———. 1987b. "Popular Culture and State Power." In *Mass Culture, Popular Culture, and Social Life in the Middle East*, ed. Georg Stauth and Sami Zubaida, 225–42. Frankfurt: Campus Verlag; Boulder, Colo.: Westview Press.

———. 1989. "L'Islam populaire dans l'Egypte et la Tunisie Rurales: l'imaginaire et structures sociales." *Bulletin du CEDEJ* 26:227–40.

Julien, Charles-André. 1985. *Et la Tunisie devint indépendante . . . (1951–1957)*. Paris: Éditions Jeune Afrique.

Kassab, Ahmed. 1979. *L'évolution de la vie rurale dans les régions de la Moyenne Medjerda et de Béja-Mateur*. Série Géographie, vol. 8. Tunis: Publications de l'Université de Tunis.

Polanyi, Karl. 1957. *The Great Transformation: The Political and Economic Origins of Our Time*. Boston: Beacon Press.

Poncet, Jean. 1963. *Paysages et problèmes ruraux en Tunisie*. 3e série, Mémoires du Centre d'Études de Sciences Humaines, vol. 8. Tunis: Publications de l'Université de Tunis.

Richards, Alan R. 1977. "Primitive Accumulation in Egypt, 1798–1882." *Review* 1(2):3–49.

Rosen, Lawrence. 1984. *Bargaining for Reality: The Construction of Social Relations in a Muslim Community*. Chicago: University of Chicago Press.

Saad, Reem. 1988. "Social History of an Agrarian Reform Community in Egypt." *Cairo Papers in Social Science* 11(4).

Schulze, Reinhard. 1981. *Die Rebellion der äegyptischen Fellahin 1919*. Berlin: Baalbek Verlag.

Scott, James C. 1985. *Weapons of the Weak: Everyday Forms of Peasant Resistance*. New Haven, Conn.: Yale University Press.

Valensi, Lucette. 1985. *Tunisian Peasants in the Eighteenth and Nineteenth Centuries*. Cambridge: Cambridge University Press; Paris: Editions de la Maison des Sciences de l'Homme.

Weber, Max. 1978. *Economy and Society*. Berkeley: University of California Press.

Willcocks, William. 1889. *Egyptian Irrigation*. London and New York: E. and F. N. Spon.

Wolf, Eric. 1969. *Peasant Wars of the Twentieth Century*. New York: Harper and Row.

Zamiti, Khalil. 1985. "La division du travail étatique: sociologie d'un barrage." In *Etats, territoires et terroirs au Maghreb*, ed. Pierre-Robert Baduel, 377–88. Paris: Editions du CNRS.

Zussman, Mira. 1986. "Pendulum Swings in Land Laws and Rural Development Policies in Tunisia: History and Consequences." In *Social Legislation in the Contemporary Middle East*, ed. Laurence O. Michalak and Jeswald W. Salacuse, 161–89. Institute of International Studies, Research Series #64. Berkeley: University of California.

13

State and Agrarian Relations Before and After the Iranian Revolution, 1960–1990

AHMAD ASHRAF

State and agrarian relations, in the recent history of Iran, have been the subject of a number of speculative and empirical analyses by journalists, politicians, and scholars. In particular, the causes, processes, and consequences of the land reform program of the 1960s have been analyzed in order either to praise the shah's benevolent reforms or to criticize them in terms of malevolent motives or negative consequences. Thus, for example, the left often ascribes the purpose of the 1960s land reform to an American design to develop dependent capitalism in the Third World, whereas militant religious circles explain it as a conspiracy of the great Satan (the United States) to bring on the decline of agricultural production and the dependency of the country on American grain and foodstuffs (e.g., Khomeini 1983: 4:24; 5:23, 39, 136; 6:181). It is often believed that the land reform program of the 1960s led to pauperization of peasants and their exodus to urban areas, factors seen as partial causes of the revolution of 1977–79. It is believed, for example, that the pauperized peasantry supported the revolution covertly in villages while they participated more overtly in the revolutionary uprisings through the mobilization of millions of rural migrants, the reserve army of the revolution (Hooglund 1980:3–6; Azar 1981:35–37). Furthermore, the peasants' potential role in radicalizing the postrevolutionary period is taken up as a major contribution of the peasantry to the revolution (Nika'in, 1981:11–26, 38–46). My purpose in this paper is to examine some of these views, still prevalent among most observers of Iran's countryside.

This paper has three parts. In the first, I examine the driving force of the

White Revolution and the land reform of the 1960s and the impact of rapid population growth and state agrarian policies upon rural class structure and agrarian relations in the 1960s and 1970s. To shed light on the nature, causes, and consequences of the shah's land reform, I lay out a context for examining and understanding recent developments in rural Iran. More specifically, my analysis of the emerging agrarian classes, including big agricultural bourgeoisie and commercial farmers, village petite bourgeoisie, middle-level and poor peasants, and landless villagers, will serve as a background to understanding the nature and forces of struggle over land and the peasant question in revolutionary Iran. In the second part of the paper, I deal with agrarian relations and land struggle in the course of revolution and under the Islamic state in the period 1977–90. Finally, I compare the state policies, agrarian relations, and land reforms under the White Revolution and in the Islamic Revolution.

Peasants and the White Revolution, 1961–1976

The driving force of Iran's land reform program in the early 1960s, the master project of the shah's White Revolution, came from two myths: one of an "impending peasant revolution" and the other of the indispensability of land reform for the development of capitalism. These myths were shared by the Kennedy administration and many Iranian Marxists in the early sixties, and the myth of the indispensability of land reform for the development of capitalism still persists in many Iranian Marxist circles (Feda'i Organization 1975:3–21; Sodagar 1979:7–38; Mo'mini 1980:161–221; Jazani 1982:50–53; Tabari 1983; Najmabadi 1987:3–42). These two myths, combined, engendered the idea of the necessity of land reform in the early 1960s.

During the 1950s and 1960s, the United States incorporated into its program of foreign aid a policy of encouraging moderate land reform in the less developed countries in order to bolster their capability to resist the so-called menace of communist encroachment. Pursuant to this policy, the United States constantly suggested to the shah the necessity of a land reform. Heartened by the American persuasion, the shah issued a decree calling for the distribution among the peasantry of some 3,000 villages held in the crown land estates. Known as Project Thirty, the crown land distribution program received technical and dollar aid from Point IV from 1952 to 1960 (Warne 1956:190–204). The 1958 revolutionary coup d'état in neighboring Iraq and the mounting propaganda campaign from the USSR against the shah's regime led American policy makers to pressure the shah to implement a reform program in Iran. One scenario that failed was General Vali-Allah Qarani's attempted coup d'état in 1959 to install an effective reform government in Iran (Cottam 1988:128). Another attempt, which proved successful, was pressuring the shah to appoint the reform cabinet of Ali Amini in 1960 (Pahlavi, 1980: Bill 1988: 142–44 Cottam 1988:128–29).

The peasant wars of this century, the relocation of the revolutionary driving force from proletariat to peasantry in revolutionary theory, the popularity of the theory of the guerrilla foco, and the challenges of the Cuban revolution all spread the fear of an impending peasant revolution in the Third World in the early 1960s. In this image of reality, Third World nations were left with two options: land reform from above or peasant revolution from below. The prevalent idea was that government and revolutionary leaders would compete for the support of the peasantry: "He who controls the countryside controls the country" (Huntington 1968:292). The peasantry can play a highly conservative or highly revolutionary role depending on its relation to land: "No social group is more conservative than a landowning peasantry and none is more revolutionary than a peasantry which owns too little land or pays too high rental" (Huntington 1968:375). This simplistic and shortsighted vision of the world was adopted by the Kennedy administration and served as the focus of U.S. strategy for progress in the early 1960s (see, for example, Humphrey 1963:5–28; Packenham 1973:59–69). The same image of social reality was held by many Marxist scholars and revolutionaries of those days (Roxborough 1979:29–32).

The idea of the necessity of land reform was predicated on a number of false assumptions: the emergence of a revolutionary peasantry in Iran; the desperate need of new industries for both cheap rural labor and the expansion of rural markets; the requirement to eliminate the old oligarchy of landowning class as the main fetter to the development of capitalism; and the necessity of land reform for primitive accumulation of capital (Feda'i Organization 1975:3–21; Sodagar 1979:7–38; Mo'mini 1980:161–221; Jazani 1982:50–53; Tabari 1983; Najmabadi 1987:33–42).

In evaluating these assumptions, it should be observed that the Iranian peasantry has shown a low revolutionary potential and a low level of participation in the country's major sociopolitical movements. Iran's nonrevolutionary peasantry was the product of a number of factors (Kazemi and Abrahamian 1978). Consisting of three strata—family small owners, sharecroppers, and landless villagers, each with, respectively, one-fourth, two-fifths, and one-third of the rural population—the village class structure prevented the emergence of either a coherent peasant community or a proletarian community—a precondition of peasant or proletarian revolution. The teamwork organization of production in sharecropping villages (the *boneh* system) led to a workable arrangement between landowner and peasant through the mediation of the village head and the heads of work teams. Hence, the extraction of surplus from the peasantry was managed by a group of prominent villagers who were at the same time the trustees of the peasants and the appointees of the landowners. The relative power of these prominent farmers and prosperous peasants, along with the weakness of the middle peasantry, further diminished the revolutionary potential of peasantry in this diffused situation. The dispersion of rural population in more than 50,000 small villages, with an average size of 50 households, scattered in a vast and mountainous country, discouraged intervillage communication and united action by the peasantry. Moreover, employment opportunity in construction sites and urban labor markets afforded an outlet for the younger generation of villagers that in turn led to the detachment of many of them from village life and agricultural activities. Also playing a part in curbing the revolutionary potential of peasantry was the Islamic notion of the sanctity of private property and sharecropping-tenancy arrangements.

Furthermore, the recent controversy over modes of transformation of European societies from feudalism to capitalism (Roxborough 1979:1–12) has led some observers to approach the Iranian land reform primarily from the perspective of labor process, i.e., in terms of the internal contradictions of the feudal mode of production as experienced, for example, by England in the course of her capitalist development. Focusing the analysis on the expropriation of peasant holdings as the necessary and sufficient condition for the formation of a free industrial working class and the accumulation of capital places undue emphasis on the role of the land reform program of the 1960s in the development of capitalism in Iran (Mo'mini 1980; Najmabadi 1987:33–42). Iran's land reform is equated in this paradigm with the historical process of enclosure in England, an analysis that neglects or underemphasizes a number of factors that influenced the nature and direction of Iran's capitalist development: Iran's specific precapitalist formation and dependent development, commercialization of agriculture long before the land reform and its role in primary accumulation of capital, population explosion, increasing oil revenues, and the technological advances of the latter half of this century.

The population explosion, coupled with the scarcity of arable lands, led to overurbanization and oversupply of cheap labor for rising industrial enterprises. The major social and economic problem on the eve of land reform was not the scarcity of a labor force but its abundance and the high rate of unemployment. The oil economy facilitated and enhanced the accumulation of capital for industrial investments. Thus, there was no need to expropriate the peasantry through land reform measures for the development of capitalism in Iran. Furthermore, on the eve of land reform, overurbanization and increasing oil revenues led to the rapid growth of urban markets to capacities quite sufficient to absorb the output of growing import-substitution industrial establishments.

Finally, in the early 1960s, the landowning class did not constitute the main obstacle to the development of capitalism in agriculture and industry. The precapitalist arrangement in agriculture was undergoing a gradual change and had adapted itself to some requirements of the market economy and the modern state since the late nineteenth century. These changes included the gradual commercializing of agriculture through development of cash crops (Nowshirvani 1981); the abolition of benefice (*tuyul*) as an intermediary institution between the state and peasantry; the commoditization of agricultural land; the rapid growth of private landownership; and the emergence of capitalist extensive agriculture with wage labor. Moreover, many large and medium-sized landowners showed a genuine interest in commercial farming even before the land reform. Hence, had there been no land reform, it is possible that more large landowners would have undertaken commercial farming with free wage labor.

Under these circumstances, the land reform was formulated and implemented from above in Iran under pressures from the Kennedy administration. Neither the peasantry from below nor the bourgeoisie from the middle participated at the initiation of the land reform (Ashraf and Banuazizi 1980). Its initiation was a political choice originating outside of the polity, but its process had not been planned. As a result, its course and outcome were influenced by the ideas and personal capability of Hasan Arsanjani, who, exploiting the opportunities of the time, emerged as the architect of Persian land reform. Arsanjani joined the reformist cabinet of Ali Amini, who enjoyed U.S. support, in May 1961 as minister of agriculture and was entrusted with the implementation of a land reform program.

Land reform was part of Amini's campaign program against Dr. Manuchehr Iqbal's cabinet and his ruling Milliyun party in the 1960 Majlis election. Amini believed in a gradual land reform program, ten to fifteen years, including a ceiling on large absentee landownership, improvement of farmers' managerial ability, and better economic productivity (Amini 1986). This approach to land reform was generally attractive to both the shah and the

Kennedy administration. In addition to appeasing the Kennedy administration and normalizing his relation with the United States, the shah's interest in the land reform was to dismantle the power base of the landowning classes and to gain the support of the peasantry for his regime, as well as to overshadow and confuse the urban opposition forces of the National Front and leftist groups (Hughes, 1965: 1–4; Hooglund, 1982: 44; Amini, 1986; Cottam, 1988: 128). The Kennedy administration favored Amini's program of land reform primarily to forestall a peasant revolution. Arsanjani's concept of land reform was, however, fundamentally different.

Influenced by the peasant wars of the twentieth century, Arsanjani advocated a version of peasant socialism and peasant power. He secured decrees, regulations, and a referendum to implement an original strategy for Iran's land reform program. He believed in the necessity of eliminating feudalism and landlord-peasant relations of production (*nizam-i arbab-ra'yati*) and in creating a self-reliant peasantry through the cooperative movement. He often criticized the idea of a revolutionary proletariat in Iran, cherished by the orthodox Marxists. "Not the industrial working class but the peasantry is the genuine revolutionary driving force in Iran," he said (Arsanjani 1962:233–38). His lifelong ambition and dream was to mobilize and lead a peasant movement and use it as a power base to seize the leadership of the state. He opposed such American methods of land reform as those applied to the Crown Land Distribution Program in the 1950s, i.e., gradual land distribution through cadastral surveys and mapping. He argued for a practical form of implementation. Arsanjani was nurtured in a farmer-bazaar milieu—his father and elder brother were farmers and his mother came from a bazaar merchant's family—where he developed a hatred of feudalism and an admiration for the peasantry. As a rural cooperative officer in 1940–41, he surveyed a number of villages and established cooperative societies in the villages of Damavand, Savih, and Najafabad. He continued to fight for the cause of the peasantry in the 1940s and 1950s in articles published in *Darya* and in cooperation with the Ahmad Qavam and Ali Razmara cabinets.

When he became minister of agriculture in 1961, Arsanjani proved to be a tough and well-experienced campaigner with clear, workable ideas. The secret to the success of his reform program lay in a simple method of land distribution that used the traditional order of landholding (*nasaq*) as its basis. In the first stage of the land reform the ceiling of landownership was one village; it covered only about 20 percent of the villages. However, Arsanjani's tactics led to a mass mobilization of the peasants throughout the countryside. He often instigated disorder by attacking feudalism, criticizing the landlord-peasant relationship, and referring to the "criminal landowners" and the "dearest peasants" in his fiery speeches to the nation (Arsanjani 1962).

Arsanjani's shock tactics alarmed the United States, the shah, and Amini. An American agent reported, "I kept asking him why there was such urgency to the land reform program?" Arsanjani replied, "The nature of the sickness required a quick solution. Why? A proper cadastral survey would have taken ten years. To break the opposition I have to destroy the power of the 100 great landowners very quickly." He scoffed at the suggestion that the Americans were responsible for the land reform program: "The first thing I did was to get rid of all the American agricultural advisors to the Ministry of Agriculture" (Wilber 1962:1, 4). Like the shah and the Americans, Amini viewed Arsanjani as suspect, dangerous, and extremely ambitious and was critical of his "urgency" in the implementation of the land distribution; he ordered the minister of information to censor Arsanjani's powerful and arousing radio speeches (Amini 1986). The shah was also alarmed by the accelerated pace of the reform and "resented and feared the power that Arsanjani was collecting independently of the throne, based on peasants and urban liberals" (Zonis 1971:60).

Arsanjani successfully organized the Congress of Rural Cooperatives in early January 1963, when some 4,700 delegates gathered in Tehran. He was also instrumental in the referendum of January 26, 1963, in support of land reform, in which the peasants actively participated. Shortly after these events Arsanjani was forced to resign. He has been described as "a tough crusader who, in his own words, pushed the land reform program 'not as Minister of Agriculture but as *rahbar* (leader)' " (Bill 1972:143–44). He was considered the "architect of land reform" who formulated and implemented "Persia's original strategy" (Warriner 1969:109–35). His effective reform measures were irreversible, and, as he prophesied after his dismissal, there would be no regression: "I have hammered the last nail of both feudalism's (nizam-i arbab-ra'yati) and Shah's coffins," he said (Amini 1986).

The land reform program was formulated and implemented in three stages. The first stage, under Arsanjani's leadership, was a quasi-revolutionary movement. The second stage, with Arsanjani out of the picture, was appropriately labeled counterrevolutionary (Mahdavi 1965). The agenda, at this stage, was suppression of the peasantry, establishment of law and order, and protection of medium-sized and small landowners (Lambton 1969:194–256). The third stage, however, was a moderate reform from above in which the state ceded ownership of the holdings under sharecropping and tenancy (rental) agreements to the occupant peasants. The state agrarian policies and strategies in the course of the White Revolution took shape in two consecutive phases, the land reform program of the 1960s and the agrarian programs of the 1970s. The implementation of these programs, along with rapid population growth, led to substantial changes in rural class structure and agrarian relations, to be examined next.

The Agrarian Classes

Persia's agrarian classes underwent two distinct periods of change and development under the Pahlavis, a relatively slow period from 1925 to 1960 followed by a period of relatively rapid transformation in the 1960s and 1970s. The first witnessed the continuation of the traditional agrarian relations of arbab-ra'yati with some modifications; the second period saw the abolition of traditional bonds and the emergence of new agrarian relations. The period from the 1920s to the 1950s witnessed the expansion and consolidation of private landownership (arbabi), for which a modern legal foundation was established by the land registration law of March 17, 1932 (Lambton 1953:182, 184–89). Furthermore, in this period, the processes of commoditizing land and commercializing agriculture which had begun in the late nineteenth century continued at a more rapid pace (Nowshirvani 1981:547–91).

In the 1930s, the new bureaucratic and mercantile elements joined the old landowning families of tribal chieftains, bureaucratic literati, and the ulama (Lambton 1953:259–62). Reza Shah himself is said to have acquired an estimated 5,600 agricultural estates (raqabas), and a number of his army generals and close associates acquired many choice properties (Lambton 1953:260–62; 1969:49–50; Nikbin 1983:102–18; Mosaddiq 1986:282, 354). Thus, in the first period under the Pahlavis, the big arbabs (including the royal household), some one hundred large landowning clans and tribal chieftains, and several hundred other families owned approximately two-thirds of the agricultural land in the country, while the shares of the state domain and charitable mortmain (awqaf) and of some three-quarters of a million petty landowners and peasant proprietors each amounted to less than one-fifth of the total (Hadary 1951:185; Arsanjani 1962:24; Iran Statistical Center 1962, vol. 15, table 101; McLachlan 1968:686–87; Khamsi 1969:4). A long-standing characteristic of the landowning class that developed further in this period was its makeup mainly of absentee landowners who lived in the capital or in major provincial towns to protect their property. The practice of absentee landownership led to the development of an intermediary group of bailiffs (mobashers). While obtaining a handsome portion of the landowners' share of the crops, in many cases the bailiffs did not hesitate to exploit the peasants and often became landowners themselves (Lambton 1953:271–72; Amini 1986).

Although the 1930s marked a decline in the political and social status of the landowning class as a whole, the big landowners reasserted themselves in the following two decades as major players on the political scene. The landowners themselves and others who came from the landowning families constituted about two-thirds of the Majles deputies from the 1920s to the 1950s (Shaji'i 1965:179, 249). These representatives repeatedly rejected or emasculated legislation that dealt with income tax, land tax, rural development acts, universal literacy programs, and land reform; they also rejected the credentials of deputies who opposed the arbab-ra'yati relations (e.g., Sayyed Ja'far Pishavari's, Hajji Rahim Kho'i's, and Sayyed Hasan Arsanjani's cases in the fourteenth and fifteenth sessions of the Majles in the 1940s; see Arsanjani 1962:23–48, 166–77, Nikbin 1983:191–92; for objection of the Majlis to the universal education bill, see Siyasi 1987: 1:126–30). The landowning class possessed even more political power at the local level; the provincial and district governors and other officials as well as the rural police were often heavily influenced by local landowners (Lambton 1953:268–74; Arsanjani 1962:150–77; Jahanshahlu Afshar 1982:191–92).

The rural population, constituting about two-thirds of Persia's total population in the 1950s, could be divided into three major classes: peasant proprietors and petty landowners; sharecroppers and family-sized tenants (*ra'yat* in its more specific connotation); and landless villagers known as *khwashnishins*, most of whom were located on the bottom rungs of the village class structure. In the early 1960s, these strata comprised, respectively, about 25 percent, 40 percent, and 35 percent of the country's rural population (estimated from Iran Statistical Center 1962:table 101; 1968:119).

The land reform program of the 1960s overhauled the traditional ties of arbab-ra'yati and introduced to rural Persia new modes of agrarian relations. It led to the sale of either whole plots or portions of plots to the occupant sharecroppers according to the traditional practice of crop division (Ashraf and Banuazizi 1980:33–35). Thus the land reform transferred the ownership of some 6–7 million hectares of agricultural land (about 52–62 percent of the total) to the occupant sharecroppers and tenant farmers (estimated from Iran Statistical Center 1962: vol. 15, table 101; Iran, Markaz 1978–85: various reports; Khosravi 1988:6–8, 63–66, 98–100, 142–45, 162–64, 189–91). After the implementation of the land reform program the social distinction— though not the maldistribution of income—among sharecroppers, peasant-owners, and small landowners was effectively eliminated, and thus small landowners and peasant proprietors formed nearly two-thirds of the rural population (see Azimi 1982:75–94). The remaining one-third consisted of khwashnishins.

In the meantime, the Agricultural Development Bank of Iran, which provided large amounts of subsidized credit, was the main vehicle for rapid growth of commercial agriculture in the private sector. From 1969 to 1980, the bank granted more than 3,000 low-interest loans (4–12 percent); together with its grants to large- and medium-scale agricultural enterprises, these amounted to the handsome total of $1.6 billion. The bank also participated in establishing six regional development banks and investment firms with a registered capital of $400 million. In the same period, the bank undertook joint projects with 46 large agricultural firms with $360 million registered capital (Iran, Agricultural 1981). To promote commercial agriculture in the public sector, the government established eight large agricultural enterprises with 155,000 hectares of highly valuable farm land and a $200 million annual budget (Iran Plan 1979). It also established 93 farm corporations with 315,000 hectares of land and 39 production cooperatives with 100,000 hectares (Ajami 1981:87–102). These quasi-public enterprises were created and managed by government agents with minimum participation by peasant shareholders. Government policies aimed at developing commercial farming and initiatives taken by prosperous peasants and commercial farmers helped bring some 4.3 million hectares of new lands under cultivation from 1960 to 1975, of which 84 percent consisted of holdings over 10 hectares. As a result, the total arable land increased from 11.4 to 15.7 million hectares and the number of holdings from 1.9 to 2.5 million units (*Agah* 1982:161–63).

Commercial farmers consisted of some 25,000 mechanized farmers, livestock farmers, and poultry farmers; at the top of the pyramid were the owners of some one hundred agroindustries and commercial farms established in the 1960s and 1970s (Okazaki 1968; Ajami 1973:1–12). Commercial farmers often came from the traditional landowning classes, traders and entrepreneurs from the top echelons of the state bureaucracy. They formed an influential core of individuals at both national and local levels (Ashraf 1982:15–17; Mahdavi 1982:59–61; and Qahraman 1982:135–54). The findings of a representative sample of 651 commercial farmers carried out in five provinces in the mid-1970s indicate that among the large-scale farmers (those with an average of 364 hectares of land), 69 percent had inherited and the balance purchased the land that they farmed, whereas in the case of other farmers, about half had inherited and the other half purchased the land that they cultivated (Qahraman 1982:139).

The *upper peasantry* consisted of several groups with different relations to rural life: the village small landowners and prosperous peasants, the village traders and owners of small capital, and the public servants. The first group came from the old small landowners, former well-to-do sharecroppers, and village traders (Lambton 1953:275–82). The land reform of the 1960s led to the expansion of these strata. This resulted from the recognition of the property rights of smallholders and the sale of nonmechanized lands to occupant sharecroppers. In addition, many owners of small capital gradually acquired some land either from the landowners or from the pauperized small owners through moneylending and preharvest purchase of crops, thus joining the ranks of the small landowners (Keddie 1972:383–88). In 1974, for example, there were some 120,000 units of agricultural production with less than 50 hectares of land that were primarily operated by wage labor. These units also sold more than half of their products to the market (Agah 1982:185). The number of prosperous peasants and small commercial farmers, who owned most of the plots from 10 to 50 hectares and 45 percent of the total arable lands, is estimated at about 400,000 households for the mid-1970s (Agah 1982:180). The village traders, moneylenders, and renters of agricultural implements (e.g., oxen, tractors, mills, and so on) constituted the second component of the village upper class. In 1976, there were some 81,000 working proprietors in the wholesale and retail trades and some 17,000 trade managers and traveling salesmen in the rural areas (Iran Statistical Center 1981a:112–13). As a group, these elements "control[led] the major portion of rural capital and credit and thus exercise[d] an influence upon the whole production system" (Hooglund 1973:232). Ranked next to the traditional landowners and their bailiffs, prosperous villagers were located in the middle level of the village hierarchy before land reform. After reform, however, these elements moved into the upper level of the village social structure, where they were able to consolidate their position by establishing a working relationship with government agents and by joining the boards of such state-initiated rural organizations as village councils, cooperative societies, houses of equity, cultural houses, and political party cells (Kishavarz 1970:118; Ashraf 1978:138–46).

The *middle peasantry* came mainly from the old sharecroppers, tenant farmers, and ordinary family small owners and peasant farmers of the era preceding land reform. The land reform program of 1960s led to a substantial increase of the family small owners and middle peasantry. In the mid-1970s, some 930,000 holders of plots from 2 to 10 hectares, who owned about 28 percent of the total arable lands, formed the main core of the middle peasantry in Persia (Agah 1982:180).

The *lower peasantry* consisted of *poor peasants* and *landless villagers*. In the mid-1970s, about 1.1 million holdings, constituting 45 percent of the total, were less than 2 hectares, and accounted for only 5 percent of the total agricultural land (Agah 1982:180). In the majority of cases, the holding was insufficient to support a peasant family. (The normal optimum size for a family was differentially determined by the availability of water, type of crops, and the technique of agricultural production.) Landless villagers were primarily the product of rapid population growth between the 1940s and the 1970s. In 1976, some 1.1 million landless agricultural workers and 1.3 million workers in industry and services totaled approximately 2.4 million employed individuals in rural areas, of whom about half a million were unpaid family workers (Iran Statistical Center 1981a:88).

Both poor peasants and landless villagers benefited from the economic boom of the mid-1960s to the late 1970s, and their income level and living standard improved substantially. The annual expenditure of rural households, at constant prices, increased from about $1,000 in 1965 to about $2,000 in 1975 (Agah 1982:186). A study of changes that occurred in two villages in the Qazvin area over a thirty-year period showed one transformed into a modern commercial enterprise, the other (with a population of about 700) into a small-holding community. In the latter case, the villagers' per capita income of $1,000 came from agriculture (21 percent), animal husbandry (22 percent), work in neighboring factories and farms (34 percent), and a combination of labor and small capital (22 percent) (Mahdavi 1982:59–64).

Another observation on a village located in one of Iran's more backward regions showed that in the fifteen years before the revolution of 1977–79, the village experienced both social change and economic growth.

By the time of the revolution, payments to the landlord, as well as his license to extort whatever he wanted, were matters of the past. The peasants were masters of their own land. Even more important, a stream of wages and salaries was transforming the village. About a quarter of the married men earned either a salary or a regular income from an enterprise, craft, or trade. The remainder of the men still pursued their peasant activities, and in addition, more than half of them earned wages from seasonal work in the cities, and many more did so from work in the village itself; also an unmarried son or daughter might contribute a wage or salary. Overall, there was hardly a household in the village which did not benefit from at least one salary or seasonal wage. ("Current Political Attitudes" 1983:5)

Still another survey of five rural areas (Savih, Tavalish, Taliqan, Sari, and Karaj and Rudihin), conducted shortly after the revolution in 1979, revealed that most of the peasants surveyed were fairly satisfied with their life conditions (Dowlat, Hourcade, and Puech 1980:19–42).

It is often concluded that the 1960s land reform led to two major negative outcomes: the fall of agricultural production, which made Persia dependent on imported foodstuffs, and pauperization of peasantry, which led to increasing rural-urban migration. Both views are simply wrong. In both cases the population explosion—from approximately 19 million in 1956 to more than 34 million in 1976—played the major part. This rapid growth, combined with rising income, led to an accelerated demand for foodstuffs that outpaced available agricultural products, even though they increased from 7 to 19 million tons in the period 1960–75 (Agah 1982:182; in the same period, agricultural land increased from 11.4 to 15.7 million hectares [ibid.:180]). As a result, the volume of imported foodstuffs leaped from less than 0.5 to over 2.5 million tons during the same period (Iran, Statistical Center 1967: 101; 1981b: 670). The rapid population growth, combined with urban pull and rural push factors, also lay behind the mass migration of villagers to the cities. Located for the most part in arid, semiarid, and mountainous areas, Iran's agrarian sector was not able to support the increasing number of villagers. In the 1940s and 1950s, the process of substantive rural-urban migration had already begun. Thus, for example, Tehran's population increased from 0.5 million in 1940 to 1.5 million in 1956 and 3 million in 1966—before land reform made its impact on rural Iran. One contributory factor was, however, the urban bias of government agencies in pricing agricultural produce below its market value. As a result the imposed price of agricultural produce lagged far behind the rapidly increasing prices of industrial products and wages, which thwarted investment in the agricultural sector. Another bourgeois bias of government agencies was the provision of generous financial aid to commercial farmers, to the relative neglect of the middle and lower peasantry. The 1960s land reform is also blamed for dismantling the grass roots work team organization known as boneh. However, the boneh system was a component of the old arbab-ra'yati mode of production in the arid and semiarid areas in which wheat culture predominated. With the abolition of the arbab-ra'yati organization of production the boneh system, initiated and safeguarded by the old landowning class, disappeared.

The socioeconomic and political changes that occurred during the Pahlavi era led to the consolidation of central power at the expense of the periphery and decreased the agricultural sector's significance as the major source of income for the privileged classes, including the royal family. These changes facilitated the implementation of the land reform program of the 1960s and

1970s, which in turn led to the downfall of the old landowning classes and the rise of new agrarian relations and social classes and strata in rural Persia, including commercial farmers, family small-holders, and wage earners (Ashraf and Banuazizi 1980:23–25). Furthermore, despite the urban bias of developmental policies and strategies in this period, rural Iran underwent modest growth and villagers of all walks of life benefited from the expanding economy and large expenditures of the public and private sectors.

The White Revolution undermined the traditional foundation of patrimonial authority—the ulama, the merchant, and the landowning classes—who had maintained linkages among the old oligarchy as well as between them and the masses of urban, rural, and tribal communities. They were replaced by new classes and groups—the infantile grande bourgeoisie, the young, Western-educated bureaucratic elites, and the new middle classes—who had weak linkages among themselves and were unwilling to or incapable of developing a strong connection with the core of the state or with the intelligentsia and other key elements in the civil society. When the revolutionary crisis came, the dominant groups were thus not able to mobilize effectively the available resources, including the peasantry, to defend their vested interests.

Peasants, Land, and Revolution, 1977–1990

As the revolution gathered momentum in the period 1977–79 in urban centers, the villagers, comprising about half the country's population, either remained indifferent to the uprising in the cities or participated in counterrevolutionary actions. A survey of modes of revolutionary mobilization shows that only 2 percent of the total of 2,483 demonstrations in support of the revolution occurred in rural areas. Furthermore, peasants were active in numerous reported cases of counterrevolutionary demonstrations by club-wielders who attacked revolutionary demonstrations and pillaged the bazaars and houses of revolutionary activists (Ashraf and Banuazizi 1985:25). A survey of five rural areas also reveals that the peasants did not participate in the revolution, and many of them confessed that they were active in pillaging the bazaars and attacking the revolutionary demonstrations. For them, land reform was an indication of the shah's good will; he removed the burden of landowners' excesses over the peasantry and distributed arable lands among them. Most peasants reported that they learned about the shah's responsibility for their ill fortune when, after the victory of the revolution, urban preachers and radio and television began to disseminate messages on the unjust character of the previous regime. Many villagers even accepted the propaganda campaign of the old regime claiming that Khomeini's aim was to return to the original owners the lands that had been distributed by the shah among the peasantry (Dowlat, Hourcade, and Puech 1980:19–42). Still another survey in the steppes at the northeastern edge of the central salt desert (*kavir*) shows that, in the fall of 1979, added to a lack of political response to the call for antiregime demonstrations was resentment at the politicization of the Ashura procession (the day of commemoration of the martyrdom of the Third Imam, Hosayn b. Ali) by Khomeini's followers (Martin 1989). A 1980 survey of political attitudes of the peasantry in a southern Zagros region shows that most adult villagers did not support the Islamic establishment and remained sympathetic to the old regime. The peasants "with virtually no exception, show unqualified disapproval of the current regime, which is perceived as a regime of mullahs. The disapproval stems mainly from conviction that this regime is responsible for the economic and social deterioration that has taken place since then" ("Current Political Attitudes" 1983:4–12).

The Agrarian Question in Postrevolutionary Iran

The revolution of 1977–79 led to a number of broad, significant social and political changes in rural Iran, including peasant uprisings in some areas, a breakdown in law and order, the expropriation of large estates, the fall of the large landowning class, the expansion of certain forms of state capitalism in agriculture, the survival of middle and many large commercial farmers, and the further growth of the middle and lower-middle peasantry.

In this critical situation, major conflicting sociopolitical forces with vested interests in the rural areas took up the land question as the prime social and political issue at the beginning of the victory of the revolution. Four major conflicting ideological approaches to this issue, all based on substantive class orientations, unfolded over the first years of the revolutionary era: the traditionalist approach of conservatives, advocated by a large segment of the ulama and traditional petite bourgeoisie; the bourgeois liberal approach advocated by commercial farmers and liberal sociopolitical forces, including the caretaker cabinet of Prime Minister Bazargan; the quasi-radical approach supported by the radical group in the ruling party; and the radical approach adopted by the young intelligentsia, organized in mushrooming leftist groups, on behalf of poor peasants and landless villagers.

The general course of sociopolitical conflict and land struggle in rural Iran, primarily directed by conflicting urban sociopolitical forces, proceeded in five main phases over the decade from 1979 to 1990: (1) the offensive launched by the radicals to mobilize the rural population against the commercial farmers, initiated at the beginning of the revolutionary era, which led to the occupation of 800,000 hectares of land by both peasants and landless villagers; (2) the defensive attempt of the commercial farmers to reestablish law and order in the rural areas, resulting in the formulation of a land reform bill by the caretaker cabinet in September 1979; (3) the formulation and enactment of a quasi-democratic Clause C of the Islamic land reform law (stipulating a ceiling on the size of landownership) by the ruling Islamic Republican party in April 1980, designed to discredit the rival liberals of the caretaker cabinet and to disarm and expel the left from rural areas; (4) the counteroffensive move of the conservative ulama and merchants, as well as the landowning classes, which succeeded in suspending implementation of Clause C in November 1980; (5) finally, after years of conflict, an uneasy truce was made by the land reform law in early 1985.

The Peasant, the Left, and the Revolution

The fall of the old regime and the victory of the revolution of 1977–79 brought the rural areas into the spotlight, and conflicting sociopolitical forces in the urban areas began to compete for the support of the villagers. At this point, two types of movements occurred in the village communities: first, political demonstrations in support of the new Islamic establishment under the leadership of opportunistic elements of the village petite bourgeoisie, functioning as the village gatekeepers; second, a socioeconomic movement in certain areas under the leadership of activist agitators and organizers from the left. The first occurred in most of the villages throughout the country, with the village gatekeepers holding the key positions in the village organizations and thus dominating the village Islamic councils and daily village affairs (see, e.g., Hegland 1980). In general, the second type of movement seldom occurred in villages dominated by small landowners and family small owners and lacking in larger landowners; such a movement was more likely in the domains of the large and even medium commercial farmers, with leadership provided by the left.

The initiative taken in early 1979 by the popular Marxist-Leninist Feda'i Organization to encourage armed struggle among the Turkoman tribes of the Gorgan and Gonbad plains—the stronghold of the commercial farmers in rural Iran—kindled the land issue in some areas. In the first weeks of the victory of the revolution, the Feda'is organized the Turkoman Cultural and Political Center and the Central Staff of the Turkoman Councils to arrange the return of the "usurped lands" to the Turkoman tillers on a communal and collective basis. Thereafter, an intensified campaign was launched against the Turkoman Councils by the landowners and the Islamic state. The conflict eventually generated a nine-day civil war in the city of Gonbad in April 1979, just three months after the victory of the revolution. Once these hostilities had ended, the Central Staff expanded its control throughout the region, a control that lasted for almost a year. Eventually, the time arrived in the winter of 1980 for a major offensive against the Turkoman radical organizations. Following prolonged clashes, four top leaders of the Central Staff, who were among the prominent militant Turkoman Feda'is, were arrested, tortured, and shot to death in the Turkoman plain on the first anniversary of the revolution in February 1980. At the same time, the offices of the Central Staff and Cultural and Political Center were looted and burned and scores of its cadres arrested by the Islamic Guards (Turkoman 1980:39–214).

Inflamed by ethnic discontent, the land struggle in the Turkoman plain and Kurdistan encouraged activists in several regions to organize radical movements. The Feda'is and the Mujahids, joined by a number of more popular leftist groups, were active in certain rural areas of the northern and western regions, dispatching students and youths of high school age to the villages. They also aggravated the land strife by dedicating a section of their daily or weekly newspapers to the peasant issue. The Tudeh (pro-Soviet Communist) party, for example, devoted a section of its daily newspaper, *Mardom,* to peasant news. An examination of one hundred issues of this newspaper, published from August 6 to December 21, 1980, shows that it carried 346 news items on the peasantry (mainly about the land struggle) and 18 articles against the landowners and in support of Clause C of the Islamic land reform law, and it included antilandowner slogans in the same issues. In addition to these activities, the Islamic committees and the Foundation for the Impoverished (*mostazafan*) confiscated agricultural establishments belonging to the royal family and the top echelons of the shah's regime who had fled the country on the eve of the revolution. This practice drastically weakened the institution of landed proprietorship and encouraged landless villagers and poor peasants to occupy the lands of landowners, including those of medium-sized owners, in many villages.

The protest movements of the peasants were thus generally oriented toward a number of demands, which, depending on the specific situation, led to one or more of the following actions: seizing lands of large landowners who had fled the country; seizing lands of medium landowners who continued to live in the countryside; seizing uncultivated lands and nationalized pastures; dissolving farm corporations and production cooperatives and distributing their lands among the shareholders; and refusing to pay back debts to institutions identified with the old regime, including the Land Reform Organization, the cooperative societies, the banks, the former landowners, the village moneylenders, and usurers. As a result, in the first two years of the revolution some 800,000 hectares of agricultural land owned by larger farmers were occupied and cultivated by peasants (Ashraf 1982:25–28).

A survey of peasant unrest during the first two years of the Islamic regime (Azar 1980:74–77) reveals that of 300 cases under study, nearly one-third were set off by undersized peasant farmers who possessed less than 2 hectares of arable land, representing about 45 percent of the country's total land holdings but only 5 percent of the arable land. Over one-quarter of the cases of unrest were started by peasants with 2–5 hectares of land, representing 20 percent of the country's total holdings and 10 percent of the arable lands. This group participated more vehemently in the peasant movements than did the smaller holders; this may be partly explained by the latter group's increasing dependence on and familiarity with nonagricultural jobs acquired both inside and outside the village communities, while the larger holders remained more attached to the land itself. The village wage-earning agricultural workers, numbering over half a million, were involved in a quarter of the total cases of unrest. The participation of the upper peasantry accounted for 14 percent of the cases for those cultivators possessing 5–10 hectares of land (17 percent of the country's total holdings and 18 percent of the total arable lands) and 3 percent of the cases for those possessing 10–50 hectares of land (17 percent of the country's holdings and 46 percent of the total arable land).

As to the form of peasant unrest, 44 percent of 285 cases surveyed consisted of such nonviolent protests as registering complaints, signing petitions, and gathering around government offices; 21 percent were peaceful demonstrations; 16 percent were violent demonstrations; 9 percent involved taking refuge in religious and public sanctuaries; and 10 percent were other forms of protest. Regarding the outcome of these unrests, 33 percent of 221 cases surveyed were continuing struggles; 34 percent attained their goals; 18 percent abandoned the struggle; 2 percent were defeated; and in 13 percent, the peasants involved were still anxiously awaiting a more favorable course of events. A significant finding of this survey is that 70 percent of these peasant struggles were fomented by radical political organizations, while the remaining 30 percent took place spontaneously, apparently growing out of events in neighboring or other rural areas. Azar's survey also shows that the peasant movements had more fervor and vigor in the provinces of Mazandaran, Gilan, Tehran, Fars, West Azerbaijan, Kermanshahan, and Hamadan (where the radical young intelligentsia was more active) than in the remaining fifteen provinces of the country. Finally, the survey reveals that in general the peasant movement throughout rural Iran tapered off in the autumn of 1979, at which time the ruling party embarked on a program of drastic land reform concomitant with the expelling of the young radicals from the rural areas (Azar 1980:74–77).

The movements of the villagers, set in motion by the left, were very threatening to the different strata of landowners, as well as to the rival political factions of the emerging Islamic state. The counteractions taken by these groups led to a number of significant ideological positions and political actions, as I discuss below.

The Landowning Classes in the Arena of Land Struggle

Following the increase in revolutionary activities in the rural areas, the various landowning classes—from the traditional landowners and large agricultural bourgeoisie down to the medium landowners and prosperous peasant farmers—found themselves increasingly the victims of uncertainty and chaos. The landowners developed two major ideological positions and action programs in response to this condition: the traditionalist reactionary or conservative approach supported by the traditional landowning classes, the modernist bourgeois liberal approach advocated by the commercial farmers.

In some regions, with the support of a group of conservative ulama, the remnants of the traditional landowning class rushed back to the distributed villages that had been their private property before the shah's land reform and reoccupied the cultivated lands, claiming the Islamic principle of the sanctity of private ownership that they believed ought to be honored in the Islamic Revolution. Though not frequent, such incidents occurred in several provinces, including Kurdistan, West Azerbaijan, Khorasan, and Baluchestan. The leading conservative ulama also actively and zealously supported private landownership by issuing edicts (*fitva*) in answer to questions about landownership raised by members of the landowning class. The most prominent ulama of the Qum theological center—the Grand Ayatollahs Ruhollah Khomeini (1980), Sayyed Kazim Shariatmadari, Sayyed Mohammad Riza Gulpayegani, and Shahab al-Din Najafi Mar'ashi—issued edicts in the first year of the revolution supporting the sanctity of private ownership. The main rules of Islamic

law concerning landownership and landlord-peasant relations were thus reaffirmed by these living ulama, to whom, as the exemplary model (*marja'-i
taqlid*), obedience is required in the Shiite sect (*Ummat*, September 24, 1980;
Kayhan, September 10, 1980).

The defense of private ownership was not confined to traditionalists, who
mainly propounded the sanctity of private landholding on the basis of Islamic
law. The modern landed bourgeoisie, including most of its medium-sized and
larger commercial farmers who survived the revolution, emphasized the functional role of modern commercial agriculture in bringing the nation to agricultural self-sufficiency—particularly, they argued, when the Islamic revolutionary community was at war with imperialism and the "great satan." A new
and significant development in this period was the emergence of an ideology
based on the cause of modern commercial farmers. A group of economists and
agroeconomists rallied around two publications—*Barzigar*, a weekly newspaper, and *Kishavarz*, a monthly journal—whose editorials, feature articles,
and news analyses tended to stress four major themes: giving priority to
agricultural production to create national self-sufficiency, as opposed to emphasizing equitable land distribution; supporting the claim that the security of
private landownership is indispensable to higher agricultural production; ide-
alizing modern technology and mechanized agriculture; and supporting a
protectionist agricultural policy aimed at curbing importation of foodstuffs,
providing commercial farmers with financial aid and low-interest credit, raising the price of agricultural products, and providing an infrastructure for
agricultural production while minimizing the state intervention.

The modern commercial farmers found allies among the ulama within
ruling and nonruling circles, the new middle classes, and the technocrats, and,
in fact, found a natural ally in the person of Ali Mohammad Izadi, the minister
of agriculture and rural development in the provisional government. Izadi, a
professor of agronomy and a successful large commercial farmer, made a
number of moves designed to safeguard modern agricultural enterprises and
private landed properties. First, he launched a propaganda campaign against
the practice of land seizure and in support of private landownership. In the
concluding session of a seminar on agricultural problems, for instance, Izadi
(*Kishavarz-i Imruz*, October 27, 1979:1) stated that "the government agricultural policy aims at full respect for landownership . . . for the fact is that
the only remedy for agricultural shortcomings is to respect private ownership
and to refrain from destroying the incentive for raising agricultural production." Second, to provide the legal basis for law and order in rural areas, he
drafted a bill to punish usurpers of arable lands. He also cooperated with the

ruling Islamic Republican party in its hostile actions against the peasant movements, which led in many cases to the dispatching of armed Islamic Guards into such troubled areas as Gonbad, Kurdistan, and Azerbaijan. Third, to meet the mounting pressure from the left while excluding private landed property from redistribution, he prepared a land reform bill that stipulated cession of wastelands, barren lands, and nationalized pastures and forests to the landless villagers. Finally, Izadi encouraged the modern commercial farmers to unite in agricultural councils (ACs), set up as substitutes for the councils of peasant farmers and agricultural workers consistently demanded by the left (*Kishavarz-i Imruz*, October 13, 1979:4). Founded in the provincial centers and most of the 165 districts throughout the country, the ACs made a number of vigorous moves in defense of the vested interests of the commercial farmers. They convened two national congresses in Tehran; bombarded the religious authorities and state officials with thousands of petitions and cables protesting the practice of land seizure and Clause C of the Islamic land reform law; drafted a land reform bill as a counterproposal to Clause C to protect private landholdings; and dramatized in their numerous resolutions, petitions, interviews, and articles the functional significance of commercial farmers for national agricultural self-sufficiency (*Kishavarz-i Imruz*, November 10, December 8, 15, 29, 1979; May 24, September 27, October 4, December 20, 1980).

Clause C: The Ceiling on Landownership

Under the leadership of the ruling Islamic Republican party and its founder and chief architect, Ayatollah Sayyid Mohammad Bihishti, then secretary general of the party, the militant ulama, and the emerging elite of the Islamic state stage-managed a civilian coup d'état against the liberal provisional government of Mihdi Bazargan by masterminding the hostage crisis in November 1979. Assured of the practical value of this crisis, enjoying the full support of the left, and calling the crisis the second revolution, the ruling party swiftly adopted a radical posture. This posture was successfully directed toward two basic goals: discrediting the liberals of the provisional government and disarming the left of its radical platform.

Responding to initiatives taken by radicals and under the mounting challenge of the left on the land issue, the ruling party decided to assume a leading role on the crucial issue of land distribution in order to expel the radical agitators from rural areas. For this purpose, it appointed Riza Isfahani (1979), the radical author of a number of works on Islamic economics and the religious conditions of landownership, as deputy minister of agriculture in charge of land affairs. At the outset, Isfahani proclaimed in an interview carried by the mass media that "under the provisions of a radical land reform the lands possessed by the big landowners would be confiscated and ceded to the peasant farmers." He added that "the equitable distribution of the arable land would be commenced in the troubled areas of Gonbad and Kurdistan," where leftist activists had fomented peasant uprisings and land struggles (*Kishavarz-i Imruz,* December 8, 1979:1, 3). Isfahani prepared a land reform bill that, after several revisions in the interests of the landowning classes, was eventually enacted by the Revolutionary Council in April 1980.

According to the provisions of the first article of this law, arable land was divided into four types: wastelands and pastures; lands formerly reclaimed by persons or firms and later confiscated by the writs of the Islamic tribunals; barren lands that had previously been reclaimed and, according to the criteria of the preceding regime, were recognized as the property of persons and firms; and lands under cultivation. The second article of the law stipulated that the lands under Clauses A and B were at the disposal of the Islamic government, which could either turn their cultivation over to private persons and firms or, as the interests of the community might dictate, allow them to be used by the public sector. The proprietors of lands under Clause C had priority for reclamation of their barren lands provided that the stipulated ceiling for cultivated land was respected. Under the fourth article of the law, the ceiling for Clause D lands was set at twice the customary average size of holdings for absentee landowners and three times that for peasant cultivators. The land left over was to be ceded to landless villagers under religious tenets issued by the highest religious authority. Land acquired legally would be compensated by the state after legal debts to the government and the religious treasury had been deducted. The customary amount of land, according to the provisions of the "Rules and Regulations for the Implementation of the Land Reform Law," would be designated in each rural area by the Commission of Seven. However, the commissions had to make sure, first, that the amount of land was large enough to support the ordinary life of a peasant household and, second, that a peasant household could cultivate it without hired labor. Furthermore, the rules and regulations of the law stipulated an important clause to the effect that landed property illicitly acquired should be confiscated and distributed among the landless villagers.

The notes of the fourth article of the law provided as follows: (1) available land under Clauses A, B, and C in any area should be given priority for distribution over land under Clause D; (2) land allocated for the forage production of livestock enterprises was to be excluded from the provisions of the law; and (3) mechanized farms should not be distributed, but turned over to cooperatives of peasant cultivators. It should be noted here that in the literature on Islamic land reform, Clause C is currently used to include a combination of Clauses C and D, referring to both barren and cultivated land subject to the stipulated ceiling of the fourth article of the law.

The rules and regulations of the law provided that an independent Central Staff for Land Distribution, consisting of five members representing the highest religious authority (*vali-yi faqih*), the Holy War for Reconstruction (Jahad-i sazandagi), and the ministries of agriculture, interior, and justice, be in charge of implementing the law. The Central Staff was to organize the Commission of Seven in all provinces and districts; these would consist of two representatives of the Ministry of Agriculture, a representative of the Holy War for Reconstruction, a representative of the religious authority, a representative of the Ministry of Interior, and two representatives of the local people. The Central Staff was established in June 1980 and by early 1981 had founded thirty-six Commissions of Seven throughout the country. These commissions were actually dominated by their staff, a group of dedicated and religiously oriented high school and college graduates organized in the Holy War for Reconstruction.

The major achievements of the Central Staff (Iran, Sitad 1981:5, 6) and its Commissions of Seven were the ceding of some 150,000 hectares of wasteland and some 33,000 hectares of barren, reclaimed, and confiscated land to the permanent possession of landless villagers and small peasant farmers. Furthermore, some 800,000 hectares of arable land, left uncultivated because of the dispute between landowners and cultivators, were temporarily transferred to peasants for cultivation. According to the Central Staff (ibid.:8, 10), the political consequences of the activities of these commissions and the holy warriors in the rural areas were the establishment of law and order in the village communities; the reduction of unrest and land strife; the extension of centralized authority over the countryside by the founding of some 19,000 Islamic village councils; and the expulsion of radical and leftist groups from the rural communities and their replacement by zealous Islamic elements.

The Struggle over Clause C

Clause C was the focal point of over a decade of conflict and struggle in rural Iran, lasting from the time of its proclamation in autumn 1979 through its suspension in autumn 1980, its reconfirmation and further legitimation by the

Islamic Majlis in autumn 1981, its rejection by the Council of Guardians of the Constitution in spring 1982, a compromise over its main provisions in the mid-1980s, and finally its demise in the latter half of 1980s. The major sociopolitical forces in society were thereby divided into two hostile camps: the exponents and opponents of Clause C. Its main supporters comprised the radical members of the new elite, a tiny segment of the ruling ulama, and the young holy warriors serving in rural areas. The left, now disarmed by the initiative taken by the governing elite and pushed aside, had no choice but to support the platform of the ruling party on the land question. The opponents of Clause C included a wide spectrum of social forces, ranging from a large group of ulama both inside and outside the ruling circles and traditional bourgeoisie to the commercial farmers organized mainly in the ACs.

The struggle of social forces over Clause C occurred at three levels: at the theological level among the ulama, at the level of general political campaigning, and at the level of violent clashes in the rural areas. At the theological level, the focus was on the legality of the clause: the sanctity of private property as one of the fundamental principles of Islamic law suggested a legal escape. This was proposed in a formulation by Ayatollah Mishkini, a prominent exponent of Clause C; it was well received by the majority of the ruling party, and was finally endorsed by Khomeini, the highest religious authority. Mishkini's proposal was based on the familiar principle of maintaining the Islamic order under the condition of overriding necessity (*zarura*), which permits the suspension of a primary rule. In the case of Clause C, the primary rule established private ownership, but its absoluteness is qualified if the ruling grand clergy, as the highest religious authority (i.e., Ayatollah Khomeini), issues an edict for such a dispensation (*Payam-i Inqilab*, January 31, 1981:64–65).

The ulama were divided into opposing camps on the question of the legality and legitimacy of Clause C. A small segment of the ruling ulama, including Ayatollahs Ali Meshkini (*Kayhan*, May 29, 1980:12), Hosaynali Montaziri, and Mohammad Bihishti, supported Clause C and for a short while enjoyed Ayatollah Khomeini's support as well (*Inqilab-i Islami*, April 14, 1981). They were opposed by a large segment of the leading ulama of the Qum and Mashhad theological centers, as well as those of other cities, who issued edicts on various occasions vigorously negating the legality of Clause C. Many others opposed Clause C, including such powerful ruling ulama as Rabbani Shirazi, member of the Council of Guardians of the Constitution; Mohammad Mohammadi Gilani, the well-known judge of Tehran's Islamic Tribunal; Shaikh Mohammad Yazdi, then deputy speaker of the Majlis and later the chief justice; and Nasir Makarim Shirazi, the editor of the monthly journal *Maktab-i Islam* (*Kayhan,* September 10, 1980:4; *Ittila'at,* January 8, 1981; Qumi 1979).

An open letter to the Islamic Majlis signed by twenty professors of theology at the Qum Theological Center (*Kayhan,* September 10, 1980:4) restated the opinion of the majority of the ulama on the land question. The authors of the letter raised two crucial points against Clause C. "The Land Reform bill," they argued, "is in contradiction with Islamic principles of ownership and the famous edicts of prominent religious authorities—particularly those of our great leader, the Imam (Khomeini)." Furthermore, they claimed, the implementation of the bill would entail heavy economic losses: "It will ruin the reclaimed lands and create diffidence in the farmers and lead to the bankruptcy and backwardness of the agricultural sector at a time when there is a need for self-sufficiency for termination of Iran's dependence on the United States of America."

The commercial farmers, organized in the ACs, began a vigorous campaign against Clause C. In one of its editorials, the weekly paper *Kishavarz-i Imruz* (December 29, 1979:1–2) gave a good account of the mounting strife between commercial farmers and the proponents of Clause C over the land question: "Thanks to Riza Isfahani, the new deputy minister of land affairs, the last week was a most turbulent week for Iranian agriculture. The small landowners, who are the members of the Agricultural Councils, instigated a widespread campaign against Isfahani and demanded his dismissal from office. They were also given audience by the Imam [Khomeini] and submitted their protests to him." The editorial further stated that the ACs of Iran, particularly those of Tehran and Fars, had made many attempts to safeguard the interests of the landowning classes, and that their representatives, organized in a group of fifty, had made several successful moves to meet with the authorities in Tehran and Qum. The chief of the Tehran AC, a highly influential and powerful individual, made considerable efforts to organize the farmers and livestock owners of Tehran, setting off an intense campaign against Riza Isfahani. In his cable to the authorities, the chief charged Isfahani with being an "antirevolutionary element" who had caused chaos and slaughter in the rural areas. In response, by using radio, television, daily newspapers, and Islamic committees of the offices and institutions of higher education, the supporters of Isfahani launched a fierce attack on the Tehran AC and labeled its members "feudal elements."

The controversy over Clause C also extended to violent confrontations in the rural areas. Following the announcement and initial implementation of the clause, hundreds of such incidents occurred. In Bujnurd, for instance, the landowners hanged the representative of the peasants at the official residence of the Commission of Seven (*Ittila'at*, February 9, 1980:10). In the provinces of Fars, Kurdistan, Khuzistan, and Azerbaijan, a number of holy warriors and members of the commissions were slain.

The united front of the conservative ulama and different strata of landowners eventually succeeded in blocking Clause C in the autumn of 1980. The Central Staff of the Land Distribution made an announcement in late October on radio and television suspending its implementation. Later, in a seminar of the Commissions of Seven convened in Tehran, Ayatollah Bihishti announced that, under current circumstances, the opinion of Imam Khomeini was that all efforts should be aimed at implementing Clauses A and B. There were four major factors, as claimed by authorities, responsible for the de facto decision to suspend Clause C: a decrease in the areas of cultivation and the volume of agricultural production; the occurrence of violent clashes in the rural areas; the weight of thousands of petitions and complaints, encouraged by landowners, addressed to the religious and state authorities to point out the poor operations of the Commissions; and, finally, the impact of the war with Iraq (*Ittila'at*, January 1, 1981:5).

The suspension of Clause C was a major setback to the Commissions of Seven and the holy warriors, who, along with various leftist organizations, began to demand its reconfirmation and reimplementation. Understandably, the main argument of the exponents of Clause C among the ruling circles was that "its continuous suspension will provide an opportunity for the leftist groups to dispatch their agents to the rural areas in order to mobilize a popular revolution through peasant movements" (*Ittila'at*, January 1, 1981:5).

To legalize Clause C further, the Ministry of Agriculture drafted a land reform bill and submitted it to the Islamic Majlis in late 1980. As members of the ruling Islamic Republican party, the majority of the deputies favored enactment of this bill. However, the twelve-man Council of the Guardians of the Islamic Constitution (with veto power over the Islamic content of the laws), consisting of six ulama and six lay judges, along with the majority of the ulama, held that Clause C was not in accordance with the Islamic principle of the sanctity of private property; thus they would have vetoed the bill had it been approved by the Islamic Majlis. Intensified conflict between the Majlis and the Council of Guardians over this issue postponed approval of the bill until late 1981. Concomitant with the suppression of the powerful and militant leftist organizations and under mounting pressure from the holy warriors serving in the rural areas, Ali Akbar Hashimi-Rafsanjani, the speaker of the Majlis, secured a decree from Ayatollah Khomeini in October 1981 that practically freed the Majlis from the veto power of the Council of the Guardians of the Constitution provided that two-thirds of the deputies voted in favor of the bill. Following two years of heated controversy and conflict, the bill was eventually enacted by the Majlis in the autumn of 1981.

As expected, the Council of the Guardians of the Constitution vetoed the bill in the spring of 1982. Khomeini changed his position once again and supported the council on the grounds of Islamic jurisprudence. Finally, the conflicting forces drafted a compromise bill that was approved by the Islamic Majlis in 1985. The new law provides, first, for the ownership by peasant cultivators of some 800,000 hectares of agricultural land (ownership that had become a matter of mounting dispute throughout the 1980s); second, the proposed ceiling on the size of landownership (Clause C) was dropped. The rival parties were not satisfied with the law; the radicals continued to fight for the rapid transfer of ownership of all occupied lands to the occupant peasants, whereas the conservatives favored the reinforcement of article 49 of the constitution according to which only lands illicitly acquired would be subject to confiscation. Thus, once again, the Council of Guardians of the Constitution objected to the bill, and in many cases the religious judges issued rulings in favor of landowners who had proved to the court that their property was acquired licitly (for the text of the 1985 law and objections by the Council of Guardians, see *Ittila'at,* May 15, 1985; for the parliamentary debates of the two opposing camps over the issue of ownership of land see *Ittila'at,* May 8, 15, 18, 1985). Heartened by the new wave of radicalization and Khomeini's personal support, the Majlis finally ratified a law in October 1986 by a two-thirds vote, allowing the transfer to some 120,000 cultivators of about 800,000 hectares of the occupied lands for a just price (for debates over this bill see Schirazi, 1987; Bakhash, 1989; see also *Iran Times,* November, 14, 1986:4).

Following his message to the pilgrims to Mecca on August 10, 1987, dubbed by the radicals the "manifesto of the Islamic Revolution," Khomeini issued a historic edict that gave unconditional authority to the Islamic state to make all manner of decisions concerning the affairs and interests of the Islamic community. Furthermore, to facilitate the enactment of radical measures, in February 1988 Khomeini created a thirteen-member Discretionary Council to review the controversial bills in the event the Majlis and the Council of Guardians should fail to reach an agreement on theological and legal points. In addition to the conservative members of the Council of Guardians, the Discretionary Council included a number of supporters of the radical measures. The limitations of Shi'i jurisprudence to manage the daily affairs of a highly complicated modern secular society had been apparent for some

time. The only available Shi'i principles were those of overriding necessity
(zarura) and preservation of the system. Deviating from the primary rules of
shari'a was possible only under emergency circumstances that would require
adopting secondary rulings to guarantee the regime's survival. In Sunni Islam
the Islamic ruler as vali-yi amr is authorized to ratify government rulings
according to the principle of masliha—the best interests of the Islamic community. Following a number of abortive attempts to apply the principle of
zarura during the ten years of Islamic rule, the Islamic regime was forced by
circumstances to adopt a Sunni principle of masliha.

The radicals hoped that this jurisprudential invention would eradicate the
Islamic barriers to moderate land reform and allow the Discretionary Council
to solve the legal problems for transferring titles of seized lands to their
occupant peasants (see, e.g., Kayhan, March 28–31, 1988:5). However, the
defeat in the Iran-Iraq war, the death of Khomeini, mounting economic problems in the postwar period, and unprecedented changes in the Soviet bloc put
the radical camp on the defensive and bolstered the clout of the moderate
bloc. The moderates, therefore, managed to resist the pressures of the radicals
and began to obstruct the implementation of the provisions of the 1986 law
concerning the ownership of the lands seized by the peasants. Referring to
article 49 of the constitution, they argued that the law applied to illicitly
acquired lands. As a result, in many cases the religious courts issued rulings
for the return of the occupied plots to the landowners who had acquired their
property licitly.

The achievement of Islamic land reform, as of the tenth anniversary of the
revolution in February 1989, was the transfer to about 80,000 peasant
cultivators of the ownership of 43,000 hectares of confiscated lands, 100,000
hectares of reclaimed and waste lands that had been seized by peasants, and
370,000 hectares of state and private barren lands. Furthermore, it was announced that the titles of the remaining 700,000 hectares of seized lands under
temporary cultivation would be transferred to 120,000 occupant peasants
(Risalat, February 13, 1989:11). The total of 0.5 million hectares of land that
has already been transferred to the peasant cultivators constitutes only 14
percent of the 3.5 million hectares of land at the disposal of the large holdings
(over 50 hectares).

Conclusions

In concluding, I will compare and contrast the land reform program of the
1960s and the agrarian program of the 1970s with the Islamic land reform and

other agrarian programs of late 1970s and the 1980s. In each case, the "non-revolutionary peasantry" was included, and instigation of the peasants came primarily from sociopolitical forces from outside the village communities. In both cases a "revolutionary crisis" in the early phase of the reform movement was followed by a "counterrevolutionary" period of suppression of peasantry and establishment of law and order in rural areas, and finally by a phase of moderate land reform from above. In both land reform programs, deviations from the Islamic principles of the sanctity of private proprietorship led to the protest movements of the ulama. In both cases, the mechanized farms, orchards, and livestock farms were, in principle, excluded from the provisions of reform (with the exception of some mechanized farms occupied by the peasants in the first two years of the Islamic revolution). In both land reform programs, family small landownership expanded. Rapid population growth, the scarcity of agricultural land, and increasing dependency upon imported foodstuffs created in both cases serious agrarian problems. Finally, urban dominance over rural society and state agrarian policies became the major factors in manipulating and resolving the agrarian problems in both land reform programs.

However, while the shah's land reform and the Islamic land reform showed certain similarities, there were also significant differences. The former was a reform from above, implemented under external pressures, to forestall the revolution from below; the latter was initiated from the middle, primarily by the young urban intelligentsia, to radicalize the whole revolutionary movement. The shah's land reform crushed the hegemony and resistance of the old landowning class to defend its vested class interest, while suppressing group conflict; the Islamic revolution unleashed the covert group conflict and led to a new struggle over land. Ironically, this led to the emergence of a heightened awareness of group interests among the commercial farmers. The shah's programs led to the fall of the old landowning class and the rise of big agricultural bourgeoisie and commercial farmers; the latter led to the fall of the big agricultural bourgeoisie and the survival of middle-sized commercial farmers. The shah's programs led to the establishment of state control over rural areas and the emergence of a state "petite bourgeoisie" in agriculture; the Islamic agrarian programs led to a much greater control by the state. The former increased the concentration of land in the larger holdings (the Gini coefficient of concentration of land distribution increased from 0.60 in 1960 to 0.65 in 1976; see Agah 1982:162); the latter decreased, to some extent, the magnitude of land concentration in larger holdings. The shah's land reform transferred the ownership of some 6–7 million hectares of agricultural land (about 52–62 percent of the total) to the occupant sharecroppers and tenant farmers; the Islamic land reform distributed approximately half a million hectares of agricultural land (3 percent of the total) among the peasants and agricultural workers who had themselves already taken the initiative to occupy and cultivate these lands. The former abolished the traditional practices of sharecropping and tenancy; the latter reaffirmed and encouraged them as Islamic institutions.

The shah's land reform led to a fundamental transformation of social structure and class relations. It eliminated the old landowning class and encouraged the rise of commercial agriculture in both public and private sectors, while expanding the family small holding. It was, thus, a true "statist-bourgeois" revolution from above without the participation of the bourgeoisie and peasantry per se. Under these circumstances, the instigation of the peasantry came primarily, in the early phase of the reform, in the person of Hasan Arsanjani, the minister of agriculture and the architect of land reform, who referred to "the criminal landowners and the dear peasants" in some of his fiery speeches to the nation.

The Islamic land reform was set in motion from the middle and below, with the revolutionary participation of activist students who incited a segment of the peasantry in some regions. It was intended and expected to go far beyond the shah's land reform. However, a number of factors led to the failure of the Islamic land reform. One major obstacle to a more radical reform policy— imposing a ceiling on the size of landownership—has been the emphatic support for the sanctity of private property in Islamic jurisprudence. Such Islamic principles must of course be honored in a political community organized under the domination of the ulama as the guardians of Islamic jurisprudence. Another crucial obstacle to the imposition of a ceiling on the size of holdings was the organized and highly effective resistance of the commercial farmers. A united front of traditionalist ulama, commercial farmers, conservative bazaaris, and a segment of petite bourgeois elements among the new elite have thus succeeded in blocking the implementation of a more radical program of agrarian reforms in postrevolutionary Iran.

The Iranian experience shows that the land question and agrarian relations have primarily been influenced by an ongoing struggle among the major urban sociopolitical forces in general and those within the regime in particular. However, the agrarian policies and strategies of both governing elites and their contenders are constrained by two main factors: the scarcity of agricultural land available for distribution among the majority of the undersized peasants and landless villagers, and the dramatic increase in the demand for foodstuffs as a result of the high rate of population growth and increasing income. Regardless of the ideological commitment of the policy makers, the question of promoting a more equitable distribution of arable land among peasantry thus will always have to be balanced against increasing the production of agricultural produce.

Author's Note

This paper was prepared for a conference on Hierarchy and Stratification in the Middle East sponsored by the Joint Committee on the Near and Middle East of the American Council of Learned Societies and the Social Science Research Council.

References

Agah. 1982/1361. *Majmu'ih-yi Kitab-i Agah: Masa'il-i 'Arzi va Dihgani* [Land and Peasant Questions]. Tehran: Mu'assisa-yi Intisharat-i Agah.

Ajami, I. 1969. "Social Classes, Family, Demographic Characteristics, and Mobility in Three Iranian Villages." *Sociological Ruralis* 9:62–72.

———. 1973. "Land Reform and Modernization of the Farming Structure in Iran." *Oxford Agrarian Studies* 11:1–12.

———. 1981/1360. "Tajdid-i Bana-yi Kishavarzi-yi Dihgani" [Reconstruction of Peasant Farming]. In *Arash* 5, 4:87–102.

Amini, Ali. 1986. Interview by Hormoz Hekmat.

Arsanjani, H. 1962/1341. *Musahibaha-yi Radiyu'i-yi Duktur Arsanjani* [Radio Interviews of Dr. Arsanjani]. Tehran: Ministry of Agriculture.

Ashraf, A. 1978. "The Role of Rural Organizations in Rural Development: The Case of Iran." In *Rural Organizations and Rural Development: Some Asian Experiences,* ed. Inayatullah. Kuala Lumpur: APDAC.

———. 1982/1361. "Dihqanan, Zamin, va Inqilab" [Peasants, Land, and Revolution]. In Agah, 7–49.

Ashraf, A., and A. Banuazizi. 1980. "Policies and Strategies of Land Reform in Iran." In *Land Reform: Some Asian Experiences,* ed. Inayatullah. Kuala Lumpur: APDAC.

———. 1985. "The States, Classes, and Modes of Mobilization in the Iranian Revolution." *State, Culture, and Society* 1, 3 (Spring): 3–41.

Azar, G. 1980/1359. "Mubarizat-i Dihqani dar Iran" [Peasants Struggle in Iran]. *Dunya* (Mehr/October): 74–77.

———. 1981. "Junbishha-yi Dihqani dar Iran" [Peasant Movements in Iran]. *Nika'in:* 27–37.

Azimi, H. 1982/1361. "Tawzi'-i Zamin va Daramad dar Astana-yi Islahat-i 'Arzi" [Distribution of Land and Income on the Eve of Land Reform]. In Agah, 75–94.

Bakhash, S. 1989. "The Politics of Land, Law, and Social Justice in Iran." *Middle East Journal* 43, 2:186–201.

Beck, L. 1980. "Revolutionary Iran and Its Tribal Peoples." *MERIP Reports* 87 (May): 14–20.

Bill, J. 1972. *The Politics of Iran, Groups, Classes, and Modernization.* Columbus, Ohio: Charles E. Merrill.

———. 1988. *The Eagle and the Lion: The Tragedy of American-Iranian Relations.* New Haven, Conn.: Yale University Press.

Brun, T., and R. Dumont. 1978. "Iran: Imperial Pretensions and Agricultural Independence." *MERIP Reports* 71 (October): 15–20.

Cottam, R. 1988. *Iran and the United States: A Cold War Case Study.* Pittsburgh, Pa.: University of Pittsburgh Press.

"Current Political Attitudes in an Iranian Village." 1983. *Iranian Studies* 16, 1–2:3–29.

Dowlat, M., B. Hourcade, and O. Puech. 1980. "Les paysens et la revolution Iranienne." *Peuples Méditerranées* 19 (January–March): 19–41.

Hadary, G. 1951. "The Agrarian Reform Problems in Iran." *Middle East Journal* 5, 2:181–96.

Halliday, F. 1979. *Iran: Dictatorship and Development.* Harmondsworth, Eng.: Penguin.

Hegland, M. 1980. "One Village in the Revolution." *MERIP Reports* 87 (May): 7–12.

Hooglund, E. 1973. "The Khwushnishin Population of Iran." *Iranian Studies* 6 (Autumn): 229–45.

———. 1980. "Rural Participation in the Revolution." *MERIP Reports* 87 (May): 3–6.

———. 1982. *Land and Revolution in Iran.* Austin: University of Texas Press.

Huges, T. 1965. *Land Reform in Iran: Implications for the Shah's "White Revolution."* Research memorandum, U.S. Department of State, Director of Intelligence and Research, February 8.

Humphrey, H. 1963. *Alliance for Progress: A First-Hand Report from Latin America.* Washington, D.C. Pamphlet.

Huntington, S. 1968. *Political Order in Changing Societies.* New Haven, Conn.: Yale University Press.

Iran, Agricultural Development Bank. 1981/1360. Unpublished materials. Tehran: Bureau of Economic Studies.

Iran, Markaz-i Tahqiqat-i Rusta'i (Vizarat-i Kishavarzi) [Center for Rural Research, Ministry of Agriculture]. 1975–84. *Barrasi-yi Mizan-i Zamini kih dar Natija-yi Ijra-yi Qavanin-i Islahet-i ʿArzi Nasib-i Zari ʾin wa Malikin Gardida Ast* [A Survey of the Amount of Land Acquired by Landowners and Peasants Due to the Implementation of the Land Reform Laws]. Tehran: published by author. A series of reports on Iran's six provinces: Isfahan, 1975–1354; Loristan, 1976/1355; Markazi, 1977/1356; Fars, 1978/1357; Bakhtaran, 1980/1359; Gilan, 1982/1361; and Mazandaran, 1984/1363.

Iran, Plan and Budget Organization. 1979/1359. *Budja-yi Koll-i Kishvar, 1358* [National Budget of 1979–1980]. Tehran: published by author.

Iran, Public Statistics. 1961. *National and Province Statistics of the First Census of Iran: November 1956.* Tehran: Ministry of Interior, Public Statistics.

————. 1962. *First National Census of Agriculture, 1960.* Tehran: Ministry of Interior, Public Statistics.

Iran, Sitad-i Markazi va Hay'atha-yi Haft Nafara-yi Vaguzari va Ihya'i 'Arazi [Central Staff and the Commissions of Seven for Transfer and Reclamation of Land]. 1981/1360. *Karnama-yi Hasht Mahih.* Tehran: published by author.

Iran, Statistical Center. 1967/1346. *Salnama-yi Amari, 1345.* [Statistical Yearbook, 1967]. Tehran:

————. 1981a. *National Census of Population and Housing: November 1976.* Tehran: Plan and Budget Organization.

————. 1981b. *Salnama-yi Amari, 1360* [Statistical Yearbook, 1981/1360]. Tehran:

Isfahani, R. 1979/1358. *Iqtisad-i Tatbiqi* [Comparative Economics]. Tehran: Ilham Publications.

Jahanshahlu Afsher, N. 1982/1361. *Ma va Biganagan, Sarquzasht* [We and Foreigners, an Autobiography]. N.p.

Jazani, B. 1982. *Capitalism and Revolution in Iran.* London: Zed Press.

Katouzian, M. A. 1974. "Land Reform in Iran: A Case Study in the Political Economy of Social Engineering." *Journal of Peasant Studies* 1, 2:219–38.

Kazemi, F. 1980. *Poverty and Revolution in Iran.* New York: New York University Press.

————, and E. Abrahamian. 1978. "The Non-Revolutionary Peasantry of Modern Iran." *Iranian Studies* 11:259–308.

Keddie, N. 1972. "Stratification, Social Control, and Capitalism in Iranian Villages: Before and After Land Reform." In *Rural Politics and Social Change in the Middle East,* ed. R. Antoun. Bloomington: Indiana University Press.

Khamsi, R. 1969. "Land Reform in Iran." *Monthly Review* 21 (July): 20–28.

Khomeini, R. 1980/1359. *Nuh Fetwa-yi Imam Khomeini* [Nine Edicts of Imam Khomeini]. Qum: n.p. (pamphlet).

————. 1983/1362. *Sahifa-yi Nur* [A Collection of Speeches and Announcements]. 18 vols. Tehran: Ministry of Islamic Guidance.

Khosravi, K. 1988/1367. *Barrasi-yi Amari-yi Vaz'iyat-i 'Arzi-yi Iran dar Shesh Ostan* [Statistical Survey of Agricultural Conditions in Six Provinces]. Tehran: Markaz-i Nashr-i Danishgahi.

Kishavarz, H. 1970/1349. *Barrasi-yi Iqtisadi wa Ijtima'i-yi Shirkat-i Sahami-yi Zira'i-yi Riza Pahlavi* [A Social and Economic Survey of Riza Pahlavi Farm Corporation]. Tehran: Institute for Social Research.

Lambton, A. K. S. 1953. *Landlord and Peasant in Persia.* London: Oxford University Press.

————. 1969. *The Persian Land Reform, 1962–1966.* Oxford: Clarendon Press.

McLachlan, K. 1968. "Land Reform in Iran." In *Cambridge History of Iran,* vol. 1. Cambridge: Cambridge University Press.

Mahdavi, H. 1965. "The Coming Crisis in Iran." *Foreign Affairs* 44 (October): 134–46.

————. 1982/1361. "Tahavvolat-i Si Sala-yi Yik dih Dar Dasht-i Qazvin" [Thirty-Year Transformations in One Village in Qazvin]. In *Agah,* 50–74.

Martin, M. 1989. "Villagers, Agriculture, and the Revolution." Philadelphia: The Middle East Center, University of Pennsylvania. Unpublished paper.

Mo'mini, B. 1980/1359. *Mas' ala-yi 'Arzi va Jang-i Tabagati dar Iran* [Land Question and Class Struggle in Iran]. Tehran: Peyvand Publications.

Mosaddiq, M. 1986/1365. *Khatirat va Ta'llomat-i Mosaddiq* [Memoirs and Sorrows of Mosaddiq]. Ed. I. Afshar. London: n.p.

Mu'assisa-yi Mutali' at va Tahqiqat-i Ijtima'i. 1965–67. Danishgah-i Tehran [Institute for Social Studies and Research, University of Tehran]. A series of survey reports on various regions, including social and economic survey of villages (*Barrasi-yi Iqtisadi va Ijtima'i-yi Rustaha-yi*); *Ilam*, 1965/1344; *Mashhad*, 1966/1345; *Sabzavar*, 1966/1345; *Arak*, 1967/1346; *Bandar 'Abbas*, 1967/1346; and *Khalkhal*, 1967/1346.

Najmabadi, A. 1987. *Land Reform and Social Change in Iran*. Salt Lake City: University of Utah Press.

Nika'in, A. 1981/1360. *Rusta-yi Iran dar Intezar-i Tahavvol* [Iran's Countryside in Expectation of Change]. Tehran: Hizb-i Tude-yi Iran.

Nikbin, B. 1983/1362. *Guzashta Chiraq-i Rah-i Ayanda Ast* [The Past Is the Light of the Future]. Tehran.

Nowshirvani, V. 1981. "The Beginnings of Commercialized Agriculture in Iran." In *The Islamic Middle East, 700–1900: Studies in Economic and Social History*, ed. A. L. Udovitch. Princeton, N.J.: The Darwin Press.

Okazaki, S. 1968. *The Development of Large-Scale Farming in Iran: The Case of the Province of Gorgan*. Tokyo: Institute of Asian Economic Affairs.

Packenham, R. 1973. *Liberal America and the Third World*. Princeton, N.J.: Princeton University Press.

Pahlavi, M. R. 1980. *Answer to History*. New York: Stein and Day.

Qahraman, B. 1982. "Do Yaddasht dar Bara-yi Kishavarzi-yi Tijari dar Iran" [Two Notes on Commercial Farming in Iran]. In Agah, 135–54.

Qumi, A. 1979/1358. *Barkhi Fatawa-yi Ayatollah Qumi* [Some Edicts of Ayatollah Qumi]. Tehran: N.p.

Richards, H. 1975. "Land Reform and Agribusiness in Iran." *MERIP Reports* (December): 3–18.

Roxborough, I. 1979. *Theories of Underdevelopment*. London: Macmillan Press.

Safinizhad, J. 1974/1353. *Bunih*. Tehran: Toos Publications.

Schirazi, A. 1987. *The Problem of the Land Reform in the Islamic Republic of Iran*. Occasional Papers, no. 10. Berlin: Free University of Berlin.

Shaji'i, Z. 1965/1344. *Namayandagan-i Majlis-i Shura-yi Melli dar Bist va yik Dawra-yi Qanunquzari* [Deputies of the National Assembly in Twenty-One Sessions]. Tehran: Institute for Social Studies and Research.

Siyasi, A. 1987/1366. *Guzarish-i Yak Zindagi* [Autobiography]. London: published by author.

Sodagar, M. 1979/1358. *Islahat-i 'Arzi, 1340–1350* [The Land Reform, 1961–1971]. Tehran: Pazand Publications.

Tabari, A. 1983. "Land, Politics, and Capital Accumulation." *MERIP Reports* (March–April): 26–30.

Turkoman, Kanun-i Farhangi va Siyasi-yi Khalq-i [Cultural and Political Center of Turkoman People]. 1980/1359. *Mubariza-yi Marq va Zindaqi-yi Khalq-i Turkoman* [The Life and Death Struggle of the Turkoman People]. Tehran: published by author.

Vieille, P. 1972. "Les paysans, la petite bourgeoisie, et l'état après la réforme agraire en Iran." *Annals* 2 (March–April): 349–77.

Warne, W. 1956. *Mission for Peace: Point 4 in Iran.* New York: Bobbs-Merrill Company, Inc.

Warriner, D. 1969. *Land Reform in Principle and Practice.* Oxford: Clarendon Press.

Wilber, D. 1962. "Memorandum of Conversation: Dr. Hasan Arsanjani, Minister of Agriculture, November 10, 1962." Personal file.

Zonis, M. 1971. *The Political Elite of Iran.* Princeton, N.J.: Princeton University Press.

14

Peasant Protest and Resistance in Rural Iranian Azerbaijan

FEREYDOUN SAFIZADEH

Studies of peasant politics since 1960 have focused attention on the social and economic background of the peasants (Alavi 1965, Moore 1966, Wolf 1969, Scott 1976, Skocpol 1979) as well as the types of production arrangements and systems that have given rise to collective political reaction and peasant participation in major rebellions (Steward, et al. 1956, Wolf and Mintz 1957, Stinchcombe 1961, Paige 1975). Recently interest has grown concerning everyday forms of peasant resistance and protest as important social phenomena (Adas 1979, 1981; Scott 1984, 1986). These phenomena include foot dragging, dissimulation, desertion, false compliance, pilfering, feigned ignorance, slander, arson, sabotage, and so on. Scott has called these activities Brechtian forms of class struggle that require little or no coordination or planning, making use of implicit understanding and informal networks and avoiding direct contact or confrontation. He states that to understand these commonplace forms of resistance is to understand much of what peasantry has historically done to defend its interests against both conservative and progressive orders (Scott 1986:6).

In the case of Iran, popular knowledge, some literary works, and most radical political statements have characterized the peasantry as apathetic, fatalistic, oppressed, servile, ignorant, passive, and disorganized (Lambton 1953:394; Sa'edi 1984). Until recently, it has not been unusual for a visitor to most rural parts of Iran to come away feeling that the peasants are bearing the burden of centuries of oppression and exploitation and, furthermore, that the situation is unlikely to change significantly in the near future. Scholarly literature has also emphasized the nonrevolutionary character of the Iranian peasantry (Kazemi and Abrahamian 1978). Kazemi and Abrahamian have argued that Iran's lack of a discontented "middle" peasantry, as well as a rural population formed of "outward-looking villages" is important in explaining the absence of large-scale peasant rebellion.[1] Some observers have attributed this absence to submissive obedience demanded by Islam. Others have seen centuries of exploitation and oppression as the cause. But as Abrahamian has stated it would be a mistake to take "the outward appearance of submission to be proof of the inward acceptance of oppression" (1982:376). It is for this very reason that I believe it is important to examine specific cases of everyday avoidance, protest, and resistance to rural Azerbaijan in considering peasant response and reaction to individuals, forces, and changes that have arisen in the past three decades.

The larger objective of this paper is to divert some of the attention from the examination of extraordinary moments in history—that is, when peasants have tried to take their destiny into their own hands—or the lack of such moments and focus it instead on the silent, anonymous, and constant forms of daily struggles over rents, crops, labor, water, taxes, and interests. The more specific aim is to examine four types of everyday forms of peasant avoidance, protest, and resistance observed in the village of Koyshan in Azerbaijan between 1979 and 1989. These peasant reactions deal with peasant-clergy, peasant-landlord, and peasant-state relations, as well as property rights. The first focuses on peasants protesting the presence of a local *mulla* (cleric), particularly his efforts to organize support for the cause of Ayatollah Khomeini at the time of the revolution; the second discusses peasants resisting other peasants considered outsiders to Koyshan because of questions concerning their transient status as worker-peasants or outmigrants; the third involves peasant resistance to the previous village landlords who still own a sizable private garden in the village; and the last deals with peasant resistance to the state and its efforts to conscript the young men of the village.

The Village of Koyshan

Koyshan is located 20 kilometers outside the city of Ardabil on the foothills of Mount Sabalan overlooking the Ardabil plain. Historically the region has been one of the agriculturally more productive areas in Azerbaijan as a result of precipitation from the Caspian Sea lowlands. The past three decades have witnessed significant growth in cash crop production in the region; however, 40 percent of family landholdings are still devoted to production for household subsistence consumption.

Koyshan is a medium-sized (1,689 persons and 294 households) and relatively well-to-do village by Azerbaijan standards. Rapid population growth,

1,860 hectares of irrigated land, the introduction of tractors, and improved seed and fertilizer have made possible the production of a reasonable surplus for the market. Koyshan did not undergo land reform (1962–72) until 1969, the final stage, because of the landlord's political influence and the village's economic and political significance in the region. When land distribution took place, 285 households, or 88 percent of the villagers, became smallholders. The average landholding per household was 2.4 hectares. Up to the time of the Islamic revolution, Koyshan, like many other rural communities throughout Iran, witnessed extensive seasonal and permanent labor migration. Consolidation of the fragmented landholding was set in motion by the process of outmigration from the village. Land reform had a significant impact on the traditional village social hierarchy, but it was the income earned by villagers from urban labor markets during the 1970s that had the most profound effect on village stratification, an important factor in precipitating the tensions and conflicts that burst into the open after the collapse of the Pahlavi government.

After the takeover by Ayatollah Khomeini and the establishment of the Islamic government, land-related confrontations occurred in many parts of Iran, including Azerbaijan, Gilan, Mazandaran, Khorasan, Kurdistan, and Fars. Land seizures were initially limited to Pahlavi family holdings, agribusiness complexes, farm corporations, and large commercial farms whose owners had fled the country, but as time went on property rights of small landowners were also threatened. The most violent and prolonged confrontations took place in Turkoman Sahra and Kurdistan as the Turkoman tribe and Kurdish villagers attempted to organize new councils to deal with old land disputes, and also, in the case of Kurdistan, to protect themselves against powerful landowners intent on reversing the outcome of the shah's land distribution.[2] Because of the involvement of leftist groups in organizing Turkoman and Kurdish councils, the Islamic government intensified its propaganda campaign against the dangers of counterrevolution and crushed these movements by force, while ayatollah after ayatollah and many nonclerical leaders issued statements concerning the sanctity of private property in Islam and the government's full respect for private ownership. In the meantime the government debated, amended, implemented, and suspended various legislation in a more equitable Islamic land reform (Ashraf 1982).

Presence of Mulla Hashim in Koyshan

In the months preceding the takeover by Ayatollah Khomeini, villagers in Koyshan did not participate in the demonstrations or other anti-shah activities that eventually led to his overthrow. When Mulla Hashim, working closely with his counterparts in the mosque network of the city of Ardabil, visited the village to inspire ideological support for the cause of Islam and encourage peasants to participate in demonstrations, many villagers maintained that he was in the outlying areas because he feared for his own safety in the city. They were convinced that when Mulla Hashim sensed an imminent confrontation between demonstrators and the shah's military, he would depart to the countryside under the pretext of recruiting more men for the demonstrations. Consequently, peasants were unwilling to risk their lives for him or for a cause that in their judgment was unlikely to bring them justice, equality, or better living conditions. The common reaction in the village was one of avoidance and behind-the-back ridicule that now and then spilled into the open, accompanied by threatening behavior. On a number of occasions the more vocal young men tried to pull the mulla off his horse when he passed through the village, while adults simply sat or stood against the buildings' mud walls watching, saying nothing, and making no effort to restrain them.

After the success of the revolution the coming and going of Mulla Hashim had to be tolerated, and the village witnessed the emergence of a faction sympathetic to the Islamic revolution. In fact in August 1979, during the month of Ramadan, a considerable number of people gathered in the mosque in the evenings to listen to Mulla Hashim, who made the rounds of villages in the district to preach and report on the latest political developments in the country. Given the turbulent political atmosphere in the country and in Koyshan, my host, Masha Rahim, suggested that the gathering in the mosque was a good occasion for me to explain the purpose of my return visit to the village. At first I was reluctant to accept the suggestion that I should appear with Mulla Hashim before the villagers in the mosque. But as this was the only occasion where I would have such a large audience, I accepted.

In the evening my assistant, Mustafa, arrived stating that we should go up to the mosque because the *rouzeh*, sermon, would be over soon. With an old oil lantern in one hand and a club in the other he led the way up the narrow, dark, and dusty passages of the village to the mosque, the only building with electric lighting. As we approached, the single bulb lighting the entrance barely illuminated the large number of young men sitting on a nearby stone wall in the darkness; still others crowded the entrance. We took off our shoes before entering the main chamber, which was well lit and well carpeted with gelims and rugs. Mulla Hashim was still up at the *manbar* (lectern), but he was listening to the conversation that was taking place among the peasants sitting on the floor in front of him. We stood near the entrance facing their

backs. The atmosphere appeared tense. Finally, Mulla Hashim recited a verse
from the Koran, ended his service, stepped down from the manbar, and
quickly made his way to the door. I anticipated an uneasy confrontation with
him, who now symbolized and represented the new Islamic regime. I expected him to ask probing questions about my presence in the village.

My uneasiness stemmed from a real concern about the major propaganda
campaign set in motion shortly after Ayatollah Khomeini's takeover, which
asserted that the counterrevolution was creating havoc in the countryside,
setting fire to the year's harvest in the village threshing grounds to destabilize
the political situation further. The new regime kept warning villagers to report
all outsiders. They had poisoned the atmosphere to such a degree that it was
difficult to provide enough evidence in time to prevent being considered a
counterrevolutionary, particularly by those who had hastily become ardent
supporters of the Islamic regime.

To my surprise, Mulla Hashim hardly stopped to talk to me as he exited the
mosque. He looked worried, and there was a flurry of talk among the people
in the mosque that quickly spread to the young men congregated outside. As
Mulla Hashim exited, my assistant quickly announced to the congregation that
I would like to take a few minutes to explain the purpose of my stay in
Koyshan. Standing at the foot of the manbar I spoke about the specifics of my
research and stated that it was essential that people have a clear idea about the
nature of my work. Furthermore, I made it clear that I was not a member or
representative of a particular political group or faction, and moreover I had
permission from the newly organized Crusades for Reconstruction and the
Commission of Seven in Ardabil to continue the research.

Later, as we walked down the dark and dusty alleys to where I was staying,
it became clear why Mulla Hashim looked so concerned. My assistant rather
contentedly stated that the men outside the mosque had cut the steering
column of his jeep, parked nearby. Then he cursed the mulla for being a
freeloader who before the change of regime came to the village only two or
three times a year, always appearing in people's threshing grounds in late
summer to collect a share for himself in the name of *imam-haqqi*, Imam's
share. Mustafa recounted the story of events at the mosque to my host in the
garden. When I inquired why the villagers were so against Mulla Hashim,
Masha Rahim replied that "he is a bastard and deserves what may happen to
him." When I asked why, his answer was "because he is the son of a *qolfat*"
(servant).

It turned out that the landlord of a neighboring village had a relationship
with a woman from Koyshan who was a servant in his house, and Mulla

Hashim is their son. Although he had not received much from his father, he had gone on to become a mulla. Masha Rahim cynically stated that "he goes from village to village begging from poor peasants for imam haqqi, and molesting people's wives while their husbands are away." I asked Masha Rahim why he did not come to the mosque, and he replied, "I never go to the mosque. It is full of two-faced people." I asked who was his *marja'e taqlid,* the ayatollah he emulates, and he said, "Mine is the great Ayatollah Kho'i in Najaf." The turn for the better in Mulla Hashim's fortune after the Islamic revolution did not last long because his marja'e taqlid was Ayatollah Shariat-madari, whom the Khomeini regime found an obstacle in the way of the creation of an Islamic government.

Migrant Villagers and Their Claims

Villagers resisted other peasants they considered to have become outsiders to Koyshan. The relationship between the landowning, city-dwelling, permanent migrants and their sharecropping partners in the village was changing. The permanent migrants maintained all or part of their village landholding through a 50–50 (*yari-yari*) post–land reform sharecropping arrangement in the region. The loss of income brought about by unemployment in the urban areas during the revolution forced many of these migrants to return to Koyshan and to depend on the income derived from their agricultural lands. This development was much resented by the villagers and intensified the already antagonistic relationship between the two groups. Their return was also an important factor in precipitating political unrest and in initiating a crisis of property rights in the village.

In later summer 1980, as the subsistence crops were being prepared for storage and the cash crop for sale, the permanent migrants or their agents were on hand to collect the usual 50 percent share of the crop or the cash value of it. The difference this year was that their village sharecropping partners were reluctant to turn over the agreed-upon share. Having anticipated just such resistance this year, many permanent migrants had returned to Koyshan as early as midspring to take charge of the situation.

A small number of permanent migrants succeeded in extracting their share of the agreement by resorting to threats or intense negotiations or because of other obligatory circumstances. Many peasants adopted the course of passive resistance and refused to pay up. The more militant sharecroppers not only refused to turn over the agreed-upon share of the crop but questioned the terms of the arrangements. Violent clashes broke out. The revolutionary guards were summoned from Ardabil and complaints lodged with the offices of Crusade for Reconstruction, Council of Seven, and the deputy governor.

The lodging complaints by the permanent migrants indicated their adoption of a new and risky strategy. In addition to having to show that they were the injured party, they had to prove a disputable point—that their primary residence was in the village and their absence from Koyshan was only temporary as seasonal migrants or visitors to other areas. These points were strongly contended by the village sharecroppers and others who claimed that the migrants had moved to the city long ago and in some cases even owned property there.

The arrival of the armed revolutionary guards in the village was a signal to the clashing parties that the Islamic government was determined to maintain order. The villagers protested that the migrant landowners "with one foot here in Koyshan and the other in Tehran enjoy the best of both worlds and exploit us more than the old landlords." The zealous guards, faced with conflicting versions of events, were in no position to establish who was at fault. Their extemporaneous verdict was that all previous arrangements had to be honored until the passage of the Islamic land reform law by the new Parliament. Furthermore, they declared that the newly created Commission of Seven (*heyat-e haft nefar-e*) was responsible for dealing with rural land disputes throughout the country, and the regional branch of the council would begin its review of rural problems and land disputes in the Koyshan area after the completion of its work in the more troublesome areas of Dashte Mughan along the border with Soviet Union.

Resisting the Landlord: The Case of Masha Rahim

Masha Rahim had been a powerful man in Koyshan. He came from one of the larger lineages, and he had two wives, a son, and a daughter from his first marriage. He was the oldest of five brothers, all well-to-do except the youngest who had a problem with opium addiction. Up to the time of the revolution, Masha Rahim was the head of the village court (*khan-e-ye ensaf*), a rural organization that came into existence as a part of the White Revolution of the shah in the 1960s, and a member of the village council (*anjoman-e deh*).

Masha Rahim was also in charge of looking after the Hosseini *bagh,* the landlord's private garden in Koyshan, a position with distinct economic and political benefits. There were the profits from the sale of fruits, nuts, wood, and hay that he divided with the landowners, but more important was the close relationship with the influential Hosseini family, whose members in Arbadil, Tabriz, and Tehran had convenient positions in government ministries. From the landlords' perspective, Masha Rahim was powerful enough to protect the garden against poachers, squatters, and those who regularly attempted to divert the garden's share of irrigation water. During the period of increased migration from the village in the 1970s, Masha Rahim's strategy was to stay put and to buy the landholdings of peasant households departing from Koyshan.

After the establishment of the revolutionary Islamic regime, its supporters in Koyshan pushed for the dissolution of various rural organizations that existed in the village. The council, the court, and the position of the village headman (*kadkhuda*) were quickly replaced by the new consultative assembly (*shora-ye deh*). Given that Masha Rahim was the head of court and also a member of the village council, he was among the traditional leaders pushed aside by the vocal adherents of the Islamic regime. Consequently, between 1979 and 1988, Masha Rahim was isolated and excluded from the new political organs in the village.

During the fall of 1979, the assembly was dissolved only six months after its establishment by the revolutionary guards, who were now involved in the affairs of the village because of the violent clashes that had taken place in Koyshan. Charges against it were that its members—who had been the economically nouveau riche but politically frustrated of the village in the years leading to the revolution—were corrupt and were misusing their positions. In its place the Islamic Council (*anjoman-e Islami deh*) was created just after the start of the Iran-Iraq War. What was important in the transition from the assembly to the Islamic council was that younger villagers with some reading and writing ability, previously unable to participate in village organizations, were selected as representatives of different lineages to the new Islamic Council.

By 1983 a new organization called *payegah-e mogavemat* (resistance center or base) was established in Koyshan. This organization was attached to the village mosque, and initially its main function was to maintain village security and to provide new recruits for the war effort. The involvement of the younger villagers in the political process made a fairly smooth transition to the payegah-e mogavemat possible. These young men were not committed to any one line nor were there major pre-existing alignments among them, even though they belonged to different village lineages. They formed the core of the payegah-e mogavemat, which, in addition to its responsibility for village security, became responsible for the distribution of nationally rationed goods. In this capacity and with the issuance of the coupon book (*daftarchay-e arzag*), payegah-e mogavemat became the central source of information with respect to household composition and consumption patterns, since rationed allocations were based on household size. Thus, payeghan-e mogavemat knew the exact profiles of each household in Koyshan. This was not really a major issue since everybody knows everybody in the village, but this knowledge was sometimes used against households, for example, in cases where young men were evading the mobilization and draft.

In early 1988, Masha Rahim joined the payegah-e mogavemat. According to his own account he was drafted by the young and hardworking core to lead this organization as its *aq saqal* (white beard or elder guide). As he said, "I am the one person in Koyshan who knows something about the city, how life is run there, how things are accomplished there." It is more likely that he joined the payegah-e mogavemat to gain political power once again in the village. It also appears that he joined to intimidate and to more forcefully resist Mr. Farzin Hosseini, a grandson of the original village landlord Hossein Agha and the present owner of the garden in Koyshan.

Masha Rahim has been the garden caretaker for a long time and feels that he has certain rights, similar to squatter rights, to the garden. As far as he was concerned the garden had been abandoned since the mid-1960s, until Mr. Farzin Hosseini's return to Ardabil in the early 1970s. Masha Rahim asserts that he saved the garden from going under and from being nibbled away by peasants and others during that period.

Since 1973, the agreement between Masha Rahim and Mr. Farzin Hosseini has been that a fixed sum per month be paid to Masha Rahim for his caretaking responsibility. In turn, Masha Rahim is supposed to make the necessary investments in irrigation, plowing, pruning, and so forth. After deducting expenses, he is to divide the profits from the sale of the garden products equally between himself and Mr. Hosseini.

During my visit to Koyshan in the summer of 1988, Masha Rahim continually cursed Mr. Hosseini for having deliberately abandoned the garden and for not having paid him the agreed-upon monthly sum. He declared angrily that "this garden is without an owner" and went on, "If it had an owner he would come to see it once in awhile, and attend to its problems. How am I going to keep up this place?" He continued, "Other villagers go and tell on me so that Mr. Hosseini will take this garden away from me and give it to someone else. I will never allow that to happen because I have wasted my life in this garden, I have protected it from every kind of danger." I asked him directly who was telling on him and what was going on. He did not want to say it, but ultimately he expressed his suspicions that his own brothers are telling on him.

Given the lack of financial support from Mr. Hosseini, Masha Rahim faced serious trouble in maintaining the garden. It costs 3,200 tomans to irrigate the garden every month, 200 tomans for the head irrigator, and 500 tomans for each of the six workers needed to irrigate the garden during their twenty-four-hour share of the water each month from mid-spring to mid-October. Masha Rahim threateningly remarked, "He sits in Ardabil twenty kilometers away and looks at his garden with a binocular, and says that my garden is going to waste and you are not taking care of it. Since you don't dare come to see it in the daylight, why don't you at least come to see it at night?"

Masha Rahim had his Uncle Taghi till the garden with his tractor for 6,000 tomans. Unfortunately, he ruined it by furrowing so deep that nothing can be done at this point. Mr. Hosseini would not pay Taghi for the tilling. When he came to the village, Taghi offended him in the public. So Mr. Hosseini decided to let Masha Rahim struggle under the burden of all the expenses of the garden, now that there is no respect left in the village.

What is interesting are the techniques of stalling, not giving a straight answer, and footdragging used by Mr. Hosseini. For example, Masha Rahim's son, who had come for a visit to Koyshan from Tehran, went to Ardabil, asking, pleading, inviting Mr. Hosseini to come to the village. Mr. Hosseini told him go back and set up the room in the garden building and said that "I will be coming this evening with the children and my wife." When Gholam told this to his father when he returned, Masha Rahim angrily replied, "Hosseini is lying, and he will never show up, he was just trying to get rid of you." Gholam lamented the wasted time and the distress and misery that Mr. Hosseini was causing his father.

But Masha Rahim is also a master of footdragging and avoiding straight answers. He was not going to let Mr. Hosseini break him financially, and when the opportunity came up he joined the payegah-e mogavemat to re-establish himself politically and use this position to intimidate and threaten his landlord. To be more specific, it is the G-3 submachine guns that the state has put at the disposal of the village payegah-e mogavemat that give Masha Rahim this aura of power. There may have been guns in the villages before but never legally and with the blessing of the state. The landlord has not been in the village for the last nine months. Masha Rahim has gone as far as Tehran to ask Mr. Hosseini's brother why he is not coming to the village and complaining that he has not been paid the monthly fixed sum agreed upon. Often, the sale of the produce of the garden does not cover its expenses, particularly the more expensive cycles of irrigation that have to be carried out. Essentially, Masha Rahim was put into a squeeze by Mr. Hosseini's willingness to see his garden dry up and turn into a wasteland because of the lack of respect shown him. Part of the pressure against Masha Rahim came from water use. If the garden was not irrigated for one or two months it would turn into a dry wasteland. The garden is too big for Masha Rahim to afford on his own. By putting this pressure on him, Mr. Hosseini choked Masha Rahim financially and protected his garden in Koyshan. On the other hand, Masha Rahim used the payegah-e mogavemat to regain his lost power and to become even more threatening and intimidating to the landlord.

Opposition and Resistance to the State

Three days before my arrival in Koyshan in early August of 1988, the revolutionary guards had surrounded the village attempting to round up draft evaders. A general mobilization was ordered because Iraq had intensified its attacks after Iran's acceptance of U.N. Resolution 598 in August. They had been unable to apprehend any of the more than 120 draft dodgers that the village is supposed to have. Finally, in the late evening they surrounded the house of Hajji Asad, beat him up, and arrested him for his three sons' evasion of service on the war front. Hajji Asad has the agency for oil distribution in Koyshan; he owns the village mill and a new tractor and recently acquired the village bath. Masha Rahim stated that Hajji Asad "has become a pig, has become a capitalist." The revolutionary guards took Hajji Asad to Ardabil to jail him until his sons turn themselves in for army service. This was to be an exemplary case for the rest of the village.

When I arrived in the village, each draft resister had a different story about how he had evaded the revolutionary guards by escaping from house to house. Many said that they were simply not going to go to war because of the time they would lose or had lost from agricultural work. There were rumors that some villagers, resentful of Hajji Asad's recent success, may have had a hand in informing the revolutionary guards that his sons have never served in the army. They had managed to evade going to the front since the beginning of the war, staying in the village to work with their father and ultimately becoming established and wealthy.

Shortly after the start of the war with Iraq, even those individuals who had already served in the army had to reenlist. Everybody is expected to pitch in with the war effort, and the mobilization of the dispossessed is very active in the rural areas. There is a lot of pressure on families to send their sons to the front. The ideology of martyrdom is strong, and it is impressed on the population by the government as well as by fathers and mothers whose sons have joined the fighting forces on their own or because of parental encouragement. In fact, once a family "gives" a martyr, pressure emanates from them toward other families to follow suit. The father of a martyr said of Hajji Asad, "How come I have lost my son; and how come we have served the cause of Islam and the country; and you have not, and you are not willing to; and in the meanwhile you are getting rich by having your sons here in Koyshan?"

Twenty-one men from Koyshan were in the army and at the front. There were three martyrs (*shahids*) from the village. Two of them were buried in the village graveyard, which I visited, and their martyr status was apparent in the special aluminum "tombstones," in reality enclosed glass vitrine where flowers and sayings from the Koran are placed. The most impressive thing is the photograph of these young dead martyrs in this glass encasement. Various Islamic and government institutions had been paying for these structures, but nowadays families themselves are forced to contribute or pay the costs, sometimes against their will. As Masha Rahim put it, there is no trace of the third martyr. The villagers have checked with the International Red Cross, but it has been determined that he is not a prisoner of war in Iraq. Masha Rahim indicated that this young man was going to marry his daughter and become his *yezn-e* (son-in-law).

By the summer of 1988, more than 125 young men from Koyshan were underground as draft dodgers. Some have gone through the initial training in military bases in Azerbaijan and Kurdistan, but as soon as they have their first leave of absence for several days, they come back and do not return. One young man laughingly remarked how he and his friends had walked off with their army boots and clothing. He stated that "the situation in the army has deteriorated to such an extent that soldiers are paid hardly anything, and are given no pocket money." In fact, a soldier's family is forced to chip in and provide clothes, food, and other care packages for these young, would-be martyrs.

Conclusion

Organized, open, and collective actions of peasants, or, as in the case of Iran, their absence, have received much attention. In my accounts of everyday forms of peasant avoidance, protest, and resistance in a small village community in Azerbaijan, I have attempted to focus attention on the so-called weapons of the weak, that is, the secret forms of self-help and noncompliance. I have also tried to counter the stereotypical images of Iranian peasantry as apathetic, fatalistic, oppressed, ignorant, and passive. The picture that emerges is a complicated one where the peasantry are not simply helpless victims of social change. Also, I have paid attention to the popular culture of resistance and the sense of justice that underlies its disguised acts of individual insubordination. The most characteristic aspect of these forms of resistance is their permanence and continuity. As Scott has observed, these daily struggles are "the stubborn bedrock upon which other forms of resistance may grow, and they are likely to persist after such other forms have failed or produced, in turn, a new pattern of inequity."

I have raised questions concerning property rights and relations, landlord-peasant relations, peasant-cleric relations, and peasant-state relations. These cases also have other implications. For example, the villagers' resistance to the permanent migrants' return to Koyshan was also an instance of peasants resisting commercial relations and the expansion of capitalist agriculture. When peasants resisted Mulla Hashim, they were questioning the alliance between the clergy and the state. When Masha Rahim resisted Mr. Hosseini, he was challenging the economic and cultural resiliency of provincial agrarian elites. Finally, the evasion of the draft and mass mobilization and the rejection of the state-supported ideology of martyrdom by many young men and their families were glaring examples of a crisis of legitimacy for the state. It is only when we have recognized the importance and multiple dimensions of the everyday struggles of the peasantry that we will not mistake the outward appearance of submission for the inward acceptance of oppression.

Notes

1. The only exception was the Jangali movement in Gilan around the turn of the twentieth century mainly because of small and independent farm ownership, relatively better precipitation and productivity, and better communications.

2. The Khomeini regime insisted that Turkoman tribesmen should refrain from seizing private property until the "original" owners could be determined, perhaps referring to the confiscation of large amounts of land in the region by Reza Shah before World War II. For an excellent study of the development of large-scale capitalist farming in the Turkman/Gorgan plain, see S. Okazaki (1968). For an in-depth study of changing agrarian relations in Kurdistan, see M. Van Bruinessen (1978).

References

Abrahamian, Ervand. 1982. *Iran between Two Revolutions*. Princeton, N.J.: Princeton University Press.

Adas, Michael. 1979. *Prophets of Rebellion: Millenarian Protest Movements against the European Colonial Order*. New York: Cambridge University Press.

———. 1981. "From Avoidance to Confrontation: Peasant Protest in Precolonial and Colonial Southeast Asia." *Comparative Studies in Society and History* 23:217–47.

Afary, Janet. "Peasant Resistance, Rebellion, and Consciousness in the Iranian Constitutional Revolution: The Case of the Caspian Region, 1906–1909." Manuscript.

Agah Publications, ed. 1982. *Agrarian and Peasant Problems*. Tehran: Agah Publications. (In Persian).

Alavi, Hamza. 1965. "Peasants and Revolution." In *Socialist Register*, 241–77. London: Merlin Press.

Ashraf, Ahmad. 1982. "Peasants, Land, and Revolution." In *Agrarian and Peasant Problems*. Tehran: Agah Publications. (In Persian).

Bruinessen, Maartin, M. Van. 1978. *Agha, Shaikh and the State: On the Social and Political Organization of Kurdestan*. Utrecht: Rijksuniversiteit.

Burke, Edmund, and Ira M. Lapidus, eds. 1988. *Islam, Politics, and Social Movements*. Berkeley: University of California Press.

Hegland (Hoogland), Mary. 1980. "One Village in the Revolution." *Merip Reports* 87:7–12.

Hobsbawm, Eric J. 1959. *Primitive Rebels*. New York: The Free Press.

———. 1967. "Peasants and Rural Migrants in Politics." In *Politics of Conformity in Latin America*, ed. C. Veliz. New York: Oxford University Press.

———. 1973. "Peasants and Politics." *Journal of Peasant Studies* 1:3–21.

Hoogland, Eric. 1980. "Rural Participation and the Revolution." *MERIP Reports* 87:3–6.

———. 1982a. *Land and Revolution in Iran, 1960–1980*. Austin: University of Texas Press.

———. 1982b. "Rural Iran and the Clerics." *MERIP Reports* 104:23–26.

Journal of Peasant Studies. 1986. Special issue on "Everyday Forms of Peasant Resistance in Southeast Asia," vol. 13.

Kazemi, Farhad. 1980. *Poverty and Revolution in Iran: The Migrant Poor, Urban Marginality and Politics*. New York: New York University Press.

Kazemi, Farhad, and Ervand Abrahamian. 1978. "The Non-Revolutionary Peasantry of Iran." *Iranian Studies* 11:259–304.

Lambton, A. K. S. 1953. *Landlord and Peasant in Persia*. New York: Oxford University Press.

Mahdavy, Hossein, 1983, "Thirty Years of Change in a Village in the Qazvin Plain." In *Agrarian and Peasant Problems*. Tehran: Agah Publications. (In Persian).

Migdal, Joel. 1974. *Peasants, Politics, and Revolution: Pressures Toward Political and Social Change in the Third World*. Princeton, N.J.: Princeton University Press.

Moore, Barrington, 1966. *The Social Origins of Dictatorship and Democracy, Lord and Peasant in the Making of the Modern World*. Boston: Beacon Press.

Najmabadi, Afsaneh. 1987. *Land Reform and Social Change in Iran.* Salt Lake City: University of Utah Press.

Okazaki, Shoko. 1968. *Development of Large-Scale Farming in Iran: The Case of the Province of Gorgan.* Tokyo: The Institute of Asian Economic Affairs.

Paige, Jeffrey M. 1975. *Agrarian Revolution, Social Movements and Export Agriculture in the Underdeveloped World.* New York: The Free Press.

Sa'edi, Gholam-Hossein. 1963. *Ilkhechi.* Tehran: Tehran University Press.

―――. 1965. *Khiav ya Meshkin Shahr.* Tehran: Tehran University Press.

―――. 1984. *Fear and Trembling.* Washington, D.C.: The Three Continents Press.

Safizadeh, Fereydoun. 1986. "Agrarian Change, Migration, and Impact of the Islamic Revolution in a Village in Azerbaijan, Iran." Ph.D. diss., Harvard University.

Salehi-Isfahani, Djavad. 1981. "The Economic Consequences of the Islamic Revolution in Iran." Paper presented at the 15th Annual Meeting of the Middle East Studies Association, Seattle.

Scott, James. 1976. *The Moral Economy of the Peasant: Rebellion and Subsistence in Southeast Asia.* New Haven, Conn.: Yale University Press.

―――. 1984. *Weapons of the Weak: Everyday Forms of Peasant Resistance.* New Haven, Conn.: Yale University Press.

―――. 1986, "Everyday Forms of Peasant Resistance." *Journal of Peasant Studies* 13:5–35.

Shanin, Teodor 1971. "Peasantry as a Political Factor." In *Peasant and Peasant Societies,* ed. T. Shanin. New York: Penguin Books.

―――, ed. 1987. *Peasants and Peasant Societies.* New York: Basil Blackwell.

Skocpol, Theda. 1979. *States and Social Revolutions.* New York: Cambridge University Press.

―――. 1982. "What Makes Peasants Revolutionary?" *Comparative Politics* 14:351–75.

Stavenhagen, Rodolfo. 1970. *Agrarian Problems and Peasant Movements in Latin America.* Garden City, N.Y.: Doubleday.

Steward, Julian H., et al. 1956. *The People of Puerto Rico: A Study in Social Anthropology.* Urbana: University of Illinois Press.

Stinchcombe, Arthur L. 1961. "Agricultural Enterprise and Rural Class Relations." In *Class, Status, and Power,* ed. Reinhard Bendix and Seymour Martin Lipset. New York: The Free Press.

Tilly, Charles. 1978. *From Mobilization to Revolution.* New York: Random House.

Wolf, Eric. 1969. *Peasant Wars of the Twentieth Century.* New York: Harper and Row.

―――. 1971. "Peasant Rebellion and Revolution." In *National Liberation,* ed. Norman Miller and Roderick Aya. New York: The Free Press.

Wolf, Eric, and Sidney Mintz. 1957. "Haciendas and Plantations in Middle America and the Antilles." *Social and Economic Studies* 6:380–412.

Contributors

AHMAD ASHRAF, managing editor of *Encyclopedia Iranica*, Center for Iranian Studies, Columbia University, is a specialist in social change and social history in the Middle East, particularly Iran.

NATHAN BROWN, assistant professor of political science at George Washington University, is a specialist in the politics of the Middle East, particularly Egypt.

EDMUND BURKE, III, professor of history at the University of California at Santa Cruz, is a specialist in the social history of the Middle East, particularly North Africa.

AXEL HAVEMANN, assistant professor of Islamic studies at the Freie University of Berlin, is a specialist in the economic and social history of the Middle East in the nineteenth and twentieth centuries, particularly Lebanon.

NICHOLAS S. HOPKINS, professor of anthropology at the American University of Cairo, is a specialist in the anthropology of the Arab world, with particular attention to agrarian change.

FARHAD KAZEMI, professor of politics and acting dean of the Graduate School of Arts and Science at New York University, is a specialist in the politics of the Middle East, particularly Iran.

TIMOTHY MITCHELL, associate professor of politics at New York University, is a specialist in the politics of the Middle East, particularly Egypt.

ŞEVKET PAMUK, assistant professor of economics at Villanova University, is a specialist in the economic history of the Ottoman Empire and economic development in the Middle East.

DONALD QUATAERT, associate professor of history and director of the South-West Asian Program, State University of New York at Binghamton, is a specialist in Ottoman social and economic history.

FEREYDOUN SAFIZADEH, assistant professor of anthropology at San Francisco State University, is a specialist in the anthropology of the Middle East, particularly Iran and Turkey.

LINDA SCHATKOWSKI SCHILCHER, assistant professor of history at Villanova University, is a specialist in Ottoman Syria, particularly its rural sector.

REINHARD C. SCHULZE, professor of Islamic studies at Friedrich-Wilhelms University in Bonn, is a specialist in the modern history of the Middle East, particularly Egypt.

KENNETH W. STEIN, associate professor of history and political science at Emory University, is a specialist in the modern history of the Middle East, particularly the Palestine mandate.

JOHN WATERBURY, William Stewart Tod Professor of Politics and International Affairs at the Woodrow Wilson School of International Affairs, Princeton University, is a specialist in the politics and political economy of the Middle East and North Africa.

Index

Note: Arabic names are indexed in the form in which they are most familiar in the West. Generally, names from earlier periods are indexed under the given or first name, while more current persons are found under the last name. Last names beginning with "al" are alphabetized according to the element following this particle. (For example, al-Khalidi is found under Khalidi, with the particle "al" retained in front of it.)